The Animation:Master Handbook

The **Animation:Master Handbook**

Jeff Paries

DISCARD

CHARLES
RIVER
MEDIA

CHARLES RIVER MEDIA, INC.
Rockland, Massachusetts

Executive Editor: Jenifer Niles
Production: Reuben Kantor
Cover Design: Monty Lewis
Cover Image: Jeff Lew
Printer: InterCity Press

CHARLES RIVER MEDIA, INC.
P.O. Box 417
403 VFW Drive
Rockland, Massachusetts 02370
781-871-4184
781-871-4376 (FAX)
chrivmedia@aol.com
http://www.charlesriver.com

This book is printed on acid-free paper.

The Animation:Master Handbook
By Jeff Paries
ISBN 1-886801-71-1
Printed in the United States of America

98 99 00 01 02 7 6 5 4 3 2

CHARLES RIVER MEDIA titles are available for site
license or bulk purchase by institutions, user groups,
corporations, etc. For additional information, please
contact the Special Sales Department at 781-871-4184.

Contents

ACKNOWLEDGMENTS. xv

FOREWORD *by MARTIN HASH* xvii

INTRODUCTION. xix

Chapter 1. Storytelling with Animation:Master. 1

EVERYONE HAS A STORY TO TELL. 2

WHAT IS A STORY?. 2

THE SIGNIFICANCE OF THE STORY 3

STORYBOARDING THE ACTION 6

WHAT TO ANTICIPATE DURING THE PROCESS OF REALIZATION 7

SUMMARY 7

Chapter 2. Core Concepts of Animation:Master 9

THE PROJECT WORKSPACE. 11

THE PROPERTIES PANEL 13

    ❍ *The Properties Panel* 13

THE WINDOW WORKSPACE. 14

    ❍ *The Window Workspace*. 15

THE STATUS BAR 16

    ❍ *The Status Bar* 16

DROP-DOWN MENUS 17

    The File Menu 18

    The Edit Menu. 19

The Project Menu. 20
The View Menu 21
The Action Menu. 23
The Tools Menu. 23
The Window Menu 31
TOOLBARS. 32
LIBRARIES 33
THE INTERFACE 33
        ○ Familiarizing Yourself with the Interface. 33
SPLINES 37
What Are Splines?. 38
What Are Control Points?. 38
What Defines a Surface? 38
SUMMARY 39

Chapter 3. Modeling Basics. 41
MODELING A SIMPLE CHARACTER WITH THE LATHE TOOL. 42
Beginning the Model 43
Modeling the Feet. 44
        ○ Modeling Feet 44
Modeling the Hands. 48
        ○ Modeling Hands 49
Modeling the Facial Features. 52
        ○ Modeling Eyes 53
        ○ Modeling the Mouth 56
MODELING WITH UNIBODY CONSTRUCTION. 58
        ○ Beginning the 20-Minute Man 59
Modeling the Legs 59
        ○ Modeling the Legs and Feet 59
Modeling the Pelvis 63
        ○ Creating the Pelvis and Torso 63
Extruding the Arms 67
        ○ Creating the Arms 67
Modeling the Shoulders, Head, and Hands 70
        ○ Modeling the Shoulders 70
        ○ Modeling the Neck and Head. 74

○ *Modeling the Hands* 75
CREATING A UNIBODY QUADRUPED 76
Beginning the Model 77
Modeling the Body 77
○ *Modeling the Body* 77
○ *Shaping the Cow's Head* 79
○ *Shaping the Cow's Body* 80
○ *Creating and Attaching the Legs* 80
○ *The Dark Side of the Moo* 83
Finishing the Cow 85
SUMMARY 86

Chapter 4. Advanced Modeling 87

HOW HOOKS WORK 88
○ *Adding a Hole with Hooks* 90
Characters with Hooks 93
USING HOOKS IN MODELING 94
○ *Beginning to Build a Dinosaur: The Tail* 95
○ *Creating the Body* 97
○ *Creating the T. rex's Arms* 100
○ *Creating the Back Legs* 105
○ *Creating the Dinosaur's Head* 108
Adding Front Claws and Back Feet 112
Finishing the Model 113
SOLVING SURFACE AMBIGUITIES 114
Common Causes and Cures for Creases 114
Non-continuous Spline along a Smooth Surface 115
Continuous Spline that Doubles Back 118
Three-Point Patch on a Curved Surface 120
MODELING THE HUMAN FACE 121
Creating a Model for the Head 121
Building the Head 122
○ *Setting Up the Rotoscopes* 123
○ *Creating a Basic Head Shape* 125
Adding Features and Resolution to the Face 127
○ *Adding Basic Features to the Face* 127
○ *Adding Resolution to the Face* 129

❍ *Closing the Patches of the Face* 133
❍ *Shaping the Face* 135
❍ *Fixing the Creases at the Mouth Corners* 137
❍ *Fixing the Surfaces around the Eyes.* 140
❍ *Creating a Nose.* 146
MODELING HUMAN EYES 150
❍ *Beginning the Creation of an Eye* 150
❍ *Creating a Pupil for the Eye* 152
❍ *Creating the Cornea Wireframe* 154
MODELING THE HUMAN BODY. 155
❍ *Beginning the Human Body: The Torso.* 155
❍ *Creating the Pelvis.* 162
❍ *Creating Arms for the Model* 164
❍ *Adding Legs to the Model.* 166
SUMMARY 168

Chapter 5. Mechanical Modeling 169

CREATING BUILDINGS. 170
❍ *Creating a Simple Building* 170
❍ *Adding Doors and Windows to Buildings* 173
MODELING AN AIRPLANE 176
❍ *Setting Up the Rotoscopes* 176
❍ *Creating the Fuselage.* 177
MODELING A SPACESHIP 183
❍ *Beginning a Spaceship* 184
Adding Detail to the Model 189
SUMMARY 192

Chapter 6. Adding Textures to Models 193

USING BASE ATTRIBUTES 194
Applying Base Attributes to the Model 194
Modifying Base Attributes 196
❍ *Applying Specularity to the Model.* 196
PATCH COLORING KILLER BEAN 198
❍ *Patch Coloring.* 199

UNDERSTANDING THREE-DIMENSIONAL TEXTURES 203
   The Checker Combiner 204
   The Gradient Combiner 207
   The Noise Combiner 208
   The Spherical Combiner 210
MATERIAL TECHNIQUES 212
   Creating Glass Materials 213
      ❍ Creating a Martini Glass 213
   Creating Metallic Materials 215
      ❍ Creating a Metal Material 215
   Complex Materials 218
      ❍ Creating a Complex Material 218
      ❍ Combining Materials 221
CREATING MATERIAL LIBRARIES 222
      ❍ Creating a Material Library 223
SUMMARY 224

Chapter 7. Decals 225
TYPES OF DECALS 226
   Color Maps 227
   Transparency Maps 228
   Bump Maps 230
   Specularity Maps 232
   Diffuse Maps 233
   Reflectivity Maps 235
   Ambiance Maps 236
   Cookie-Cut Maps 238
   Displacement Maps 239
   Fractal Maps 240
DECALING TECHNIQUES 240
      ❍ Decaling Curved Surfaces 241
      ❍ Decaling using Flatten 243
      ❍ Creating a Brick Wall 246
   Antialiased versus Non-antialiased Image Maps 249
USING ALPHA CHANNELS IN DECALS 251
TIPS FOR CREATING DECALS 253

○ *Creating a Head Image Map in Photoshop* 254

TEXTURE MAP ALTERNATIVES 257

SUMMARY 258

Chapter 8. Constraints 259

UNDERSTANDING CONSTRAINTS. 260

TYPES OF CONSTRAINTS 261

   Aim At Constraints. 261
     ○ *Using the Aim At Constraint* 261
   Kinematic Constraints 265
     ○ *Kinematic Constraints* 265
   Path Constraints. 268
     ○ *Path Constraints* 269
   Translate To Constraints 272
     ○ *Translate To Constraints* 273
   Orient Like Constraints 275
     ○ *Orient Like Constraints* 277
   Aim Roll At Constraints 277
     ○ *Aim Roll At Constraints*. 277
   Spherical Limits 279
     ○ *Spherical Constraints*. 279

USING MULTIPLE CONSTRAINTS 281
     ○ *Using Aim At and Orient Like Constraints Together* 282
     ○ *Using Path and Aim Roll At Constraints Together*. 283

ANIMATING CONSTRAINTS. 285
     ○ *Animating Constraints*. 285

TARGET BONES. 287
     ○ *Target Bones* 288

SUMMARY 288

Chapter 9. Bones 289

UNDERSTANDING JOINTS 290
     ○ *Two-Bone Joints* 291
     ○ *Three-Bone Joints* 293

BONE HIERARCHIES. 296

A STANDARD NAMING CONVENTION FOR BONES 297
BONING A BIPED 298
   ◯ *Boning Killer Bean* 299
   ◯ *Finishing Bones* 303
BONING QUADRUPEDS 305
   ◯ *Adding the Basic Bones* 306
   ◯ *Adding Bones to the Legs* 308
   ◯ *Adding Bones to the Tail* 309
BOOLEAN OPERATIONS 311
   ◯ *Simple Boolean Operations* 311
SUMMARY 314

Chapter 10. Path Animation 315

SIMPLE TRANSLATIONS FOR MOTION 316
   ◯ *Simple Translations* 317
CREATING A SIMPLE PATH 318
   ◯ *Creating a Simple Path* 318
   ◯ *Translate Only* 323
ADVANCED PATH ANIMATION 324
   ◯ *Advanced Path Animation Example 1* 324
   ◯ *Advanced Path Animation Example 2* 326
CONTROLLING ANIMATION ALONG A PATH 327
  Using Ease 327
   ◯ *Using the Ease Channel* 328
SUMMARY 331

Chapter 11. Creating Actions 333

CREATING SKELETAL ACTIONS 334
   ◯ *Creating a Simple Walk Cycle* 334
  Using Stride Length 338
   ◯ *Stride Length* 339
  Skeletal Squash and Stretch 343
   ◯ *Skeletal Squash and Stretch* 343
CREATING MUSCLE ACTIONS 348
   ◯ *Creating a Simple Muscle Motion* 349

Naming Groups 350
POSES. 351
CREATING POSES 351
    ○ *Creating Emotion Poses* 351
LIP-SYNCH 354
    ○ *Simple Lip-Synch* 355
    LipSYNC 357
    ○ *LipSYNC* 357
MOTION LIBRARIES 359
SUMMARY 360

Chapter 12. Environments 361
WHAT CONSTITUTES AN ENVIRONMENT? 362
CREATING SIMPLE ENVIRONMENTS 363
    Simple Ground Planes 363
    ○ *Simple Ground Planes* 363
COMPLEX ENVIRONMENTS. 368
    ○ *More Complex Ground Plane*. 368
    ○ *Using Grid Maker to Create Ground Planes* 372
    Cylindrical Backdrops. 375
    ○ *Creating Cylindrical Backdrops* 376
    Dome Backdrops 381
    ○ *Environment Maps* 381
    ○ *Decaling a Dome*. 383
    Spherical Backdrops 386
    ○ *Spherical Environments* 386
    Front Projection Mapping 390
    ○ *Using Front Projection Maps* 390
SUMMARY 395

Chapter 13. You as Director. 397
DIRECTION AND THE MOOD OF THE STORY. 398
THE CAMERA 399
    ○ *Tracking Objects with the Camera* 399

Multiple Cameras 401
    ○ *Multiple Cameras* 402
LIGHTING 403
    ○ *Basic Lighting Technique* 406
FOG AND BACKGROUND COLOR 410
MOTION BLUR 411
SUMMARY 412

Chapter 14. Rendering 413
THE HYBRID RENDERER 414
    Flat Shading 414
    z-Buffer 415
    a-Buffer 416
    Gouraud Shading 417
UNDERSTANDING FINAL OUTPUT 418
    AVI 418
    QuickTime MOV 419
    TGA (TARGA) File Format 419
ALPHA BUFFER 420
MOTION BLUR 421
    ○ *Using Motion Blur* 422
SUMMARY 423

Chapter 15. Compositing 425
THE ART OF DIGITAL COMPOSITING 426
    Scene Composition 427
THE MULTIPLANE INTERFACE 429
    The Menu Bar 430
    The Composition Window 432
    The Tool Panel 433
    The Attribute Panel 433
    The Object List 435
LAYER ANIMATION 435

❍ *Layer Animation* 435
WORKING WITH MULTIPLE LAYERS 436
❍ *Multilayer Compositions* 437
EXAMPLE EFFECTS 440
❍ *Color Key* 440
❍ *Lens Flares* 442
SUMMARY 444

About the CD-ROM 445

Index 447

Acknowledgments

For my Dad, who went through a lot of trouble a few years back to get me a piece of software for Christmas — software that has changed my life.

For my Mom, who (of course) always supported me in my many failures as well as my many successes.

SPECIAL THANKS:

To Hash, Inc. and everyone there, without whom this book and one killer piece of software would not exist.

To CONIX, both for awesome OpenGL for the PowerMac, and even more for allowing me to include the extension with this book.

To Steve Sappington, for helping me decide just exactly what would be useful to cover, and helping me work out some of the finer technical details.

To Tim Elston, for much of the technical editing, and help in providing me with a different point of view.

To Kim, Michael, Katie, Michele, Jason, Brittany, Cody, Brandon, Gerry, Hank T., Jeff L., Todd S., and Tommy D. for support and contributions.

To Becky and Sasha, who seemed to understand why they weren't getting regular walks and their usual attention from me while I was working, and still remained my buds.

And of course, to all of you Hash fanatics out there who have supported me in my efforts. Keep spreading the word.

Finally, big thanks to Charles River Media, for helping me every step of the way in getting a long overdue book published and distributed.

FOREWORD

BY MARTIN HASH

I've never believed in psychometry (the description of a person based on a psychic examination of the items that person's touched), but I can tell a lot about you who are reading this book, because you are a lot like me — you want to create.

Odds are, you're a better artist than I am. I vividly remember the days of my youth, bent over my artist's table, painstakingly trying to mimic the trend-setting pencils of Barry Smith from "Conan the Barbarian," or Gil Kane from the 100th issue of "Spiderman." My teenage dreams of being a comic-book artist and writer stayed with me into college, though I had long come to the conclusion that I as a single artist could never finish a complete book, let alone my ultimate goal of making fulfilling animated cartoons. Simultaneously, the birth of computers was upon us and my eyes were keen for any hint of help from that direction.

In retrospect, it seems amazing that I and others were able to keep the faith of computer animation during those ancient days of memory measured in "Ks" (not megs) and processor speeds of a single megahertz (not hundreds of mega-hertz). In 1987, a frame from one of my first animations appeared on the cover of *Commodore Magazine* as one of the "Best Products of the Year." That anima-tion, "Dragonrider," was created with my first commercially available 3D ani-mation product, "Animation Apprentice." No one should ever get the misim-pression that any of these early programs (ultimately there were ten released on the Amiga) made me any money. The goal was the animations, and secondarily to meet people who want to make animations. To this day, I call people I met then my friends.

Some of those friends later collaborated with Hash Inc. to make several award-winning animations ("Fluffy"), a children's book and accompanying game (*Why Does the Wind Blow?*), and even a feature-length movie (*Telepresence*). These were our first professional efforts that provided more of a sense of fulfillment than monetary success. Also, the weaknesses inherent in earlier versions of our program "Martin Hash's 3-Dimensional Animation" (MH3D), came to light. I assure you we strived vigorously to overcome every limitation. (We want our next movie to be awesome.)

I used to say, "You're still the animator, the computer can't do it for you." But now that distinction is blurring: More and more, the computer *is* the animator. Your role increasingly becomes one of directing. As programs like MH3D get more and more sophisticated, you become a storyteller rather than a technician. But, however powerful and all-knowing computers may become, the stories still have to come from you. Even if you are the only one who ever sees the results, every finished story counts in the great tally book of your life.

Martin Hash

Introduction

Hash Inc.'s Animation:Master has been around in one form or another for more than 10 years. In that time, it has established itself as a leader in character animation because of its favorable price and robust feature set. Version 5 is the next step in the evolution of Animation:Master, incorporating many revolutionary features never before available in any 3D software package at any price. This provides a unique opportunity for you. For less than the cost of a used Volkswagen Bug, you can learn to make movies on the desktop.

3D Is Everywhere You Look

It is virtually impossible to sit down and watch even 30 minutes of television without seeing some form of computer animation. Many shows are digitally enhanced to provide objects that cannot be created easily or at an effective cost level, and many of the commercials television viewers are bombarded with are created entirely on someone's dining room table.

Movies are no exception. The myriad films featuring visually stunning digital effects have paved the way for digital artists to emerge as an essential part of the production team. There is no doubt that these effects are here to stay, as evidenced by the continued success of this market.

Throughout the animation industry's growth, Hash Inc. has continued to provide the only low-cost solution for character animation, pioneering the ability to produce quality animation on the desktop. Many consumers previously unable to afford the high cost of animation software have turned to Animation:Master and found that it contains many of the powerful features available in high-priced software at just a fraction of the price. Keep this in mind as you increase your sophistication through the exercises and information contained in this book. You are gaining valuable knowledge that just may lead to something great.

WHO IS AN ANIMATOR?

Bear in mind that just because an individual is an exceptional artist does not mean that he or she will make a good animator. The reverse is also true. Artists and animators are closely related, but both art and animation are very individual, and require very separate skills that take time and patience to develop. Both artists and animators have a well-trained eye for their craft that took years to develop. Accomplished artists can learn to become capable animators; likewise, proficient animators can become skillful artists. The trade-off for the acquisition of any skill is an investment of time, patience, and money. This book is going to help you increase your sophistication level with Animation:Master while saving the enormous amount of time it would have taken you to discover these techniques on your own.

WHAT YOU CAN EXPECT FROM THIS BOOK

This book is intended to raise the skill level of any user of Martin Hash's 3-Dimensional Animation or Animation:Master by providing explanations and tutorials that illustrate many advanced techniques used to create believable characters and stunning images.

This book also provides an excellent desktop resource for users who are already familiar with Hash's software by expanding their knowledge of the software and providing alternative methods of modeling and animation.

Since Animation:Master runs on both the PC and the PowerMac, the information contained in this book is applicable to both platforms. PowerMac users need to be familiar enough with the software to be able to compensate for the differences between PCs and Macs — most notably, the right-click of a PC mouse.

Both the PC and PowerMac versions of the software have the same tools located in the corresponding parts of the interface.

WHAT YOU WILL NEED

Since this book is targeted at intermediate to advanced users, a solid underlying knowledge of Animation:Master and how it works is necessary. This includes knowing how to get around the interface, as well as the use of the available tools. Some items, such as constraints, will be covered in a little more depth, since they can be difficult to understand fully.

Several of the examples include the creation and manipulation of image maps, making it beneficial to own and be familiar with a paint program such as Photoshop or Fractal Design Painter. This will help you understand the full process of creating and applying image maps.

ABOUT THE CD-ROM

The CD-ROM included with this book contains many of the models shown in the tutorials, so that you can open and examine them within Animation:Master. These models are provided in Animation:Master v5 format as a learning tool for your private, noncommercial use and may not be distributed or converted to other formats.

Wherever possible, all supporting image maps, materials, and patch color information is included with the model files, so that you can fully understand the construction of these characters and how each of these parts combine to achieve the final goal. Also included are several example animations created with Animation:Master that show the capabilities of the software. These are for private use as well and may not be distributed or converted to any other format.

A FINAL NOTE

Animation is hard.

If you're familiar with Hash Inc., you've heard that one before. There is no doubt that through practice, patience, and understanding, you will become successful at producing images that satisfy your desires.

As a truly extraordinary individual once said:

"Hang in there, you'll be famous."

Believe it.

CHAPTER 1

Storytelling with Animation:Master

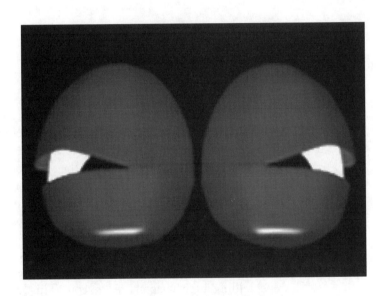

This chapter introduces you to the process of creating storyboards and developing a story and characters. It also tells you a little about what to anticipate during the creation of the animation.

The chapter covers the following items:

- Everyone Has a Story to Tell
- What Is a Story?
- The Significance of the Story
- Storyboarding the Action
- What to Anticipate During the Process of Realization

EVERYONE HAS A STORY TO TELL

It's true. Some stories may be more interesting or involved than others, but when you boil it all down, everyone has a story to tell. We can go as far back as prehistoric times. The people who lived then communicated using paintings on the cave wall, some of which still speak to us today. The ancient Egyptians told their stories in great detail on the walls of tombs. They paid so much attention to detail that an ancient recipe for beer found in one tomb was fairly easily recreated in modern times. The great Anasazi Indians gathered in the deserts of New Mexico thousands of years ago for ceremonies in the great kivas that brought stories to them in visions.

Every religion on the face of the planet tells a story. Many cultures have handed stories down from generation to generation, with each new story-teller adding a few chapters to the epic. This amazing progression in the creation of stories has made storytelling an art form as individual as the person telling the story.

WHAT IS A STORY?

So exactly what is a story? Very simply, a story communicates ideas or events from one person or group of people to another person or group of people.

Have you ever come home from the grocery store telling anyone who would listen how you were about to pull into a parking spot when someone came racing up the aisle to steal it from you at the last second? Or perhaps the time you went to an amusement park and one of the rides made you sick? This is storytelling in a basic form. However, these stories are not the kind that will captivate an audience and stand the test of time.

To become a great storyteller, you must be able to see the tragic, funny, terrifying, or thrilling aspects of a situation, then express those in your story and make the audience feel them. All those times when someone says "We'll laugh about this someday" — those are what make great stories. Perhaps the time you came home and found that your dog had ripped open your couch and spread shredded foam all over the living room floor. Or the time a pipe broke under the kitchen sink and water came cascading out into your kitchen.

Take these situations one step farther by embellishing the story to make it alluring, and you've got a story to tell. Give the dog that shredded the couch the personality of a child. Perhaps it was a temper tantrum that caused this deviant behavior. Better still, perhaps the dog planned to clean the mess up before you came home, but you showed up early and caught her red-pawed.

What about the broken pipe? Hardly a funny situation. Until you think about what that overweight plumber looked like in his tee-shirt and loose blue jeans while crouching on his hands and knees beneath your kitchen sink in an inch of water, commenting on the "large crack under the sink" that was to blame for the leak.

Now you're on the right track.

THE SIGNIFICANCE OF THE STORY

Animation:Master was created with the sole intention of helping you tell your stories. In developing a story for any purpose, especially animation, you must put special thought into the idea or concept around which the story is to be built. Unless you are interested in animation purely as a hobbyist, you need a story that most people can relate to. Make it too vague and either you'll come off as a strange human being, or everyone will leave scratching their heads trying to decipher what it was that they just saw.

With this in mind, it is important to remember that "private" or "inside" jokes, no matter how funny they may seem, very often make no sense to anyone other than those involved. There are so many things that we as a society, and that each individual culture within our society, have in common that creating a story around a familiar object, place, situation, etc., can be fairly easy.

Storytelling through animation can be accomplished by following a few simple steps. First, you need an idea. Coming up with the idea is often the hardest part of telling a story. It's important to recognize and develop an idea when it hits. Ideas can come from dreams, wishes, family members, pets, surroundings, experiences, likes and dislikes, etc. Anything you do, at any time, can spark an idea that might be the next great animation waiting to happen.

Keep a pencil and paper next to your bed and record any dreams that have the potential to become a story. Think about things that happened while you were growing up. Consider your travels; look at your pets; look in the mirror. It may help to carry a small notebook and pencil around and take notes if something strikes your fancy. Sit down and ask yourself what stories you have to tell.

Once you have an idea, character development comes next. You need to decide what each character is going to be like. For example, Lassie and Benji are both dogs, but Lassie is bigger, has longer hair that is much lighter in color, has a longer snout, and can communicate well. Benji, on the other hand, is small, has dark fur and a short snout, and can do a ton of neat tricks.

Ask yourself as many questions about your character as you can while you are in this stage. It will save you much time and trouble later on. Some questions to get yourself started may include:

- Is the character humanoid, or not?

- If it is humanoid, is it male, female, or androgynous? What does the skin look like? What kind of hair does it have? What do the eyes look like? What does the nose look like? How tall is this character? What kind of teeth does it have?

- If you're building a monster, does it have tentacles, claws, or both? Can it breathe fire, a freeze ray, or neither? Does it have long sharp fangs? How about a huge sucker with tiny barbs that inject digestive fluid into your body, so that you're digested inside your own skin, after which the monster sucks the juice back out?

Once you've decided on each character's look, you must also make some decisions about its personality. Remember Gizmo in *Gremlins*? All cute and fuzzy unless you broke the rules. Those rules were part of his personality — things that made him who he was, and made the story happen. There are several characteristics that can help to stereotype your characters' personalities so that they drop into particular categories very quickly for the viewer.

One of the most obvious is the eyes. Eyes can show such a wide range of emotions that they lend a lot to the personality of characters. If the eyebrows are furrowed and the eyelids are down low, there is no doubt that the character is angry. If the eyelids are open and the brow is raised, the character has an inquisitive or curious look.

Other properties that enhance characters' personalities are their mannerisms. Do they eat with their bare hands, making grunting noises while shoveling food into their mouths? Do they walk with a gait that shows confidence, or do they shove their hands deep into their pockets and look at the ground while shuffling their feet?

Using Gizmo as an example again, imagine removing his quiet, gentle nature and replacing it with an obnoxious, flatulent, cigarette-smoking tangle of hair. Would he still be as cute? Maybe to some, but certainly those changes in his mannerisms would remove the previous image you had of him. They would make it more difficult for his story to be compelling to the majority of potential viewers.

Finally, think about the voice of your character. Many characters have no voice at all, which makes the previously discussed characteristics all that much more important. If your character does have a voice, give it a lot of thought, because it helps to make the personality of your character live. Remember the little song that Gizmo would whistle? That and the high-pitched exclamation "Bright light!" were pretty much all the voice he needed.

Keep in mind that smaller characters tend to have higher voices, and larger characters deeper ones. What does it say if the tentacled monster described earlier has a sleek and sexy female voice to help it attract its victims? Perhaps it indicates that this is a devious monster that knows how to capture prey in its current environment.

Now that the characters have been developed, you can move on to storyboarding your animation. Once you reach this point, the really hard part is done, and it's time to have some fun.

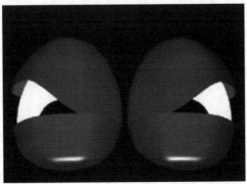

FIGURE *An angry pair of eyes.*
1.1

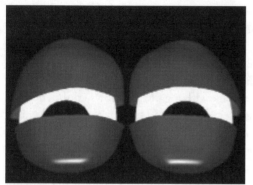

FIGURE
1.2　*A frightened pair of eyes.*

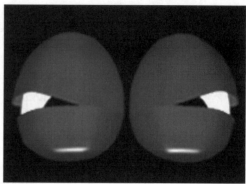

FIGURE
1.3　*A stern pair of eyes.*

STORYBOARDING THE ACTION

Storyboards don't really need to be anything more than several sketches that show the action in each scene of the animation as you would like it to occur. Don't worry if you're not an excellent pencil-and-paper artist. It is acceptable to draw your storyboards as stick figures if you need to. Storyboards don't have to be fancy, high-detail works of art that take weeks to complete. The important thing to remember when storyboarding is that you are developing a visual guide upon which you will build your animation and develop your story. You must understand clearly what each frame in the storyboard is showing to have a solid base upon which to build your story. Storyboards also need to contain notes with additional information or thoughts concerning a particular scene's lighting, dialogue, action, or camera movement.

The information contained in the storyboards will make it easier to develop the actual animation, because storyboards give definition to the project. Using storyboards is much more developmentally efficient than trying to sit down and drop objects into a scene until it looks good.

If it's possible, hang the storyboards on an empty wall in clear view of your computer. This will help you to visualize the entire project, making it easier to understand at what point you are, and in what direction you are heading. Once the storyboards are completed, the process of bringing your concept to realization comes next.

WHAT TO ANTICIPATE DURING THE PROCESS OF REALIZATION

The process of developing a story into a full-blown animation can be long. Be patient. Expect it to take time and for mistakes to happen. After all, you're only human. Sometimes, the story will come easily and develop quickly, and the characters will more or less "tell" you their personalities, making them easy to work with. At other times, it may take years to develop and bring a story to fruition.

Not everyone will like or accept your stories. This is just a basic fact of human nature. Things that one person finds hilarious are often repulsive and tasteless to another. If you know your audience well, then you will be able to tailor your story to fit their needs.

Finally, while you are working, try to set manageable deadlines for yourself. The worst possible thing to do is to take a job, then decide to learn a complex new feature of the software for use specifically in that job. This particular situation almost guarantees failure. As you progress in your knowledge of Animation:Master, always know your limits, and try not to exceed them with the jobs you perform.

SUMMARY

Understanding how to spot and develop a story and the characters that play a part in it will help you become a great storyteller. This information is important to keep in mind, since each individual interprets events differently, resulting in the creation of unique storytelling styles.

Now that you have a little background information to assist you as you start down the long road of animation, it's time to review the interface and toolset available.

CHAPTER

2

Core Concepts of Animation:Master

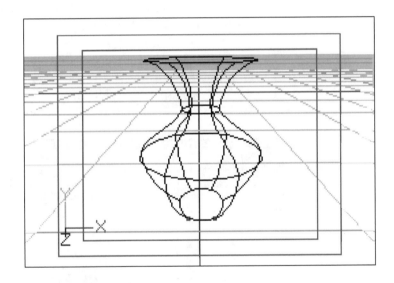

This chapter discusses the layout and configuration options of the Animation:Master interface. You'll need to understand the parts of the interface, as well as the terminology used throughout the program, to be able to handle the exercises in this book.

To work comfortably within the interface, your screen resolution must be at least 800 × 600, preferably 1024 × 768 or higher. This requires a video card with at least 4MB of RAM on it, which will allow you plenty of room to work without constantly having to drag panels around to get them out of your way.

The interface is intuitive and should be easy to learn. It adheres to many standards such as drag and drop, dockable tool panels, and many of the keyboard shortcuts you're already familiar with from using other applications.

This chapter covers the following items:

- The Project Workspace
- The Properties Panel
- The Window Workspace
- The Status Bar
- Drop-Down Menus
- Toolbars
- Libraries
- Splines

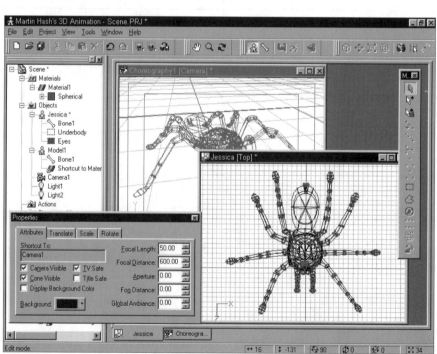

FIGURE *The Animation:Master interface.*

2.1

Figure 2.1 shows an image of the entire Animation:Master interface, the parts of which are described in detail in the next few sections.

THE PROJECT WORKSPACE

The **Project Workspace** is the large area with the white background that appears on the left side of the screen when the software is first started, shown in Figure 2.2.

It's important to be familiar with what you can do in the **Project Workspace**. You'll spend a lot of time working with the different items in this area.

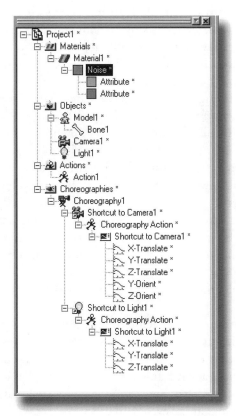

FIGURE
2.2
*The **Project Workspace**, where a "tree" view shows all of the models, materials, actions, lights, etc., in any given project.*

When you begin a new project, the **Project Workspace** will display the project name (which defaults to "Project1"), followed by icons for *Materials, Objects, Actions,* and *Choreographies*. Each of these icons is a header to a particular section of items (categorized by name), which are all empty at the start of a new project. When Materials are created, they appear in the **Materials** section. Models, lights, cameras, and null objects appear in the **Objects** section, Actions appear in the **Actions** section, and Choreographies appear in the **Choreographies** section. As you become familiar with the software, you'll notice the placement of other objects within these sections, such as Decals, Bones, and Choreography Actions.

To view the available sections, start Animation:Master, then select **New** from the **Project** drop-down menu. A project tree will appear in the **Project Workspace**.

As you add items to each of these sections, you can expand or collapse the branches that contain the individual items to suit your needs. Throughout the software, right-clicking (Command-clicking on PowerMac) on items opens up various menus that will save you a lot of time in utilizing certain tools or features. For example, clicking the **New** button (the button with a blank page on it) allows you to create a new Choreography, Model, Action, or Material. If you wanted to create a new Material, you could also right-click on the *Materials* icon in the **Project Workspace** and select **New Material** from the available menu. Take a moment to right-click each of these icons to view the options for each. For the most part, at this level, you're only allowed to create new items or import existing ones. However, as you continue to add items, create actions, and so on, more options will become available to you.

For organization's sake, items that are added to a project can be renamed easily. Simply click the item you wish to change, then press the **F2** key to edit the name. After you type in a new name, press **Enter** to save the changes. The default icons (*Materials, Objects, Actions,* and *Choreographies*) can't be renamed, and the Project item name will change only when the Project is saved.

You may notice as you work that asterisks appear after the names of certain items in the **Project Workspace**. These asterisks mark the items that have been changed, but have not yet been saved. It's a good idea to save often by clicking the **Disk** button on the **Standard Toolbar**. Everyone who has ever used a computer has lost data at one time or another. Saving often will reduce the amount of hard work that you lose in the event of a crash.

Now that you're familiar with the types of items that appear in the **Project Workspace**, the next section describes the **Properties Panel**, where changes to many of the settings for different items are made.

THE PROPERTIES PANEL

The **Properties Panel** is the rectangular box shown in Figure 2.3.

FIGURE   *The **Properties Panel**, where changes are made to many*
2.3   *settings for different items. This image shows a model*
Properties Panel.

The **Properties Panel** updates to show the options for each item that is selected in the **Project Workspace**. Many, many different settings are controlled on the **Properties Panel** — lights, cameras, object colors, embedding options for files, and more.

The following exercise will help you get acquainted with the **Properties Panel**.

EXERCISE

THE PROPERTIES PANEL

1. From the **Project** drop-down menu, select **New**.

2. Right-click (Command-click on PowerMac) the ***Objects*** icon in the **Project Workspace**, then select **New, Light** from the available menus.

3. Notice how the **Properties Panel** updates to show the options available for the new item. These include the Light Type, Shadows, Color, Intensity, Width, Distance to Fall-Off, and a couple of additional ghosted options that do not apply to the default light type.

4. Click on the light button to the far left (Klieg-type light), and notice that the previously ghosted options on the panel become active.

5. Click on the **Color** chip to change the light color. A default 20-color palette window pops up. Click the **Other...** button at the bottom of

this window to open a standard system color picker. Here you can enter color values, or select one from the onscreen palette that matches your system settings.

6. When you're finished, click **OK**. The changes you made will be reflected on the **Properties Panel**.

The **Properties Panel** settings affect many of the objects in the main window area of the interface, called the **Window Workspace**. The next section describes some of the options available to you here.

THE WINDOW WORKSPACE

The **Window Workspace** is the large area of the screen where the windows in which you will be working will appear, as shown in Figure 2.4. The **Window**

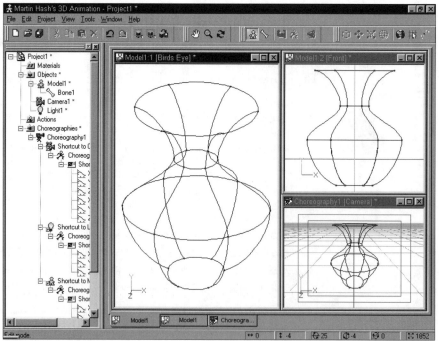

FIGURE *The **Window Workspace** can have any number of windows open, in any configuration*
2.4 *that you wish.*

Workspace allows you to open as many windows as you like and arrange them in any way you need in order to work efficiently.

The following exercise will help you understand how to work with the Window Workspace.

EXERCISE

THE WINDOW WORKSPACE

1. To experiment with the **Window Workspace**, begin by selecting **New** from the **Project** drop-down menu.

2. Right-click (Command-click on PowerMac) the ***Objects*** icon in the **Project Workspace** and select **New, Model** from the available menus. An empty **Modeler** window will open in the **Window Workspace**, and the toolbar will change accordingly.

3. From the **Window** drop-down menu, select **New Window**. This opens a second occurrence of the model window. Any changes you make to a model in one of these windows are reflected in any other open windows of the same type. For example, if you manipulate a model in the second window, the first will update to show the changes being made.

4. More control over the organization of windows can be found in the **Window** drop-down menu. Take a moment and experiment with the different configurations available. Also, notice that the very bottom of the **Window** drop-down menu contains a list of open windows, from which you can select the window you wish to become active.

5. The look of the **Window Workspace** can be changed by using something called **Workbook** mode. Workbook mode will arrange the windows you have opened on "pages," each with its own tab located along the bottom portion of the interface. To activate **Workbook** mode, select **Workbook** from the **View** drop-down menu. The **Window Workspace** will then be bordered by tabs containing the name of the window to which they're attached (refer to Figure 2.4). In **Workbook** mode, selecting the window in which you wish to work is as easy as clicking the appropriate tab.

The **Project Workspace**, **Window Workspace**, and **Properties Panel** are all very important to the entry and control of data for different items. However, helpful information can also be found in a bar across the bottom of the screen called the **Status Bar**. The next section describes the type of information found on the **Status Bar**, and how it relates to different items in the software.

THE STATUS BAR

The **Status Bar** is a small gray bar across the very bottom of the interface. It looks similar to Figure 2.5. The **Status Bar** contains useful information such as keyboard shortcuts, frames per second (in relation to the drawing times for on screen models), and the **View Settings** for the selected window.

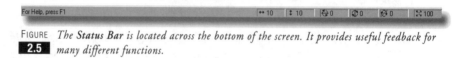

For Help, press F1

FIGURE *The **Status Bar** is located across the bottom of the screen. It provides useful feedback for*
2.5 *many different functions.*

The following exercise will help you recognize the type of information you can expect to find on the **Status Bar**.

EXERCISE

THE STATUS BAR

1. Select **New** from the **Project** menu.

2. Right-click the **Objects** icon in the **Project Workspace**, and select **New, Model** from the available menus.

3. Select **New Window** from the **Window** drop-down menu. This will create a second occurrence of the currently open **Modeling** window.

4. Press the **6** key on the numeric keypad to change to a side view.

5. To see what kind of feedback the **Status Bar** provides, move the pointer around the screen. Notice that as you position the cursor over different areas of the interface, the messages on the **Status Bar** update with relevant information.

6. Click one of the active tools on the **Tools** toolbar. Notice that the **Status Bar** updates with information about options for the selected tool.

7. Located at the right of the **Status Bar** are the **View Settings**. These boxes contain the **X** and **Y Offsets**, **X**, **Y**, and **Z Rotate**, and **Zoom** values for the currently selected window.

8. Click any of the **View Settings**. The dialog shown in Figure 2.6 will open.

9. A dialog will open showing each of the view options and their current values. You can directly enter data into any of these fields by

FIGURE
2.6
*The View Settings dialog box, which contains
information about X and Y Offsets, X, Y, and Z
Rotates, and the Zoom value for the selected window.*

double-clicking in the one you wish to change, then typing in the
new value and pressing **Enter**.

NOTE

The information that appears in the **View Settings** dialog is the same
that appears in the **Status Bar**. Therefore, changing a windows view by
using the **Turn**, **Move**, or **Zoom** tools will change the values in both of
these locations.

As you've no doubt noticed while working through the exercises in this
chapter, many items are accessed from the drop-down menus located on the
menu bar along the top of the screen. The next section describes the tools that
are located in the drop-down menus and gives a little information about what
each of them does.

DROP-DOWN MENUS

Drop-down menus are located on the bar along the top of the interface, as
shown in Figure 2.7.

FIGURE
2.7
*The default drop-down menus. As you navigate the
interface, the available menus will change accordingly.*

The drop-down menus contain options for file management, editing tools, interface customizing options, and help. Many drop-down menu items have shortcut keys assigned to them. The keyboard shortcut is shown on the right side of the drop-down menu, on the same line as the option.

The next few sections describe each of the drop-down menus and briefly describe the functions of the available tools in each menu.

THE FILE MENU

Figure 2.8 shows the **File** drop-down menu.

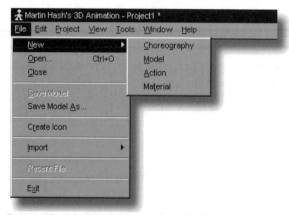

FIGURE   *The **File** drop-down menu for a Model.*
2.8

As shown in the figure, selecting **New** from the **File** menu allows you to choose to create a new Choreography, Model, Action, or Material. These are the same options that appear if the blank-page (**New**) button is clicked.

Open allows you to open a Project, Choreography, Model, Action, or Material. This can be used if you wish to make changes to an item without having to open the entire Project with which it is associated.

Close will close the selected window or file on which you're working. For example, if you select the **Project1** item in the **Project Workspace**, then select **Close**, the project will be closed and the software will remain open.

Save allows you to save the currently open item. Clicking the **Disk** button will save any changes you have made to any of the open files. **Save As** is very similar to **Save**, but it allows you to save a new version of an item without losing the original.

The Create Icon feature allows you to create an icon for a particular Model, Action, Pose, etc. Rendering a selected window (for example, a **Model**), then selecting this option from the **File** menu would cause the software to replace the default model icon in the **Project Workspace** with a small version of the rendered image. This makes it easy to distinguish among many models, actions, materials, or poses.

The **Import** options are sensitive to the active area of the program. For example, if you select **File**, **Import** from an active **Model** window, the options will allow import of another Model, or a v4.xx Segment. However, opening the **File** menu from an active **Choreography** window shows that the **File** menu does not contain an **Import** option at all.

The **Recent Files** list makes it easy for you to recall a previous file without having to browse your hard drive for it. Simply select **File**, then the file you wish to open from the **Recent Files** list, and the selected file will open.

Selecting **Exit** from the **File** menu will close all open windows and exit the Animation:Master program. Selecting this option should be avoided, unless you definitely are ready to exit.

Now that you've reviewed the **File** menu options, the next section describes the options found in the **Edit** menu.

THE EDIT MENU

Figure 2.9 shows the **Edit** drop-down menu.

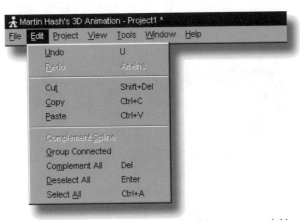

FIGURE   *The **Edit** drop-down menu. Many of the options available*
2.9   *from this menu only apply to the Modeler.*

Undo and Redo allow you to undo and redo changes you make to your Models. These options contain levels, meaning you can select Undo three times and undo the last three changes you've made to your Models.

Cut, Copy, and Paste are used for modeling. These three options affect only a selected point or group of points.

Complement Spline selects all of the control points on the currently selected spline. This is useful in modeling when changes need to made along an entire spline.

Group Connected groups all of the control points that are connected to the selected spline. This means that if you have a face model and select one control point on the chin of the model, then choose Group Connected, all of the points that make up the head will be selected.

Complement All inverts all control points. Those that aren't selected will become selected, and those that are selected will become deselected.

Deselect All deselects all control points that are currently selected. Select All selects all of the control points of a given model.

Snap Group to Grid is useful in mechanical modeling, or in modeling objects that need to be measured with the grid. Choosing this item when a group of control points is selected will cause the selected points to jump, or snap, to the nearest grid intersection.

Generally, Edit menu options are active only during Modeling and Action. They will appear ghosted if another part of the program is active.

The next section describes the Project menu options.

THE PROJECT MENU

Figure 2.10 shows the Project drop-down menu.

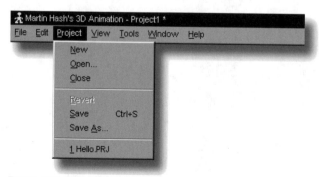

FIGURE   *The Project drop-down menu.*
2.10

Project files are Animation:Master's way of saving files. A Project file incorporates all of the Models, Materials, Lights, Cameras, Actions, Choreographies, and Poses for any given scene. The component files can be saved individually as well. However, Projects provide a great way to organize data, since there are no confusing directories to swim through in order to locate important files. Project files are very easy to work with, because all of the data is stored in one place. Selecting **New** from the **Project** menu will create a new Project. If a Project is already open, you'll be prompted to save it before the new Project is begun.

Open allows you to open an existing Project from your hard drive. **Close** closes the currently open Project and prompts you to save any unsaved changes before closing.

Revert reloads the last saved version of the current project. This is useful if you're working to position camera and lights in a choreography and you make a mistake that causes the scene to look bad. Selecting **Revert** drops all of the changes you've made since the last time you saved and reloads the last saved version of the project.

Selecting **Save** saves any unsaved changes made to the currently open Project. Unsaved changes are marked with asterisks (*) following the items that have been changed.

Save As lets you save any unsaved changes made to the currently open Project, as well as changing the name of the Project. This is useful if you want to experiment, but are afraid to overwrite previously saved data. You can create your Project, save it, then use **Save As** and enter a new name. Now any changes you make to the Project will affect only the second file, not the original.

The **Recent Files** list makes it easy for you to open recently used Projects when you enter the software, or when several Projects are related and you need to move from one to the next easily.

The next section discusses the **View** drop-down menu.

THE VIEW MENU

Figure 2.11 shows the **View** drop-down menu.

Selecting **Toolbars** from the **View** drop-down menu allows you to select which toolbars are visible at any given time. A dialog similar to the one shown in Figure 2.12 will open. Clicking in the checkboxes will allow you to toggle the different toolbars on and off.

The **Status Bar** option toggles the **Status Bar** along the bottom of the screen on or off. Although the **Status Bar** contains useful information, more experienced users may prefer the extra screen space.

FIGURE   *The **View** drop-down menu. This menu controls much of*
2.11   *how the interface looks and "feels."*

FIGURE   *The **Toolbars** dialog. The checkboxes allow*
2.12   *you to decide which toolbars are visible.*

The **Workbook** option, as discussed earlier, allows you to toggle workbook tabs along the bottom of the screen. This option can help you stay organized and makes it easier to switch between windows.

The **Refresh** item redraws the active window. This option is especially useful when you're modeling. At times, the screen may have modeling artifacts on it that become confusing. Pressing the space bar or selecting **Refresh** from the **View** drop-down menu will redraw the screen, eliminating any drawing artifacts.

The **View** drop-down is normally followed by the **Tools** drop-down, with one exception. When you're working on an Action, an additional drop-down appears on the menu bar. This drop-down is called **Action** and is discussed in the following section.

THE ACTION MENU

Figure 2.13 shows the **Action** menu. The options in the **Action** drop-down only affect the action in the active **Action** window.

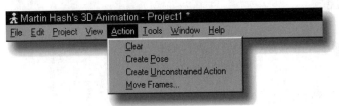

FIGURE   *The **Action** drop-down menu. This drop-down only appears on the*
2.13   *menu bar when an **Action** window is active.*

Selecting **Clear** will clear all of the keyframes in the Action, allowing you to begin a new action. **Create Pose** will make a Pose (a one-frame Action) from the current frame. Poses are saved with the model itself and appear in the **Objects** section of the **Project Workspace**. Poses are covered more in depth later in this book.

Create Unconstrained Action allows you to create an Action that does not use constraints. The **Move Frames** tool allows you to move a set of frames from one part of an Action to another, making it easy for you to reorganize the way an action works.

Muscle Mode is another Action area of the program. These same four options are available there as well.

The next section discusses the **Tools** menu, and how you can modify the look of the software with the options available there.

THE TOOLS MENU

Figure 2.14 shows the **Tools** drop-down menu.

Selecting **Customize** opens a dialog similar to the one shown in Figure 2.15. You shouldn't customize the interface too much until you're comfortable with how to get around and where the different tool sets are located. The exercises in this book use default keyboard commands and can easily be confusing if you've reassigned many keys or moved tools from one toolbar to another.

The **Toolbars** tab, shown in Figure 2.15, allows you to select which toolbars are visible, what they look like, and how they're named. You can also create your

2.14   *The Tools drop-down menu contains only two options. Selecting either of these will open
another dialog that allows significant control and customization of the interface.*

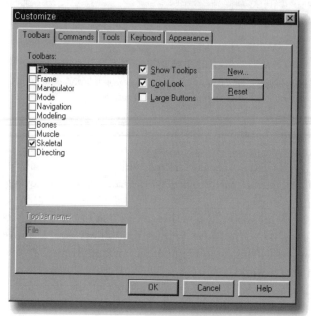

FIGURE   *The Customize dialog. Here you can make often-used programs available to you from*
2.15   *within the Animation:Master interface, through the change keyboard shortcuts, and by
customizing the available tools on each toolbar to modify the look of the interface.*

own, custom toolbars with this panel. The **Commands** tab, shown in Figure
2.16, allows you to move buttons between toolbars, including any custom ones
that you may have created.

The **Tools** tab, shown in Figure 2.17, allows you to add shortcuts to programs that you use often in conjunction with Animation:Master. For example,
if you spend a lot of time in an effects package, you can click the **Add** button
and fill in the required information. A shortcut to the newly added program
will appear in the **Tool** menu of Animation:Master, allowing you to launch
that program from within the interface.

Figure 2.18 shows the **Keyboard Shortcuts** tab of the **Tools, Customize**
panel.

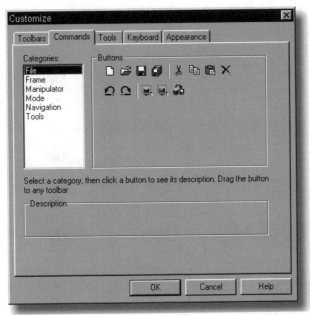

FIGURE
2.16
*The **Commands** tab of the **Tools, Customize** panel. Here you can move tools from toolbar to toolbar.*

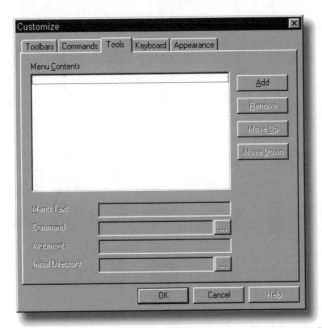

FIGURE
2.17
*The **Tools** tab of the **Tools, Customize** panel. This dialog is used to create shortcuts to other programs that appear in the **Tools** drop-down menu.*

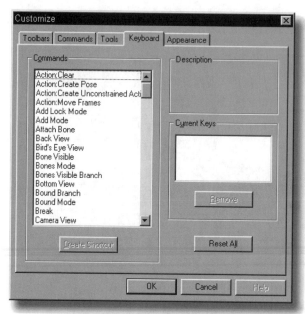

FIGURE **2.18** *The **Keyboard Shortcuts** dialog. Here you can create new keyboard shortcuts, or reassign ones used in the software.*

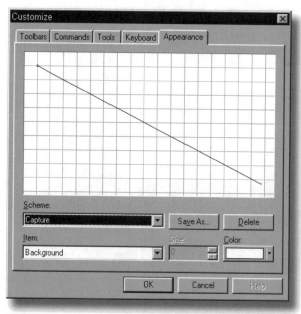

FIGURE **2.19** *The **Appearance** dialog, where you can change the colors of the interface elements and save them.*

The **Keyboard Shortcuts** tab shown in Figure 2.18 displays a list of all of the available keyboard commands, their description, and the shortcut key that is currently assigned to each. If a command has no shortcut key, one can be assigned by clicking the command name, then clicking the **Create Shortcut** button. A box will pop up requesting that you press the new shortcut key. A shortcut key can also be reassigned in this manner, once the default or previous one has been removed.

Figure 2.19 shows the **Appearance** section of the **Tools, Customize** panel.

The **Appearance** tab shown in Figure 2.19 allows you to make changes to the color of the interface, as well as many other elements within the software. Once you have a setup you're happy with, you can save your color scheme for easy recall if you decide to change it later.

Selecting the **Options** item from the **Tools** drop-down menu will allow access to additional settings for different tools in the program. When you first select **Tools, Options**, a dialog similar to Figure 2.20 will open.

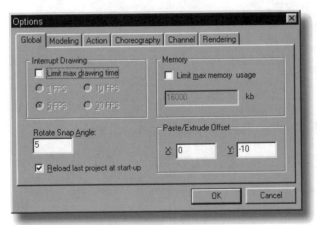

FIGURE *The Global Options tab. Values changed here affect every*
2.20 *part of the software.*

The **Global** tab contains options that affect every part of the software. **Interrupt Drawing** modes can help complex models or slower machines draw faster by limiting the time allowed to draw the screen.

Limiting memory usage allows you to set a limit on how much of your system's memory the software can use. On most systems, this option should not be used, since the operating system will allocate memory.

The **Rotate Snap Angle** makes the **Rotate Manipulator** rotate in the value entered here. For example, the default 5 makes it very easy to rotate a selected object 90 degrees, since after a certain number of 5-degree increments, the rotation value lands exactly on 90.

The **Paste/Extrude Offset** will offset pasted or extruded splines from the original position. This can help avoid confusion if you accidentally click outside of an object manipulator, deselecting all. If a pasted or extruded group of control points is not offset, it will be placed exactly on top of the original spline.

Reload Last Project at Startup is useful if you have work to continue on a given project from day to day. When this box is checked, launching the software will automatically open the last Project that you were working on.

The next tab is the **Modeling Options** tab, shown in Figure 2.21. The options that you can change on the **Modeling Options** tab will affect any modeling windows in the current Project.

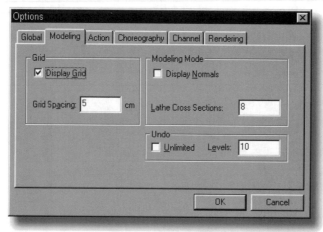

FIGURE   *The **Modeling Options** tab. Values changed here affect any*
2.21   *Modeling windows.*

The **Display Grid** option toggles the grid drawn in the background on and off. **Grid Spacing** is measured in centimeters and can be changed by simply typing a new value into the **Grid Spacing** field.

The **Display Normals** checkbox toggles on the display of the models normals. Normals are essentially the direction that a surface is pointed. When this option is turned on, yellow lines are drawn in the direction that the surface is facing.

The **Lathe Precision** field allows you to change the number of cross-sections that are created when a spline is lathed. The default of *8* is enough for most models, but sometimes more or fewer are needed.

The **Undo** portion of this tab allows you to control the number of undo levels available in the software. It's unlikely that you would want to go beyond 10, which is the default.

The next tab is the **Action** tab, shown in Figure 2.22.

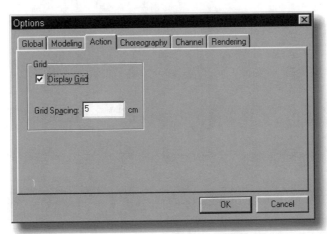

FIGURE *The Action Options tab. Values changed here affect any*
2.22 *Action windows.*

The **Action Options** tab allows you to toggle a visible grid on or off in an **Action** window, as well as changing the scale of the grid by manually entering a value into the **Grid Spacing** field.

The next tab is the **Choreography Options** tab, shown in Figure 2.23.

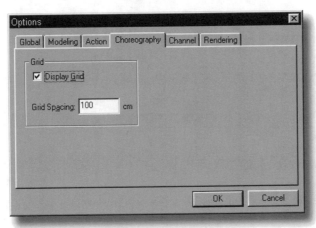

FIGURE *The Choreography Options tab. Values changed here affect*
2.23 *any Choreography windows.*

The **Choreography Options** tab allows you to toggle a visible grid on or off in any **Choreography** windows, as well as changing the scale of the grid by manually entering a value into the **Grid Spacing** field.

The next tab is the **Channel Options** tab, shown in Figure 2.24.

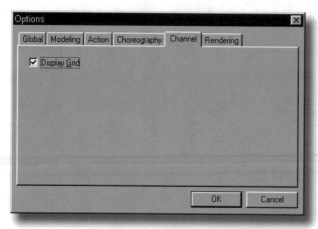

FIGURE
2.24   *The Channel Options tab. Values changed here affect any Channel windows.*

The **Channel Options** tab allows you to toggle a visible grid on or off in any **Channel** windows. The grid spacing can't be changed in a **Channel** window, since the window already displays a set value for any given option.

The final tab is the **Rendering Options** tab, shown in Figure 2.25.

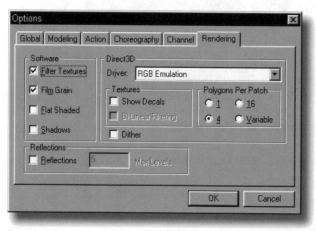

FIGURE   *The Rendering Options tab.*
2.25

The **Rendering Options** tab allows you to fine-tune the rendering quality within the interface. This tab also contains various real-time options, such as the subdivisions per patch (quality) and **Decals**. These options are discussed throughout the course of this book.

The final drop-down menu that appears in the menu bar across the top of the interface is the **Window** drop-down menu. The next section describes the options available from the **Window** drop-down.

THE WINDOW MENU

Figure 2.26 shows the **Window** drop-down menu.

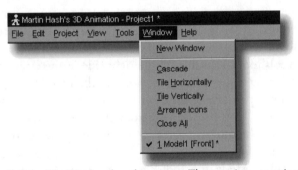

FIGURE   *The **Window** drop-down menu. The menu items contained*
2.26   *here make it easier for you to work by letting you open more*
         windows or helping you arrange the ones that are already open.

Selecting **New Window** from the **Window** drop-down opens another occurrence of the active window. You can open as many of any given window type as you choose. This is useful if you want to see several views of a model at the same time.

Cascade and the tiling options are different preset window arranging options. **Arrange Icons** organizes the windows that are minimized along the bottom of the screen.

The **Available Windows** list contains a list of every open window, so that you can quickly and easily select the window in which you need to work. This option is similar to the **Workbook** tabs from the **View** menu, except that it does not take up any screen space.

Each of the drop-down menus has now been described in detail to make it easier for you to locate the option you need. The next section briefly discusses each of the toolbars and their functions.

TOOLBARS

Now that you're familiar with the drop-down menus and their contents, there are ten different toolbars that you should also get to know. Understanding which tools are located on each toolbar and what function each tool performs will make it easier for you to use the software effectively. Details of the operation of each tool are provided in the online help.

The toolbars are *dockable,* meaning that they can be "stuck" to the sides of the interface if you like. They can also be rearranged, stretched out, or hidden to suit the way you prefer to work.

All of the toolbar options can be accessed by right-clicking the border of any toolbar. Selecting **Hide/Unhide** from a right-click menu will affect only the toolbar you're clicking on.

The **File** toolbar defaults to the upper left-hand corner of the interface. It contains buttons for **New, Open, Save, Cut, Copy, Paste, Undo, Redo, Preview Render, Progressive Preview Render,** and **Render to File.**

The **Tools** toolbar defaults to the right side of the interface, and the available buttons change depending on which of the five available modes is active. If you need to open several different toolbars at once (such as the **Bones** and **Modeling** tools), you can do this from the **View, Toolbars** menu. Keep in mind that only the toolbar related to the mode in which you are working will become active.

In **Modeling Mode,** the **Tools** toolbar contains buttons for **Edit, Add, Add Lock, Insert, Delete, Break, Detach, Peak, Smooth, Group Mode, Lasso Mode, Hide, Extrude, Lathe,** and **Flip Normals.** In **Bones Mode,** the **Tools** toolbar contains buttons for **Edit, Add, Delete, Attach, Detach, Group Mode,** and **Lasso Mode.**

In **Directing Mode,** the **Tools** toolbar contains buttons for **Edit** and **Add Path.** In **Skeletal Mode,** the **Tools** toolbar contains **Edit** and **Lock Bone** buttons. Finally, in **Muscle Mode,** the **Tools** toolbar contains **Edit, Group Mode, Lasso Mode,** and **Hide** buttons.

The **Frame** toolbar defaults to near the bottom of the screen. Most often, the **Frame** toolbar is used to step through the frames of an animation or action, or to mark keyframes as you create an action.

Additional buttons on the **Frame** toolbar give you control of keyframing (such as constraints or Muscle movement), a **Scrub Bar** that is used to easily move through frames, and a **Delete Keyframe** button.

The **Mode** toolbar defaults to the top of the interface, following the **Standard** toolbar. It has five buttons that are used to change modes throughout the program. The available modes are **Modeling Mode, Bones Mode, Muscle Mode, Skeletal Mode,** and **Directing Mode.**

The **Navigation** toolbar defaults to the top of the interface, following the **Mode** toolbar. This toolbar contains buttons for **Turn, Move,** and **Zoom.** These buttons affect the view into the window in which they're used.

The **Manipulator** toolbar defaults to the top of the interface, following the **Navigation** toolbar. The toolbar contains buttons to switch among **Standard, Translate, Scale,** and **Rotate** manipulators, as well as **World Space, Snap Manipulator to Grid,** and **Show Bias** buttons. The manipulators are used frequently throughout the exercises in this book, so you may want to take a moment to experiment and become comfortable with their operation.

The toolbars can be moved anywhere on the screen. This helps you to access the tools you use most often while you work. The next section discusses **Libraries,** an easy way to organize and recall data.

LIBRARIES

The **Libraries** window generally appears docked along the left-hand side of the interface below the **Project Workspace.** It helps you organize and easily recall data that you've created. As your collection of Models, Materials, and Actions grows, you'll find that using libraries is a big help. Review the **Libraries** options in the online help once you're familiar with the general operation of the software.

THE INTERFACE

Now that you are familiar with the general parts of the interface, a little practice is in order before you really get to work. The following exercise will help you get rolling in the A:M interface.

EXERCISE

FAMILIARIZING YOURSELF WITH THE INTERFACE

1. From the **Project** drop-down menu, select **New**. A project tree will appear in the **Project Workspace**.

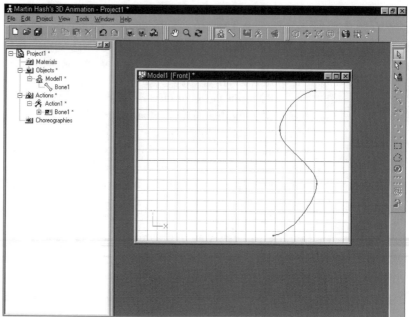

FIGURE   An "S"-shaped spline created using the **Add Lock** tool.
2.27

2. Right-click the **Objects** icon in the **Project Workspace**. Select **New**, then **Model** from the available menus. A modeling window will open, and the **Tools** toolbar will change appropriately.

3. Click the **Add Lock** button, then click near the top of the window. Notice that a control point appears in the modeling window, and a spline follows the pointer wherever you move it within the window. Move the pointer appropriately and click three more times to form an "S" shape, similar to the one shown in Figure 2.27.

5. From the **Tools** menu, select **Options**. Click the **Modeling** tab. Enter 6 into the **Lathe Precision** field, then click **OK**.

6. Click any point on the "S"-shaped spline, then click the **Lathe** button. The result should be something that looks like a vase.

7. Click the **Bones Mode** button. Notice the default bone in the center of the model. Move the top (thin end) of this bone down toward the center of the model by dragging it with the mouse.

8. Click the **Add Bone** button, then click near the top of the existing bone. Drag the mouse upward to position the bone within the top half of the model.

NOTE

Notice that the second bone you added is a different color than the first. As you build more and more complex models, you'll find that as you add bones, each is a different color. This makes it easy for you to distinguish the different parts of a model and to select individual bones when you create Actions.

9. Right-click the *Choreographies* icon in the **Project Workspace** and select **New Choreography** from the available menu. A **Choreography** window will open, containing a default camera and light.

10. Click on the **Model1** item in the **Project Workspace**, and while holding the mouse button down, drag the item over the **Choreography** window. Release the mouse button to drop the model into the **Choreography** window.

11. Right-click the *Materials* icon in the **Project Workspace** and select **New Material** from the available menu. Click the plus (**+**) to the left of the **Material1** item to expand the item's branch.

12. Right-click the **Attribute** node, then select **Change Type To, Checker** from the available menus. Click the plus (**+**) to the left of the **Checker** item to expand that branch.

13. Click the first **Attribute** node beneath the **Checker** item in the **Project Workspace**. On the **Properties Panel**, click the **Attributes** tab.

14. Click the **Color** chip, then click the **Other** button near the bottom of the color palette. In the system standard color picker, enter *10, 158,* and *248* into the **Red**, **Green**, and **Blue** fields, respectively. Click **OK**.

15. Click the second **Attribute** node beneath the **Checker** item in the **Project Workspace**. On the **Properties Panel**, click the **Attributes** tab once again.

16. Click the **Color** chip, then click the **Other** button near the bottom of the color palette. In the system standard color picker, enter *219, 57,* and *109* into the **Red**, **Green**, and **Blue** fields, respectively. Click **OK**.

17. If the **Material Preview** window does not show a checker material (if it is black), press the **Spacebar** to refresh the window. Click the **Checker** item in the **Project Workspace**.

18. On the **Properties Panel**, enter *15* into each of the **Translate** fields, *25* into each of the **Scale** fields, and *60* into the **Blur** field. Notice how the entry in each of these fields changes the look of the material.

19. Click on the **Material1** item, hold the mouse button down, and drag the material over the **Model1** item in the **Project Workspace** (the pointer will change to a shortcut pointer). Release the mouse button to apply the material to the vase model.

20. Click on the title bar of the **Choreography** window. Select the Vase model by clicking on it (a yellow manipulator box will appear). Drag the model toward the camera.

21. Change to a side view by pressing the **6** key on the numeric keypad. Press **Shift+Z** to zoom to fit the scene within the window. The view should look something like Figure 2.28.

22. Notice that the camera is much higher than the Vase model, and that the model does not fall within the camera cone (the purple pyramid).

23. Click the camera to select it, then use the mouse to drag it downward until the Vase model is within the field of view.

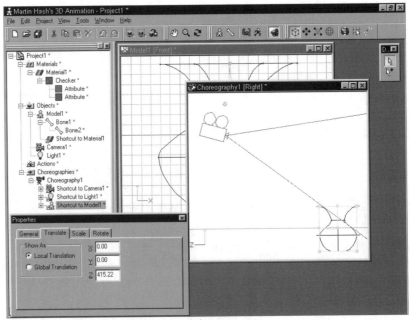

FIGURE   *A side view of the Vase model and the camera.*
2.28

24. Right-click in the **Choreography** window and select **View**, then **Camera1** from the available menus. This will change to a camera view of the scene.

25. You should see the Vase model within the camera's field of view. Click the **Render** icon, then click in the window to render the scene. It will probably turn out a little dark. Take a few moments to experiment with moving the default light around the screen. This is done by clicking on the light, then dragging it to a new location. Continue once the render looks satisfactory to you.

26. Right-click the **Project1** item in the **Project Workspace**, then select **Save As** from the available menu. Point to where you would like to save this project, then type in *My First Foray* and click **OK**.

Many explanations and details were omitted from the preceding exercise. However, it should have helped you get used to moving around the interface, clicking the right mouse button, and using the drag and drop capabilities of the software. It would be a good idea to play around a while longer, adding several more instances of the Vase model to the choreography (drag and drop), experimenting with the light settings (on the **Properties Panel**), and making camera movements (drag).

When you're comfortable with the interface, move on to the next section, which explains a little about control points, splines, patches, and surfaces.

SPLINES

This section describes the type of modeler that Animation:Master uses. It should help you understand what makes a surface that will render.

There are many different kinds of 3D modelers, the most common being the *polygon editor*. Polygon editors can be difficult to work with: They create surfaces with a series of small polygons (most often, triangles), and polygonal objects often render with rough or faceted edges, since it is difficult to make complex smooth surfaces with them.

The modeler in Animation:Master is different because it is *patch-based*. The curved lines and smooth edges the modeler uses are excellent for creating organic shapes. The modeler can also create mechanical objects just as easily as polygon modelers, since patch modelers are much more powerful than polygon modelers.

The first thing you need to understand about the modeler is what a *spline* is. The term has certainly been tossed around enough that you may have heard of it. The following section describes the splines that are used within Animation:Master.

WHAT ARE SPLINES?

The ease of finely adjusting smooth, curved, three-dimensional splines is what makes patch modelers so powerful and easy to use. Essentially, *splines* are just smoothly curved lines that you adjust with control points. To create a model, you use splines to form *patches,* and patches to form the model.

Splines are very different from the vectors used in polygon modelers in that moving one spline is equivalent to moving dozens or even hundreds of polygons simultaneously. Spline models have densities much lower than those of equivalent polygon models, making them easier to work with, and easy on storage space.

As splines are added to a model, their curvature is controlled at certain locations along the spline. These locations, called *control points,* are discussed in the following section.

WHAT ARE CONTROL POINTS?

Splines are lines drawn between *control points,* the individual red or green squares that make up a spline and indicate where you can click to move or adjust that spline. Splines are directional: They enter a control point on one side and exit it on the other. Changing the shape of a spline in the modeler is quite easy. Simply point at the control point you wish to move, press and hold the mouse button, then drag the point to a new location. Creating objects will, of course, take a little more time and practice, but it's nice to know the modeler won't waste your practice time.

There is a fundamental concept that you must understand to use splines effectively to model: What makes a surface that will render? The next section discusses the rules for creating legal (rendering) patches.

WHAT DEFINES A SURFACE?

Probably the most difficult thing you will ever do is to create your first patch. Almost everyone just sits right down to begin their 3D adventures by constructing their own heads. Many become frustrated when creating a single patch seems so difficult. Many even break down and read the documentation.

It seems a waste to get frustrated over something such as a single patch, when they're very rarely used. Experience with the modeler will make it easier for you to understand what will create a surface, and what would be the best way to manipulate that surface. As you gain experience and continue to create and attach splines, a model will take form.

As the complexity of a model increases, so will the possibility of surface ambiguities. *Surface ambiguities* occur when connected control points can be either filled by a patch or left open. The software decides which connected control points define patches, consistent with the three rules for creating patches. This means that if you keep the following three rules in mind, creating a surface will be much easier for you (or at least you will understand why your model doesn't render):

1. All open and closed splines when extruded have patches on the extruded sides. This means that any splines that are extruded will create legal patches automatically.
2. All open and closed splines when lathed have patches on the lathed sides. This means that performing a Lathe operation on a spline will also result in automatic creation of legal patches.
3. Any closed combination of three or four control points defines a patch, *unless* all three or four control points are in the same spline. This is to minimize unwanted interior patches.

Don't expect just to sit down and model away. Good modeling skills take time and practice to develop, and at times you'll become frustrated. Remember, animation is hard, and part of animation is modeling.

SUMMARY

You have now read about and experimented with many of the tools and options available to you within the software. As you continue to gain experience, you'll become more comfortable with the navigation of the interface, and many operations will become considerably easier for you. Remember that practice makes perfect, and practice equals experience.

The next chapter will get you rolling by describing modeling basics. This chapter will lay the foundation for the great storytelling achievements that lie ahead of you.

3 Modeling Basics

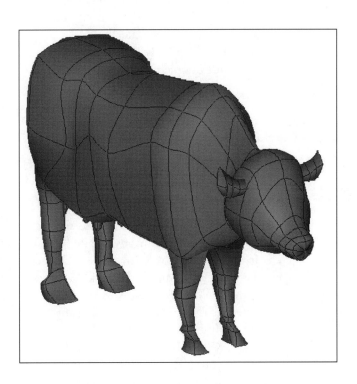

This chapter discusses the modeling of simple characters that don't require the use of any special techniques such as hooks, magnitude adjustments, or "hanging" splines. Instead, they're built using basic modeling techniques such as lathing, rotation, and translation of groups. As you'll discover while working your way through this book, the techniques you learn here are built on in later chapters to create increasingly complex objects.

Keep in mind as you work through this chapter that it's designed to teach you commonly accepted approaches to modeling cleanly and efficiently. It is by no means the only way to create any given model.

This chapter covers the following techniques:

- Modeling with the Lathe Tool
- Modeling a Unibody Biped
- Modeling Simple Quadrupeds

MODELING A SIMPLE CHARACTER WITH THE LATHE TOOL

Advertising professionals often use simple characters, because most of the everyday objects seen in advertising are simple: a bottle of weed killer, a credit card, cereal boxes, etc. These characters aren't complex; in fact, they can be built and animated quickly and easily. They are fantastic learning tools, from which you can gain the fundamentals of creating an animatable character. This is because in advertising, most objects of this type are given human qualities.

Jack "Killer" Bean is quite possibly the best starting point for you in expanding your knowledge of the Animation:Master modeler. The fact that he has no complex joints or connected parts, as well as the low patch count required to create him, makes him a perfect character to practice animation techniques on. For this exercise, Jack Bean will be used strictly as a modeling example. Later chapters cover his texturing and the application of bones. Figure 3.1 shows a character sketch of Jack "Killer" Bean. The Killer Bean character is made up of a series of simple shapes that are easily created with the lathe tool.

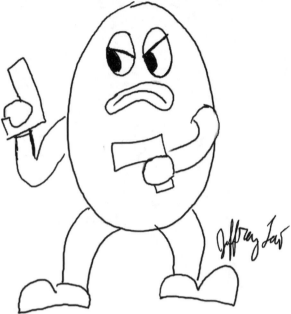

FIGURE *A character sketch of Jack "Killer" Bean.*
3.1

BEGINNING THE MODEL

Generally, the torso or pelvic area is where the modeling begins on a charac-ter. The pelvis is generally assigned as the patriarch when bones are applied (meaning that when the pelvis is moved, all other parts of the model will move as well).

Jack's body is somewhat less than statuesque, making him unfit for swim-suit competition, but quite capable of taking the abuse that often comes his way. Killer Bean's body is created by lathing a spline around the Y-axis. This type of modeling is common in the creation of heads, torsos, and appendages, such as arms and legs.

Start by opening *Killer Bean.MDL* from the accompanying CD-ROM. You can see that Jack already has his torso, arms, and legs modeled (see Figure 3.2). The next sections show you how to create the feet, hands, and facial fea-tures used in the Jack Bean model, and how to put them together to form the character.

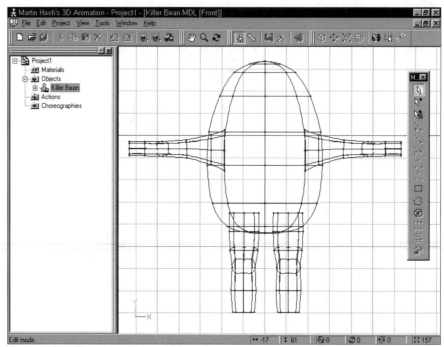

FIGURE *The* Killer Bean.MDL *model from the accompanying CD-ROM.*
3.2

MODELING THE FEET

Don't let the size of Bean's feet fool you! The Bean is quick on his feet and a pair of sensible shoes is a must in his line of "work." This exercise will walk you through the creation of Jack Bean's feet.

EXERCISE

MODELING FEET

1. Open *Killer Bean.MDL* from the accompanying CD-ROM, if it isn't open yet. Use the **Move** tool to drag the window downward until the body section is no longer visible to avoid getting the screen cluttered up.

2. Begin the shoes by creating a 9-point spline to the right of the Y-axis marker, as shown in Figure 3.3. Select any point along the spline by clicking it, then click the **Lathe** button.

3. Use the **Group** tool to select the top cross-section of the foot. Enter *1* into the **X** and **Z Scale** fields on the **Properties Panel**. Repeat

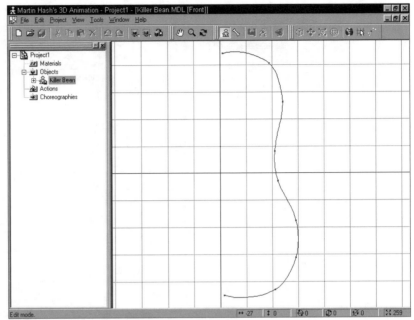

FIGURE *Spline shape used to create Killer Bean's feet.*
3.3

this procedure to "close" the bottom cross-section of the foot. It may be necessary to make adjustments to the end cross-sections to round out the surface of the model. This is done by selecting the cross-section with the **Group** tool and using the arrow keys to move the control points to an appropriate position. The foot should be shaped like a peanut, as shown in Figure 3.4.

4. Use the **Group** tool to select the entire foot, then type *90* into the **X Rotate** field on the **Properties Panel**. This will orient the foot properly along a horizontal plane.

To make the bottom of the foot flat, you'll need to remove the splines creating the curvature along the bottom of the foot. The best way to visualize the correct splines for the purpose of this exercise is to picture the face of a clock over the view you currently have of the foot: 12 would be straight up, 6 straight down, 3 to the right, and so on.

5. The splines that need to be removed are at 5, 6, and 7 o'clock. Use the **Group** tool to select these three splines and press the **Delete** key. The object should now look similar to Figure 3.5.

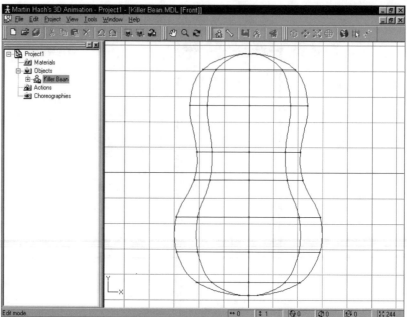

FIGURE **3.4** *Lathed "peanut" shape of the feet.*

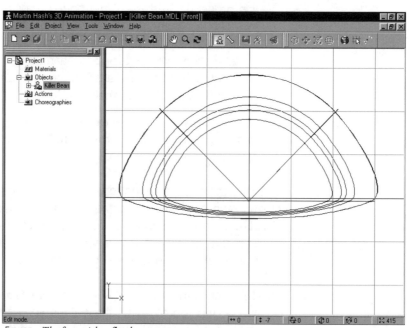

FIGURE **3.5** *The foot with a flat bottom.*

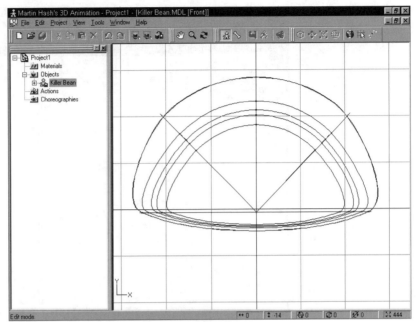

FIGURE
3.6 *Front view of foot after making adjustments.*

6. From the front view, shape the foot by selecting the lowermost outer control points and translate them inward. The foot should look similar to Figure 3.6 at this point.

7. Change to the **Top** view by pressing the **5** key on the numeric keypad. Make adjustments by grouping and translating the points along the sides of the foot until it more closely resembles a foot shape. You can do this by shaping the inner side of the foot with a slight inward curve, and by making some slight adjustments to the outer edge of the model.

Since "side view" is never specified throughout the course of this tutorial (everyone has his or her preferences),you need to verify that the foot is correctly oriented. Select a side view and **Zoom** out until both the foot and the body are visible. The fat part of the foot is the front or toe. If the foot is pointed toward the back of the body, use the **Group** tool to select it and enter *180* in the **Y Rotate** field on the **Properties Panel**.

8. Once the foot is oriented correctly, select it with the **Group** tool and drag it into position relative to the leg. Verify the position of the foot

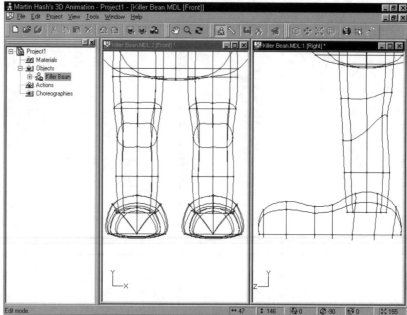

FIGURE *Both a front and side view of the feet attached to the legs.*

3.7

from both **Front** and **Side** views to make sure you get the right foot on the right leg.

9. With the foot still grouped, select **Copy**, then **Paste** from the **Edit** menu. Right-click the **Group** name in the **Project Workspace** and select **Flip, X-axis** to create the model of the second foot. Use the mouse or arrow keys to translate the second foot into position.

The feet are now done and in position, so save your work by clicking the **Disk** button. The next exercise will walk you through adding hands to the model.

MODELING THE HANDS

Killer Bean's hands are strong from gripping his handguns. While the description of how to create them may sound complex, the hands themselves are just simple "mittens." Jack Bean wouldn't have it any other way, because more fingers can get in the way of the trigger.

MODELING HANDS

1. Continue from the previous exercise. Make some room to work by using the **Move** tool to drag the window downward until none of the model is visible.

2. Create a straight vertical spline with 11 control points off-center of the **Y Axis** marker. You can adjust the size of the hand later if necessary, so this positioning is not crucial. Take care, however, to ensure that the spline is far enough from the Y axis to create some thickness to the model.

3. Select any point along the spline by clicking on it with the mouse, and click the **Lathe** button.

4. Both the top and bottom of the cylinder that was just created can be closed by selecting them with the **Group** tool, and entering *1* in the **X** and **Z Scale** fields of the **Properties Panel**.

5. Use the arrow keys to "tuck" the ends into the cylinder slightly and create a nice rounded edge to each end of the tube.

6. Select the entire cylinder with the **Group** tool and enter *90* in the **Z Rotate** field on the **Properties Panel**.

7. Begin shaping the hand by selecting the seven vertical cross-sections starting from the right side of the model, including the end points. (See Figure 3.8.)

8. Rotate this group by entering *25* in the **Z Rotate** field on the **Properties Panel**. Reposition the group so that it follows the curvature of the spline without folding over itself.

9. Continue by selecting the six vertical cross-sections starting at the same end and working your way inward, once again including the end points. Rotate the group by entering *25* in the **Z Rotate** field on the **Properties Panel** once again. If necessary, reposition the group with the mouse or arrow keys. (See Figure 3.9.)

10. Next, select the five vertical cross-sections starting at the same end and working your way inward, including the end points. Rotate this group by entering *45* in the **Z Rotate** field on the **Properties Panel**.

11. Repeat this rotation after selecting the three vertical cross-sections starting at the same end and including the end points. (See Figure 3.10.)

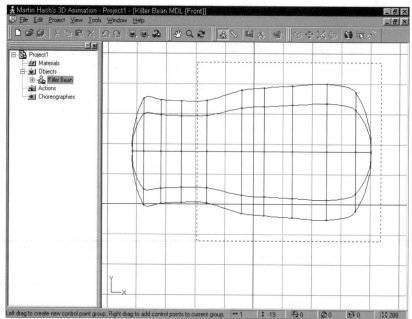

FIGURE
3.8
These cross-sections form the hand when rotated.

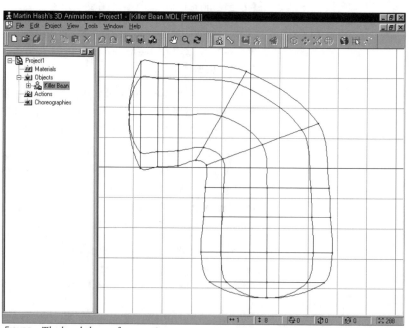

FIGURE
3.9
The hand shape after step 9.

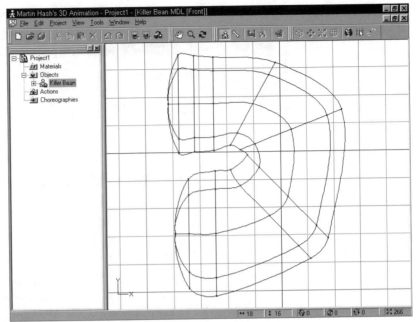

FIGURE   *The hand shape after step 11.*
3.10

Figure 3.10 shows the shape of the model at this point, which is clearly out of scale. Scaling adjustments can be made to the lower half of the hand at this time. The idea at this point is to make the model look somewhat like a mitten, the thumb being created by the lower part that was formed by the groups rotated in steps 7 through 11.

12. Complete the hand by selecting the three vertical cross-sections starting from the left end of the hand. Enter *–20* into the **Z Rotate** field on the **Properties Panel** to create some curvature to the upper part of the hand.

13. Select the thumb with the **Group** tool from a front view. Switch to a top view, and translate the thumb slightly off center using the mouse or arrow keys.

    Make any other necessary adjustments until your model matches the one shown in Figure 3.11.

The hand is now completed and needs to be positioned on the body. The newly created hand belongs at the end of the right arm, intersecting the arm to about the third spline. Verify proper placement from both the front and top views.

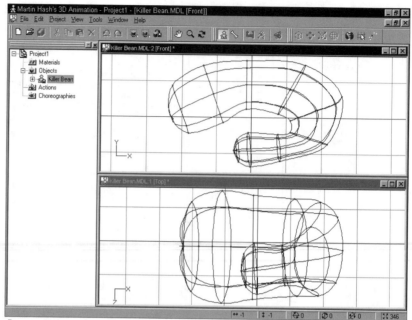

FIGURE *Front and top views of the completed hand model.*
3.11

Create the left hand by selecting the right one with the **Group** tool and choosing **Copy**, then **Paste** from the **Edit** menu. In the Project Workspace, right-click the new group name and select **Flip, X axis**. If the left hand does not flip into proper position, adjust it with the mouse or arrow keys.

Now that you've completed the body, you can add the face to the model. Click the **Disk** button to save your work before you go on.

MODELING THE FACIAL FEATURES

The cold, hollow look in Killer Bean's eyes comes from years of evening the score. He has the blank, unfeeling stare of death.

Many different types of eyes can be constructed for any given character. Killer Bean's eyes are simple half spheres that have some scaling distortion to elongate them.

EXERCISE

MODELING EYES

1. Continue from the previous exercise. Begin the eyes by selecting any point on the torso and pressing the **/** key to **Group Connected**. The entire body should be selected.

2. Select **Copy**, then **Paste** from the **Edit** menu.

3. Translate the new group up and away from the main torso to avoid any confusion while modeling.

4. Scale the eyes down to fit the body proportions by entering *19, 15,* and *19* into the **X, Y,** and **Z Scale** fields, respectively.

Although the simple torso shape was copied to create the eyeballs, it contains some unnecessary resolution that can be removed.

5. To remove some of the resolution from the eyes, switch to the top view. Using the analogy of a clock face as in the foot exercise, select the splines at 12, 2, and 10 o'clock. Then press the **Delete** key.

6. Press the **2** key on the numeric keypad to switch back to a front view. Use the **Group** tool to select the third horizontal cross-section down from the top of the eye. Press the **Delete** key to remove the selected spline.

7. Similarly, select the fifth cross-section down from the top of the eye and press the **Delete** key to remove the selected spline.

8. Translate the control points of the eye until it has an egg shape.

9. From a side view, adjust the shape of the eye into an oval.

10. Use the **Group** tool to select the entire eye.

11. Enter *20* into the **X** and *–5* into the **Y Rotate** fields on the **Properties Panel**. This will tilt the eye back somewhat, and turn it to match the curvature of the head more closely.

Figure 3.12 shows both front and side views of the eye segment for reference in shaping.

12. Group the eye shape and position it from a front view centered on the fourth spline down from the top of the body segment. From the side view, the eye should be intersected halfway into the wireframe of the body. If necessary, use the **Zoom** tool to magnify the eye area to make the proper adjustments.

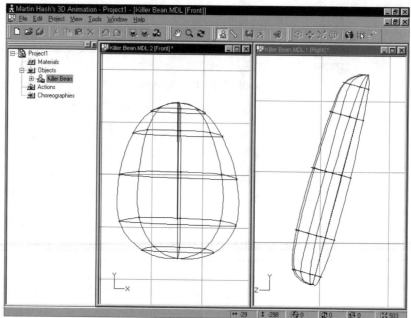

FIGURE 3.12 *Front and side views of Eye shape for modeling reference.*

13. Create a pupil by making an 8-point spline in the shape of a C. The end points of the C-shaped spline should be placed very near the Y axis marker without crossing over.

14. Click any point along the pupil spline, then click the **Lathe** button to create the sphere.

15. Select the sphere with the Group tool and enter *15* and *90* into the **X** and **Z Scale** fields on the **Properties Panel**.

16. Position the pupil from the front view roughly halfway between the fourth and fifth horizontal cross-sections of the eye. From the side view, the pupil should intersect halfway into the eye.

17. Create an eyelid by grouping the top five horizontal cross-sections of the eye and selecting **Copy**, then **Paste** from the **Edit** menu.

18. Scale the eyelid up to fit around the eyeball by entering *110* in both the **X** and **Y Scale** fields on the **Properties Panel**, and *120* in the **Z Scale** field.

19. Change to a side view and adjust the eyelid to look similar to the one shown in Figure 3.13.

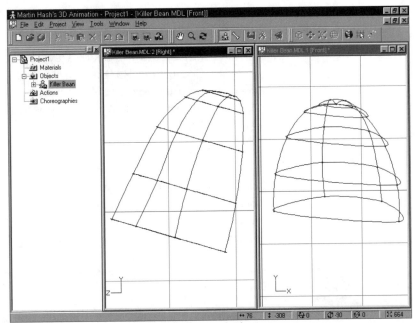

FIGURE *The eyelid shape from both the front and side views.*
3.13

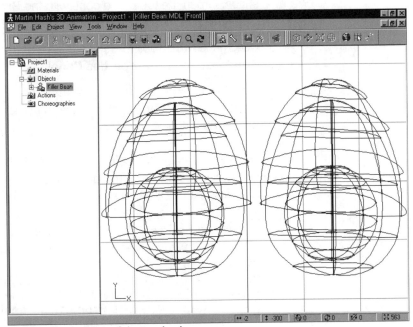

FIGURE *Close-up view of the completed eyes.*
3.14

20. Once you've shaped the eyelid, position it from the front view over the eye. Check from a side view as well to ensure proper positioning.

21. You can now create the second eye by selecting this one and choosing **Copy**, then **Paste** from the **Edit** menu. Right-click the group name in the **Project Workspace**, and select **Flip, X-axis**. Make any necessary adjustments to position the eye correctly. (See Figure 3.14.)

The eyes are now finished, and it's on to the mouth to complete this model. Click the **Disk** button and continue.

Killer Bean doesn't need a fancy mouth because he is concise and to the point when he speaks. In fact, Killer Bean's mouth is made up of a simple torus, or doughnut shape, that was modified by scaling.

EXERCISE

MODELING THE MOUTH

1. To create the mouth, set the **Lathe Precision** to *7* and draw a diagonal spline with just two control points.

2. Select one of the points and click the **Lathe** button to create a cone shape. Group the top of the cone with the **Group** tool and press the **Delete** key, leaving just a ring of control points.

3. Use the **Group** tool to select this ring and enter *90* into the **X Rotate** field on the **Properties Panel**.

4. Translate the ring to the right of the green Y axis marker with the mouse or arrow keys. Click outside the yellow **Manipulator** box to deselect the ring of control points.

NOTE

You must first deselect all points, then reselect the spline on which the lathe operation will be performed, because lathes are performed on a spline level. This is also the case with the **Extrude** tool.

5. Set the **Lathe Precision** to *10*. Select any point on the ring by clicking on it with the mouse. Then click the **Lathe** button to create a torus to form this character's mouth.

6. Select the entire mouth with the **Group** tool, and enter *90* into the **X Rotate** field on the **Properties Panel** to orient the mouth vertically.

7. Flatten the mouth into a more oval shape by grouping the two cross-sections that make up the top lip and translating them downward. Likewise, group the two cross-sections that form the bottom lip and move them upward. If necessary, make slight adjustments to the individual splines to even out the mouth shape.

8. Switch to a side view and group all of the points above the center spline of the mouth. Enter –45 into the **X Rotate** field on the **Properties Panel**. This will give the mouth some curvature.

9. Group all of the points below the center spline of the mouth. Enter 45 in the **X Rotate** field on the **Properties Panel** to curve the bottom part of the mouth similarly to the top.

10. Use the Group tool to select the entire mouth and enter 15 into the **X Rotate** field on the **Properties Panel**. This will tilt the mouth backwards slightly to match the angle of the body. Figure 3.15 shows a front view of the completed mouth.

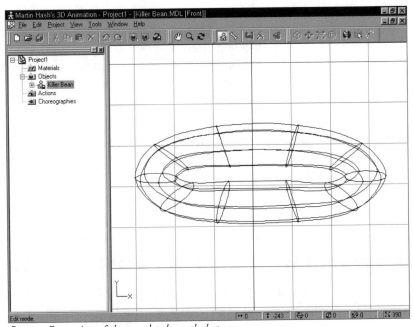

FIGURE *Front view of the completed mouth shape.*
3.15

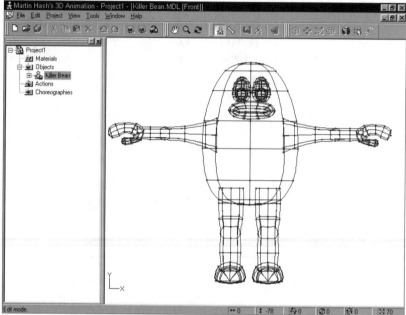

FIGURE *The Killer Bean.*
3.16

11. Use the **Group** tool to select the entire mouth and position it from the front view just below the eyes. From a side view, the mouth should intersect the body roughly three splines. Figure 3.16 shows the complete model from a front view.

As you can see from these exercises, using Animation:Master's modeling tools, you can create a simple character quickly and easily. Proficiency is achieved through practice, and the next exercise will prove that proficient use of the available tools can produce excellent results lightning-fast.

MODELING WITH UNIBODY CONSTRUCTION

One of the more potent capabilities of Animation:Master v5 is the ability to build and animate one-piece models, referred to as *unibody construction*. Unibody construction has many long-term benefits, such as *reusable motion libraries, surface integrity,* and *model flexibility.*

The method used to construct the next figure as a unibody model uses lathes that take into account the resolution of the adjoining parts of the model before they are added.

The 20-Minute Man exercises are a step up from Killer Bean: The shoulder and leg joints are more complex, since both are connected directly to the body. The joints used on the 20-Minute Man are simple but effective for the difficulty level of the character. As you work through these exercises, don't worry if your proportions are off or your character looks out of scale. The proper proportioning of characters and controlling them within Animation:Master will be covered later in the book.

EXERCISE

BEGINNING THE 20-MINUTE MAN

1. Start Animation:Master, and begin by selecting **New** from the **Project** drop-down menu. Save the project as "20-Minute Man."

2. Expand the project list by clicking the plus (**+**) sign to the left of the "20-Minute Man" item in the **Project** window.

3. Right-click the **Object** list and select **New, Model**.

Unibody construction is an excellent way to gain enough resolution to construct a model entirely of 4-point patches in very little time.

MODELING THE LEGS

The 20-Minute Man is built quite literally from the ground up, beginning with a leg, then continuing up the body to the head.

EXERCISE

MODELING THE LEGS AND FEET

1. Continuing from the previous exercise, use either the normal **Add** mode or the **Add Lock** mode to create a vertical spline with 8 control points to the right of the green Y axis marker. Select any point along the spline by clicking on it, then click the **Lathe** button.

2. Group the bottom cross-section of the resulting cylinder and enter *1* in both the **X** and **Z Scale** fields on the **Properties Panel**.

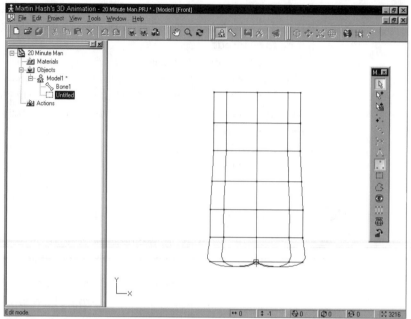

FIGURE   *The beginning of a leg.*
3.17

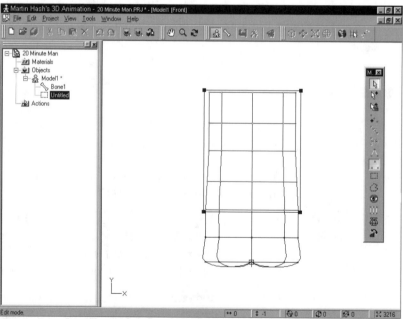

FIGURE   *Leg points to group in forming the upper leg.*
3.18

3. Use the arrow keys to move the selected group upward until it is even with the next spline on the model, as shown in Figure 3.17.

4. Use the **Group** tool to select the points shown in Figure 3.18.

5. Enter *60* in both the **X** and **Z Scale** fields on the **Properties Panel** to scale the upper part of the leg down. The value of 60 is an approximation used here based on the distance of the original spline from the Y axis marker. It may or may not work well with your model.

6. Translate the selected group downward with the mouse or arrow keys until it forms a smooth curve above the nonselected points. Switch to a side view and translate the selected group backward along the Z axis until it's centered over the back of the remaining points, forming the shape of a leg over the back end of a foot.

7. From the front view, use the **Group** tool to select the control points shown in Figure 3.19. These points will form the foot of the 20-Minute Man.

8. From the top view, use the scale manipulator to scale the foot down along the X axis only, until it is in the shape of an oval.

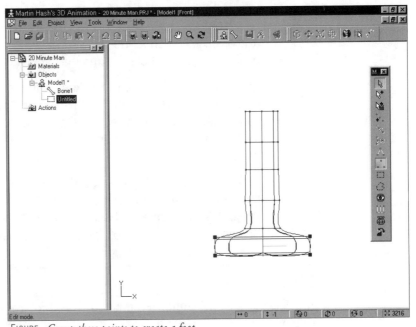

FIGURE *Group these points to create a foot.*
3.19

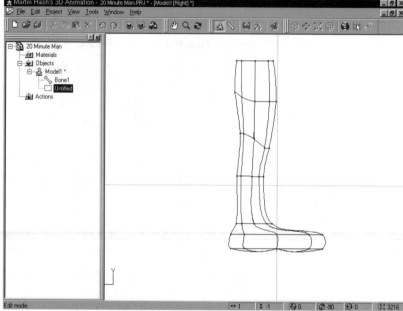

FIGURE *A side view of the completed leg.*
3.20

9. Shape the leg by manipulating the control points from the front view first. Make the ankle and calf areas a little thinner, and the thigh area a little wider. Switch to the side view and move the calf spline back a bit to create a slight curve along the back of the leg.

10. Select the spline that forms the knee with the **Group** tool, and enter *45* in the **X Rotate** field on the **Properties Panel**. Make any adjustments necessary to correct any deformations that occurred as a result of rotating the knee spline. Figure 3.20 shows a side view of the completed leg.

11. Create the second leg by grouping the first, then selecting **Copy**, then **Paste** from the **Edit** menu. Right-click the group name in the **Project Workspace** and select **Flip, X Axis**. If the pasted group flips and remains on top of the original leg, use the mouse or arrow keys to translate it to the right.

The legs are now complete, so take a second to save your work before continuing on to the pelvis.

MODELING THE PELVIS

The 20-Minute Man model differs from the Killer Bean in that the legs of this model are connected directly to the body. The legs of the Killer Bean model were simply intersected into the body, which is an effective method in simple characters, but does not illustrate a good technique for unibody modeling.

EXERCISE

CREATING THE PELVIS AND TORSO

1. Select the top splines of both legs with the **Group** tool and click the **Hide** button to hide the rest of the model.

   To create a seamless joint with the pelvis, the resolution used on the previous step needs to be accounted for here. Doing this will maintain a clean, 4-point patch construction.

   Calculate the resolution by counting the control points around both of the rings from the legs. You can also figure the resolution by multiplying the number of legs created (2) by the lathe precision used to create them (8). Therefore, the next step will require you to set the **Lathe Precision** to *16* (8 points × 2 legs).

2. Draw a diagonal spline that begins near the Y axis marker and extends out as far as the outside edge of one of the leg cross-sections. While one of the points on this spline is selected, click the **Lathe** button. The model should look similar to Figure 3.21.

3. Select the top of the cone with the **Group** tool and press the **Delete** key.

4. Use the **Group** tool to select the remaining ring.

5. Switch to a top view and use the scale manipulator to scale the selected group down in the Z axis only until it is in the shape of an oval. Figure 3.22 shows the group after scaling.

   To connect the new spline cross-section to the top of the legs, it will be necessary to connect several 2-point splines between the two. It may be helpful to use **Turn View** to change to a bird's-eye view of the model while doing this.

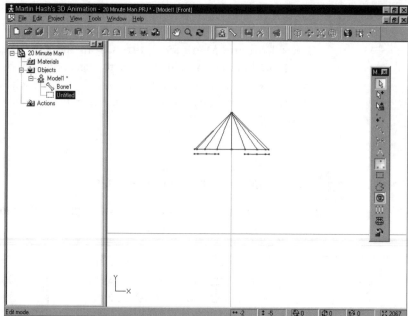

FIGURE
3.21
Matching the leg resolution for the pelvis.

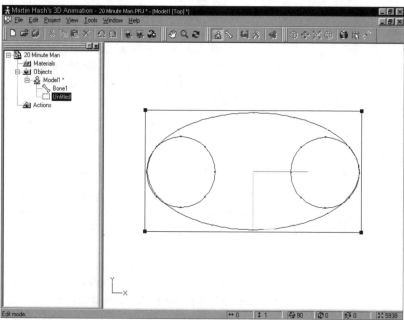

FIGURE
3.22
Creating an oval pelvis shape by scaling.

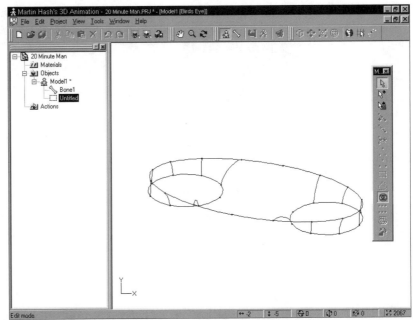

FIGURE
3.23
Bird's-eye view of waist cross-section and upper leg cross-section.

6. Starting with the outermost control points (the ones that would run down the outside of each leg), connect a 2-point spline between the corresponding control points on the leg cross-section and the pelvic ring. Continue around each cross-section, connecting 2-point splines between corresponding control points. Don't connect any splines to the innermost two points (the ones that would run down the inside of each leg). Figure 3.23 shows an angled view of the model at this point.

7. Switch to a top view and connect the two innermost control points from each leg cross-section.

8. Close the area by adding a 3-point spline that leads from the back control point on the pelvis cross-section, to the just-joined thigh control points, and then to the front control point on the pelvis cross-section.

9. Shape the circles that form the top of the thighs more naturally by selecting control points around these rings and translating them until they look more organic. Figure 3.24 shows the model after these adjustments.

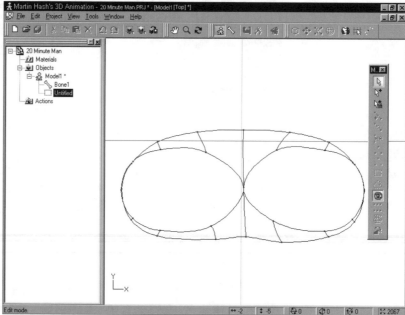

FIGURE **3.24** *Top view of waist area after splines between waist cross-section and leg cross-sections are joined.*

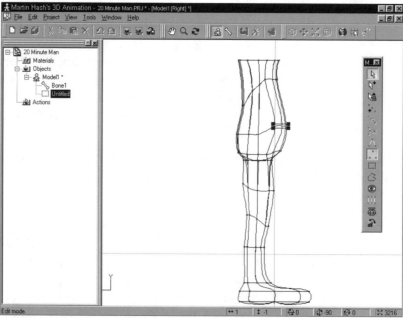

FIGURE **3.25** *Translate these control points to form a belly and add shape to the torso.*

The waist area is now complete, and you can see how the transition was made between the legs and the pelvis. Click the **Disk** button to save your work, and move on to the torso.

10. Switch to a front view and press the **H** key to unhide the rest of the model. Group the top cross-section of the model and extrude it three times vertically to form a torso.

11. Use the **Scale** manipulator to shape the torso thicker toward the pelvis, thinner just above the stomach, and thicker toward the top spline.

12. From a side view, select the control points shown in Figure 3.25. Translate them away from the body to form a bit of a gut. You can also make other adjustments at this point, such as rounding out the buttock area and shaping the back.

Now that the torso is done, the next step will be to create the shoulders for the model. Save your work before continuing.

EXTRUDING THE ARMS

The next exercise describes how to add arms to the model by using the **Extrude** tool. Once the basic shape of the arm where it connects to the body is established, the arm will be extruded away from the body.

EXERCISE

CREATING THE ARMS

1. Switch to a front view and use the **Group** tool to select the control points shown in Figure 3.26.

2. Click the **Extrude** button, and without moving the group, enter *45* into the **Z Rotate** field on the **Properties Panel**.

3. Click the **Extrude** button once more, without moving the selected group, and enter *45* into the **Z Rotate** field on the **Properties Panel**. If either of the rotations of the extruded cross-sections causes the new splines to cross over or deform existing splines, adjust their position now. You may have to use the **Zoom** tool to magnify the shoulder area.

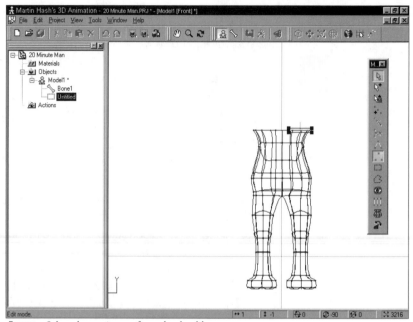

FIGURE *Select these points to form the shoulder area.*
3.26

4. Use the **Group** tool to select the far right cross-section (the last extrusion) and press the **H** key to hide the rest of the model.

5. Switch to a side view. The visible cross-section will become the joint where the arm connects to the body. As you can see, there is currently only half of a "ring." Since a full circle of control points is needed to form the arm, add a 7-point spline to the model. Join the end points of this spline to the end points of the cross-section, and shape the remaining five control points to complete the circular shape needed for the arm. Verify proper positioning of the additional control points from the front view. If they're misaligned, make adjustments as necessary.

6. After you complete the circle, select the entire arm hole with the **Group** tool from the front view. Use the **Scale Manipulator** to scale the selection in the Y and Z axes until it more closely matches the body proportions.

7. With the arm hole still selected, use the **Extrude** tool to extrude once for the biceps, again for the elbow, again for the forearm, and once more for the wrist.

8. Make any adjustments to the Y and Z scale that are necessary to correctly shape the arm.

NOTE

You can make effective hinge-type joints by rotating the spline that will be at the center of the joint to a 45-degree angle. This tilted spline will cause knee and elbow joints to bend more smoothly when manipulated. This technique also causes a bump to show on the outside of the joint and a curvature to form on the inside.

9. Select the spline that will be the elbow joint. Enter *–45* in the **Y Axis Rotation** field on the **Properties Panel**. Correct any deformation that occurs.

10. From a top view, verify that the arm is shaped correctly. Make any adjustments that are necessary to give it a suitable look.

Figure 3.27 shows the completed arm, after all adjustments to scale and position have been made.

11. To create the other arm, repeat steps 2 through 10 on the other side of the body. The extrusions that form the arm hole will need to be rotated –45 in the Z axis, since it is the opposite side of the body. Likewise, the elbow spline will need to be rotated 45 in the Y axis.

Figure 3.28 shows the model after the second arm has been modeled.

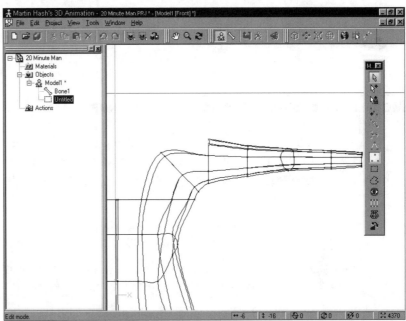

FIGURE *A view of a completed arm and how it attaches to the body.*
3.27

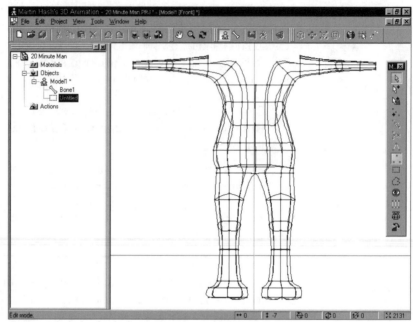

FIGURE *The body after both arms have been added.*

3.28

Now that you've added the arms and shoulder areas to the model, the shoulder area will come next. Save your work before going on.

MODELING THE SHOULDERS, HEAD, AND HANDS

The next exercise focuses on reducing the resolution around the shoulder area of the model so that you can model the neck and head without too many splines. It is somewhat similar to the way you created the waist area.

EXERCISE

MODELING THE SHOULDERS

1. Select the points shown in Figure 3.29 with the **Group** tool and press the **H** key to hide the rest of the model.

2. Set the **Lathe Precision** to *8* and make a single diagonal spline over the selected points.

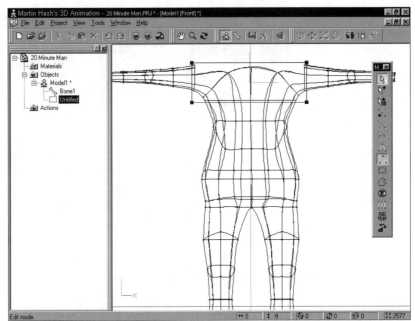

FIGURE *The control points from which the neck will be formed.*
3.29

3. Click the **Lathe** button to form a cone shape over the shoulder area. Select the top of the lathed cone and press the **Delete** key.

4. Select the remaining ring of points with the **Group** tool. Switch to a top view and center the selected points over the body.

5. Switch back to the front view and select the control points shown in Figure 3.30. Press **Shift+H** to hide more. Change back to the top view.

Closing the shoulder area of the model with patches is easy, but you must pay attention to avoid connecting splines to the wrong control points.

6. Start by adding two 3-point splines that are not attached to anything. Connect one across the back of the model, and one across the front.

7. Now add two 2-point splines between the neck ring and the body: one in the front center, and one in the back center. Use Figure 3.31 for reference.

8. Continue closing the patches by adding six 2-point splines as shown in Figure 3.32.

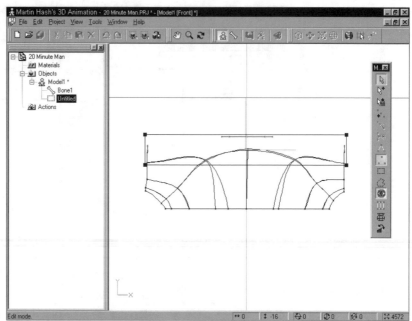

FIGURE
3.30   *The neck and shoulder cross-sections of the model.*

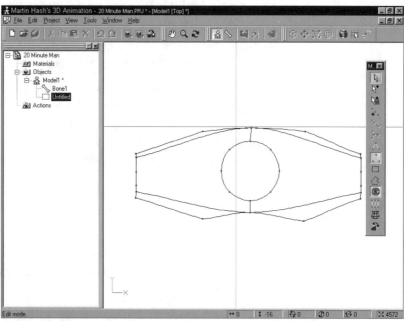

FIGURE
3.31   *The first two splines to connect to begin attaching the neck to the body*

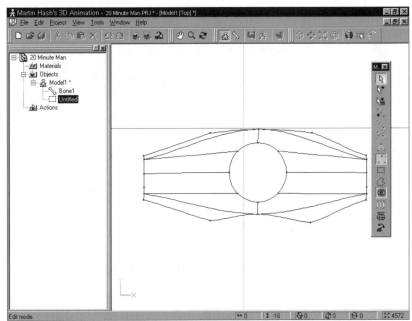

FIGURE **3.32** *Adding splines to close the surface of the neck.*

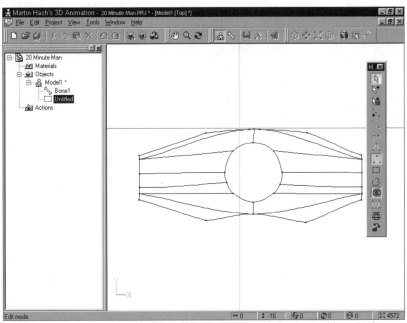

FIGURE **3.33** *Two control points inserted, and the final two splines for the shoulders added.*

Notice that there are still two control points without splines attached to them. To form clean, 4-point patches, two control points need to be added to the neck ring.

9. Add two control points by clicking the spline onto which they are going to be inserted, then pressing the **Y** key.

10. Once both control points have been added, close the surface with two more splines between the open control points. Use Figure 3.33 as a reference for adding the control points and splines.

The shoulder area is now complete, and it should be fairly obvious in what direction the model will be completed. The next exercise explains the creation of the neck and head.

MODELING THE NECK AND HEAD

EXERCISE

1. From a front view, use the **Group** tool to select the uppermost cross-section on the body (the neck ring).

2. Click the **Extrude** button and drag the extrusion upward to form the neck.

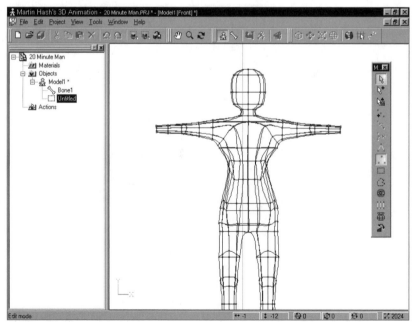

FIGURE *The shape of the head.*

3.34

NOTE

This would be a good time to take a look at the model as a whole and make any adjustments to body scale, since the entire body is easily available. In this exercise, the body was scaled down to 80% along the X axis to thin it out.

3. Continuing from the previous step, use the **Group** tool to select the top cross-section of the neck.

4. Extrude the selected spline four times, dragging each extrusion upward slightly.

5. Group the top cross-section of the head and enter *1* in both the **X** and **Z Scale** fields on the **Properties Panel**.

6. Scale and shape the remaining cross-sections appropriately to form a somewhat spherical head shape.

Figure 3.34 shows the model after the head has been added and shaped.

Now that the head and neck are done, you can finish the model by adding some hands. Click the **Disk** button to save your work, then go on to the next exercise.

EXERCISE

MODELING THE HANDS

The hands are created in much the same way as the head.

1. Use the **Group** tool to select the wrist cross-section.

2. Extrude four times, dragging the extrusions out horizontally.

3. Close off the tip of the hand by grouping the end cross-section, then entering *1* in both the **Y** and **Z Scale** fields on the **Properties Panel**. Scale and shape the remaining cross-sections appropriately to form a curved hand shape. Figure 3.35 (on the following page) shows the complete model.

The first few times you run through this exercise, you may have some difficulty with the view angles needed to connect splines, or with getting all of the cross-sections in the correct position to connect them. Once you get a feel for the technique, however, and fall into a modeling "groove," you should be able to run through it in 15 to 20 minutes.

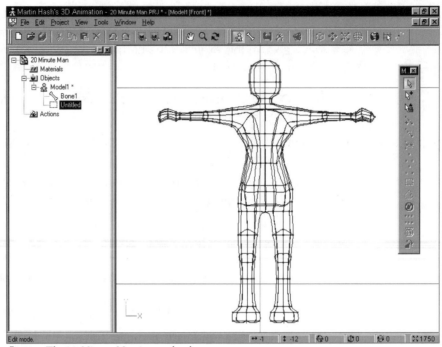

FIGURE   *The 20-Minute Man is completed.*
3.35

Unibody construction is useful because it maintains the integrity of the model's surface while keeping the resolution of the model down. Now that you've created a simple biped and a unibody biped, the next exercise will walk you through creating a quadruped.

CREATING A UNIBODY QUADRUPED

Quadrupeds have become a quite popular game for animators. Dogs, horses, sheep, cows, cats, and any other number of four-legged creatures roam the earth, waiting to be digitally immortalized. These obvious quadrupeds will inevitably lead to more complex objects, such as dragons, dinosaurs, and other mythical creatures.

You have now modeled a character whose extremities only intersected the body (Killer Bean), as well as a model constructed as one piece (20-Minute Man). The object of the next section is to create a quadruped by forming the legs and body separately, then connecting them together.

The cow used in the following exercises is a simple model formed by once again using the Lathe tool. This model is the first that takes advantage of Animation:Master's rotating pivot, which allows lathing around any axis at any angle.

BEGINNING THE MODEL

To keep the resolution down and make the model easier to study for future reference, the head was not created with very much detail. The final model in this case ended up being created out of only 368 patches.

1. Start Animation:Master, and begin by selecting **New** from the **Project** drop-down menu. Save the project as "Cow."
2. Expand the project list by clicking the plus (+) sign to the left of the "Cow" item in the **Project** window.
3. Right-click the **Object** list and select **Import Model**. Open *Cow Body Spline.MDL* from the accompanying CD-ROM. This is the spline that will form the main body, correctly oriented from the top view.

EXERCISE

MODELING THE BODY

This spline was added from the top view in the correct orientation for a cow's body (horizontal rather than vertical). The next few steps describe orienting the pivot to match the body spline's orientation before lathing.

1. Pivot rotation works best (is least confusing) from a slightly angled view, so use the **Turn** tool to rotate the modeler window to a convenient view.

2. Click any point on the spline and press the **/** key to **Group Connected**. Click the **Rotate Manipulator** button. Use the green handle on the pivot to rotate the pivot –90 degrees X (watch the **Properties Panel** for the correct value if necessary) until the green Y axis is running parallel to the spline. Figure 3.36 shows the pivot after it has been rotated.

3. Switch to a top view and translate the pivot toward the Z axis marker.

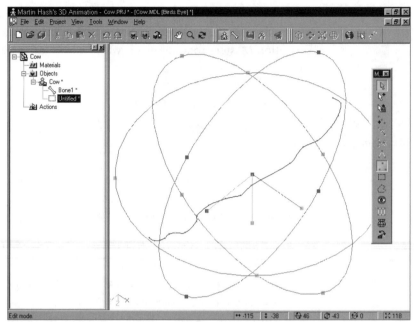

FIGURE *Pivot rotated to match horizontal orientation of spline.*
3.36

At this point, the pivot is oriented such that a lathe function will occur along the Z axis. When the pivot is rotated, its rotation value only references the selected point or group of control points. Once you deselect the point or group of points, the default orientation of the pivot returns.

4. Set the **Lathe Precision** to *7 cross-sections.* Click the **Lathe** button. You should end up with something that resembles a cow torpedo.

5. Because the model was offset slightly from the Y axis of the pivot when it was lathed, there are holes at either end of the torpedo that need to be closed. Use the **Group** tool to select the "snout" cross-section and enter *1* in both the **X** and **Y Scale** fields on the **Properties Panel**.

6. With the closed snout of the model still selected, **Zoom** in until you have a clear view of the model's head. If the snout area appears to be "tucked in" to the face of the model, use the arrow key make any necessary adjustments to smooth the surface out.

The head of the model is still somewhat round because it was created using the lathe. The next exercise will explain how to shape the model to look more like a cow.

EXERCISE

SHAPING THE COW'S HEAD

1. Use the **Group** tool to select the eight cross-sections that form the head and rotate them roughly –25 degrees in the X axis. This will cause the head to turn downward slightly. You may notice that the points "travel" a bit when they are rotated. This can be corrected by selecting the **Translate** or **Standard Manipulator** and moving them back into position.

2. To make the head look like a cow's head will require a little shaping. Use the **Group** tool to shape the head from the side, then switch to a top view and make adjustments. Use Figure 3.37 for reference.

3. Complete the head by scaling the last cross-section down slightly, to thin out the neck end of the head.

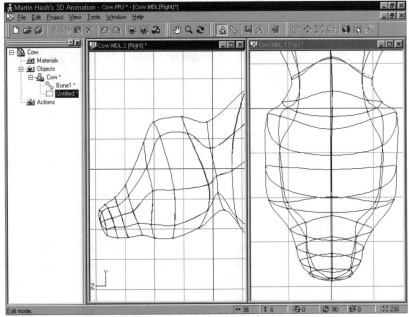

FIGURE *Side and top view of the cow's head, for shape reference.*
3.37

4. With the cross-section still selected, click the **Hide** button and switch to a front view. Translate the sides of the neck cross-section inward to square it up a bit.

The basic shape of the head of the cow is now done. As you can see, the shaping goes rather quickly once the basic body has been created. Click the Disk button to save your work and continue on to the next exercise, which will walk you through shaping the body.

EXERCISE

SHAPING THE COW'S BODY

A cow's body is blocky or squarish, except for the bony protrusions at the shoulder blades and the pelvic area. This cow looks a little scrawny. Scaling up the back of the neck and the first few cross-sections of the body will "beef" up the model and give it some weight.

1. In the front chest area of the model, pull the points that make up the center spline running along the bottom of the cow's body forward and down a bit to give a little more muscular look to the chest.

2. Use the **Group** tool from a side view to group the cross-sections of the body one at a time. Hide the rest of the model, and "square" up the model slightly by translating the outside control points of these cross-sections inward.

3. From the side view, pull the control points that form the shoulder area upward to add a bump for the shoulder blades.

The front end of the body is now shaped correctly. In the next exercise, you'll add front legs to the cow. Click the **Disk** button to save your work before continuing.

EXERCISE

CREATING AND ATTACHING THE LEGS

The legs for the cow were created by lathing a 6-point spline to a precision of 5. The legs were shaped and rotated as needed, then saved as *Cow With Legs.MDL* on the accompanying CD-ROM.

1. Open the file *Cow With Legs.MDL* from the CD-ROM.

2. Use the **Group** tool to select the points shown in Figure 3.38 and click the **Hide** button to hide the rest of the model.

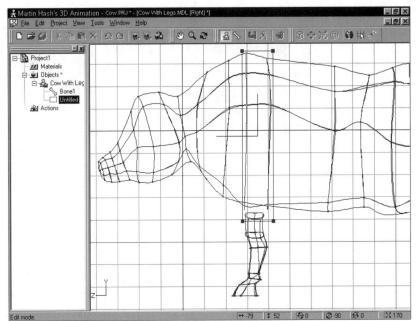

FIGURE 3.38 *Grouping the shoulder and leg cross-sections to attach the legs to the body.*

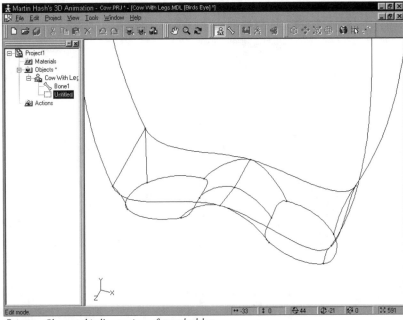

FIGURE 3.39 *Close-up bird's-eye view of attached legs.*

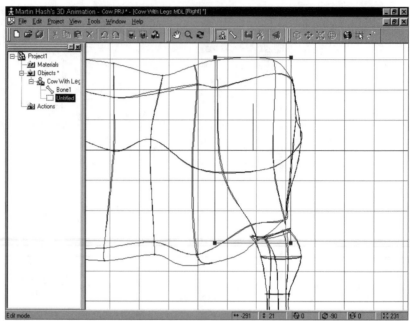

FIGURE   *Control points needed to attach the back legs.*

3.40

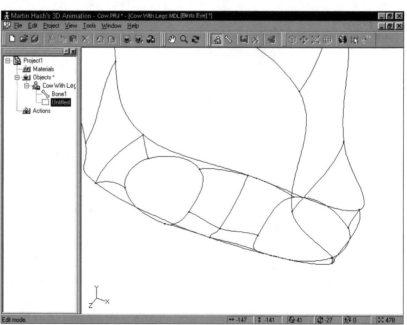

FIGURE   *Close-up bird's-eye view of the attached back legs.*

3.41

3. Before you can attach the legs to the body, you need to insert a control point along the spline that runs along the bottom of the cow's body. Select the control point at either end of this spline, and press the **Y** key to insert a point.

4. Begin attaching the legs by adding a 3-point spline from the inside middle control point of one leg, to the middle point that was just added, and finally to the middle point of the opposite leg.

5. Continue attaching the legs by adding 2-point splines around the top cross-section of the leg and the corresponding body control points. Figure 3.39 shows a close-up bird's-eye view of the attached legs.

6. Click the **Hide** button to unhide the rest of the model, and select the control points shown in Figure 3.40.

7. Click the **Hide** button to hide the rest of the model.

8. Attach the back legs to the model the same way the front legs were attached. Remember to insert an extra control point in the middle spline of the cross-sections that make up the back leg. Figure 3.41 shows a bird's-eye view of the attached back legs.

Being able to add parts to a segment when they have been built separately is an important part of modeling capability. Click the Disk button to save your work, then continue to the next exercise, which will describe adding a tail to the model.

EXERCISE

THE DARK SIDE OF THE MOO

The final exercise on the cow describes how to add a tail to the model. Although the tail is created similarly to the legs (lathe, then shape), it is connected to the body in a different manner.

1. Begin creating a tail by adding a 5-point spline similar to the one shown in Figure 3.42.

2. Set the **Lathe Precision** to *4*, select the **Translate Manipulator**, and move the pivot toward the rear end of the cow slightly.

3. Click the **Lathe** button and shape the tail thicker at the top, and wide at the bottom (that fuzzy end part on a cow's tail).

4. Use Figure 3.43 to attach the tail to the appropriate control points. Note that the top cross-section of the tail was rotated in the X axis

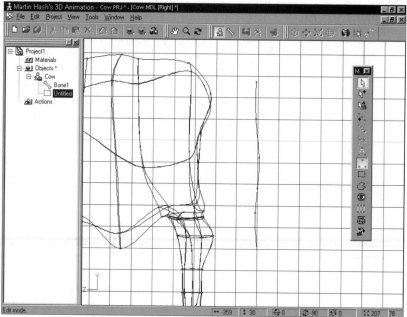

FIGURE *Spline used to create a tail.*
3.42

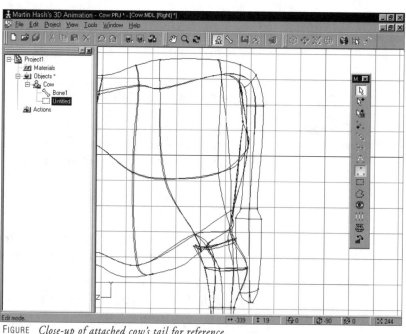

FIGURE *Close-up of attached cow's tail for reference.*
3.43

to a vertical position, making for a smoother curve from the tail to the body. Once the rotation was performed, the top cross-section was then extruded toward the body of the cow.

5. Two-point splines can now be added from the top of the tail to the top middle control point between the hip bones of the cow, from the two side control points of the tail to the two back control points on the hips, and from the lower edge of the tail to the next control point down in the middle spline of the cow's body.

To create a smooth curve like the one shown here, it may be necessary to translate some of the control points that make up the tail.

FINISHING THE COW

For a little more detail on the cow's body, a simple lathed object was added to create an udder. It was then copied several times and placed accordingly.

Simple lathing was also the technique used for the addition of the ears.

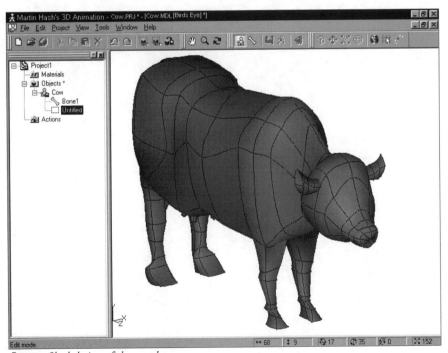

FIGURE *Shaded view of the complete cow.*
3.44

Neither the udders or the ears are actually attached to the model. Although they are part of the model and will move with it, they are simply intersecting the surface of the cow's body, much like many of the parts of Killer Bean.

Figure 3.44 shows a bird's-eye view of the completed cow wireframe model. Decals will be added later for the Jersey cow look.

SUMMARY

This chapter has covered some of the most common techniques for modeling simple, but usable, characters. You can build on the techniques used to create these characters to develop very complex models.

Chapter 4 builds upon the techniques learned in Chapter 3 and moves on to some more complex modeling issues, such as hooks, surface creasing, and creating models with compound curves.

4 Advanced Modeling

This chapter discusses the creation of complex objects. Models that are labeled "complex" don't necessarily have an immense amount of data in them. Instead, they use techniques such as hooks, hanging splines, and multipart construction. They also require a little knowledge of spline direction.

Complex characters take time to develop, so their use is generally reserved for digital movie and TV effects. Animation:Master v5 can easily create complex characters in a short time when it's used effectively. Some people have a natural ability to look at a wireframe representation of a 3D object and very easily discern what needs to be done to get it where it should be. Others need a little practice.

The tutorials that follow build on the techniques you learned in Chapter 3. This chapter describes what hooks are used for, walks you through using hooks in modeling a dinosaur, describes how to construct and control spline directions in modeling a human face, discusses modeling a human body, and demonstrates techniques for effective-looking eyes.

It takes time to reach an advanced level of modeling. The following pages contain some fairly complex models created with techniques that were developed with hours of use and practice.

This chapter covers the following techniques:

- How Hooks work
- Using Hooks in Modeling
- Spline Direction and Creases
- Spline Direction in Modeling a Human Face
- Modeling with Multiple Parts
- Modeling the Human Body

HOW HOOKS WORK

One great advantage of modeling with patches is the ability to create a low-density model easily. Low-density models have small patch counts and take up very little physical storage space. Anyone familiar with 3D can figure out that low density equals easy manipulation.

While traveling the learning curve associated with spline modeling, you'll discover that certain occurrences of adjoining patches cause creases along the surface of the model. These creases can be fixed easily, but only when you've gained some modeling experience and know what to look for. Animation:Master v5 has implemented a very special tool that helps reduce the resolution of adjoining parts of a model, because surface integrity is often lost in the quest for a decent low-density model.

The special tool in Animation:Master v5 that can reduce such creases is called a *hook*. Hooks allow the extra splines associated with variable-density patches to be connected directly to the center of another spline. In an area that has been hooked, the software interpolates the surface between the two adjoining patches to provide a clean surface that reduces resolution. Hooks are not a visible tool; there are no buttons to click, no shortcut keys to press. They simply connect to the center of a spline, just as any control point connects to another control point.

The following exercise will introduce you to hooks and one way they can be used. Figure 4.1 shows a simple lathed vase created from a 4-point spline.

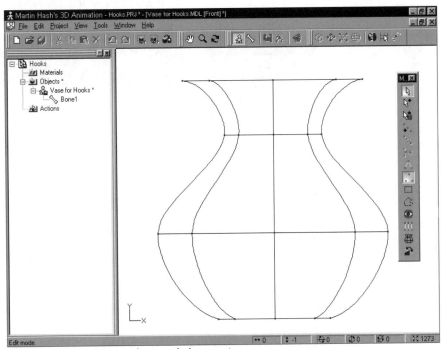

FIGURE *A simple vase created using a lathe operation.*
4.1

ADDING A HOLE WITH HOOKS

As a simple exercise in using hooks, assume that for some reason it was decided that the model in Figure 4.1 was to have a spout. The following exercise will explain how to add a hole to the side of the vase that can be extruded to form a spout.

Open the model *Vase.MDL* from the accompanying CD-ROM before you begin.

1. From the front view, use the **Group** tool to select half of the model and click the **Hide** button to hide the other half.

2. Create a spline loop by lathing a diagonal spline and removing the top control points of the cone that is formed. Select the remaining control points and enter *90* into the **Z Rotate** field on the **Properties Panel** to stand the ring on end. Switch to a side view.

   Figure 4.2 illustrates the difficulty in dealing with attaching the ring of control points to the body of the vase, because of the varying resolution. Six of the eight control points on the ring have cor-

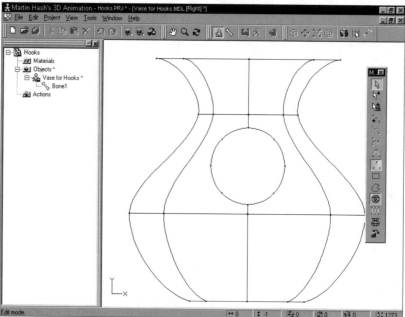

FIGURE *Viewing the spline ring and vase from the side.*

4.2

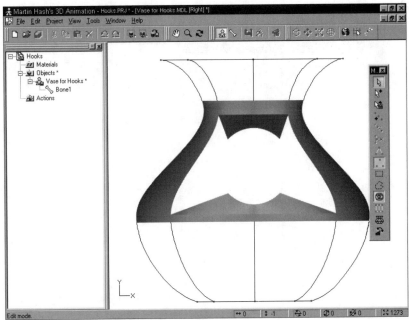

FIGURE **4.3** *Rendering of ring partially attached to vase.*

responding points on the vase body (top, bottom, lower left, lower right, upper left, and upper right), but what about the other two?

If the vertical center spline that was occupying the center patch of the vase is removed and the surfaces are closed between the vase and ring's corresponding points, rendering will yield results similar to Figure 4.3.

The holes created by the two 5-point patches on either side of the hole look dauntingly large, but using hooks could make it easier to close the surface.

In this situation, you can apply hooks by first inserting a control point onto the vertical spline on either side of the spline ring. Then add a spline from the ring to the newly added point, and finally hook into the next spline around the body of the vase.

3. To use a hook, attach the control point at the end of one spline to the center of the target spline, exactly as you would normally glue control points. When the spline hooks, the control point at the hooked end of the spline will disappear. This is because a hook is not a control surface.

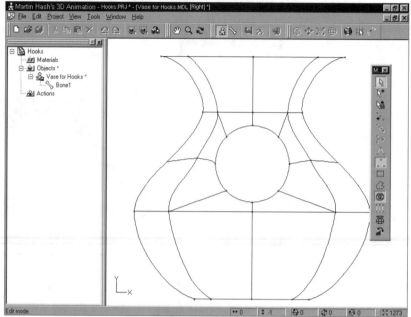

FIGURE *Wireframe view of the vase showing hooks.*
4.4

NOTE

Remember when you work with hooks that the hooked end of a spline can attach at 1/4, 1/2, or 3/4 of the way along the target spline. This allows you better control over which adjoining surfaces the hooked surface will be averaged from, and also allows multiple hooks into a single spline.

4. A good technique to provide a smooth surface is to continue the spline that will be hooked over an extra spline on the model. This will greatly reduce any surface ambiguities that might occur.

Figure 4.4 shows the wireframe of the vase with hooks. Making adjustments from the front and side views will give you a clean connection on the side of the vase.

The simple example in the preceding exercise illustrates the usefulness of hooks in modeling. However, this example is not a situation that would occur often, if at all.

Reducing geometry is common in all types of models and can be clearly illustrated with examples from a typical bipedal form. Shoulders, the back of a head, and complex hand shapes that connect to the wrist are all examples in which hooks can be of benefit. All of these locations have areas of high resolution that need to attach to adjoining parts of lower resolution.

Now that you've experienced hooks on a simple level, the next section discusses using hooks in a more common, practical manner: the Thom model.

CHARACTERS WITH HOOKS

For this section, open the *Thom.MDL* on the CD. Thom, the yellow Animation:Master mascot, is an excellent example of real-world usage of hooks.

Look closely at his waist area and notice how hooks were used to give a clean transition from the splines in the legs to those in the torso. The wireframe close-up in Figure 4.5 shows the hooks in Thom's waist, and Figure 4.6 shows a rendered view of the hooked area.

NOTE

Note that if you're creating models intended for export as DXF files, you should not use hooks in the models you create. The hooked areas won't export as polygonal surfaces.

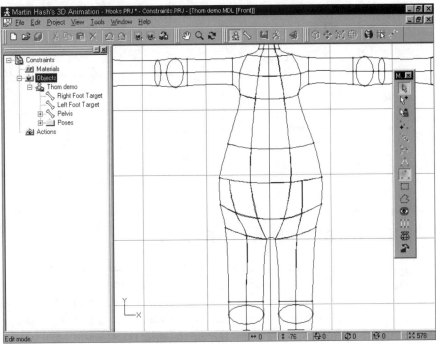

FIGURE   *Close-up view of waist with hooks.*

4.5

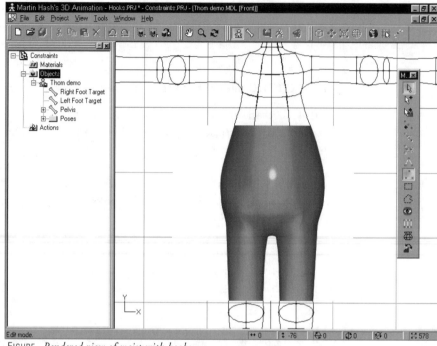

FIGURE *Rendered view of waist with hooks.*
4.6

Because hooks create a surface averaged from the two adjoining surfaces, it takes some time and a little practice to be able to use them effectively. The next section describes the creation of a dinosaur from scratch to review some of the tools used in the previous chapter, as well as to give you some practice in using hooks correctly.

USING HOOKS IN MODELING

Dinosaurs have become popular applications of computer graphics. Fantastic effects like those seen in *Jurassic Park* and several other movies have led to a lot of interest in building dinos ur models in 3D. Such models can help you learn how to use a technique s ch as hooks to construct a popular character. And they give you a chance to l uild a different type of biped or quadruped.

The following exercise, wh ch describes how to model a *Tyrannosaurus rex* from scratch, uses hooks exter ively.

BEGINNING TO BUILD A DINOSAUR: THE TAIL

1. Start Animation:Master, and begin by selecting **New** from the **Project** drop-down menu. Save the project as "Trex."

2. Expand the project list by clicking the plus (**+**) sign to the left of the **Trex** item in the project window.

3. Right-click the object list, and select **New, Model**.

4. Right-click the **Model** name and select **Save As**. Enter *Trex* as the name.

Now that the project is set up, you're ready to begin modeling the *Tyrannosaurus rex*.

Unlike many of the other models you've created throughout the exercises in the book, the *T. rex* will be built from the back forward. The bulk of a dinosaur's body can easily be created from a single lathed shape, but the purpose of this exercise is real practice using hooks to join together variable-resolution patches:

5. Begin in the side view, and create a horizontal spline with 13 control points on it.

6. Set the **Lathe Precision** to *10*.

7. Select any point on the spline by clicking on it, and press the **/** key to Group Connected. Click the **Rotate Manipulator** button and rotate the pivot –90 degrees X.

8. Translate the pivot to just above the highest point in the tail spline. Refer to Figure 4.7 for the correct positioning.

9. Click the **Lathe** button to create the tail shape.

10. Use the **Group** tool to select the open end of the tail. Then click the **Extrude** button. Enter *1* into both the **X** and **Y Scale** fields on the **Properties Panel**. Make any necessary adjustments to position the tail cross-section properly.

11. Shape the tail by selecting each cross-section with the **Group** tool and adjusting it similarly to Figure 4.8. Most of the cross-sections shown here were rotated between 15 and 25 degrees X. After you rotate each cross-section, make any necessary adjustments to its scale.

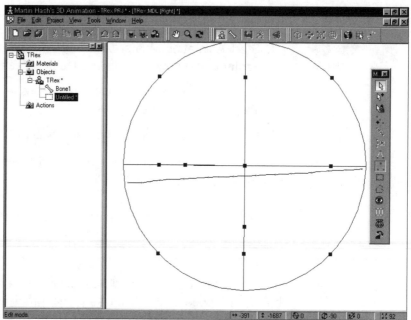

FIGURE *Placement and rotation of Rotate Manipulator.*
4.7

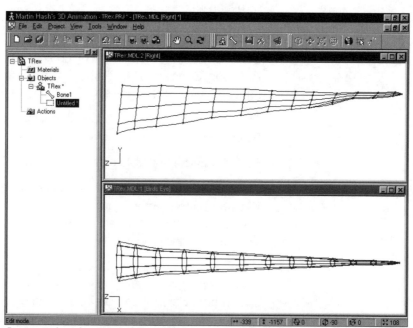

FIGURE *Side and top view of the tail shape.*
4.8

The tail is now complete. The next section walks you through creation of the dinosaur's body, then discusses how to connect the tail to the body piece.

CREATING THE BODY

As with most of the other models you've created to this point, the torso area of the dinosaur takes up the bulk of its size. As you're constructing the body of the *Tyrannosaurus rex*, keep in mind that it's a very large and muscular dinosaur. Muscular characters' surfaces rarely appear smooth; rather, they often look "lumpy."

1. To build the body of the dinosaur, create a horizontal spline with 13 control points.

2. Set the **Lathe Precision** to *12*.

3. Click on any control point along the body spline, press the **/** key to Group Connected, then click on the **Rotate Manipulator** button. Rotate the pivot –90 degrees X and translate it to a position similar to that shown in Figure 4.9. This pivot position will create a wide body shape when lathed.

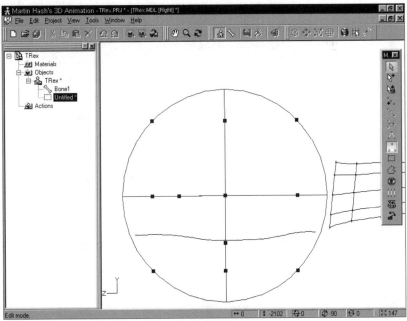

FIGURE *Pivot rotation and translation for body spline.*

4.9

4. Click the **Lathe** button.

5. Begin connecting the body and the tail by selecting the two cross-sections to be joined, in addition to the next two cross-sections up. Click the **Hide** button.

6. Starting from the middle horizontal spline, begin connecting 2-point splines between corresponding control points along the tail cross-section and the body cross-section, as shown in Figure 4.10.

7. Close off the tail by inserting a control point along the next open spline on the tail. Continue the spline from the body cross-section across this new control point, and hook it into the next cross-section on the tail piece. You can complete this procedure easily if you first group the top of the model and hide the rest, then attach the hook from the top view.

8. Repeat step 7 to attach the open bottom spline of the body to the tail. When you're finished, the model should look similar to Figure 4.11. Figure 4.12 shows a bird's-eye view of the shaded wireframe of the model for reference.

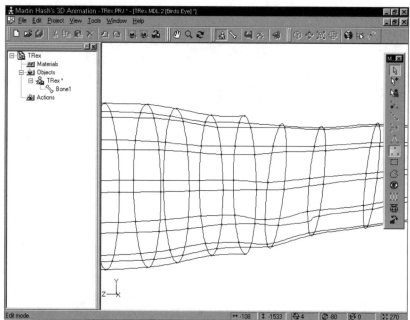

FIGURE *A bird's-eye view of splines attached between the tail and body cross-sections.*
4.10

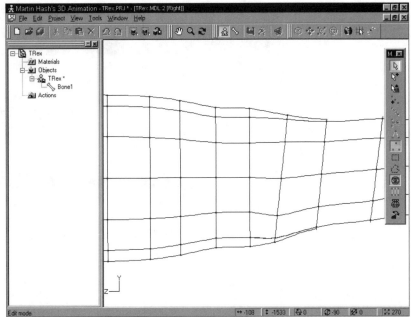

FIGURE
4.11
Side view of the body using hooks to connect to the tail.

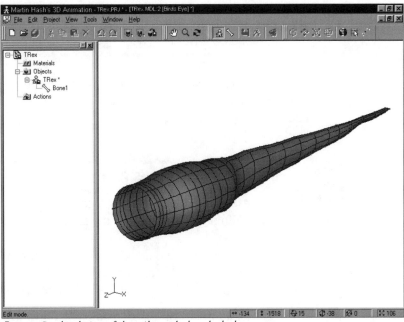

FIGURE
4.12
Rendered view of the tail attached to the body.

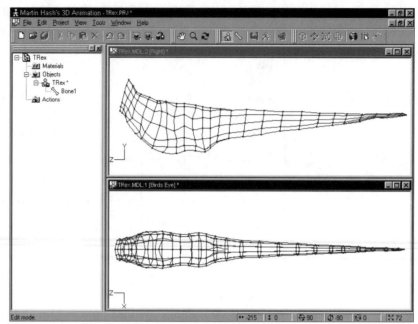

FIGURE *Side and top view of the body shape for the* T. rex.
4.13

9. Shape the body from the side view. Make it thicker toward the back of the body where the thighs will be, thinner in the midsection, and tapered toward the neck end, as shown in Figure 4.13.

Once you've shaped the body similarly to Figure 4.13, you can save your work and move on to the next section, which will walk you through the creation of "arms" for the dinosaur.

EXERCISE

CREATING THE *T. REX*'S ARMS

This exercise continues to add to the model created in the previous steps. The next step is to add the arms onto the model.

1. Begin creating the dinosaur's arms by adding a spline with 10 control points on it. Click any control point along this spline and press the **/** key to Group Connected. Click the **Rotate Manipulator** button.

2. Rotate the pivot –90 degrees X to orient it for proper lathing of the arms. After rotating, translate the pivot upward.

3. Set the **Lathe Precision** to 6, then click the **Lathe** button.

4. From the top view, position the arm in front of the body and slightly off to the side. The arm should not be left located near the middle of the body where it will appear when lathed.

5. Select the entire arm with the **Group** tool, and select **Copy**, then **Paste** from the **Edit** menu. Right-click the group name in the **Project Workspace**, and select **Flip, X Axis**.

6. Switch to a side view and use the **Group** tool to select the control points shown in Figure 4.14.

7. Click the **Hide** button to hide the rest of the model.

8. Attach four 2-point splines between the arm cross-section and the patch where the arm is supposed to connect.

    The process of connecting the arms to the body can be tricky, so if you're not comfortable with the view you're working in, use **Turn View** to rotate the view to a satisfactory angle. The important thing is to be sure that you're connecting the correct splines. Hiding different parts of the model may also be useful.

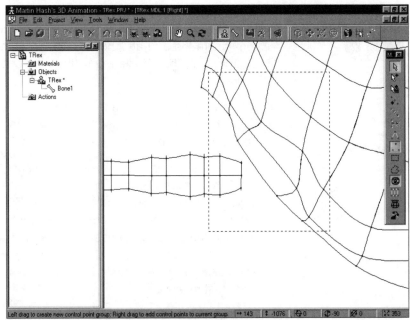

FIGURE *Group these points to begin attaching the arm to the body.*
4.14

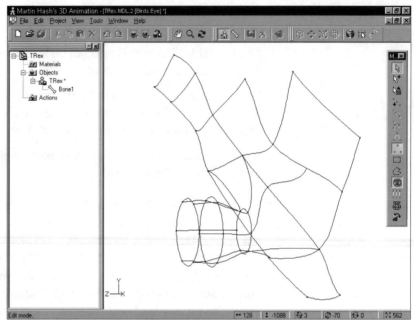

FIGURE *Using hooks to attach the arm to the body.*
4.15

9. Insert a control point on the next cross-section out on the body from where the arm attaches. Attach a spline from the arm to this control point, then hook it onto the next open spline as shown in Figure 4.15.

10. Unhide the model and change to a top view. Use the **Group** tool to select the half of the model that you've attached the arm to. Click the **Hide** button to hide the rest of the model.

11. Group just the splines that make up the arm, then rotate them with the **Rotate Manipulator** in the Y axis only until they match the angle of the body. This rotation will most likely cause some distortion in the joint where the arm attaches. Correct the distortion by grouping the shoulder splines and click the **Hide** button while holding down the **Shift** key. From the front view, translate the points that make up the arm circle until they are close to the side of the patch that meets it.

12. From the side view, make any rotations necessary to match the angle of the body.

13. Repeat steps 8 through 12 to attach and position the other arm.

14. Once you've attached both arms, switch to a side view and Group the front half of the model. Click the **Hide** button and switch to a front view.

15. Zoom in to the center of the chest, where both arms attach to the body.

16. Insert a control point along the center spline that runs between the arm holes. Add a 3-point spline across this control point and to the two remaining open control points on the arm cross-sections.

17. Zoom out from the model. Now broaden the chest area of the dinosaur by grouping the arms one at a time and translating them away from each other. Doing this may cause distortion along the adjoining body splines. Adjust to correct any distortion that occurred. Moving the arms outward should result in a side view similar to the one shown in Figure 4.16. Figure 4.17 shows a shaded bird's-eye view of the model at this point.

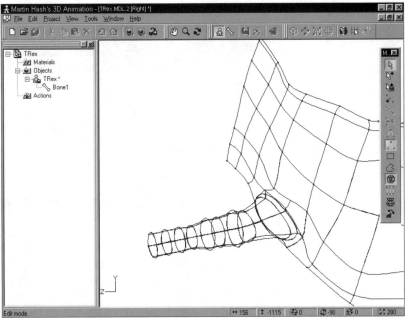

FIGURE *Side view of arms connected to body.*
4.16

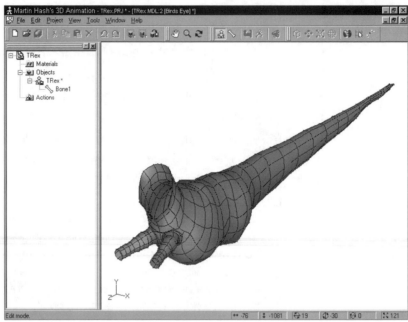

FIGURE   *Bird's-eye view of the shaded model.*

4.17

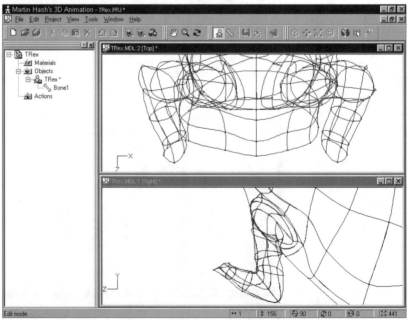

FIGURE   *Side and top views of front arm shape.*

4.18

The final phase of adding the arms is to shape them. Figure 4.18 shows both top and side views of the arms for reference in shaping.

The arms are now complete. The next section will walk you through adding the dinosaur's hind legs. Click the **Disk** button to save your work before continuing.

CREATING THE BACK LEGS

This section continues to build on the dinosaur model that you've created to this point. The next steps explain how to add the back legs onto the model.

1. Begin creating the back legs by adding a spline with 17 control points on it. This spline should be oriented vertically. Set the **Lathe Precision** to *10,* click any point along the spline, press the **/** key, then click the **Rotate Manipulator** button.

2. Translate the pivot a little away from the selected spline and click the **Lathe** button.

3. From the front view, use the **Group** tool to select the newly lathed leg. Translate the leg into proper position along the side of the dinosaur's body.

   Figure 4.19 shows both the side and front views for shaping the back leg.

4. Once you've shaped the back leg similarly to the screen shots, select it with the **Group** tool, then select **Copy** and **Paste** from the **Edit** menu. Right-click the group name in the **Project Workspace** and select **Flip, X Axis** to create the second leg. Switch to the front view and translate the new leg into position.

5. Begin attaching the back legs by switching to a top view and grouping the body splines near the thigh area and the first cross-section on the leg.

6. Switch to a side view and break the body splines that fall within the leg cross-section area, shown in Figure 4.20. Observe the remaining splines and control points and notice how the "corners" of where the leg will attach will be 5-point patches.

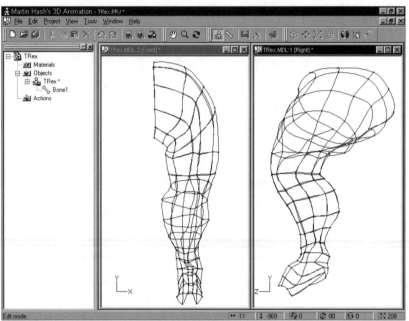

FIGURE
4.19
Side and front views of back leg shape.

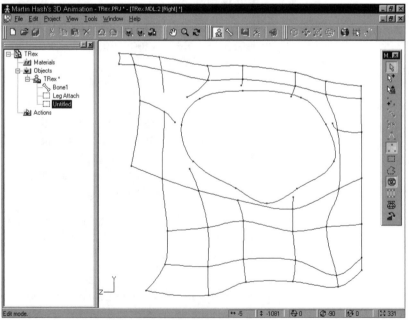

FIGURE
4.20
Broken splines where the leg will attach.

7. From the side view, begin closing the surface between the body and the leg by attaching splines between corresponding control points along the leg and body cross-sections. Five control points should remain open. You'll use hooks to close the surface.

8. Unhide the model, switch to a front view, and group the body and upper two cross-sections of the back leg.

9. Select a view that's comfortable for you to work in. Now attach hooks to close the surface around the back leg using the techniques you learned in attaching the body to the tail and the arms to the body. You may have trouble discerning the surfaces in Figure 4.21, but you can follow the splines along to locate where they connect.

10. From the side view, tuck the "corners" of the body patch where the leg was attached behind the area where the thigh meets the body. This will help keep the surface of the model looking smooth.

11. Repeat steps 5 through 9 to attach the other leg. Figure 4.22 shows a shaded view of the model with both legs attached.

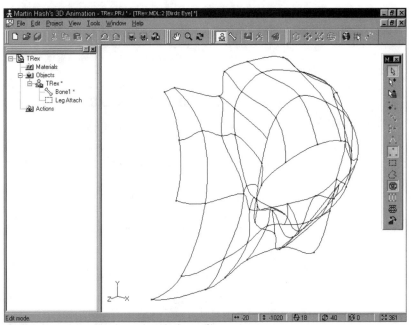

FIGURE *Locations of hooks to close the leg surfaces.*
4.21

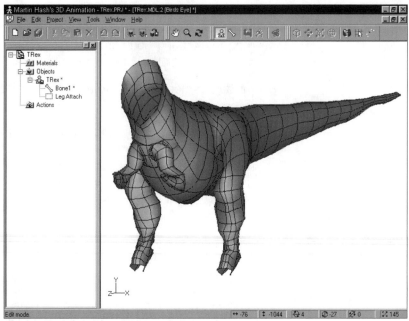

FIGURE *Shaded model with legs attached.*
4.22

The back legs of the dinosaur are done for now, and the next section will walk you through adding a head to the dinosaur. Click the **Disk** button to save your work before continuing.

EXERCISE

CREATING THE DINOSAUR'S HEAD

The head for the dinosaur is created with the long splines (the ones that run up the body) continuing to form the head. Once again, this exercise utilizes hooks in attaching the body parts together.

1. Create a horizontal spline with 12 control points on it. Select any point along this spline and press the **/** key. Set the **Lathe Precision** to *10* and click the **Rotate Manipulator** button.

2. Rotate the pivot 90 degrees in the X axis to correctly orient it for lathing the head spline. Translate the pivot as shown in Figure 4.23.

3. Click the **Lathe** button.

4. From the side view, shape the newly lathed spline into a head for the dinosaur.

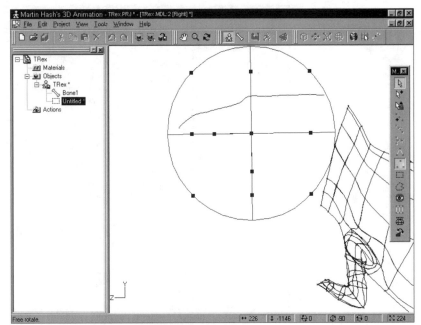

FIGURE *Spline used to create the* T. rex *head.*
4.23

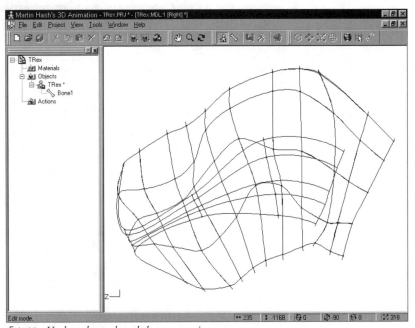

FIGURE *Unshaped mouth and throat extrusions.*
4.24

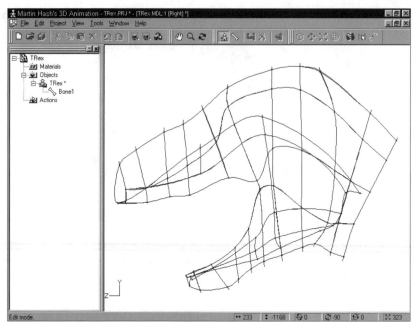

FIGURE
4.25
Shaped mouth and throat area.

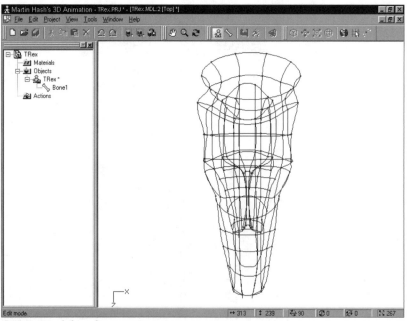

FIGURE
4.26
Head shape from top view.

5. From the side view, group the spline toward the open end of the mouth. Click the **Extrude** button and pull the extrusion back into the mouth of the dinosaur. Extrude once again and pull the new extrusion back farther into the head to form the beginning of the throat area. Figure 4.24 shows the mouth with the new extrusions.

6. Select the head of the model with the **Group** tool and click the **Hide** button. Working from Figure 4.25, shape the head and mouth area of the dinosaur. Remove the splines that run vertically between the upper and lower inner mouth by breaking them. Notice that the nose area was modified slightly, and the throat was curved down the back of the neck of the model.

Figure 4.26 shows a top view of the head to assist in proper shaping.

Attach the head to the body of the model by grouping the cross-sections in that area, then click the **Hide** button. Add splines between corresponding control points on both the head and body cross-sections, and use hooks to match resolution and close any remaining open control points. Figure 4.27 shows a close-up view of the head attached to the body.

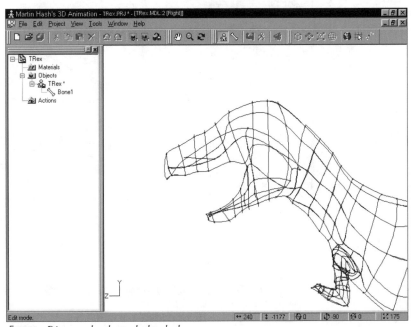

FIGURE   *Dinosaur head attached to body.*
4.27

The main body of the dinosaur is now complete, and there are just a few more details to add before the model is done. Save your work and continue to the next section, which will describe how to add the front claws and back feet to the dinosaur's arms and legs.

ADDING FRONT CLAWS AND BACK FEET

To create the claws for the arms of the dinosaur, extrude the end cross-section of the arms several times. Form these extrusions into a claw shape. The second claw on each hand was created by lathing a simple cone shape, then attaching it to the hand. Figure 4.28 shows a close-up of the dinosaur's hand.

The back feet of the dinosaur were created similarly to the front claws, but when the second toe was added, room was made for a third toe to be inserted. The third toe was created from a simple lathed cone shape. Figure 4.29 shows a side, top, and front view of the foot to help you in modeling.

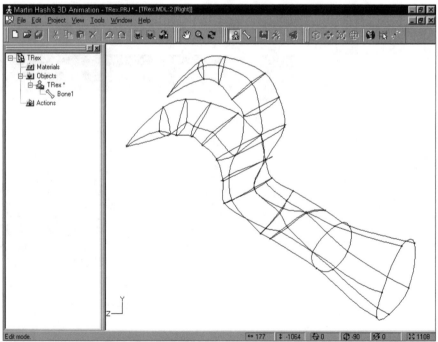

FIGURE *Close-up of dinosaur's front claws.*
4.28

A crease occurs where a spline entered one side of a control point and ended. This results in a different spline coming out the other side of the same control point.

Most often, the actual cause of this is partial construction of a model. You might create part of a model, then leave it while you construct other parts. When you return to this point, the center control point of another spline is connected to this intersection, and a crease results.

Actually identifying the point that is causing the crease is the most difficult part of fixing this problem. It can be quite a chore on a complex model to locate a single control point that has one spline coming in and another going out. To eliminate this crease, two control points are added to either side of the center control point, as shown in Figure 4.32.

The next step is to break the splines between the newly added control points as shown in Figure 4.33.

After the splines have been broken, the two control points hanging from the center point can be deleted.

Finish by gluing the two remaining control points together, then connect the newly glued control point back to the original model (Figure 4.33).

Figure 4.34 illustrates the clean, crease-free rendering.

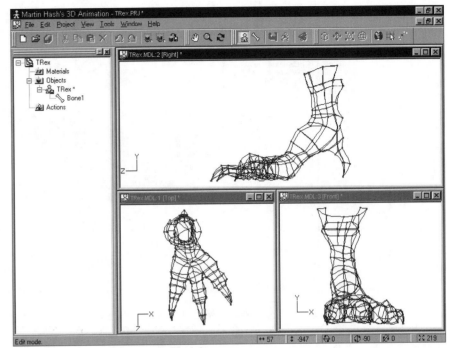

FIGURE 4.29 *Side, top, and front view of back foot.*

FINISHING THE MODEL

A few minor details will add much to this model. Teeth were added by creating a small lathed cone shape that was curved toward the back of the mouth to give the head a ferocious look. The tooth shape was repeated many times to fill the mouth with teeth.

The model does not have eyes at this point, but they could easily be added using hooks or one of the other modeling techniques described in previous tutorials.

Figure 4.30 shows a shaded view of the final *Tyrannosaurus rex* model.

The dinosaur provides an example of using hooks to connect parts with varying resolution. As you can see, hooks, when used correctly, can create a clean, low-resolution surface. However, even with hooks, it's still possible to end up with creases in the surfaces of your models. The next section deals with the common causes of surface creases, as well as how to spot them, and how to eliminate them.

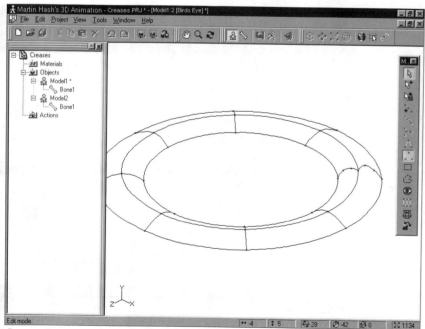

FIGURE 4.32 *Insert control points.*

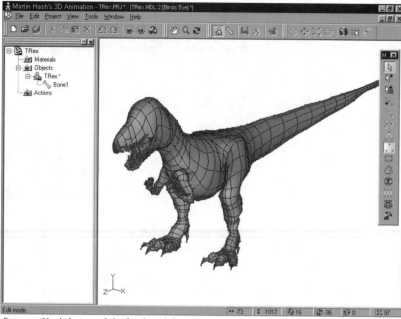

FIGURE *Shaded view of the final model.*
4.30

SOLVING SURFACE AMBIGUITIES

All of the models discussed so far have been relatively simple: only a few compound curves were used. However, more complex models require more patches, eventually reaching the point where closing a given patch can cause surface ambiguities. Consider it "modeling yourself into a corner."

The renderer in Animation:Master v5 recognizes both 3- and 4-point patches as legal patches, so they will generally render smoothly. Using the patches incorrectly will, however, still lead to creasing on the surface of a model. This section identifies the common causes of surface creases, as well as how to get rid of them easily.

COMMON CAUSES AND CURES FOR CREASES

In the heat of modeling, considering each attachment of one spline to another and whether or not it will cause a problem is the last thing on anyone's mind.

Most times, there will be no problem w
with legal patches. Eventually, however
models. The following section describes
creasing, and how to solve the problems.

NON-CONTINUOUS SPLINE ALO

The most common cause for creases alor
noncontinuous spline along a smooth
wireframe and a rendered view of a mo
the right side of the model in the rende
in the surface.

The giveaway to be looking for wit
smooth spline in the area where the cre
the wireframe image in Figure 4.31 exp
the right side of the model. Dragging th
make the splines traveling through the
thing you don't want on the smooth surf

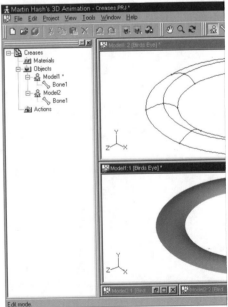

FIGURE *Wireframe model with rendering crease.*
4.31

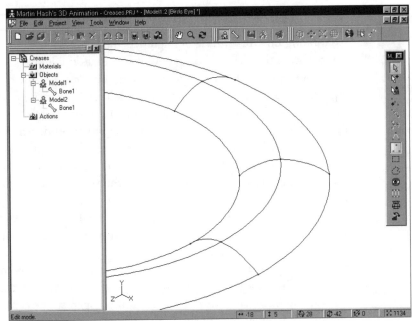

FIGURE *Connect the newly glued control point to the model.*
4.33

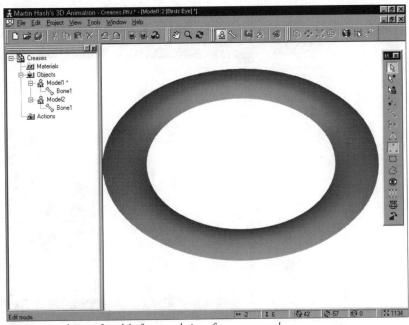

FIGURE *Rendering of model after completion of crease removal.*
4.34

CONTINUOUS SPLINE THAT DOUBLES BACK

Continuing on with surface ambiguities, the second most common cause for a bad surface is the use of a continuous spline that doubles back on itself. This use of a spline causes a flat area to render along the surface of the model: the offending spline renders as a flat patch while the adjoining splines are often curved.

Figure 4.35 illustrates the wireframe of the bad patch, as well as a rendering in which a crease is visible. Luckily, this situation doesn't come up as often as the previously discussed one, because it requires a little more work to correct. In this situation, the only way to fix the offending patch is literally to disassemble that area of the model, correct the spline that doubles back on itself with extra resolution, then re-form clean patches.

This example could be corrected by first breaking the offending spline, then adding a spline that continues from the open control point down toward the next spline, as shown in Figure 4.36. Continue by inserting a control point onto the lower spline, then attaching the hanging control point to this point (Figure 4.37).

Next, insert one control point on each of the two remaining vertical splines, and finish by attaching the remaining open spline across the just-added control points. Figure 4.38 shows the final wireframe, as well as a render of the now-clean surface.

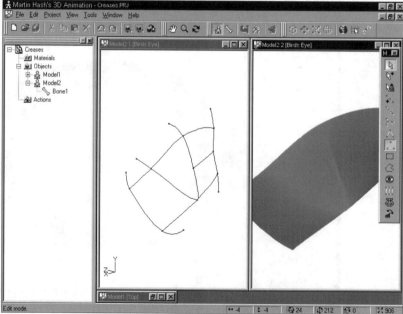

FIGURE   *Crease caused by the doubled-back spline in the center of the wireframe.*
4.35

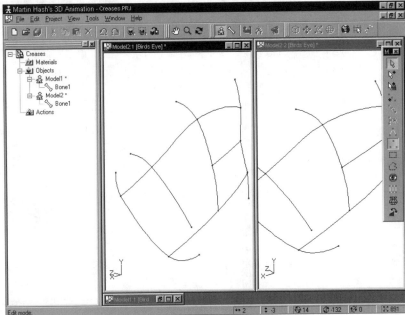

FIGURE   *Adding a spline that continues from the open control point after breaking the*
4.36   *doubled-over spline.*

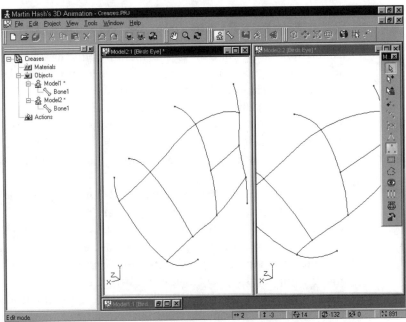

FIGURE   *Insert a control point and attach the hanging spline to this control point.*
4.37

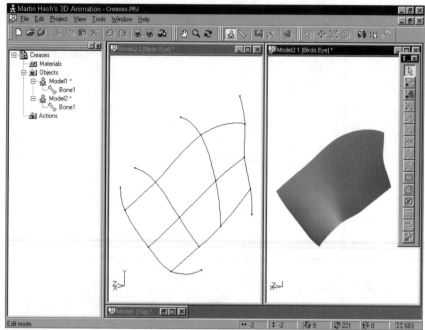

FIGURE *The final wireframe and rendered view after correcting the crease.*
4.38

THREE-POINT PATCH ON A CURVED SURFACE

Animation:Master contains one of the few spline-based modelers on the market that allow you to use 3-point patches when creating models. Unfortunately, that doesn't mean that they will always render cleanly.

Figure 4.39 shows both a wireframe and shaded view of a curved surface where a 3-point patch was used. Obviously, the best way to avoid these creases is to avoid 3-point patches. This, however, is not always possible, and it's not easy trying to plan them for an inconspicuous place on your model.

To minimize the creasing caused by 3-point patches, avoid having two of them adjoining as they are here. If you can keep it to one 3-point patch surrounded by legal 4-point patches, the effects will be less exaggerated.

The next section shows you how to create a human face, which is a considerable step forward from the models thus far in that a face contains many compound curves, making a surface that can be difficult to control. The human face model will also provide a practical example of patch creases and how to remove them without adding unnecessary resolution to the model.

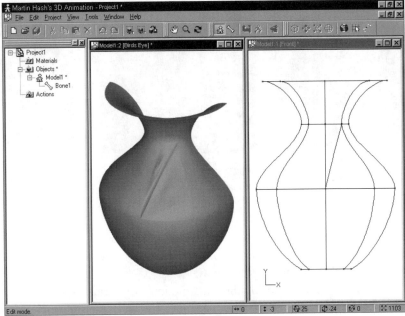

FIGURE   *Curved surface with a 3-point patch causing a crease.*
4.39

MODELING THE HUMAN FACE

Human heads are one of the most difficult models to build, yet they seem to be near the top in demand. People want to create their heads in 3D and show them off to anyone who will watch. Unfortunately, few users succeed in creating a useable rendition of a human head. Many become frustrated with one aspect or another during the creation and just simply give up.

You'll need patience while working on a complex model like this. Getting the model to look "right" will require hours of fine-tuning of the individual control points making up the model. The following section was designed with the easiest way to create a head in mind. This technique should make it easier to create human heads that have low patch counts and smooth surfaces.

CREATING A MODEL FOR THE HEAD

One of the best ways to create an accurate human head model is to start with one. Find a friend or relative who is willing to be the guinea pig for your

FIGURE **4.40** *Front view of Martin Hash.*

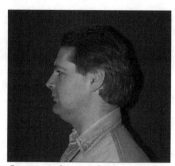

FIGURE **4.41** *Left view of Martin Hash.*

FIGURE **4.42** *Right view of Martin Hash.*

modeling escapades. At the least, if no one you know is willing to pose for you, find someone who understands what you want and is willing to help by taking photographs of you.

The setup for the construction of a head begins with three images of the head you want to build: a front view and one from each side of the head. The subject of this modeling exercise is Martin Hash, the creator of Animation:Master. Mr. Hash was kind enough to stand in front of a blue screen at Hash Inc. and pose for the pictures shown in Figures 4.40, 4.41, and 4.42.

The preceding images were taken with a Kodak digital camera, and then read into a PC using the software provided with the camera. Ideally, you should use a well-lit environment that avoids the dark shadows in these images. However, because the images will serve only as rotoscopes (background images), the shadows are not a major concern.

While you take these photographs, it's vitally important to remain the same distance from the subject for each picture. Otherwise, creating an evenly scaled model will be quite difficult.

BUILDING THE HEAD

Finalizing the images for use consisted of opening them one at a time in Adobe Photoshop and scaling them to 200 percent. This gave the images some size so that the rotoscopes wouldn't distort and pixelate because of low resolution. Both the Magic Wand and Paths in Photoshop were utilized extensively to remove the background of the images to white. The background color used is pure white (255,255,255) so that it can easily be removed in Animation:Master. The final images were saved as .*TGA* files.

Now that the rotoscopes for the head have been created, set up the Project files as described in the following exercise.

EXERCISE

SETTING UP THE ROTOSCOPES

1. Start Animation:Master and begin by selecting **New** from the **Project** drop-down menu. Save the project as "Martin."

2. Expand the project list by clicking the plus (**+**) sign to the left of the **Martin** item in the project window.

3. Right-click the **Object** list, and select **New, Model**.

4. Right-click the **Model** name and select **Save As**. Enter **Head** and press **Enter**.

5. Right-click the **Head** item in the model section of the **Project Workspace**. Select **Import, Rotoscope** from the available options.

6. Use the **Open File** dialog to locate the *Martin Hash Front View.TGA* rotoscope on the accompanying CD-ROM. When the rotoscope opens, select white for the transparent color on the **Properties Panel** to tell the software not to draw any white pixels. This will help to make the image manageable.

7. Repeat step 6 for both the *Martin Hash Right View.TGA* and *Martin Hash Left View.TGA* rotoscopes.

8. As they open, the rotoscopes will stack on top of one another, making them all visible from the current view. After opening all three of the rotoscopes, use the mouse to drag them apart, to provide a view that allows easy alignment.

9. Select a few points that are easily visible on all of the rotoscopes. Create three 2-point splines and "stretch" them in a straight line between the selected points on the three images, using the front rotoscope for original reference points.

10. With the reference splines in place, use the mouse to drag the rotoscopes into a position in which all three images are aligned. If necessary, make any scaling adjustments to the rotoscopes. Figure 4.43 shows the final alignment of the rotoscoped images.

11. Each rotoscope's name appears in the **Project Workspace**. The rotoscopes for the side views must be "turned" to be visible from

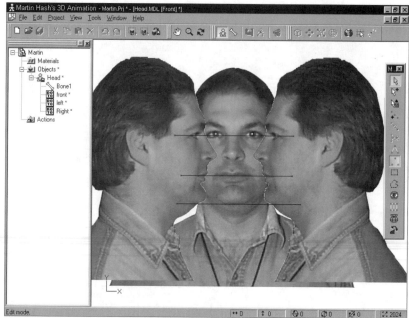

FIGURE *Aligned rotoscope images with reference splines.*
4.43

the sides, rather than the front. Orient the left and right rotoscopes by clicking them one at a time, selecting the **General** tab on the **Properties Panel**, then selecting the corresponding view from those available in the drop-down list.

12. Animation:Master uses the *right-hand rule* coordinate system, so for the left rotoscope, select the right view, and for the right rotoscope, select the left view. When you choose to view the model from the right view, you'll be viewing the model from your right side.

13. After the rotoscopes are in their final positions, select each one and uncheck the pickable box on the **Properties Panel** to prevent the rotoscope from being inadvertently selected while modeling.

The setup stages for modeling a head are now complete. This would be a good time to click the **Disk** button to save your work before continuing on to begin modeling the head. Save the model in your **Master** folder under the name "Head." In the next exercises, you learn how to model the head's shape and add some basic features to it.

EXERCISE

CREATING A BASIC HEAD SHAPE

The basic head shape is created by tracing the contours of the roto-scope images.

1. Begin modeling the head by creating a horizontal line beginning at the tip of the nose and ending near the ear.

2. Set the **Lathe Precision** to *26,* click a point on the horizontal spline, and click the **Lathe** button.

3. Group the newly lathed spline and enter *90* into the **X Rotate** field on the **Properties Panel**. Use the **Group** tool to select the inner set of control points, and then press the **Delete** key.

4. Depending on your positioning of the initial spline before lathing, it may be necessary to scale the lathed spline to make it fit the outline of the face. Once the spline is scaled near the correct size, use the mouse to start pulling the points in until they match up with the edges of the face. Outline the face roughly along the hairline, down

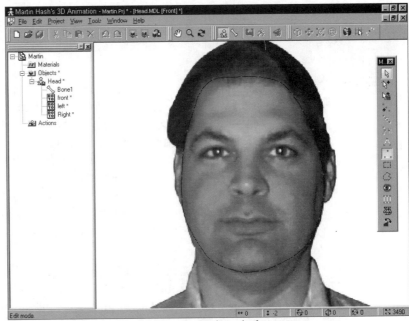

FIGURE   *Front view showing the spline that outlines the face.*
4.44

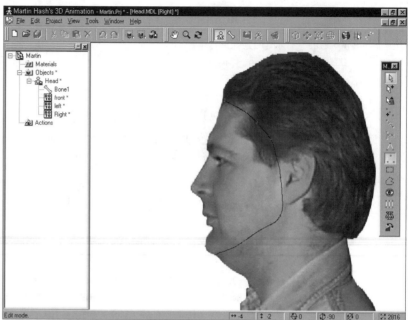

FIGURE   *Side view alignment of outline spline.*
4.45

the cheek to the jawbone, and across the tip of the chin. Figure 4.44
shows the spline that outlines the outside of the face.

5. Remembering that there is depth to the model, switch to a side view
   and translate the points along the Z axis until they match up with the
   corresponding areas of the face. The adjustments made from the
   side view work well: grouping the points from the side means that
   adjustments are made to both edges at once.

   Figure 4.45 shows the outline spline from the side view once it
   has been adjusted. The adjustments made from the side view will
   misalign the outline spline from the front view (most likely around the
   jaw line and chin area), making it necessary to go back to the front
   view and align the control points once more.

The basic outline of the face that you just created will serve as a basis for
shaping the face as you continue to build it. The outline spline can affect the
final look of the head model fairly significantly, because it controls how much
of the side of the head is seen.

The next section will describe how to add features to your newly created
head.

ADDING FEATURES AND RESOLUTION TO THE FACE

Now that you've created the basic head shape, you're ready to add some basic features to the face. As you'll learn in the following exercise, photorealistic eyes require a little more detail than you learn here, but these tutorials will get you on your way to sharpening your skills. The second exercise will help you fine-tune the features that you added, and the remaining exercises help you to shape the face to be more realistic, as well as to resolve any surface ambiguities.

EXERCISE

ADDING BASIC FEATURES TO THE FACE

As stated earlier, making the eye area of a face look photorealistic requires more detail than you'll create in this tutorial. If you ever need to build such a model, use the technique described in the first few steps that follow to add cross-sections to the inner area of the eye. You can shape the additional spline as you continue modeling the head:

1. Trace around the eye just outside of the eyelids with a 7-point spline. Position the seven points so that there is one in each corner of the eye, two across the top, and three across the bottom.

2. Select a point along this spline by clicking on it, then click the **Extrude** button. Scale the extrusion down until it fits inside the first spline, then press the **Enter** key to Deselect All. Use the mouse to translate the points of the newly lathed spline to outline the eyeball. Figure 4.46 shows a close-up of the eye after step 2 is completed.

3. Complete the outlines for the eyes by grouping the splines that outline the eye, then select **Copy** and **Paste** from the **Edit** menu. With the newly pasted group selected, right-click the group name in the **Project Workspace** and select **Flip, X Axis**. Position the new group and make any necessary adjustments.

The basic outline for the eyes is now complete. The next steps walk you through how to outline the lips of the model. Save your work before continuing.

There are several different possibilities in modeling the mouth. It seems easiest to outline the mouth first, then shape the lips:

4. Begin by creating a horizontal spline with two control points, and lathe it to a precision of *16*.

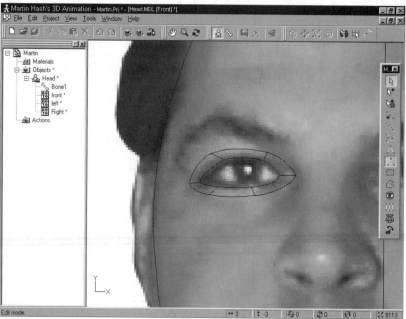

FIGURE *Close-up view of splines tracing the contour of the eye.*
4.46

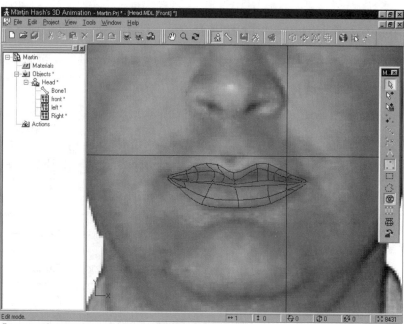

FIGURE *Close-up view of splines tracing the contour of the lips.*
4.47

5. Rotate the new cross-section 90 degrees in the X axis to orient it correctly, and shape the outer spline around the outside of the mouth. Of the 16 points, there should be one for each corner, 9 across the top, and 5 across the bottom.

6. Shape the inner spline along the middle of the lips themselves, then select this inner cross-section and extrude it.

7. Scale the extrusion down to fit inside of the previous cross-section, then arrange these points along the line where the lips meet. This spline will later form the entrance of the mouth, so you can give it a flatter shape to fit the mouth opening.

Figure 4.47 shows a close-up of the mouth splines once they have been positioned and shaped to fit the template.

The layout for the face is now complete, and the real work is about to begin. Now that you've outlined the lips and eyes, you need to add resolution to the face to close the surfaces. The next exercise walks you through this.

EXERCISE

ADDING RESOLUTION TO THE FACE

At this point, the model is nothing more than a simple outline of the important features. You'll need to add resolution to be able to complete the face.

1. Start with the file last saved in the previous exercise. To begin adding more resolution to the model, group the outermost spline by clicking any point along it, then pressing the **/** key.

2. Select **Copy**, then **Paste** from the **Edit** menu, and scale the selected group of points down to fit inside the original outline. Position these points to form a contour inside the previous outline, placing the points that lie at the corners of the eyes halfway between the outside corner of the eye and the existing spline that makes up the outline of the face.

3. After you position the previous cross-section, select it by clicking any point on the spline, and press the **/** key. Once again, select **Copy**, then **Paste** from the **Edit** menu. Then scale this group down until it fits inside the previous contour, and the points near the corners of the eyes are just beginning to touch the eye itself.

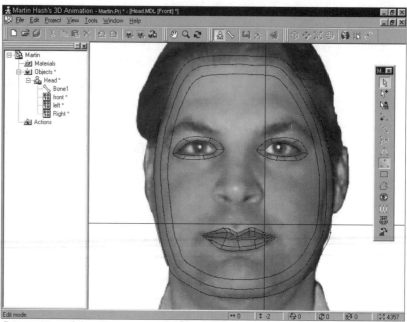

FIGURE *View of the spline contours of the face model.*
4.48

Figure 4.48 shows the model after the two inner contours have been added to the face.

4. Make any minor adjustments that are necessary to fit the two inner contour splines more closely to the chin area.

5. Translate the main control points that make up the forehead area downward toward the center of the forehead.

6. Select the innermost contour of the face by clicking any point along the spline and press the **/** key. Select **Copy**, then **Paste** from the **Edit** menu, and scale down the new contour until all of the control points lie inside of the previous contour spline.

7. Use the **Group** tool to select the five lowest control points on the newest contour and press the **Delete** key. Deleting these five control points will cause a straight spline to connect across the lower mouth area. Select this spline by clicking on it, and press the **K** key to Break the spline. Figure 4.49 shows the model after the Break has been done.

8. Connect each of the two open control points to the corresponding corner of the mouth on the face. Make any necessary adjustments to the remaining control points along this spline to create a smooth,

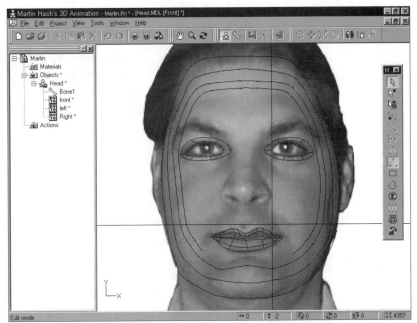

FIGURE
4.49
Broken spline tracing the contour of the face near the mouth.

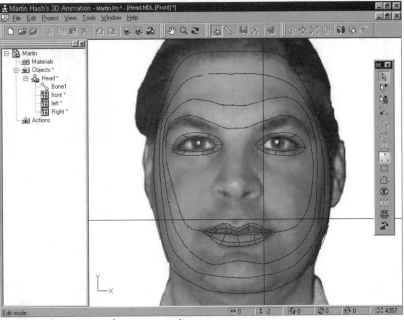

FIGURE
4.50
Adjustments made to contour splines.

even contour that traces up the outer cheek area to the eye sockets and around the brow.

9. Adjust other existing splines in the forehead area to cover more of the forehead. As you arrange these control points, make sure that the control points are close to lining up. Figure 4.50 shows the face after these adjustments to the forehead contour splines.

10. Starting from the outside cross-section of the face and working inward, add splines between the available control points. It's best to start outside the outermost cross-section and leave an extra control point hanging for surface control. As you work your way around the perimeter of the face, make any adjustments necessary to smooth the spline contours. When you reach the middle of the face, leave an extra control point hanging on a spline.

Figure 4.51 shows the model with splines added across the contours. Notice how some of the control points along the inner contours were repositioned to provide better-looking contours and easier control of muscles at a later time.

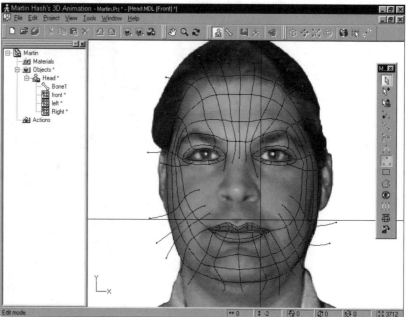

FIGURE   *View of face model with closed contour splines.*
4.51

Now it's time to move on to closing the inner surfaces of the face. The next exercise teaches you how to close the patches of the face. Click the **Disk** button to save your work before continuing.

EXERCISE

CLOSING THE PATCHES OF THE FACE

Now that you've closed the external part of the face completely with legal patches, you'll need to add some resolution to the inner contours to complete the surfaces.

1. Continuing from the previous exercise, locate the three control points hanging near the center of the model. Continue the ends of these splines and connect them to three middle control points along the top lip.

2. Next, continue the two splines that run through the corners of the eyes and connect them to the next two available control points along the upper lip.

3. Add two splines between the bottom two control points of the eye outline and continue them down to the remaining control points on

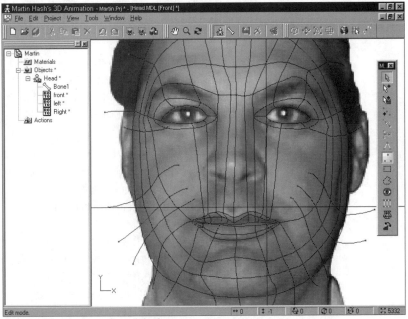

FIGURE *Closing the surface of the face.*

4.52

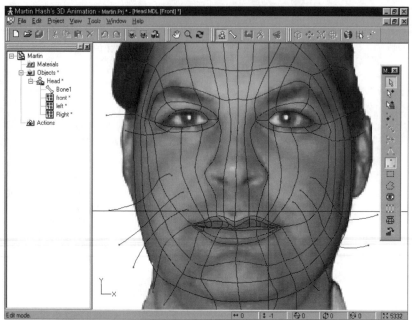

FIGURE *Insert and arrange four control points on each open vertical spline.*
4.53

the upper lip. After you finish this step, the model should look something like the one shown in Figure 4.52.

4. Notice that there are three horizontal splines still to be connected. These splines will form the roundness of the face. Begin closing the cheek area by inserting four control points to each one of the vertical splines running between the mouth and eyes that were just closed. Figure 4.53 shows the model after these control points have been inserted and arranged.

5. Once you've positioned the inserted control points, you can continue the horizontal hanging splines on across the face to close the remaining open patches. After you've added the horizontal splines, the model should look similar to Figure 4.54.

In Figure 4.54, notice that an extra control point has been added at the intersection of the uppermost horizontal spline where a spline was left hanging. The hanging spline will preserve the continuity of the surface. If this control point hadn't been added, and the spline had just stopped when it entered the control point, a crease would have developed in the surface of the model.

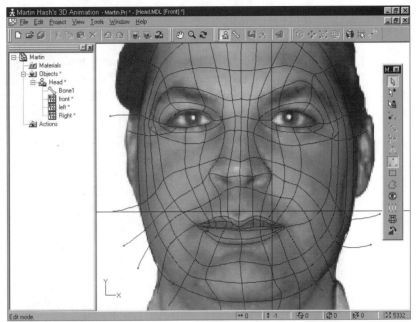

FIGURE *The closed patches of the face.*
4.54

Also observe that several more control points were added between the eyes on the vertical splines traveling along the nose. A spline was also added to close the surface of the model in that area.

That concludes the closing of the surfaces that will form the face. As you can see, the model has remained low-density to this point, and there's enough resolution to provide accurate muscle movement representations if the model is to be animated in such a manner. Save your work and continue to the next exercise, which will walk you through shaping the face.

EXERCISE

SHAPING THE FACE

Although adding the resolution to create the contours of the model is a relatively easy task, it's this exercise that is the hardest: It requires the artist in you to come out, even if it is just for a bit. You'll have to rely on your eye to tell you whether the model looks correct.

1. Begin making adjustments to the model by selecting the outermost ring of control points on the face. The easiest way to do this is to

select any control point on the outer contour, then select
Complement Spline from the **Edit** menu.

2. Switch to a side view and verify that the "depth" of the selected control points is still correct. While in the side view, group and translate the extra splines that were left hanging off of the outer contour behind the face.

3. Select each of the next two contour splines on the face and adjust them similarly. It may be useful for this step to have two modeling windows open, one with a front view and one with a side view. The second contour spline in should be pulled back just beyond the corners of the eyes from the side view. This is where the face curves back to somewhat straight sides. The third contour spline should be translated back from the side view to the edge of the eyebrow.

4. While in the side view, select all of the control points that extend beyond the nose in the rotoscope image and translate them back along the Z axis until the farthest point out is aligned with the tip of the nose.

5. From a front view, select just the middle vertical spline and click the **Hide** button. From a side view, shape this spline to follow the contour of the nose on the rotoscope.

6. From a front view, unhide the model and select the three splines running vertically in the center of the model. Switch to a side view and click the **Hide** button once again. Make adjustments to these splines to form a nose shape for the model.

7. After you've worked through and shaped all of the vertical splines in the model, start selecting the horizontal splines and adjust them from the top view. Adjusting these splines from the top view can get tricky, because there is no rotoscope to aid in the proper positioning of the control points.

   If you think you'd benefit from a rotoscope in the top view, have your subject lie flat on the ground, facing up. Measure off the same distance you used for the original rotoscopes, then lie down at the head end of your subject and take as straight a picture as you can manage. You can now clean this rotoscope in the same manner as the previous ones and open it in the top view for reference.

This will be a difficult area as you model your first few heads. It can eventually lead to hours of adjusting one control point at a time until the model looks right.

Every so often it's a good idea to stop working and take a step back to look at your model. A model looks quite a bit different when you're more than 12 inches away from it. Once you're comfortable with the shape and contour of the face you've created, continue to the next exercise, which describes fixing creases that form at the corner of the mouth.

If you render your model at this stage, several obvious problems will show in the surface of the model. The corners of the mouth, the eyes, and the lack of a nose would be the most obvious. This following exercise explains how to fix these areas, and how to finish them without significantly increasing the resolution of your model.

EXERCISE

FIXING THE CREASES AT THE MOUTH CORNERS

Figure 4.55 illustrates the creases that form in the corner of the mouth where several splines meet at one control point. The way to fix this problem is to continue the splines along the contour of the face that best fits their curve.

1. Begin by breaking the splines that join to the corner of the mouth, as shown in Figure 4.56.

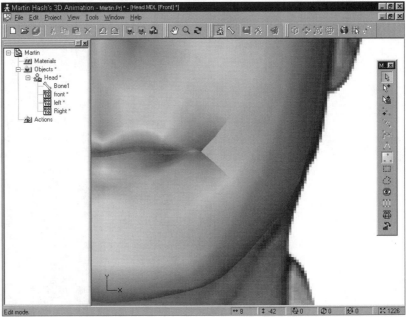

FIGURE   *Creases formed in the corner of the mouth.*
4.55

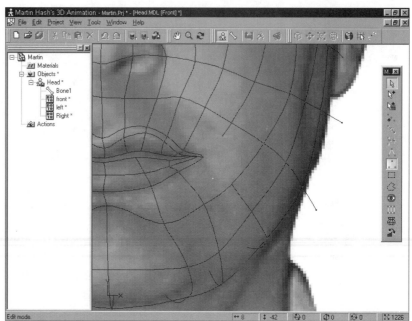

FIGURE *Break the splines that form the corner of the mouth.*
4.56

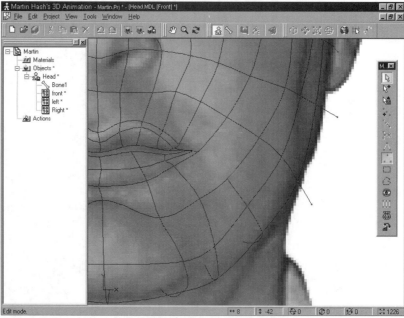

FIGURE *Spline added to the horizontal spline in the corner of the mouth.*
4.57

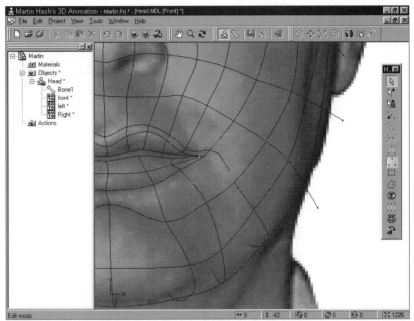

FIGURE *Spline added across upper lip with two hanging control points.*
4.58

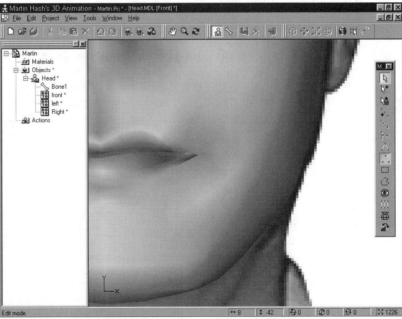

FIGURE *Render of mouth corner after reorganization of splines.*
4.59

2. Next, add a spline that continues the horizontal spline at the corner of the mouth, as shown in Figure 4.57.

3. Connect the newly added spline to the contour that traces up the cheek of the face. Break the spline across the outer top cross-section of the lips, between the corner and the next control point.

4. Add a spline to the broken upper-lip cross-section with two control points hanging off of it, as illustrated in Figure 4.58.

5. Connect the two control points of the hanging spline across the corner of the mouth and the open spline that runs out to the edge of the face. Rendering this area at this point should give a result like the one shown in Figure 4.59.

6. As you can see, this has greatly reduced the creases that formed at the corner of the mouth. Repeat this procedure on the other corner of the mouth, then move on to the eyes. Remember to save your work occasionally.

As you can see, the creation of the mouth led to creases in the surface of the model that were not apparent as the model was created. Now that the mouth has been fixed, the area around the eyes also has some surface ambiguities, which will be corrected in the next section.

EXERCISE

FIXING THE SURFACES AROUND THE EYES

Because of the resolution of the eyes, and the fact that there are several splines running around the eye area, creases tend to form along the eye-socket edges as well. Rendering the eye area at this point produces an image similar to Figure 4.60.

1. To correct this problem, begin by deleting the spline that hangs through the control point where three facial splines come together.

2. Continue by breaking the two splines that join at the remaining control point, as shown in Figure 4.61.

3. Glue the ends of the two hanging splines to each other, then to the original control point, as shown in Figure 4.62.

4. Continue the spline from the control point on the eye contour shown in Figure 4.63 to the control point to which the previous control point connected.

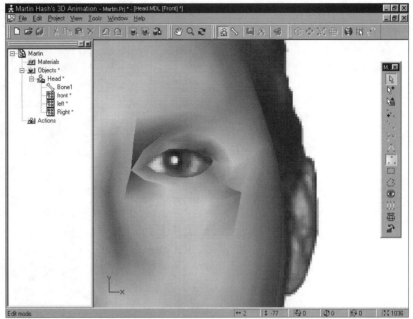

FIGURE 4.60 *Rendering of eye artifacts.*

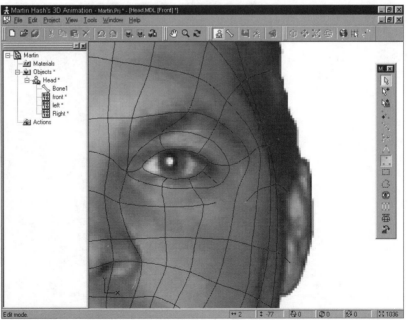

FIGURE 4.61 *Hanging spline removed, and adjoining splines broken from remaining control point.*

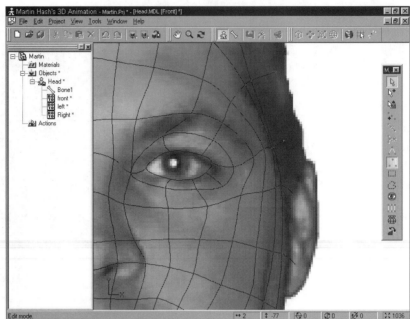

FIGURE
4.62
Hanging splines first glued together, then glued to the original control point.

FIGURE
4.63
Continuation of eye contour spline to close surface.

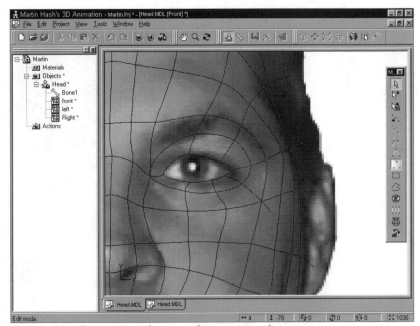

FIGURE
4.64
Control points inserted on eye and nose contour splines.

5. Insert five control points along the left side of the eye, on the eye and nose contour splines shown in Figure 4.64.

6. Add a 5-point spline across these points to create 4-point patches.

7. Next, break the splines that form the inner corner of the eye.

8. Attach a spline between the corner control point of the eye and the open control point on the eye contour spline. Figure 4.65 illustrates this.

9. Join the end point of the spline hanging from the eye outline spline to the end point of the spline that runs along the edge of the nose. Once you've connected them, glue them to the control point that forms the corner of the eye, as shown in Figure 4.66.

10. Figure 4.67 shows a shaded render of the face with the wireframe visible. Notice the holes along the upper edge of the eye socket. The deletion of the control point at the lower right corner of the 4-point patch that adjoins the holes, coupled with the addition of a spline between the eye orbit and the eye contour as shown in Figure 4.68, closes the hole in the eye socket.

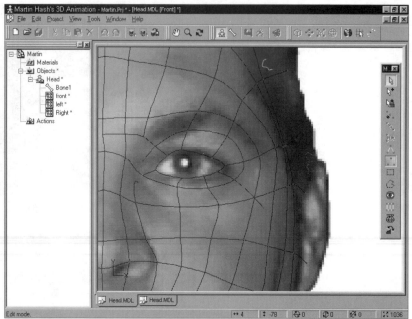

FIGURE   *Addition of spline from corner of eye to next adjoining control point on eye contour*
4.65   *spline.*

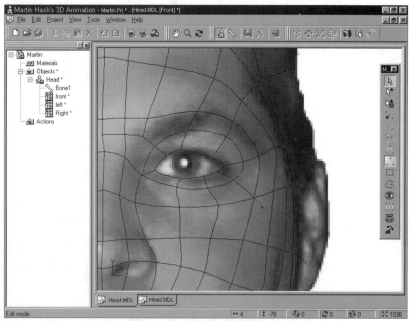

FIGURE   *Closing the corner of the eye.*
4.66

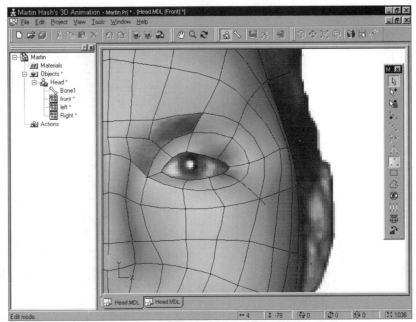

FIGURE   *Holes in the surface of the model.*
4.67

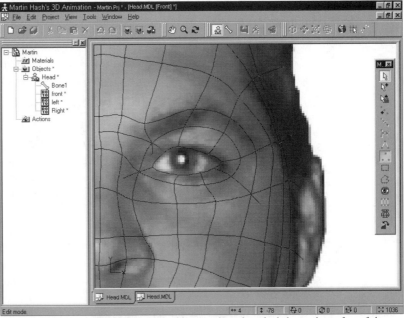

FIGURE   *Deleting a control point and adding a spline close the holes in the surface of the*
4.68   *model.*

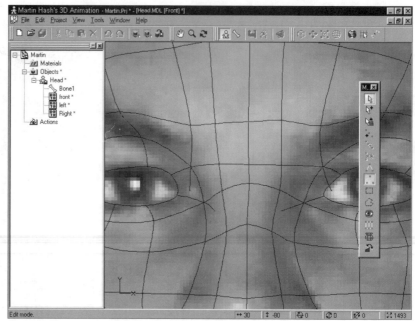

FIGURE
4.69
Close-up view of the bridge of the nose after both eyes are completed.

Figure 4.69 shows a detail close-up of the bridge of the nose, and how it will look when both eyes have been corrected.

11. You can further reduce any artifacts remaining on the eyes by making slight adjustments to the gamma and magnitude of the spline curves. The area around the eyes won't look like a trouble spot once you've applied image maps to the face.

By now, you've added almost all of the necessary resolution to the face, and you're on the home stretch. The next exercise will describe how to manipulate the existing splines and add just a little more resolution to form a nose.

EXERCISE

CREATING A NOSE

Continuing on with the model created in the previous exercise, the model should render similarly to Figure 4.70 after you've completed the eye artifact corrections. The last feature you'll add to this face is a nose. The actual shape of the nose can be difficult to pin down, because it deals with several compound curves. Usually, it's best to work on one

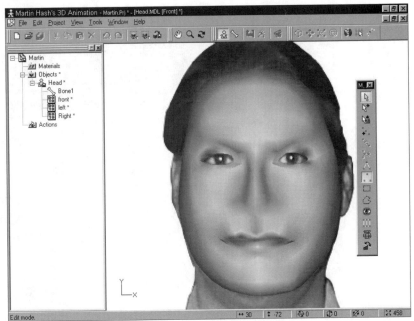

FIGURE *Rendered image of face with no nose.*
4.70

nostril until it's shaped correctly, then adjust the control points of the other from a side view, making them identical.

1. Begin defining the nose on the face by inserting control points along the splines between the nose and lips. Then add a spline across them, as shown in Figure 4.71.

2. Shape the nostrils by pulling the two points shown in Figure 4.72 upward into the nose. Translate the center point to the tip of the nose to form the beginning of the nostril shape.

3. Shape the surrounding splines to the shape of the nostril and the underside of the nose. Figure 4.73 shows how the final wireframe should look.

4. The final rendering of the face you've just created is shown in Figure 4.74. A few more hours of adjusting the control points along the sides of the face, and it will be very close to the original head. Mapping images onto this model will be covered in a later chapter.

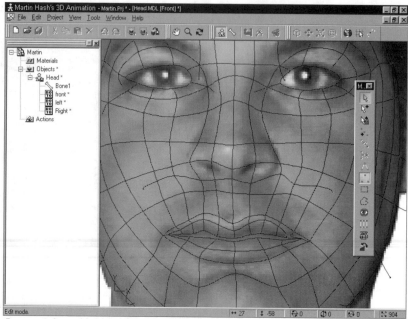

FIGURE *Spline added between nose and lips.*

4.71

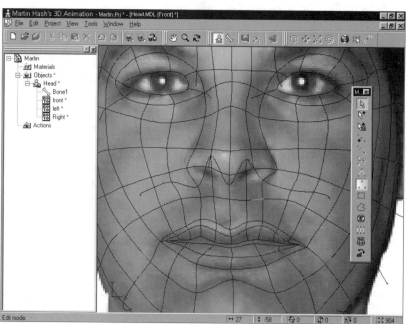

FIGURE *Control points translated upward to form nostrils.*

4.72

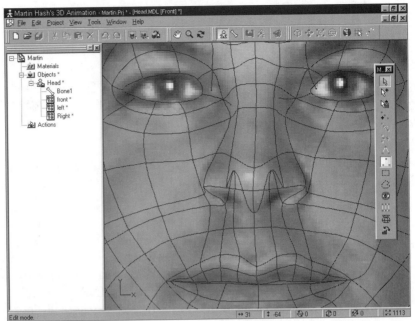

FIGURE
4.73
The close-up wireframe view of the final nose shape.

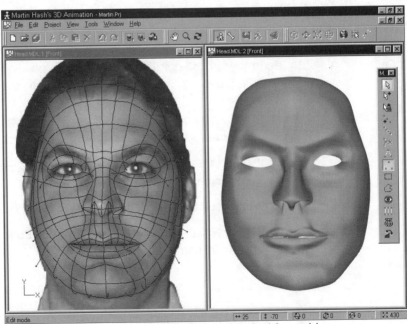

FIGURE
4.74
Side-by-side wireframe and shaded view of the final face model.

In this chapter, you've learned how to create and shape a human head, as well as add features and resolution to the face. The face gave you practice in creating complex surfaces, and in removing ambiguities that come up during the modeling process.

Another advanced technique is the combination of separate parts to create one model. Realistic eyes provide an excellent opportunity to practice just that.

MODELING HUMAN EYES

There is a saying that eyes are windows to the soul. Considering the size of the eye compared to the rest of the human body, that is a pretty broad and encompassing comment. The eyes often tell a story without a word.

The following section examines a technique for creating great-looking human eyes easily and quickly. The CD-ROM in this book contains a library of eye color maps that you may use to enhance the looks of your models.

EXERCISE

BEGINNING THE CREATION OF AN EYE

Whether we're happy, sad, angry, thrilled, or whatever — our eyes give it away. It's important to remember that when you work to create realistic heads and bodies. Don't let your work be sold short by flat-looking eyes. People will notice quickly if the eyes don't look right. Therefore, this exercise describes a technique for creating realistic eyes easily:

1. Start Animation:Master, and begin by selecting **New** from the **Project** drop-down menu. Save the project as "MakeEye."

2. Expand the project list by clicking the plus (**+**) sign to the left of the **MakeEye** item in the **Project Workspace**.

3. Right-click the **Object** list and select **New, Model**.

4. Right-click the model name and select **Save As**. Enter *Eyeball* as the model name.

The model of the eye created in these exercises has three separate pieces. Each plays an important role in the final look of the model. The first part of the eye that will be created is the eyeball itself:

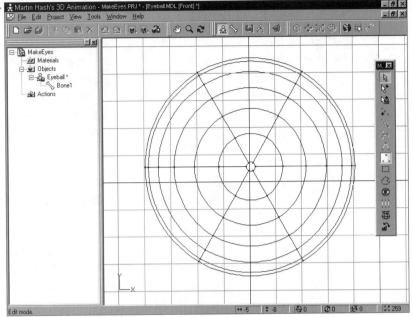

FIGURE *Eyeball model oriented properly.*
4.75

5. Create a spline with seven control points on it, shaped in an arc similar to one-fourth of a circle.

6. Select the spline by clicking any point on it and pressing the **/** key. Switch to the **Translate Manipulator** and orient the pivot just to the left of the spline.

7. Set the **Lathe Precision** to *6,* and then click the **Lathe** button.

8. Select the entire model with the **Group** tool and enter *–90* into the **X Rotate** field on the **Properties Panel** to orient the model vertically as shown in Figure 4.75.

9. Group the entire model and name the selected group "Eyeball."

That completes the creation of the first of the three parts needed for the eye model. Notice that the center of the wireframe has a hole in it. This hole will serve as the iris for the eye and can be manipulated in **Muscle** mode to create a dilating effect. The next section continues with the creation of the Pupil section.

CREATING A PUPIL FOR THE EYE

Much of what makes computer animation work is what a viewer can't see. In the case of the eye, the eyeball is really only a hemisphere, which, if viewed from the proper angle, would give a view through the iris directly into the inside of the head. In this model, the possibility of this happening is eliminated by creating a closed sphere that will sit inside the eyeball itself. Eventually, this sphere will be colored black to represent the pupil:

1. Continuing from Step 9, switch to a side view and select the entire eyeball wireframe with the **Group** tool. Select **Copy**, then **Paste** from the **Edit** menu.

2. While in the side view, select the **Translate Manipulator** button, and translate the pupil back along the Z axis outside of the eyeball.

3. Group the cross-section closest to the eyeball (the front of the pupil), as shown in Figure 4.76, and enter *1* into both the **X** and **Y Scale** fields on the **Properties Panel**. This will close the opening at the front of the pupil.

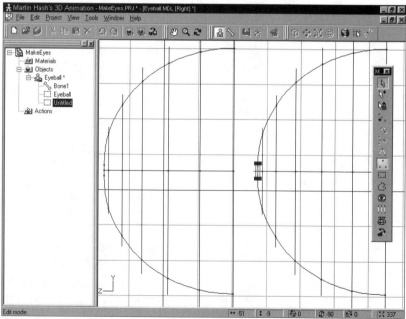

FIGURE *Group the front cross-section of the pupil wireframe.*
4.76

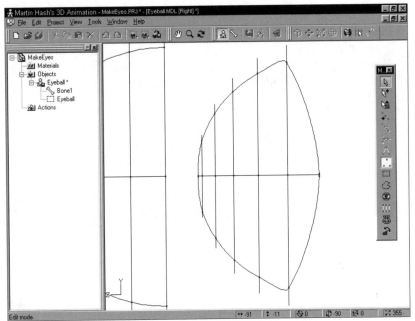

FIGURE *View of modified pupil wireframe.*
4.77

4. Repeat Step 12 after grouping the cross-section on the pupil oppo-site the one that was just scaled.

5. To fit the model correctly inside the eyeball without causing any crossing surfaces, select the entire pupil wireframe, and enter 90 into the **X**, **Y**, and **Z Scale** fields on the **Properties Panel**. Figure 4.77 shows what the model should look like now.

6. With the pupil wireframe still selected, click the **Translate Manipulator** and move the pupil along the Z axis until it fits inside the eyeball. Name the selected group "Pupil."

7. Make any necessary adjustments to the last few cross-sections of the pupil to avoid any overlapping surfaces. Be sure to check from both the side and top views.

The second of the three parts of the eye is now complete. The final piece of the eye is the cornea. It's necessary to build this piece to get the proper effect on the eye. Like the pupil built for the model, a real eye's pupil is a hole in the surface of the eye. At most times, specular highlights can be seen on that surface (the "twinkle" in someone's eyes), even over the pupil.

Click the **Disk** button to save your work before continuing to the next exercise.

CREATING THE CORNEA WIREFRAME

The final step for the eye is the creation of the cornea wireframe. The cornea consists of a sphere that surrounds both the eyeball and pupil wireframes. The sphere that forms the cornea is oriented vertically to avoid any visible inconsistencies at the poles of the lathed sphere.

1. Continue from the previous exercise. Create a spline with 13 control points, similar to the one shown in Figure 4.78. Take care to form the spline into a smooth curve.

2. Select the entire spline by clicking any point on the spline. Then press the **/** key.

3. Set the **Lathe Precision** to *8* and click the **Lathe** button.

4. Check from the side view to make sure that the cornea wireframe does not overlap the eyeball wireframe.

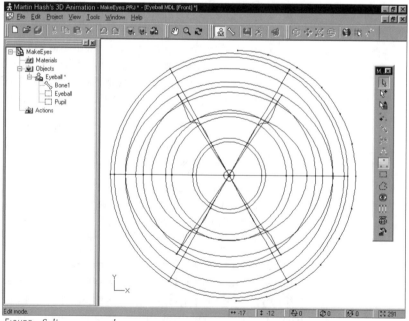

FIGURE *Spline curve used to create cornea.*
4.78

5. When you're satisfied with the look of the eyeball wireframe, select the cornea wireframe and name the group "Cornea."

Now that you're familiar with modeling a human face and an effective eyeball, the next exercise moves on to modeling the human body. Although the human body uses techniques similar to those used when creating simple characters in Chapter 3, the human form has much more shape and elegance.

MODELING THE HUMAN BODY

Unless you'll never need more than a floating, speaking head, your next logical step is modeling the human body. Humans come in so many different shapes and sizes that they can be difficult to build.

The following exercises deals with the construction of a female body. This is because the female form has a considerably higher number of compound curves, leaving the male figure essentially a subset of the female. Wherever possible, any issues in modeling the differences between the two forms will be pointed out and discussed. This will help you in the future if you choose to model a male figure. Mind you, the most obvious anatomical differences have been skipped in this exercise.

EXERCISE

BEGINNING THE HUMAN BODY: THE TORSO

1. Start Animation:Master, and begin by selecting **New** from the **Project** drop-down menu. Save the project as "Human."

2. Expand the project list by clicking the plus (+) sign to the left of the **Human** item in the **Project Window**.

3. Right-click the **Object** list and select **New, Model**.

4. Right-click the **Model** name and select **Save As**. Enter **Body** as the name.

The project is now set up, and you're ready to begin modeling. The Human figure will begin with the torso. Much like the rest of the tutorials on building full characters that you've walked through, the Human body starts at the torso or pelvis. We now start modeling the torso, and later exercises will build down through the pelvic area:

5. Begin constructing the torso of the model by setting the **Lathe Precision** to 8. Draw a short horizontal spline that begins near the Y axis marker and extends a short way along the X axis.

6. Click the **Lathe** button, then switch to a top view. Select the inner ring of control points that the lathe formed with the **Group** tool, and press the **D** key to delete them.

7. While still in top view, translate the center point inward slightly to form a curve, and adjust the outline of the spline to more closely resemble the waist area of a human body. Figure 4.79 shows the shape of the newly created cross-section after it has been formed.

8. Because this spline will serve as the waist of this model, switch back to a front view and translate the two end control points upward slightly, forming the shape of the upper leg area.

9. From a side view, use the **Group** tool to select the waist spline. Click the **Extrude** button, then click inside the yellow manipulator box and drag the extrusion upward a short distance.

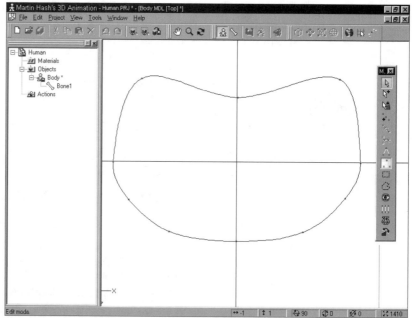

FIGURE *Top view of waist spline.*
4.79

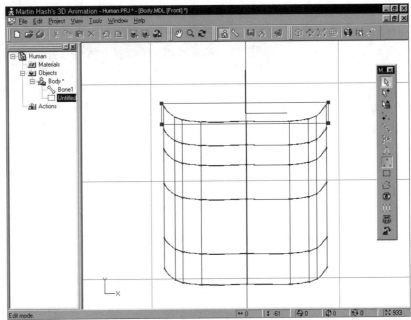

FIGURE *Three more extrusions to form the torso.*

4.80

10. While the newly extruded spline is still selected, click the **Extrude** button once again and drag the new cross-section roughly twice as far up as the first one was placed.

11. You'll need to perform three more extrusions to create enough resolution to form the torso. The model should then look similar to Figure 4.80.

12. Use the **Group** tool to select the top cross-section of the model, and enter 25 in both the **X** and **Z Scale** fields on the **Properties Panel**. Since the model looks very cylindrical, take a few moments to shape the body from both front and side views similarly to the one shown in Figure 4.81.

NOTE

The spline traveling down the center of the model will form the backbone curvature along the back, so it was translated in slightly. The upper torso was scaled up slightly, and the ring of control points that form the neck hole was cleaned up by straightening the control points on that spline. The spline that was running horizontally across the center of the body was adjusted to give more of an indentation to the chest area of the model. If the model were male, this spline would be more pronounced

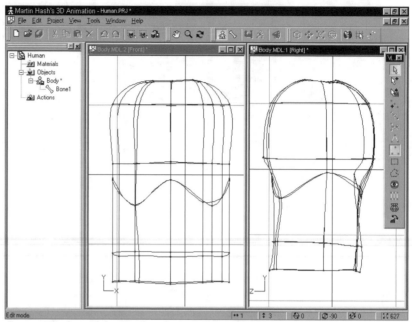

FIGURE *The shape of the torso from both the front and side views.*
4.81

to start forming some musculature in the chest area. The shoulders would also be broadened. Translating the back spline inward would create a more sculpted look to the back of the model.

Before continuing, the model was also adjusted from the top view and formed to a more circular shape.

13. Continue working on the model by selecting the lowest spline in the torso with the **Group** tool. Enter *100* in both the **X** and **Z Scale** fields on the **Properties Panel** to widen the hips of the model. If necessary, they can be adjusted again at another time.

14. Switch to a side view and zoom in on the chest area of the torso. Create a spline with seven control points similar in shape to the one shown in Figure 4.82.

15. Select the spline from which the breast will be formed with the **Group** tool. Click the **Rotate Manipulator** button and rotate just the pivot –90 degrees along the X axis. This will change the orientation of the Roll axis. Translate the pivot upward until the center line of the **Rotate Manipulator** sphere is just above the highest point of the spline to be lathed, as shown in Figure 4.83.

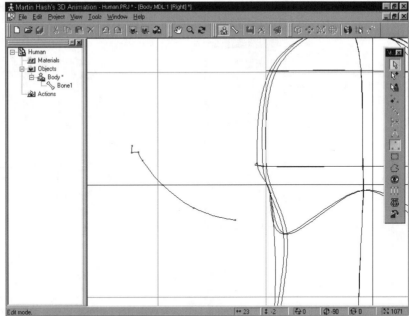

FIGURE *Spline used to form a breast.*
4.82

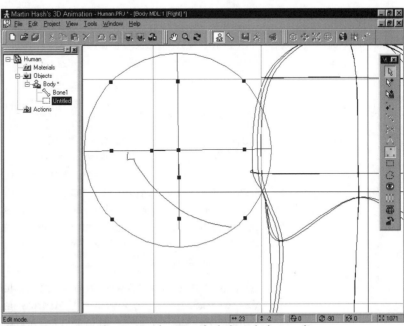

FIGURE *Proper pivot alignment and position for lathing the breast spline.*
4.83

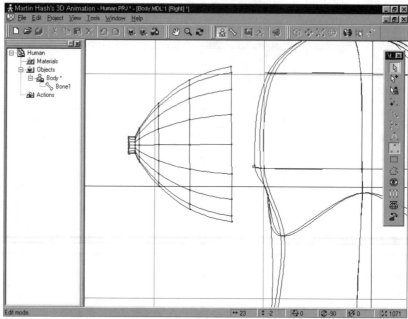

FIGURE *Lathed breast shape.*
4.84

16. Click the **Lathe** button to create the breast shape. It should look similar to the shape shown in Figure 4.84. At first glance, it's obvious that some scaling and translation adjustments need to be made to properly form the breast.

17. Begin correcting the breast by scaling it to match the body proportions of the model more closely. Those of you who are big fans of the movie *Weird Science:* Here's your chance to play. Now that you've scaled the breast to fit the body, switch to a side view and rotate the end of the breast upward slightly. Translate the front of the breast downward until it matches curvature of the body. Switch to a front view and adjust the outermost cross-section to match the previous translations. Translate the top spline upward to give a smoother transition when the breast is attached to the body. Use Figure 4.85 for reference in making these adjustments.

18. Now that the breast has a more natural look, select it with the **Group** tool. Enter *15* into the **Y Rotate** field on the **Properties Panel** to rotate the breast to match the angle of the body.

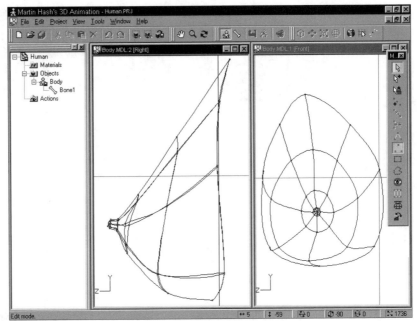

FIGURE *Front and side views of the breast shape.*
4.85

19. With the breast still selected, select **Copy**, then **Paste** from the **Edit** menu. Right-click the group name in the **Project** workspace, and select **Flip, X Axis**.

20. The next step is to attach the breasts to the torso. From a side view, select the ring of control points at the base end of both breasts using the **Group** tool.

21. Select **Copy**, then **Paste** from the **Edit** menu. Use the **Group** tool with the right mouse button to add the front half of the body to the selected group. Click the **Hide** button to hide the rest of the model.

22. Refer to Figure 4.86 in attaching the newly copied spline loops to the chest area of the torso. Begin by connecting splines between corresponding control points on the torso and the spline rings.

23. Now that you've attached the spline loop to the torso, delete the splines between the control points along the innermost ring of the breast wireframes. These splines need to be removed to avoid attaching two copies of the spline ring on top of one another.

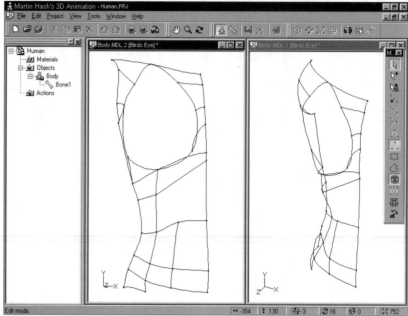

FIGURE *Attaching the spline ring to the torso.*
4.86

24. Once you've removed the splines, attach the control points hanging off the breasts to their corresponding control points along the spline rings on the torso.

That completes this exercise, so click the **Disk** button to save your work, and continue to the next exercise, which describes the creation of the pelvic area.

EXERCISE

CREATING THE PELVIS

1. Begin creating the pelvis by using the **Group** tool to select the lowest cross-section of the torso.

2. Click the **Extrude** button and drag the extrusion downward slightly to form the hips and crotch area.

3. Extrude the selected spline downward two more times to provide adequate resolution.

4. From the front view, use the **Turn** tool to slightly turn the view to bird's-eye. Insert a control point onto the splines that run along

either side of the center spline forming the bottom of the pelvis. It's necessary to do this for both the front and the back of the pelvis cross-section, so you'll add four control points in all.

The control points added in step 4 will provide enough resolution in the pelvic area to let you add the legs onto the figure. You could use hooks in this situation. They'd be effective if the splines being hooked continued upward toward the stomach area before hooking.

5. Continue by hiding all of the model except the lowest cross-section of the pelvis.

6. Switch to a top view and connect a 2-point spline between the center control point in the front and the control point in the back of the pelvis.

7. Connect two 2-point splines between the corresponding control points added in step 4 in the front and back of the pelvis.

8. Insert one control point on each of the three splines running through the center of the pelvic cross-section.

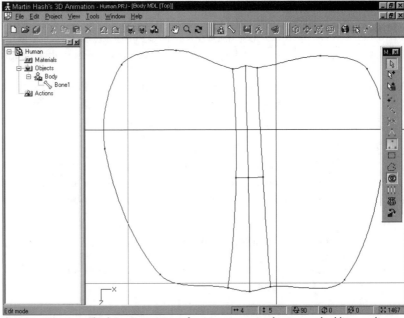

FIGURE *Top view of pelvic cross-section after inserting control points and adding a spline.*

4.87

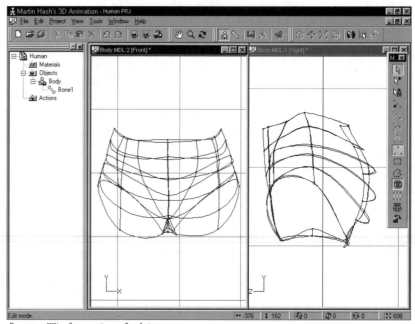

FIGURE *Wireframe view of pelvis area.*
4.88

9. Add a 3-point spline that connects across the control points added in step 8. Figure 4.87 shows a top view of the new spline that was just added to the center of the pelvic area. The holes that will form the legs are easily discernible, as is the crotch area of the model.

Figure 4.88 shows both a side and front view of the completed pelvis area of the model. To shape this area, the buttocks were rounded out, and the spline running up the front of the crotch was translated forward slightly.

The pelvic area is one of the places where taking the time to properly adjust the control points will give a nice smooth look to a model. That completes the pelvic area, and the next exercise will describe adding arms to the model.

EXERCISE

CREATING ARMS FOR THE MODEL

The arms are added on to this model in much the same way as the breasts:

1. Create the arms by lathing an 8-point spline into a cylinder with a **Lathe Precision** of 6.

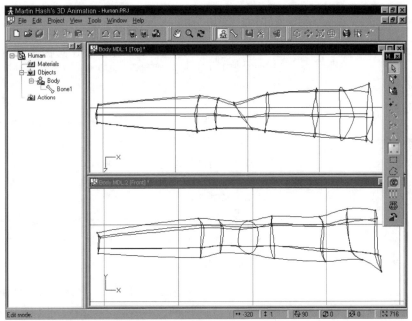

FIGURE   *Front and top views of the arm's shape.*
4.89

2. Shape the arm from both the front and top views. Once you've reached a satisfactory shape, copy, paste, and flip the complete arm to form the other one.

3. For shape reference, Figure 4.89 includes both a front and a top view of the final arm. Notice that the elbow spline was rotated 45 degrees in the Y axis to make an effective elbow joint, and that the entire forearm was rotated downward slightly to make it look a little more natural.

4. Now that the arm is complete, copy and attach the end cross-section toward the shoulder of the model to the torso using the same technique as the breast in the previous section. Use the same procedure to attach both of the arms.

Once the arms are attached, you'll need to make minor adjustments to scale and translation to properly fit them to the body.

The next step in this section is the addition of legs to the pelvic area of the model. Save your work before continuing.

ADDING LEGS TO THE MODEL

The leg should be shaped, then copied, pasted, and flipped to form the second leg. The legs are created for this model in the same manner as the arms:

1. Create the legs by lathing an 8-point spline into a cylinder with a **Lathe Precision** of 6.

2. Now shape the leg from both front and top views. Once you reach a satisfactory shape, copy, paste, and flip the complete leg to form the second leg.

3. For shape reference, Figure 4.90 includes both a front and a top view of the final leg. Notice that the knee spline was rotated in the X axis to make an effective joint.

Once you've completed the leg, you can attach it to the pelvis by breaking the splines between the control points of the top leg cross-

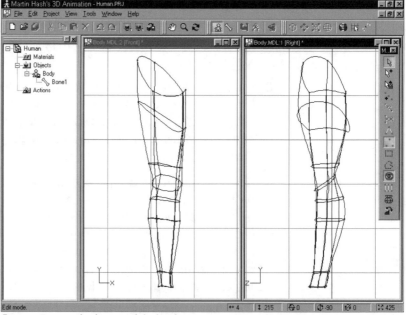

FIGURE   *Front and side view of the leg shape.*
4.90

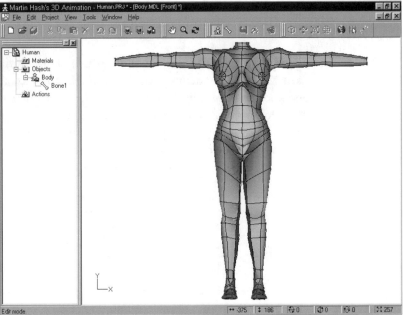

FIGURE *Shaded wireframe view of the final model.*
4.91

section and connecting the hanging control points to the corresponding control points of the pelvis. Attach both legs in this manner, then make any necessary adjustments.

You can construct simple feet for this model by extruding the end cross-section of the leg and rotating the extrusions as they're created. Close off the ends of the feet by scaling those cross-sections to 1 along both the X and Y axes.

Figure 4.91 shows the final shaded wireframe for this model.

Some work still can be done to making adjustments to the body that offer a little more anatomical correctness, but the modeling technique was the important knowledge to gain here.

Although frustrating at times, human figures are fantastic modeling exercises. To get some experience in modeling human forms, it may be beneficial to photograph someone against a wall or blue screen and use the photograph as a rotoscope.

SUMMARY

Organic modeling takes time and practice. The tutorials in this chapter have used advanced modeling techniques such as hooks, multipart construction, and knowledge of spline direction to make modeling complex objects as easy as possible. As you practice and gain experience with the modeler, you'll discover your own techniques that will help in defining your style of modeling.

The next chapter describes how to model some nonorganic or mechanical models, such as spaceships, buildings, and airplanes.

5 Mechanical Modeling

This chapter discusses the creation of mechanical objects. Models labeled "mechanical" are not necessarily machines. Rather they are usually symmetrical or contain many flat surfaces.

Mechanical objects are used in all types of computer animation, from high-end digital film effects to desktop demonstrations and visualization. Although polygonal modelers have been the mainstay of mechanical modeling, splines are useful in many situations, allowing a wide range of flexibility and a lower model resolution. Previously discussed techniques can be used in Animation:Master to create mechanical objects quickly and easily.

This chapter describes some techniques used to create buildings, explains how to model an airplane, and gives a method for creating spaceships.

The chapter covers the following techniques:

- Creating Buildings
- Modeling an Airplane
- Modeling a Spaceship

CREATING BUILDINGS

Although they aren't a mainstay by any means in character animation, buildings and surrounding areas provide backdrops and locations where most character action takes place.

Taking advantage of the way the modeler interprets splines makes it easy to create holes for doorways and windows on close-up shots.

The following exercises will describe how to create simple buildings, as well as how you can easily add doors and windows to walls.

EXERCISE

CREATING A SIMPLE BUILDING

Most of the detail on a building could easily be represented with image maps, making it unnecessary to create every window and door. This exercise will concentrate on creating the building's shape. Mapping can provide the detail.

1. Create a new project and select **Save As** from the **Project** drop-down. Type *Building* for the project name and press **Enter.** Right-click the **Object** button in the **Project Workspace** and select **New, Model**. Click the plus (+) sign to the left of the **Object** button to

expand the object list. Right-click the model name, and select **Save As**. Enter *Building.MDL* and press Enter.

2. Under **Tools**, select **Options**, then click the Modeling /. Turn the Grid on if it's not already visible, and enter *20* into the **Grid Spacing** field.

3. From a top view, add a single vertical spline that is two grid units long. Press the **/** key to select the spline you just added, then click the **Extrude** button. Drag the extrusion two units to the right, creating a square with rounded corners.

4. Press the **/** key to **Group Connected**, then press the **P** key to Peak all of the selected points. With the control points still selected, right-click within the yellow bounding box and select **Snap to Grid** from the available menu. You should now have a square, with each of the four points sitting on a grid intersection.

5. Change to a front view and use the **Group** tool to select the entire spline you just created. Zoom out enough to see between six and eight grid squares vertically on the screen.

6. Click the **Extrude** button, change to a **Translate** manipulator by pressing the **N** key, and translate the extrusion along the Y axis only three grid spaces.

7. With the extrusion still selected, click the **Extrude** button a second time. On the **Properties Panel**, enter *80* into both the **X** and **Z Scale** fields to create the second tier of the building.

8. Click the **Extrude** button once again, and translate the new extrusion in the Y axis only, upward two grid units. Press the **/** key to **Group Connected**, then press the **P** key to Peak all of the points in the building. The model should look similar to Figure 5.1 at this point.

9. Continue by using the **Group** tool to select the top cross-section of the building. Click the **Extrude** button, then enter *80* into the **X** and **Z Scale** fields on the **Properties Panel**.

10. Click the **Extrude** button once again and translate the extrusion two grid units upward along the Y axis.

Although this model doesn't give the most visually realistic results possible, it serves as a simple building, and it's made up of only 26 patches. You could add image maps to create a more realistic result. Extra detail such as a sunken rooftop and several antennas would also help.

You can throw in some variation to make the building a little more realistic by scaling it down in the Z axis to make it wider than it is deep.

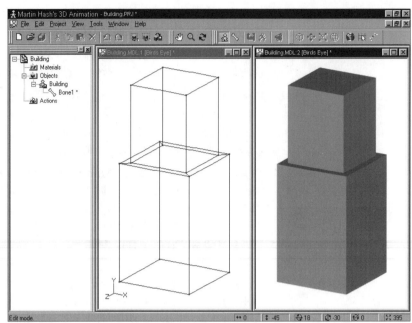

FIGURE *Both a wireframe and rendered view of the building with two tiers built.*
5.1

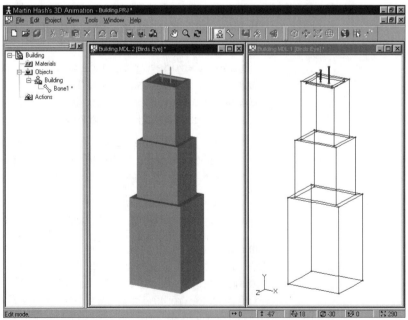

FIGURE *Both a wireframe and a rendered view of the completed building.*
5.2

Since most of the detail of buildings is best added with image maps, it's very easy to create many variations of a single building in a short time. Good-looking buildings are quick and will be very useful in filling out scenes.

For close-ups or inside shots of buildings, partial models can be built that will adequately represent the whole. For example, if the script calls for the camera to zoom in to an apartment window and view inside the apartment, it makes no sense to build the entire apartment complex, since it won't be seen. You can easily add doors and windows to models without adding unnecessary resolution by taking advantage of the way the modeler interprets legal patches.

EXERCISE

ADDING DOORS AND WINDOWS TO BUILDINGS

The fact that Animation:Master interprets a single closed spline as a hole can be to your advantage in adding doors and windows to models. Although you could use transparency maps, they can cause some confusion if you intend to add windowsills or glass, or to position other objects in relation to the window (since you can't see the hole until you render).

1. Start Animation:Master, and begin by selecting **New** from the **Project** drop-down menu. Save the project as "Wall."

2. Expand the project list by clicking the plus (**+**) sign to the left of the **Wall** tag in the **Project Workspace**.

3. Right-click the **Object** list and select **New, Model**.

4. Right-click the **Model** name and select **Save As**. Enter "Wall" as the name.

Now that the project is set up, you're ready to begin creating a wall with a doorway.

5. From the **Tools** menu, select **Options** and click the **Modeling** tab to verify that the Grid Spacing is set to the default 5. From a front view, create a single vertical spline, seven grid spaces long.

6. Click the **Extrude** button and drag the extrusion to the right eight grid spaces. Press the **/** key to **Group Connected**, then press the **P** key to peak all of the points. This rectangle represents a "wall" to which a door will be added.

7. In the center of the model, create a single 5-point spline in a circular shape. Glue the end points together to form a single 4-point, closed spline.

NOTE

Animation:Master interprets patches as four control points on two different splines. The fact that the spline used to create a 4-point patch in step 7 was a single spline will cause the modeler to create a hole where this spline is attached to a model.

8. With any point of the new spline selected, press the **/** key to **Group Connected**, then press the **P** key to Peak all of the points.

9. Position the points as shown in Figure 5.3. The grid was turned off in this image for clarity. The spline is positioned so that it's two grid spaces wide and just under three spaces high.

10. To attach the doorway to the wall, you'll need to add several control points to the wall splines. Select each side of the wall, one spline at a time, and insert two control points on each with the **Y** key.

11. Add 2-point splines between each of these new control points and the corresponding points on the door. Figure 5.4 shows the wireframe of the model after these splines have been added.

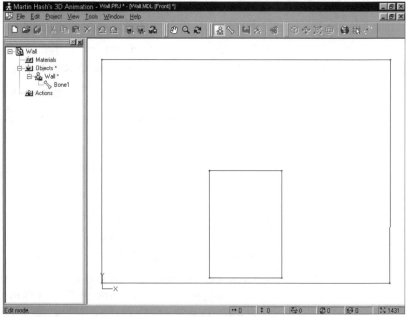

FIGURE   *Placement of the closed spline loop that will form a doorway.*
5.3

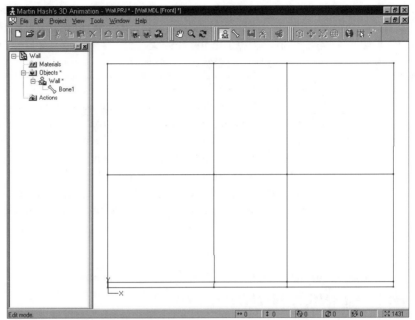

FIGURE *Wireframe view of wall with doorway attached.*
5.4

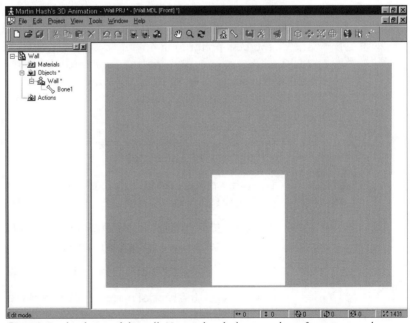

FIGURE *Rendered view of the wall. Not much to look at now, but a few textures and some*
5.5 *trim will make an excellent doorway.*

The bottom of the doorway can be grouped and translated downward so it won't form an obstruction. The only patch that will not render in this wall is the one you created as a single spline. Figure 5.5 shows the final render of the wall.

Now that you've seen how to take advantage of nonrendering splines for doorways, keep in mind that you can make windows in exactly the same manner. Adding some trim and wall textures will make a huge difference in setting the mood of the scene you're working on.

Since buildings are something of a requirement in creating complete scenes, they're used quite often. Another much-desired mechanical object is the airplane. A technique for creating airplanes is discussed in the next section.

MODELING AN AIRPLANE

This exercise will discuss the creation of a jet airplane. One of the benefits of modeling mechanical objects such as this with a spline modeler is the somewhat organic look that's maintained. Many modern aircraft have very smooth and curved surfaces that are well suited to spline modeling.

The SR-71 Blackbird is not just a beautiful aircraft to look at — it's also one of the best-performing aircraft ever flown. The SR-71 can fly well over 2,000 miles per hour, can climb at 30,000 feet per minute, and has a ceiling of 85,000 feet and a range of over 3,000 miles. Such impressive statistics are worthy of this reconnaissance aircraft, which will be modeled in the following exercise.

EXERCISE

SETTING UP THE ROTOSCOPES

1. Start Animation:Master, and begin by selecting **New** from the **Project** drop-down menu. Save the project as "SR-71."

2. Expand the project list by clicking the plus (**+**) sign to the left of the **SR-71** tag in the **Project Window**.

3. Right-click the **Object** list and select **New/Model**.

4. Right-click the **Model** name and select **Save As**. Enter *SR-71a* and press **Enter**.

5. Right-click the **SR-71a** item in the **Objects** section of the **Project Workspace**. Select **Import, Rotoscope** from the available options.

6. Use the **Open File** dialog to locate the *SR71 Front.TGA* rotoscope on the accompanying CD-ROM.

7. Repeat step 6 for both the *SR71 Side.TGA* and *SR71 Top.TGA* rotoscopes.

8. Each rotoscope's name appears in the **Project Workspace**. The rotoscopes for the side and top views must be "turned" to be visible from the correct angles, rather than the front. Orient the side rotoscope by clicking it, selecting the **General** tab on the **Properties Panel**, then choosing the right view from those available in the drop-down list. Repeat this process for the top rotoscope, selecting the **Top** view from the drop-down list.

9. After the rotoscopes are in their final positions, select each one and uncheck the pickable box on the **Properties Panel** to keep you from inadvertently selecting the rotoscope while you're modeling.

The setup stages for modeling the SR-71 are now complete. This would be a good time to click the **Disk** button to save your work before continuing on to begin modeling the plane. In the next exercise, you learn how to model the fuselage shape and add the wings to it.

EXERCISE

CREATING THE FUSELAGE

The basic fuselage shape is created by tracing the contours of the rotoscope images.

1. Begin modeling the airplane from the top view. Add a spline with 13 control points that traces along the right hand side of the airplane's body, ignoring the wings. Figure 5.6 shows the spline, with the rotoscope hidden for clarity.

2. Set the **Lathe Precision** to *12,* click any point on the spline, and press the **/** key to **Group Connected**. Change to a **Rotate** manipulator and rotate the pivot –90 degrees in the X axis. Use the mouse to translate the pivot away from the spline in the X axis until it's lined up just outside the innermost control point near the nose of the plane.

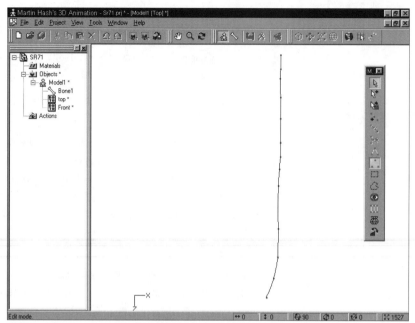

FIGURE   *The 13-point spline from which the body of the airplane will be created.*
5.6

3. Click the **Lathe** button to create the plane's body. Use the **Group** tool to select the end cross-section at the nose of the plane. Then enter 1 into both the **X** and **Y Scale** fields on the **Properties Panel**.

4. From a front view, translate the entire fuselage down along the Y axis until the center point of the wireframe nose lines up with the template's nose. Use the **Group** tool to select and translate the control points that make up the fuselage until they look similar to Figure 5.7.

5. Change to a side view. Continue to shape the model with the **Group** tool and translate points to match the rotoscoped image.

6. After you've shaped the model from the side view, change back to a top view and use the **Group** tool to select the first cross-section in front of the wings. Position this cross-section along the Z axis so that it lies just in front of the wings. Use the **Group** tool to select the next cross-section back and position it along the Z axis just behind the previous cross-section. Figure 5.8 shows the location of these splines for reference.

7. Working from the top view, use the **Group** tool to select the points along the edges of the fuselage and translate them outward to match the shape of the plane's wing, as shown in Figure 5.9.

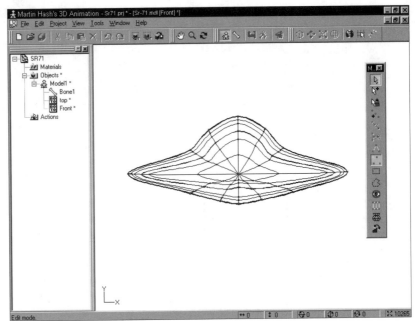

FIGURE   *The shape of the SR-71 fuselage from a front view.*
5.7

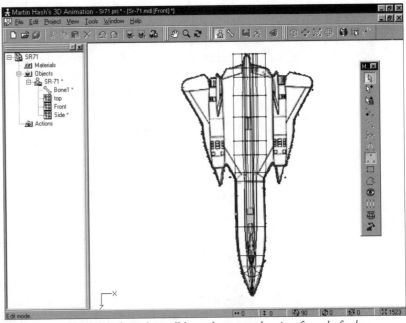

FIGURE   *Position of the splines that will be used to create the wings from the fuselage.*
5.8

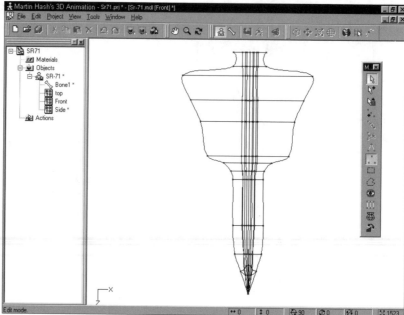

FIGURE
5.9
The shape of the SR-71 wings pulled from the fuselage shape. In this screen shot, the rotoscoped image was hidden for clarity.

8. Toward the back of the model, arrange the points to trace the gaps on the wings where the engines are located. Use the **Group** tool to select the last cross-section of the fuselage and extrude it twice to provide adequate resolution to finish the fuselage shape.

Figure 5.10 shows a bird's-eye view of the model after step 8.

9. The SR-71 is powered by two Pratt & Whitney JT 11D-20B Turbo Ramjet Engines that produce 32,500 lb of static thrust with afterburners. The engines on this model are created separately from the body. Create a single 2-point spline to the side of the model. Group this spline with the **Group** tool, then click the **Hide** button to hide the rest of the model.

10. Add several control points to this spline to make it a 5-point spline. Shape it along the side of the left engine rotoscope from a top view.

11. With any of the control points on this spline selected, press the **/** key to **Group Connected**. Switch to the **Rotate** manipulator and rotate the pivot –90 degrees in the X axis. Translate the pivot to the center

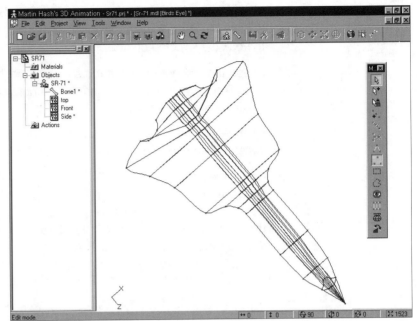

FIGURE *Bird's-eye view of the fuselage model with the wings created.*
5.10

of the engine, verify that the **Lathe Precision** is set to 8, and click the **Lathe** button.

12. Use the **Group** tool and the mouse to make any necessary adjustments to the size of the engine, from both the top and side views.

The cones at the front and back of the engine are created by simply lathing a 2-point spline, shaping it as necessary, and positioning it on the engine.

When the first engine is complete, select it with the **Group** tool and choose **Copy**, then **Paste** from the **Edit** menu. Right-click the new **Untitled** group name in the **Project Workspace** and select **Flip, X-Axis** from the available menu. If necessary, use the mouse or arrow keys to position the second engine correctly.

13. The last parts that need to be added to the plane are the fins that sit atop either engine. Start by creating a simple cylinder with several cross-sections from the side view.

14. Group the top of the cylinder and scale it to 1 along both the X and Z axes. Press the **/** key to **Group Connected**, then press the **P** key to Peak the selected points.

15. Shape the cylinder to match the shape of the fin from the side view, extruding where necessary to shape the notch at the back of the fin where it meets the engine.

16. Change to a front view and scale the fin down along the X axis until it matches the thickness of the fin in the rotoscope.

17. Group the entire fin. Enter *–15 degrees* in the **Z Rotate** field on the **Properties Panel** for the left fin, or *15 degrees* if you created the right fin first. With the entire fin still selected, pick **Copy**, then **Paste** from the **Edit** menu. Right-click the **Group** name in the **Project Workspace** and choose **Flip, X-Axis** from the available menus. Use the mouse or arrow keys to position the newly created fin if necessary.

The SR-71 shows how an airplane can be built easily in Animation:Master. This model was completed in under an hour and is made

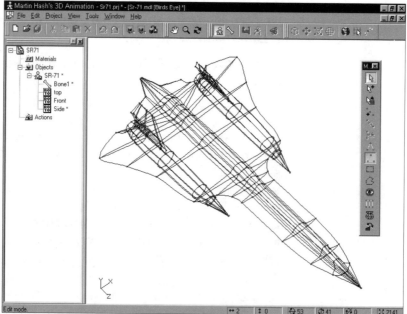

FIGURE   *A wireframe view of the completed SR-71 model.*
5.11

FIGURE *A rendered view of the SR-71 model in "flight."*
5.12

up of only 328 patches. More detail can be added with image maps for realism if the need arises.

Recently, television shows such as *Babylon 5* and *Star Trek* have made spaceships hugely popular. They are used extensively in professional production, and when set in the correct scene, they look very believable. The next section of this book will describe how to recreate a spaceship used by Hash, Inc. for the movie *Telepresence*.

MODELING A SPACESHIP

One of the major benefits to modeling spaceships is the freedom they allow you as an artist. Nobody can stand over your shoulder and tell you that the model doesn't look right, because there is no reference (at least none that the government is willing to admit).

In this exercise, you'll again see the beauty in modeling mechanical objects with a spline modeler, and the wonderful organic quality that is preserved.

EXERCISE

BEGINNING A SPACESHIP

1. Start Animation:Master and begin by selecting **New** from the **Project** drop-down menu. Save the project as "Alien Ship."

2. Expand the project list by clicking the plus (**+**) sign to the left of the **Alien Ship** item in the **Project Workspace**.

3. Right-click the **Object** list and select **New, Model**.

4. Right-click the **Model** name and select **Save As**. Enter *Spaceship* as the name.

The project is now set up, and you're ready to begin modeling. The spaceship figure begins with the main hull of the ship, and the details are added later.

5. Begin constructing the hull of the model by setting the lathe precision to 22. From the front view, create a spline with 12 control points shaped similarly to the one shown in Figure 5.13.

6. Select any point along the spline by clicking on it, then click the **Lathe** button.

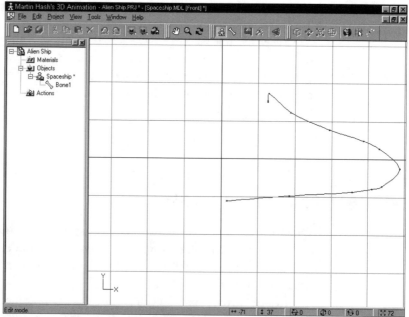

FIGURE *Front view of the spline used to create the ship's hull.*
5.13

7. From the front view, select the lowermost cross-section with the **Group** tool. Enter *1* into both the **X** and **Z Scale** fields on the **Properties Panel**. Translate the selected points upward with the arrow keys until the bottom of the hull is flat.

8. Change to a side view and use the **Group** tool to select groups of control points near the back of the ship, then translate them with the mouse to shape the model similarly to Figure 5.14. This will create an area suitable for an engine "glow."

9. Still working from a side view, use the **Group** tool to group the top three cross-sections of the model. Shape them similarly to Figure 5.15 to form a window in the hull.

10. Change to a top view and round out the back of the ship. Translate the sides of the hull inward to create a more round look to the ship.

11. Translate the points that make up the window in the hull into a rectangular shape with rounded corners. Group the two cross-sections at the front of the ship and translate them toward the back of the ship, forming an indentation in the hull.

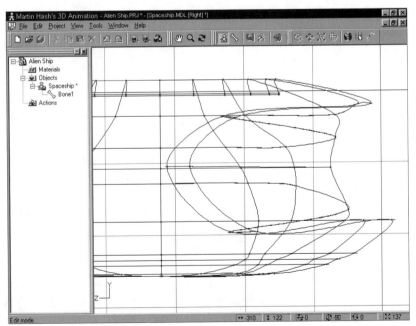

FIGURE   *Side view of the hull shape.*
5.14

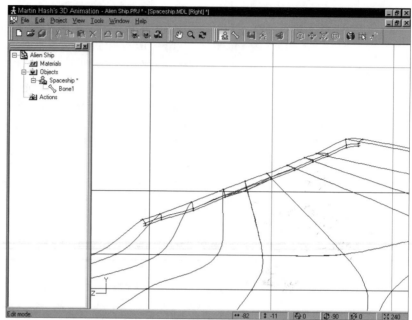

FIGURE *Side view of the window in the front of the hull.*
5.15

The main part of the hull is complete, but it's still necessary to add the fins to the front of the ship. At this point, the model should look similar to Figure 5.16.

12. Begin adding the fins to the front of the ship by "fanning out" the front of the ship slightly. Set the lathe precision to 7 and add a 5-point spline similar to the one shown in Figure 5.17.

13. Click any point along the spline and press the **/** key to **Group Connected**. Click the **Rotate Manipulator**, and rotate the pivot –90 degrees in the X axis. From the top view, translate the pivot to the right of the selected spline. Click the **Lathe** button.

14. Shape the model from both the top and side view similarly to the one shown in Figure 5.18.

15. Break the spline on the hull of the ship that leads from the center indented points toward the inside edge of the fin. Attach a spline between this broken spline and the inside control point on the fin to form a continuous spline from the hull to the fin.

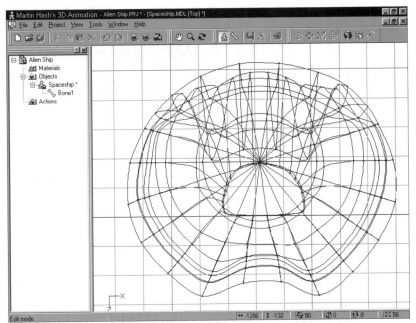

FIGURE *Top view of the hull shape, as well as the rounded rectangular window.*
5.16

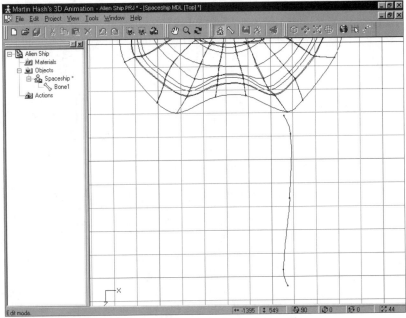

FIGURE *Top view of the spline used to create the fins on the spaceship.*
5.17

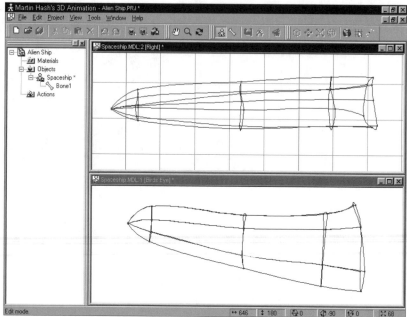

FIGURE *Both a top and a side view of the fin shape.*
5.18

16. Break the outside spline on the body and connect it to the outside control point of the fin to create a continuous spline around the outside of the fin. The rest of the control points should more or less line up with the points that they will be connecting to. If necessary, use Figure 5.19 for reference.

17. Group all of the original fin shape and select **Copy**, then **Paste** from the **Edit** menu. Right-click the **Group** name in the **Project Workspace** and select **Flip, X-Axis** from the available menu. Use the mouse or arrow keys to move the new fin into position on the opposite side of the ship.

18. Attach the opposite fin by repeating steps 15 and 16.

19. From the front view, two holes are formed in the hull where the fins meet the body. These 5-point patches can be resolved easily by adding a spline and hooking it to the center of the next spline down.

The main hull of the ship is now complete, and the only parts of the model left to build are for detailing, such as the gun turrets, canopy, and some surface detail. All of the techniques for adding detail to the model

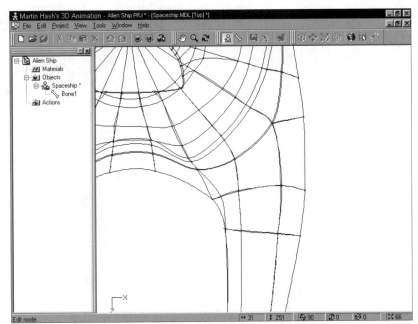

FIGURE Top view of the fin connected to the hull of the spaceship.
5.19

have been used throughout this book; the next section contains explanations of the methods used. This would be a great time to take a second to click the **Disk** button and save your work before continuing.

ADDING DETAIL TO THE MODEL

The hull was the hard part of this space ship, but don't let that fool you. The details may be simple to create, but it can be difficult to add them correctly to a model without inadvertently crossing parts, or completely missing joining them together. If you're careful, take your time, and view the model from several different angles, you should keep any possible problems to a minimum.

As you can see in Figure 5.20, the surface detail was added symmetrically. It was created for one side of the ship, then copied, pasted, and flipped to form the other side.

Most of the detail used on spaceships comes from image maps (covered in Chapter 7). However, some things, like the large pipes along the sides of the ship, must be added by hand.

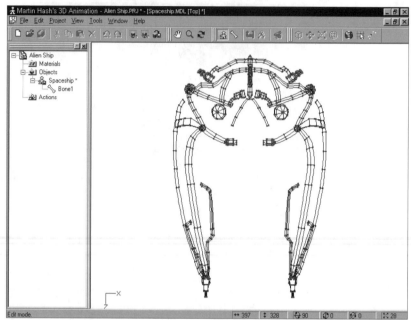

FIGURE
5.20

Top view of the detailing added to the hull of the ship.

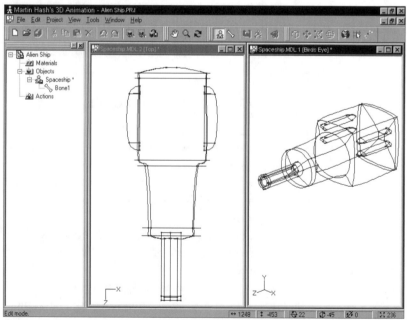

FIGURE
5.21

Both a top and bird's-eye view of the gun turrets attached to the end of each fin.

Keep in mind when you're adding detail that mechanical objects are usually manmade, so the detailing on them is very regular. Cones, cylinders, and cubes are commonplace for detailing.

The pipes along the hull of the ship were created by lathing a spline to a precision of 4, then deleting one of the sides from the resulting cylinder (to cut down on unnecessary resolution). The cross-sections were then grouped and translated into position.

The gun turrets, shown in Figure 5.21, are created from simple lathed shapes, adjusted to fit the shape of the gun.

More detail was added by creating several simple cone shapes as well as a few rectangular objects toward the back of the hull.

The canopy, shown in Figure 5.22, was created by extruding a 4-point spline. The canopy shape was adjusted to match the curvature of the hull of the ship, then translated into position.

The final model, shown in Figure 5.23, is made up of 1,451 patches, most of which came from the detail added after the model was shaped. Higher patch counts are normal in mechanical objects and rarely cause any problems, since few mechanical objects are animated in a way other than simple rotations or translations.

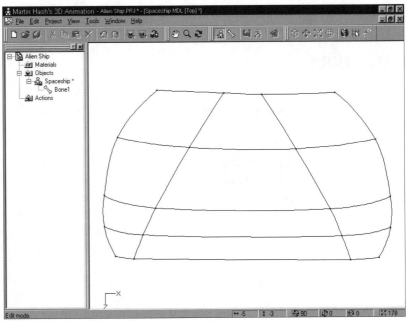

FIGURE *Front view of the canopy for the spaceship.*
5.22

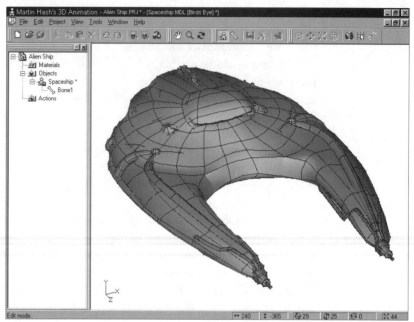

FIGURE *Bird's-eye view of the completed spaceship.*
5.23

SUMMARY

Mechanical modeling covers a wide range of possibilities, from buildings to airplanes to spaceships. A big part of success in modeling mechanical objects is to be careful not to add too much detail to the model, but to know when to say when and use an image map. Take the capabilities afforded to you in models created from splines and use them to your advantage. For example, imagine the SR-71 taking off by flapping its wings smoothly like a bird, or the building swaying gently in a breeze.

Now that you've gained a little experience with the main types of models used, it's time to start applying textures to the models you've created. The next chapter discusses the Materials Editor in Animation:Master.

6 Adding Textures to Models

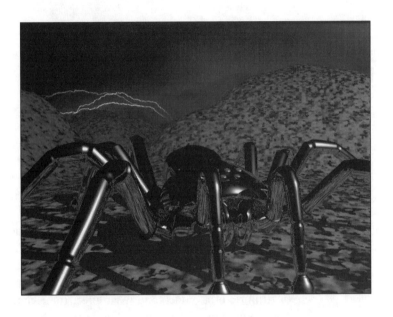

This chapter will help you understand the use of Base Attributes, patch colors, and the Materials Editor to apply textures to your models. **The chapter covers the following techniques:**

- Texturing with the Base Attribute
- Texturing with Patch Colors
- Understanding Three-Dimensional Textures
- Material Techniques
- Complex Materials
- Material Libraries

USING BASE ATTRIBUTES

Every model has a set of *Base Attributes* associated with it that can be modified to help get the model looking the way you want. Base Attributes are different from the materials discussed later in this chapter in that they're used only on one model, and they affect the entire model.

As you gain experience creating models, you'll notice that the default color is white, and that no properties such as Specularity or Ambiance are applied to the model.

To change the default attributes for your models, click on the model name in the **Objects** section of the **Project Workspace**. The **Base Attribute** settings will appear on the **Properties Panel**, allowing you to make changes.

The following exercise describes how to make changes to the Base Attributes of a model, and what effect these changes have on that model. The model used in this exercise is Thom, the mascot for Animation:Master.

APPLYING BASE ATTRIBUTES TO THE MODEL

1. Start by opening the *Thom No Color.MDL* file from the accompanying CD-ROM. For reference, Figure 6.1 shows the full model.

Rendering at this point would lead to a plain white model that is somewhat less than exciting. To change the color of the entire model, click the name **Thom No Color** in the **Objects** section of the **Project Workspace**, then select the **Attributes** tab on the **Properties Panel**.

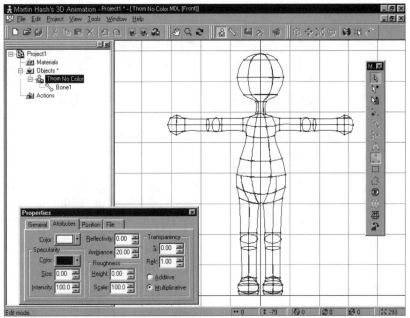

FIGURE
6.1
The Thom No Color.MDL *model from the accompanying CD-ROM. On opening,
all of the* **Base Attributes** *are set to their default values.*

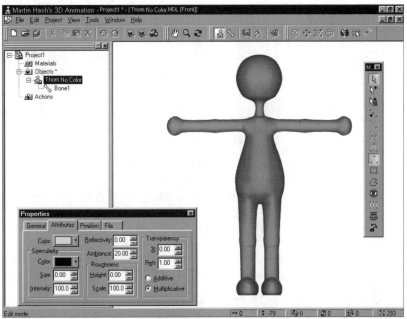

FIGURE
6.2
A rendering of the Thom model after the **Base Attribute** *color is set to yellow.*

2. Click on the color chip to the right of the **Color:** item on the **Properties Panel**, and select the yellow swatch near the bottom right of the palette that appears. If you prefer to type the value in, click the **Other** button near the bottom of the palette and enter *255, 255, 0* into the **Red**, **Green**, and **Blue** fields, respectively.

3. Render the model by clicking the **Render Mode** button and clicking anywhere in the model window. As easily as that, you've just changed Thom's coloring to all yellow, and on rendering should see results similar to those shown in Figure 6.2.

There are many other fields on the **Properties Panel** that can be changed to modify the look of a model as a whole, including **Specularity**, **Reflectivity**, **Ambiance**, **Roughness**, and **Transparency**. The next section describes the **Specularity** values.

MODIFYING BASE ATTRIBUTES

Beneath the **Color** item on the **Properties Panel** is an item called **Specularity**. This item allows you to specify how shiny your model looks. *Specular highlights* are the bright areas that appear on shiny objects. Most often, specular highlights occur on curved objects, when the light from a light source bounces off a model's surface and goes directly into the camera. As a general rule, the harder the object, the higher its specularity.

The **Color** field in the **Specularity** section of the **Properties Panel** allows you to change the color of the specular highlight that appears on your model. This means that you can modify the color of the highlight to match different colored lights in a choreography. If no changes are made to the Specular Color, the specular highlight will shift from the color of the Base Attribute toward white.

The **Specular Size** field determines how big a specular highlight will appear on your model, and the **Specular Intensity** determines how intense the specular color will appear. There are no limits to the values that can be entered into these fields, but values much beyond 100 will generally yield unusable results.

The next exercise will walk you through making changes to the specularity values of the Thom model.

EXERCISE

APPLYING SPECULARITY TO THE MODEL

1. The Thom model has a surface that is somewhat shiny (specular). To change the Specularity, click the color chip to the right of the **Color:** item in the **Specularity** section of the **Properties Panel**.

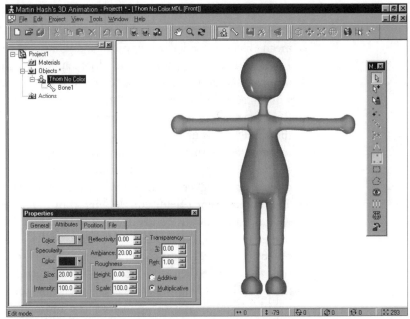

FIGURE
6.3
The Thom model rendered with a small amount of specularity applied. Notice the white highlights on the head, on the hands, and in the waist area.

2. Select white from the palette that appears. This causes the color on Thom's body to shift from yellow (the Base Attribute) to white (Specular Color) wherever a specular highlight appears.

3. To make highlights appear, enter a value of *20* into the **Specularity Size** field.

4. After entering the Specular value into the field on the **Properties Panel**, render the model and see how the surface color and texture were affected. Figure 6.3 shows a rendering of the model at this point. Take a few moments to experiment with different specular values and see how the changes affect the final rendering.

The remaining fields available on the **Properties Panel** help to control how every model you create will look:

• **Reflectivity** will cause your model to reflect the environment around it. *Reflectivity* is based on a percentage value from 0 to 100, 0 being no reflections and 100 being a perfect mirror. High reflectivity values will come at the price of slowing the renderer.

- **Ambiance** controls how bright an object appears when no light is hitting it. Acceptable Ambiance values range from 0 to 100. A value of 0 will mean that the model will appear totally dark when no light is cast on it and a value of 100 will make an object appear to glow from within. Keep in mind that even though a value of 100 makes an object *appear* to glow, it will not actually give off any light.
- **Roughness Height** and **Scale** control a turbulence function that perturbs the surface of your objects. The default value of zero will cause an object to be perfectly smooth, whereas larger roughness values cause the surface of model to appear rougher. Values for roughness can go well into the thousands or higher if you desire, so experiment with this item.
- The **Transparency** fields control how transparent your object appears, as well as how much it bends light (refraction). A **Transparency** value of 0 makes a model appear totally opaque, while a value of 100 makes an object completely transparent. The **Refraction** values are based on a real-world index between 1 and 2. A **Refraction** value of 1 causes very little bending of light, whereas a high value such as 2 would cause an upside-down image to appear in the model, essentially turning the model into a lens.

As you can see from working with Thom, Base Attributes make it easy to apply attributes to your model on a global level. However, attributes can also be applied to the individual patches that make up a model, allowing for a wide variety of surface texture possibilities.

The next section describes how to changes the attributes of a model on a patch level.

PATCH COLORING KILLER BEAN

Although Base Attributes allow some flexibility in the way a character looks, you won't always want to apply attributes on a global level (to the entire model). In most cases, the surfaces of your models will be a diverse mixture of colors, textures, image maps, etc. One of the techniques used in Animation:Master to create more diverse surface textures is called Patch Coloring. Patch Coloring is a way of defining colors for a patch or group of patches. The next exercise will describe how to create and apply color to patches.

The Killer Bean model created earlier in this book is an example of a model that can be textured by applying patch materials to named groups. Named groups are an important concept in Animation:Master because they offer flexibility for muscle motion, Poses, coloring the surfaces of models, lip synching, and in the modeling process itself. The next few steps describe how to create named groups for the Killer Bean model.

EXERCISE

PATCH COLORING

1. Open the *Killer Bean No Color.MDL* file from the accompanying CD-ROM. If the model doesn't open in a modeling window, right-click the model name in the **Objects** section of the **Project Workspace**, and select **Edit** from the available menu. Figure 6.4 shows a rendering of the complete model, with no coloring applied.

2. As you're naming groups with the intention of creating patch colors for a model, it can be helpful to note which parts of a model will be

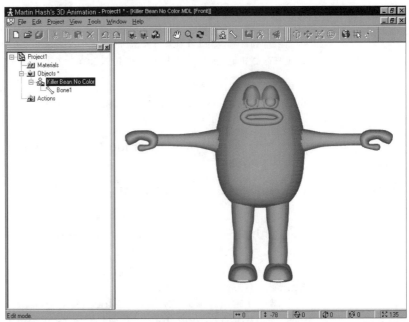

FIGURE   *The rendered* Killer Bean No Color.MDL *model from the accompanying CD-ROM.*
6.4

colored the same. This can save a lot of time in the process. On this model, both of the hands and both of the feet are the same color. To begin creating a named group, hold down the **Shift** key, since there will be multiple points selected, then click on any point in the right hand, any point in the left hand, any point in the right foot, and any point in the left foot.

3. Press the **/** key to **Group Connected**. The control points that make up the hands and feet should turn green, indicating that they're grouped.

4. Examine the **Project Workspace**. Notice that a group named **Untitled** has appeared and is highlighted. Click on the name once to select it, then press **F2** to edit the name. When a blinking cursor appears in the name field, type in *Hands and Feet,* then press **Enter**.

You just created a named group! Notice that after you press **Enter**, an asterisk appears following the name you typed in. This asterisk reminds you that unsaved changes have been made to this model. Right-click the model name and choose **Save As** from the menu that appears. Decide where you would like to put the model, enter a name, and click **OK** to save the model to your hard drive.

5. It is always a good idea first to name all of the groups in your model before applying textures to them. Press **Enter** to **Deselect All**.

6. Use the **Zoom** tool to magnify the area around the eyes of the model. Hold down the **Shift** key and click on one control point in each pupil.

7. Press the **/** key to **Group Connected**. Name the selected group **Pupils**.

8. Press **Enter** to **Deselect All**.

9. Hold down the **Shift** key and click one control point on each eyeball. Press the **/** key to **Group Connected** and name the selected group **Eyeballs**.

10. Press **Enter** to **Deselect All**.

11. Click any control point in the mouth shape and press the **/** key to **Group Connected**. Name this group **Mouth**.

12. Press **Enter** to **Deselect All**.

You should now see four named groups in the **Project Workspace**. This is all you need for this model. To apply colors to the named groups, select them one at a time and make the appropriate entries into the **Properties Panel**.

The main body, arms, legs, and eyelids are all the same color and make up the majority of the model, so their coloring will be left to the Base Attribute in the final step of the exercise.

13. Continuing from the previous step, click on the group named **Hands and Feet** in the **Project Workspace**. The points that you selected for this group should turn green to indicate that they're selected.

14. Click the **Attributes** tab of the **Properties Panel**. Notice that all of the fields are ghosted. This is because the selected points are currently getting their attributes from the Base Attribute settings.

15. Click the checkbox to the left of the **Color:** item. All of the options on the **Properties Panel** will activate, allowing changes. This checkbox specifies that you want the settings you're about to make to override the Base Attribute on the selected patches.

16. Click the color chip, then click the **Other** button when the default color palette opens. Enter *63* for the **Red Value**, *0* for **Green**, and *128* for **Blue**. Click **OK** to close the color palette. The color chip next to the color checkbox turns purple, indicating the color of the selected patches.

17. To set the rest of the attributes, begin by changing the **Specular Color** to white and entering *80* for the **Specular Size**. The **Specular Intensity** can be left at the default **100**.

18. Enter *20* into the **Ambiance** field and leave the rest of the settings at their defaults.

Rendering the model at this point should produce an image similar to the one shown in Figure 6.5.

19. The final step in coloring the Killer Bean is to set the Base Attribute. Click the **Killer Bean** item in the **Objects** section of the **Project Workspace**.

20. Select the **Attributes** tab on the **Properties Panel** and set the **Color** to *179* **Red**, *0* **Green**, and *0* **Blue**. Change the **Specularity**

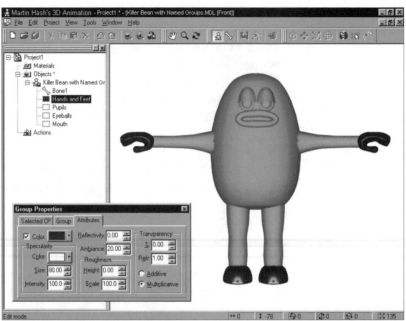

FIGURE **6.5** *The rendered Killer Bean model after attributes are added to the hands and feet.*

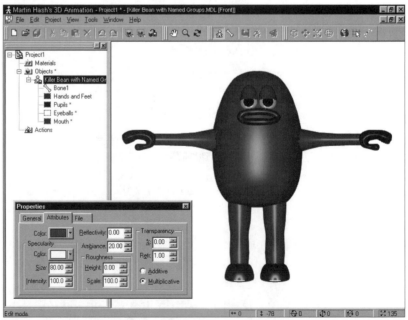

FIGURE **6.6** *The completed Killer Bean model, with attributes applied to named groups.*

Color to white and Size to *80*. Figure 6.6 shows a render of the model, completely colored. Since the image is black and white, you'll have to refer to your rendering.

You've now used the Base Attribute, as well as the capability to color individual patches along the surface of a model. Up to this point, you've used only simple colors with some specularity. The next section will help you to understand how to create more complex textures with the materials editor.

UNDERSTANDING THREE-DIMENSIONAL TEXTURES

The very first step in using the *materials editor* effectively is to understand exactly what it is you're doing when you choose to create a new material. Many people misunderstand just exactly how the material is being created. This can be frustrating, making it hard to continue using materials as a practical alternative to image maps.

When you first choose to create a new material, the material appears in the **Project Workspace** as a single simple attribute. This means that you can make changes to the attributes of the material by clicking the **Attribute** item and changing the values on the **Properties Panel**. The default attribute settings are **Color**; **Specular Color, Size,** and **Intensity**; **Reflectivity**; **Ambiance**; **Roughness Height,** and **Scale**; **Transparency**; **Refraction**; and **Transparency Type**.

More complex materials are created by using *combiners,* which are simply different methods of combining material attributes. For example, the Checker Type material uses two attribute nodes, which can be set independently. When you apply the material to a model, it will create a checker pattern that alternates between the two attributes. The available combiner types are *Checker, Gradient, Noise,* and *Spherical,* and to mix things up even more, *Turbulence* can be added. The combiner type can be selected by right-clicking the Attribute node you wish to change, then selecting **Change Type To** from the available menu.

Even more complex materials can be created by specifying attribute nodes as another material type, making for a very complex texture. As you can probably imagine, this allows for a considerable range of materials.

With all the different possibilities, you might think that materials are the answer to your texturing prayers. However, although they're very powerful, and very useful, every method of texturing models has its advantages and disadvantages.

There are some big advantages to using materials created in the materials editor. The textures are independent of resolution, meaning you can get as close as you want to the model and not lose any of the texture's fidelity (it will remain sharp even at high resolution, close up). Also, it's fairly easy to make changes to the materials if necessary. They can be changed even after they're applied, and they can be reused on any object with no major modifications. The biggest disadvantage of using materials is an increase in render time.

The following sections will help to illustrate how the different combiner types will affect a model.

THE CHECKER COMBINER

All of the materials created in the materials editor are 3D. To understand the Checker combiner, imagine you had cubes of two different colors that were 10 cm each. Now imagine taking these cubes and arranging them into a larger, 3D cube, such as the one shown in Figure 6.7.

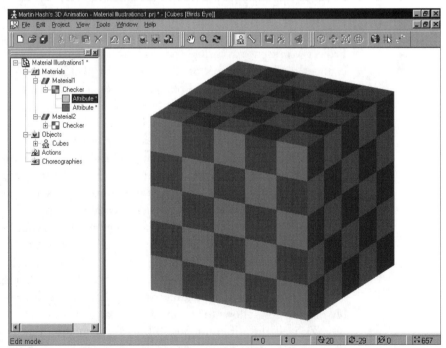

FIGURE   *Two differently colored cubes arranged into a larger 3D cube.*

6.7

NOTE

Notice the area along the right side of the cube, toward the top, where the colors don't seem to match up correctly. Remember that these materials are three-dimensional. Where the dark cube meets the light cube in the front upper corner, the dark part is actually an infinitely thin slice of the next block to the right of the light-colored one.

Now, imagine these cubes stacked into infinity in all three dimensions. This is the Checker material type. When you apply this material to a model, you're specifying what part of this infinite 3D space appears on the model. Making changes to the Translate values of the material moves the material in 3D, not the object.

To illustrate further, imagine that you wanted to apply this material to a simple sphere. Figure 6.8 shows the location of the Checker material in relation to the sphere, and Figure 6.9 shows the material on the sphere.

Finally, to clarify exactly what effect the texture had on the model, the infinite rows of cubes are removed, and a slice of the sphere is cut off, as shown in Figure 6.10.

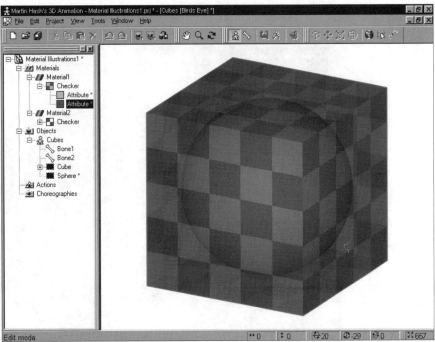

FIGURE   *The 3D Checker material positioned about a sphere model.*
6.8

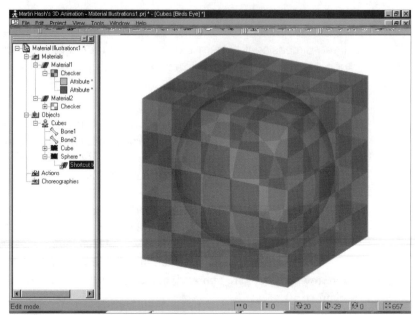

FIGURE
6.9   *The effect of applying the 3D Checker material to the sphere. If you look carefully, you can see how the sphere is "cut out" of the 3D texture.*

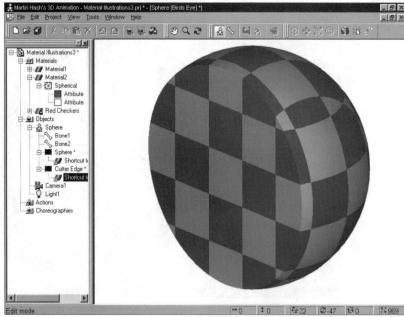

FIGURE
6.10   *The sphere model with a slice cut out of it to illustrate the 3D Checker combiner type.*

You can change some properties of the Checker material, such as the X, Y, and Z size of the cubes, the Translate value of the material, the scale, and the Blur value, which helps to blur the lines between the cubes for a more organic quality. Experiment with these properties and see what kind of effects you can produce.

The second type of combiner is called a Gradient. The next section discusses the Gradient combiner type.

THE GRADIENT COMBINER

The *Gradient* combiner has two Attributes that can be adjusted. A gradation will be created between these two Attributes when the material is applied.

Generally, the Gradient combiner is used in one of two ways. The first is in creating standard linear gradients from a given starting point to a given ending point, such as the one shown in Figure 6.11.

The second way a gradient can be used is to adjust a value called *Edge Threshold*. When no start or end positions are specified for the gradient, you

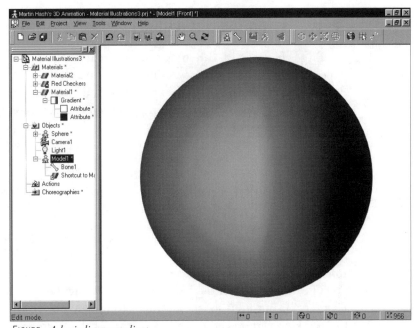

FIGURE *A basic linear gradient.*
6.11

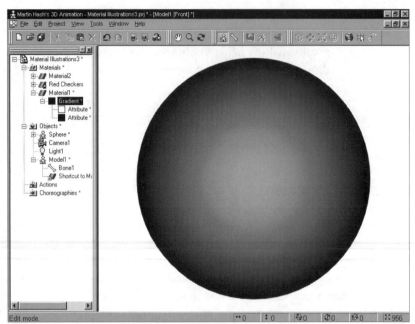

FIGURE *A Gradient combiner applied to a sphere. No start or end positions were specified*
6.12 *for the gradient, and an Edge Threshold of 50 was set.*

can use Edge Threshold to cause the specified attributes to gradate toward the
edges of the object, as shown in Figure 6.12.

Edge Threshold can be used to create some interesting effects.
Experiment with transparency values of the attributes used for the gradient.
Remember when you're working with Gradient combiners that the first
Attribute node is used at the starting position, and the second Attribute node
is the ending position.

THE NOISE COMBINER

Like the Checker and Gradient combiners, the Noise combiner also has two
Attributes that you can adjust. When applied to a model, the two attributes are
combined using a noise algorithm.

The default look of the Noise combiner is interesting in itself, as shown in
Figure 6.13. But even so, the default setting may not be what you're looking
for. Working with the adjustable properties of the Noise combiner will yield a
wide variety of interesting textures.

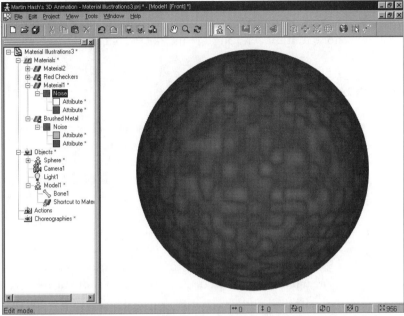

FIGURE
6.13
An interesting pattern is created when the Noise combiner is used with default settings.

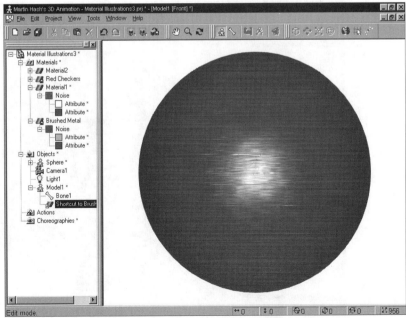

FIGURE
6.14
A brushed metal look created by setting a Noise combiner with a large X-scale value.

Scale adjustments in any of the three directions are the most common. Setting the scale value along one axis much larger than the others will cause the noise to streak, creating a result like the one shown in Figure 6.14.

THE SPHERICAL COMBINER

The Spherical combiner has two Attributes that can be adjusted. When applied to a model, the Spherical combiner will create an effect similar to a jawbreaker candy. However, if you apply the material to a spherical model, but apply no translations, the model will appear to be a single color, as shown in Figure 6.15.

Cutting away part of the model shows the effect the material is actually having, shown in Figure 6.16.

Translating a Spherical material applied to a sphere demonstrates how the material will react three-dimensionally. Figure 6.17 shows this effect.

There are other settings for the Spherical combiner, such as Ring Size, Blur, and Scale, that can be used to create a wide variety of textures.

Now that you have a basic understanding of the materials editor and how it works to create materials, the next section will describe some techniques used to create more realistic material types.

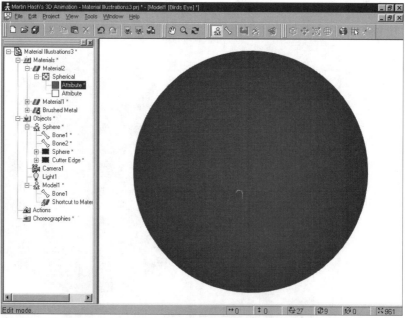

FIGURE *A Spherical combiner will appear as a flat color if no translation is specified.*
6.15

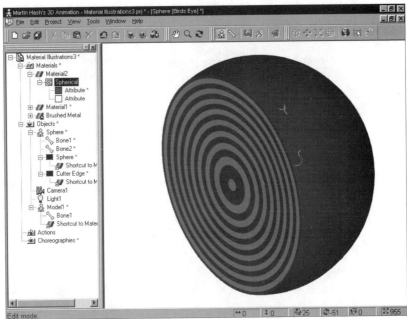

FIGURE
6.16
Part of the sphere cut away, showing the effect the spherical material has on a model.

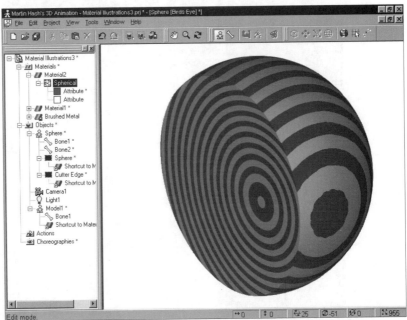

FIGURE
6.17
The effect that translating the spherical material has on the object to which it's applied.

MATERIAL TECHNIQUES

Obviously, not everything you're going to build will be a flat color. Sometimes you'll use decals, and sometimes more complex materials. One thing you'll want to keep in mind as you plan your materials is to observe real-life objects. Remember that in real life, you would select the material, then create the object from the material. It's exactly the opposite on the computer, where you first create the model, then apply the material. It will become easier for you to create realistic materials once you have some practice and understanding of the combiner types in the materials editor and how they affect each other.

In the real world, two particular classes of materials deserve special mention because of their unique properties: glass and metal. These two types of materials are more difficult to create than most others because they don't have a bunch of set attributes you can use to create them (for example, what color is chrome?).

With that in mind, the next two exercises will describe the creation of materials that will point you down the right path in creating objects that look like glass and metal.

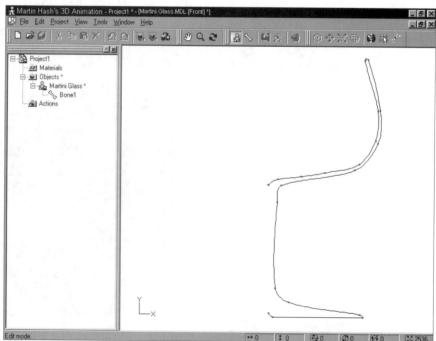

FIGURE 6.18 *A spline used to create a margarita glass. Simulated glass objects must have thickness to render correctly.*

CREATING GLASS MATERIALS

A few things are very important to keep in mind if you're planning to create a glass material for an object. One of the most important is the construction of the object itself.

Objects that are to look like glass need to have thickness to the walls (see Figure 6.18). Otherwise, they will tend to appear flat or will incorrectly refract the surrounding environment.

EXERCISE

CREATING A MARTINI GLASS

1. Open the *Martini Glass.MDL* model from the CD-ROM accompanying the book.

2. Click the **Martini Glass** item in the **Objects** section of the **Project Workspace**, then click the **Attributes** tab on the **Properties Panel**.

In preparing to apply attributes to this model, think for a moment of what your answer would be if someone placed a drinking glass in front of you and asked you what color it was.

Clear?

If that's your answer, you're right, but you won't be able to locate the color "clear" on any palette on the computer. Instead, clear is no color, which is represented by 0, 0, 0, RGB.

Consider some of the other qualities of glass. It's hard and smooth, very specular, and bends light (most glass bends light slightly, and liquids refract more heavily since they're thicker). With that in mind, attributes can be estimated and entered into the appropriate fields on the **Properties Panel**.

3. Continuing from step 2, click the **Color** chip on the **Properties Panel** and select the **Black** color swatch.

4. Set the **Specular** color to white (*255,255,255*), and the **Specular Size** to *100*.

5. Leave the **Reflectivity** at *0* and set the **Ambiance** to *20*.

6. For the **Transparency**, enter *97%*, and *1.1* for **Refraction**.

7. For the type of transparency, check the **Additive** radio button. This will cause the renderer to take the color of the object and add

50% of the color that lies behind the object, giving a realistic look to the glass. This effect can be seen most prominently on colored glass.

The Attributes for the glass are now set. Rendering in the **Modeler** window will not produce much, because glass objects rely on the surrounding environment to make them show up well. Once in a scene, however, the proper lighting and surroundings can provide excellent results, like those shown in Figure 6.19.

A little bit of color and just a little reflection on the glass objects would go a long way toward adding realism. As you've seen, reflective values will cause the renderer to slow down. When you combine them with transparency and refraction, you should expect a fair increase in render times.

Both glass and metallic objects share very similar attribute settings. However, metallic objects don't require the special "double wall" construction discussed in the previous exercise. The following exercise describes how to create a simulated metallic material.

CREATING METALLIC MATERIALS

As you're planning objects that will have simulated chrome materials applied to them, the most important thing to keep in mind is the environment surrounding the object. Just as glass won't appear without an environment to refract, chrome needs an environment to reflect, or else it will just appear as a flat color in a scene.

The following exercise offers a few tips to get you started in creating simulated chrome materials.

EXERCISE

CREATING A METAL MATERIAL

1. Open the *Metal Materials.PRJ* file from the CD-ROM accompanying the book. Right-click the **Choreography1** item in the **Choreographies** section of the **Project Workspace** and select **Edit** from the available menu.

2. Press the **1** key on the numeric keypad to change to a camera view. You should see a scene that contains a simple cylinder sitting on a ground plane. When rendered, the scene should look similar to Figure 6.20.

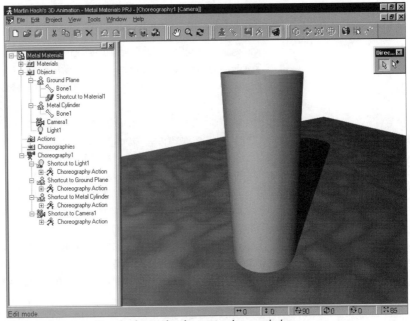

FIGURE *A nonmetallic cylinder rendered on a simple ground plane.*
6.20

Before you apply any attributes to the model, it's time to sit back and think again for a moment. *What color is chrome?* It takes a while to come up with an answer, which usually ends up being "chrome" when you get tired of thinking. Like "clear," chrome is not part of the palette that is available to you, so you'll have to come up with something else.

The logical answer to the question is that chrome is the color of the objects reflecting in it. There is never a part of a chrome object in the real world that doesn't reflect something. Therefore, as with the glass material, all color is once again removed, represented by 0, 0, 0 RGB.

Now for some of the additional qualities of chrome objects. Like glass, chrome is very reflective, and very shiny. This should be a good start in setting the chrome materials attributes.

3. Continuing from step 2, click the **Metal Cylinder** item in the **Objects** section of the **Project Workspace**. Click the **Attributes** tab on the **Properties Panel**.

4. Click on the **Color** chip on the **Properties Panel** and select the black color swatch.

5. Set the **Specular Color** to white (*255,255,255*) and the **Specular Size** to *100*.

6. Set the **Reflectivity** to *90* and the **Ambiance** to *20*.

7. Make sure that the **Reflections** box on the renderer is on by selecting **Tools, Options**, then click the **Render** tab. The **Reflections** checkbox is on the left side of the panel under the **Reflections** section.

NOTE

Complex scenes can take an extremely long time to render when heavy reflection values are used and many objects are present. In most cases, checking the **Reflections** box and leaving it at the default *5* will be adequate for a realistic render. Users with slower computers, or those who don't want to wait, can drop the value down. The value that you enter causes the ray that is cast to reflect only the number of times specified.

8. Render the image and examine your results. You should see similar output to that shown in Figure 6.21. Notice that closer to the bottom of the cylinder, the reflection of the ground plane bends.

Remember that chrome objects depend on a full environment to look right. There are ways around this that will be discussed in later chapters,

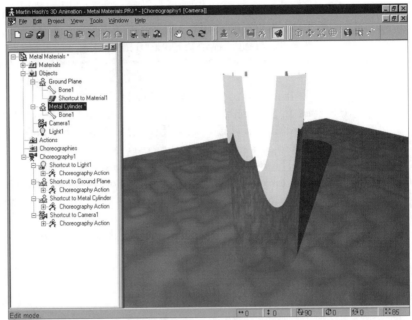

FIGURE **6.21**   *A rendering of the cylinder with the metallic material applied to it.*

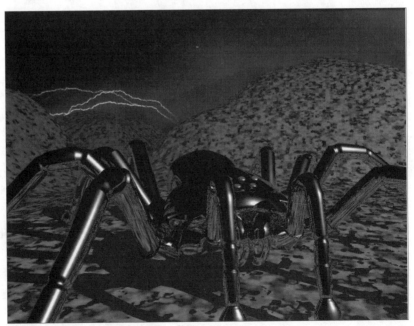

FIGURE **6.22**   *"Jessica" Copyright ©1994 Jeff Paries.*

but it's still an important piece of information. Proper lighting and an ample environment will pay off with excellent chrome effects, similar to the ones shown in Figure 6.22.

It can be tricky to plan ahead for both glass and metallic objects, because you might begin some models with the intention of deciding on textures at a later time. As you've seen, if you don't plan ahead for a glass object, you might need to do a serious modeling overhaul.

The two special types of materials covered here will get you rolling in the right direction. Keep in mind that observation of the real world and experimentation are the keys to creating successful materials. As your experience grows, don't rely on materials to do the whole job of texturing for you. Often, you'll want to consider adding more detail with image maps.

The next section describes how to create complex materials by using combiners as attribute types, as well as how to add several materials to a single object.

COMPLEX MATERIALS

It's easy to forget that you can change attributes within a combiner type material to another combiner type, allowing you to create a very complex material. This is how the most effective-looking materials are created.

One of the best examples of a complex material type is wood, since it generally has a multicolored grain in addition to the wood color itself. The following exercise will discuss the creation of a simulated bark material.

EXERCISE

CREATING A COMPLEX MATERIAL

1. Click the **New** button and select **Material** from the available menu. Click the plus (**+**) to the left of the **Material1** item to expand the material tree.

2. Right-click the attribute node and select **Change Type To, Noise** from the available menu. Click the plus (**+**) to the left of the **Noise** item to expand the material tree further.

3. Right-click the first attribute that appears beneath the **Noise** node, and select **Change Type To, Noise** from the available menu. Repeat this step with the second attribute.

4. Expand the material tree by clicking the plus (**+**) to the left of each of the **Noise** nodes. You should now have a material tree that consists of a **Noise**-type material created with two **Noise**-type nodes, each with two attributes.

5. Select the first **Attribute** node beneath the first **Noise** node by clicking on it, then select the **Attributes** tab of the **Properties Panel**.

6. Click the color chip, then click the **Other** button on the color palette. Enter *95, 23, 23* into the **Red**, **Green**, and **Blue** fields, respectively. Set the **Specular Color** to white, and the **Specular Size** and **Intensity** to *100*. All of the other items can be left blank, except for **Ambiance**, which should be set to *5*.

7. Select the second **Attribute** node beneath the first **Noise** node by clicking on it, then select the **Attributes** tab of the **Properties Panel**.

8. Click the color chip, then click the **Other** button on the color palette. Enter *129, 89, 66* into the **Red**, **Green**, and **Blue** fields, respectively. As with the previous Attribute, the **Specular Color** should be set to white, and the **Specular Size** and **Intensity** to *100*. Enter *5* into the **Ambiance** field.

By looking at the sphere in the material preview window as you're creating your material, you can get a rough idea of how the changes you're making are affecting the look of the material. If necessary, you can Turn, Move, and Zoom the sphere. You can also click in the preview window to move the light source around.

9. Select the first **Attribute** node beneath the second **Noise** node by clicking on it, then select the **Attributes** tab of the **Properties Panel**.

10. Click the color chip, then click the **Other** button on the color palette. Enter *165, 40, 40* into the **Red**, **Green**, and **Blue** fields, respectively. The **Specular Color** should be set to white, the **Specular Size** set to *20,* and **Intensity** to *100*. Enter *5* into the **Ambiance** field.

11. Select the second **Attribute** node beneath the second **Noise** node by clicking on it, then select the **Attributes** tab of the **Properties Panel**.

12. Click the color chip, then click the **Other** button on the color palette. Enter *219, 146, 111* into the **Red**, **Green**, and **Blue** fields,

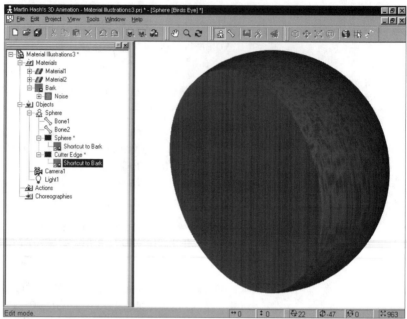

FIGURE   *A rendered cutaway view of the Bark material created in the previous exercise.*
6.23

respectively. Once again, you should set the **Specular Color** to white, the **Specular Size** to *20,* and **Intensity** to *100.* Enter *5* into the **Ambiance** field.

13. The creation of the material isn't finished just because you've set all of the attributes for the noise combiners. Each **Noise** item in the material tree has its own set of properties that can be adjusted. In this particular material, the properties for the **Noise** nodes are all identical. Set the Noise Properties by selecting a **Noise** node. Then, on the **Properties Panel**, leave the **X**, **Y**, and **Z Translate** at *0* and enter *60, 6000, 60* for the **X**, **Y**, and **Z scales**, respectively.

Figure 6.23 shows a rendered cutaway view of the final Bark material. To save this material, right-click the **Material1** item in the **Project Workspace** and select **Save As** from the available menu.

The method just described is very effective for creating interesting, complex materials. However, as you can probably figure out, the trees for materials created in this manner can become very complex very quickly, and as such, can be difficult to keep track of when you're making modifications. Another way to use materials is to apply several materials to an object, keeping the complexity of the material down, and making it easier to make any necessary changes. You can create a material almost identical to the one just discussed by applying two separate Noise materials to the same object.

The following exercise will discuss the creation of two separate Noise materials combined on a model to create a simulated bark material.

EXERCISE

COMBINING MATERIALS

1. Click the **New** button and select **Material** from the available menu. Click the plus (**+**) to the left of the **Material1** item to expand the material tree.

2. Click the **New** button once again and select **Material** from the available menu. Click the plus (**+**) to the left of the **Material2** item to expand the material tree.

3. Right-click the attribute node beneath the **Material1** item and select **Change Type To, Noise** from the available menus. Click the plus (**+**) to the left of the Noise item to expand the material tree further. Repeat this step on the attribute node beneath the **Material2** item.

4. The first attribute beneath the **Noise** node in **Material1** should be set to *95, 23, 23*, **Red**, **Green**, and **Blue**, respectively. The **Specularity Color** should be set to white, and both the **Intensity** and **Size** to *100*. Enter *5* into the **Ambiance** field.

5. The second attribute beneath the **Noise** node in **Material1** should be set to *129, 89, 66*, **Red**, **Green**, and **Blue**, respectively. The **Specularity Color** should be set to white, and both the **Intensity** and **Size** to *100*. Enter *5* into the **Ambiance** field.

6. Click the **Noise** node beneath the **Material1** item. Set the **X**, **Y**, and **Z Scale** to *60, 6000,* and *60*, respectively.

7. Set the first attribute beneath the **Noise** node in **Material2** to *165, 40, 40*, **Red**, **Green**, and **Blue**, respectively. The **Specularity Color** should be set to white, **Size** to *20*, and **Intensity** to *100*. Enter *5* into the **Ambiance** field.

8. Set the second attribute beneath the **Noise** node in **Material2** to *219, 146, 111*, **Red**, **Green**, and **Blue**, respectively. Once again, set the **Specularity Color** to white, **Size** to *20*, and **Intensity** to *100*. Enter *5* into the **Ambiance** field.

9. Click the **Noise** node beneath the **Material2** item. Set the **X**, **Y**, and **Z Scales** to *60, 6000,* and *60,* respectively.

10. You can now apply the materials to a model. Do this by dragging the material from the **Materials** section of the **Project Workspace** and dropping it onto a model name in the **Objects** section of the **Project Workspace**. The materials will be added to the model in the order that they're applied.

NOTE

When you're applying several materials to a single model, it is not necessary to use the same type of combiner on each material. For example, you can combine simple attributes with Spherical, Checker, Gradient, or Noise combiners, or other simple attributes. Keep this in mind as you develop materials.

Materials can be created and saved off fairly easily, and as you can imagine, the number of materials you have can grow very quickly.

Now that you've learned how to create and work with basic materials, you need a way to organize them. The next section will explain how to catalog them with Libraries for future use.

CREATING MATERIAL LIBRARIES

Material libraries are a way for you to group or catalog sets of materials to make them more accessible. Consider how easily materials could be applied to models if there were a "Metal" bin from which a simulated metal material could be grabbed, and a "Weathering" bin from which a simulated rust could be taken and applied to the metal. This is exactly the idea behind creating material libraries. When you create new materials, it's easy to add them to a library. Likewise, when a library is open, it's easy to introduce the materials into your project.

The following exercise describes how to create your own material libraries, how to add materials to the library, and how to utilize a material from a library in a project.

EXERCISE

CREATING A MATERIAL LIBRARY

1. Depending on the layout of the interface that you prefer to work with, the **Libraries** window may not be open. If it isn't, right-click any toolbar and check the **Libraries** item. This will cause an empty **Libraries** window to open.

2. Right-click in the **Libraries** window and select **Add/Remove Libraries** from the available list.

3. Click the **New** button, type *Materials,* and press **Enter**. A dialog box will open asking if you'd like to create a new library with this name. Click **Yes**.

4. As easily as that, your new library has been created. Click the **Close** button to go back to the main library window. You'll see a tab across the bottom with the name "Materials" on it.

5. To add materials to the library, simply drag and drop them onto the **Libraries** window. The name of the material will appear beneath the material icon.

6. To insert a material into a project, right-click a material name in the **Libraries** window and select **Insert Into Project** from the available menu.

7. You can remove materials from a library altogether by right-clicking the material name in the **Libraries** window, then selecting **Remove From Library** from the available menu.

Libraries are a powerful tool to help you keep your materials organized. You can easily create custom material sets that match your needs for any given model. For example, mechanical objects might use a library called "Metals," which contains gold, silver, copper, brushed metal, and rust, while a Foliage library might contain different types of bark and several different colors of leaves.

Your collection of materials will likely grow very quickly. The use of libraries will help you keep them organized and accessible. Remember that having many materials can become confusing, so use as descriptive a name as possible for each one.

SUMMARY

You should now be familiar with materials and how they can affect models as a whole (Base Attribute), as well as on a patch level. You should also have a deeper understanding of the 3D nature of materials, and just what it is you're doing when you're creating a material. The exercise on unique material types such as glass and metal will help to get you on track with observing the world, and applying those observations when you create your own materials.

As your material collection grows, remember that libraries are an effective way to keep materials organized and easy to use. Libraries are quick to create and will help you to work more efficiently.

Although materials add detail and a unique look to a model, relying on them alone won't get you to the next level. When it comes to creating eye-popping graphics, texture maps are truly the king of the hill. The next chapter describes how to create and use image maps effectively.

Decals

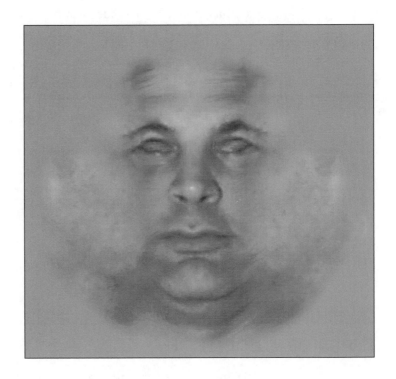

This chapter discusses the types, use, and application of image maps as decals. Effective use of decals is the real trick to making any 3D model really pop off the screen. *Decals* are a type of image map that you apply directly to the surface of a model, in such a way that whenever the surface of a model bends, twists, or distorts throughout the course of an animation, the map will do likewise. For example, imagine a character with stubble on his face. Once you've mapped the stubble on, any time the model opens his mouth to speak, yawn, or holler, the stubble will stretch and deform accordingly. This makes for a very realistic effect — and it makes decals indispensable for character animation.

Decals actually got their name from the small sheets of decals that come in plastic modeling kits. The idea behind them is to use an image map in 3D just as you'd use those decals you apply to plastic models (except it isn't necessary to wet them down first). Decals provide incredible control over placement and size, they're easy to edit without having to reapply them time and time again, and you can animate them by using sequences of image maps.

This chapter covers the following techniques:

- Types of Decals
- Decaling Techniques
- Anti-aliased versus Non-antialiased Image Maps
- Using Alpha Channels in Decals
- Tips for Creating Decals
- Texture Map Alternatives

TYPES OF DECALS

Ten different types of decal maps are supported in v5 of Animation Master. Rule number one for using them effectively is to stick to the *TARGA (.TGA)* image format. TARGA is the most flexible and efficient as far as usability and crossing platforms is concerned, because both the PowerMac and PC support the TARGA format well. TARGAs are also read and written by all of the major paint programs available on the market today, as well as many shareware ones.

To open an image as a decal, right-click the model name in the **Project Workspace**, then select **Import, Decal**. The **Properties Panel** will change to show the **Decal Properties** and **Options**, including the **Type** drop-down list that allows you to select the way the map is to be applied.

COLOR MAPS

The first type of image map is called Color. *Color maps* are the most-used type of map and can contain any number of colors on up to a 32-bit image (16.7 million colors plus an alpha channel).

Generally, for higher resolution renderings, you should use 24-bit color maps (16.7 million colors). Figure 7.1 shows an example color map, and Figure 7.2 shows the map applied to a model of a Dalmatian.

Remember that the renderer will take care of the *anti-aliasing* (jagged edge removal) for you, so it isn't necessary, and in fact is sometimes detrimental, to create anti-aliased image maps. This is discussed further later in this chapter.

FIGURE *An example of a Color-type map. This image will be used to decal a Dalmatian.*
7.1

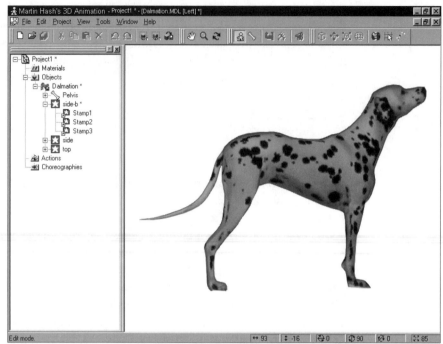

FIGURE   *The Dalmatian color map applied to a model of a dog.*

7.2

TRANSPARENCY MAPS

The second map type is a *transparency map*. Transparency maps define transparent areas on the surface of a model using shades of gray. Black areas on the image map will be cause the underlying model's surface to become completely transparent, and white areas will cause the underlying surface to become opaque. Variations of gray throughout the image create varying levels of transparency.

Generally, transparency maps should be grayscale or black-and-white images to work correctly. This map type is very effective for creating odd-shaped holes in objects, or creating such things as windows in buildings without unnecessarily increasing the resolution of the model.

FIGURE
7.3
A black to white gradient image that will be used as a transparency map.

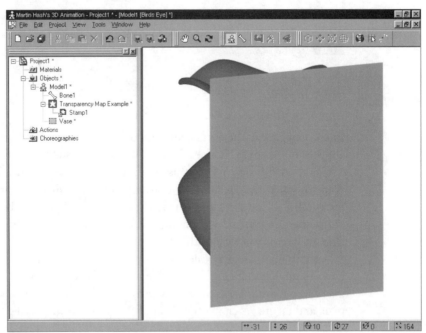

FIGURE
7.4
A scene with a flat plane placed in front of a vase.

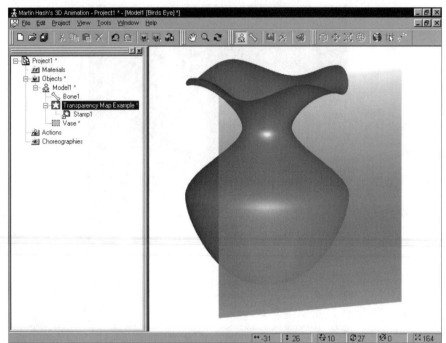

FIGURE *The same scene shown in Figure 7.4, with the transparency map shown in Figure 7.3*
7.5 *applied to the plane model.*

BUMP MAPS

Bump maps cause the surface of a model to appear to have bumps. When you apply a bump map, it doesn't actually alter the surface of the model. Bump maps are used often. You can usually create them easily from the original color map to which they relate. For example, a brick wall would have a color map for the bricks, and a bump map to make the wall appear bumpy. You could create the bump map by changing the color map to grayscale, then making any necessary modifications to the map.

Bump maps are grayscale images in which the different gray values determine how "bumpy" a surface will look. White areas will appear raised, and gradations of gray cause varying levels of bumps to appear. Figure 7.6 shows an example bump map, and Figure 7.7 shows the effect of applying this map to a plane.

NOTE

Bump maps *require* gradation between shades of gray to work correctly. A common mistake that newer users make is to expect that a black line on a white map would cause a deep depression in the object to which it was applied. However, since there is no gradation between the black and white,

FIGURE
7.6
An example of a bump map that can be used for a brick wall.

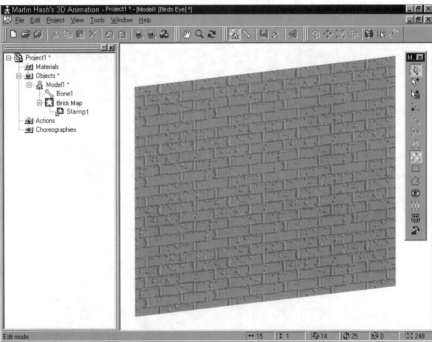

FIGURE
7.7
The bump map shown in Figure 7.6 applied to a flat plane. Even though the model appears to be bumpy, if it were rendered from a side view, no bumps would be visible.

the map will do nothing. An easy way to make an effective bump map is to create the design you need, then apply a blur filter to it in whatever paint program you're using. A slight Gaussian blur from Photoshop is usually enough to create an effective bump map.

The three previously mentioned decal types are the most commonly used, but they're far from the limit of the decaling capabilities in Animation:Master. It would be wise to be familiar with the three types of maps mentioned to this point, as almost every model could easily use at least one of the three.

SPECULARITY MAPS

The next type of map is a *specularity map*. Specularity maps define areas on the surface of an object that are specular or shiny. These maps are grayscale images in which the different gray values determine how shiny a surface will look. White areas of an image map will make the underlying model's surface 100% specular, and gradations of gray will give the model's surface varying levels of specularity. Figure 7.8 shows an example specularity map, and Figure 7.9 shows the effect of applying this map to a simple model to which no Specularity attribute was applied.

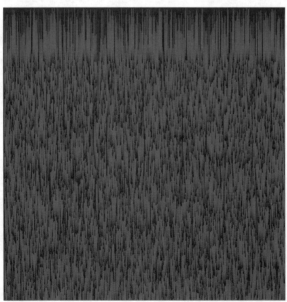

FIGURE *An example of a specularity map.*
7.8

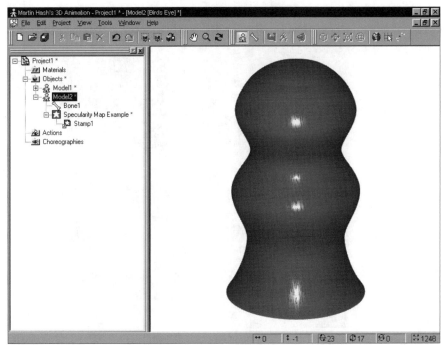

FIGURE
7.9
A simple model with the specularity map applied. Notice how the map causes "broken" or uneven specular highlights along the surface of the model, even though the model has no Specularity attributes set. Specularity maps are good for aging or beating up older objects.

A good way to picture what a specularity map does is to imagine an old, worn-out wooden table. The surface of the table would be uneven or scuffed up, and the scuffed areas reflect less light than the polished or less worn areas. A specularity map could be used to simulate these scuffed areas.

DIFFUSE MAPS

The next type of map is called a *diffuse map*. Diffuse maps work well in almost any situation for one good reason: They make objects look dirty or worn by breaking up the surface color of the underlying object. Since virtually every real-life object has some variation in surface color, diffuse maps are an effective way to simulate these variations.

Diffuse maps are grayscale images in which the different gray values determine how much the color of a model's surface will change. White areas of the map cause no change in the underlying surface color; shades of gray cause the underlying surface to darken. Figure 7.10 shows an example diffuse map, and Figure 7.11 shows the effect of applying this map on a simple vase model.

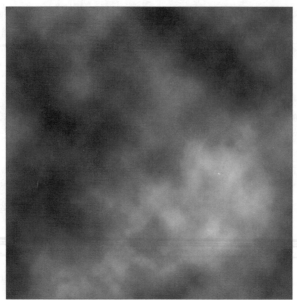

FIGURE   *An example of a grayscale diffuse map.*
7.10

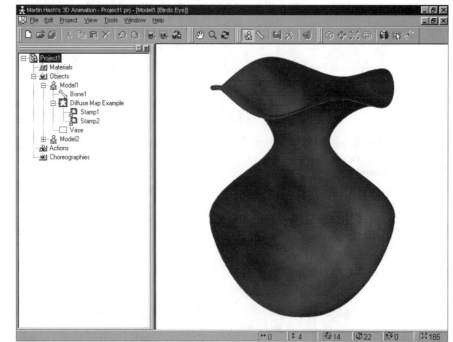

FIGURE   *The map shown in Figure 7.10 applied to a simple vase model. Notice how the map makes*
7.11   *the model appear worn-out and dirty.*

NOTE When you create a detailed diffuse map, try to use an **Airbrush** tool if your paint program has one. This will allow a softer, more realistic look to the map than using a tool such as a **Pencil** or **Paintbrush**. For overall coverage, rendering a Difference Cloud in a program such as Photoshop will provide effective maps.

REFLECTIVITY MAPS

The sixth type of map is called a *reflectivity map*. Reflectivity maps are grayscale images in which white causes the surface of the model to become 100% mirror, and black causes no reflectivity at all.

Reflectivity maps are often used in conjunction with specularity maps to create realistic surfaces (scuffed areas of objects do not reflect well). A clear example of where these two maps could be used in conjunction would be the metal plate screwed to the wall of many gas-station restrooms that is supposed to serve as a mirror. It has some weak reflective qualities, as well as some shiny spots.

NOTE The value field for reflectivity maps determines how much effect the grayscale image has on the model's surface. A higher number would make the surface appear more reflective. Reasonable values for reflectivity maps are from 1 to 1000%.

FIGURE *An example reflectivity map.*
7.12

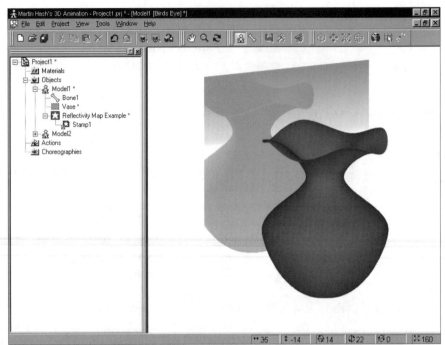

FIGURE *A plane behind a vase model. The map shown in Figure 7.12 is applied to the plane.*
7.13 *Notice that the detail of the reflection is greater toward the bottom of the plane, where the amount of reflectivity acquired from the image map creates a good mirror.*

AMBIANCE MAPS

The next type of map is called an *ambiance map.* Ambiance maps are so named because they alter the *ambiance,* or brightness, value of the object to which they're applied. This map type is also grayscale, where lighter colors in the image map denote higher ambiance values, and darker colors have lesser effect.

The most common and recognizable example of ambiance maps would be the lit windows of a skyscraper at night. Photos and renderings of such buildings show many rows of both lighted and unlit windows.

NOTE

Keep in mind that ambiance maps, like the Ambiance attribute, can make an object appear to glow. However, the object itself will not actually cast any light.

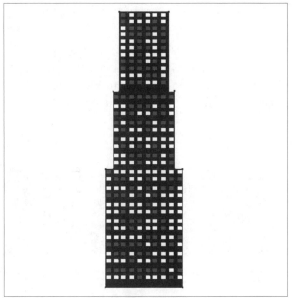

FIGURE
7.14
An example of an ambiance map that could be used on the building modeled in Chapter 5.

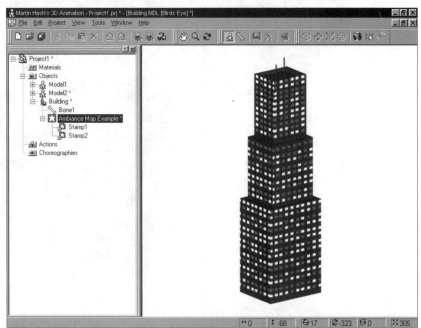

FIGURE
7.15
The ambiance map in Figure 7.14 applied to the building that was modeled in Chapter 5. Different levels of gray were used in the map to simulate dark windows.

COOKIE-CUT MAPS

The eighth type of map is called a *cookie-cut map*. Cookie-cut maps are most effective when a 32-bit TARGA file is used. The software will automatically use the alpha channel in the decal to cut away the surface of the model to which the decal is applied. This lets you make "cutout"-type background

FIGURE   *An example of a logo cookie-cut map.*
7.16

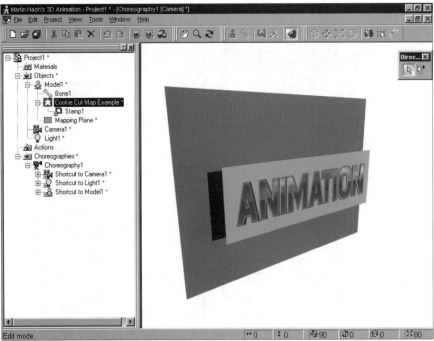

FIGURE   *The logo image from Figure 7.16 applied to a flat plane that lies in front of another plane.*
7.17   *This image shows a rendering of the map as a color map.*

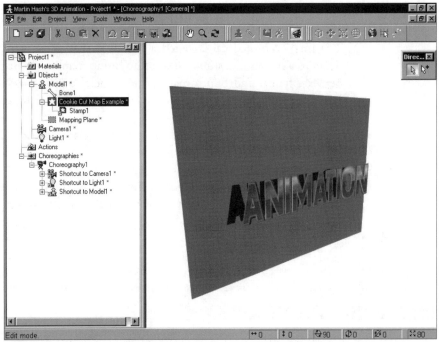

FIGURE   *Once the map was specified as a cookie cutter, the alpha channel in the decal image was*
7.18   *cut away, leaving only the logo behind.*

objects, realistic leaves, or logo-type decals with clean edges, and without adding any unnecessary resolution to your scene.

DISPLACEMENT MAPS

Displacement maps are the ninth type of image-mapping method available to you. *Displacement maps* work exactly like bump maps, except that they actually cause the surface of the model to deform, or displace, according to the shades of gray in the image map.

Because of the spline-based nature of Animation:Master, displacement maps work in a unique fashion. When you apply the map, you won't see any changes on the model until render time. This is quite different from the way displacements work in polygonal-based modelers. As a displacement is applied to a polygonal model, the surface of the model will deform according to the values contained within the image map. Displacement maps are an effective technique for modeling in polygonal programs, since the data is less tactile and more difficult to manipulate than it is in a spline-based program.

FRACTAL MAPS

The final type of decal is called a *fractal map*. Fractal maps are used to add detail to a model in a similar fashion to bump mapping. The major distinction between fractal and bump maps is that fractal maps shade to show different levels of depth on an object — unlike bump maps, which raytrace the appearance of surface ambiguities.

Both fractal and displacement maps are rarely used. Essentially, they appear in the software to appease the feature junkies out there who don't want to miss out on the buzzword of the day.

Now that you have an idea of how each of the map types will affect the surface of a model, the next section will describe techniques used to apply decals effectively to objects.

DECALING TECHNIQUES

Understanding how each type of decal affects the model to which it's applied is only half the battle when it comes to effective image mapping. There are subtle nuances you have to consider, such as the shape of the surface to which the map is to be applied, the value of maps such as bump maps, and whether or not an alpha channel would help make your job easier in the long run.

When applying decals, you should keep in mind that a single patch is infinitely thin. This means that if you were to take a flat plane and apply a decal to it, the map would look satisfactory from the front view and appear backwards on the back side of the model, as shown in Figure 7.19. Although this would not create a problem for something like a window decal or painting, it could become confusing if you're attempting to make a thin model like a credit card that would need to have different image maps on both sides. Models such as the credit card need to be created with "thickness" so the decals don't show through.

As you experiment with decals, one problem you're likely to encounter is the decaling of a curved surface or object. This is an important issue, because most models have some curvature to them and will benefit from at least one image map. The way the software handles image maps as decals tends to stretch or smear them if the image is applied over a surface that bends too much. You'll need to take some care to avoid this. The next exercise describes one way to decal a curved surface.

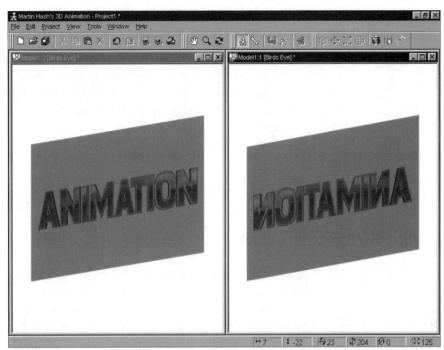

FIGURE **7.19** *An example render of both the front and back of a flat plane with an image map applied as a color decal. Notice that the image appears backwards when the plane is viewed from the back.*

EXERCISE

DECALING CURVED SURFACES

1. Open the *Curved Surface.PRJ* file from the accompanying CD-ROM. The project will open to a front view of a modeling window that contains a simple cylinder.

2. Change to a top view by pressing the **5** key on the numeric keypad. Use the **Group** tool to select the front half of the cylinder model. Click the **Hide** button to hide the back half of the model.

3. Press the **2** key on the numeric keypad to switch to a front view.

4. Right-click the **Cylinder** item in the **Objects** section of the **Project Workspace** and select **Import, Decal**. Locate the *Cylinder Map.TGA* file on the accompanying CD-ROM.

NOTE

The image map loaded in step 4 was created by taking a screen shot of the completed cylinder model, opening it in Photoshop, selecting an area larger than the wireframe, then filling the area with a texture provided by Adobe.

5. On the **General** tab of the **Properties Panel**, use the **Type** drop-down list to select **Bump** from the available items. Enter *500* into the **Value** field.

6. Select the bright green swatch from the default palette for the Transparent color. This is a color that doesn't appear in the image map. That will ensure that no pixels are dropped from the grayscale image that is being used.

7. Right-click the **Cylinder Map** item and select **Position** from the available menu. Use the mouse to position the map as shown in Figure 7.20. When the map is in place, right-click within the image map manipulator and select **Apply** from the available menu. Right-click within the map manipulator once again and select **Stop Positioning** from the available menu.

Now that you've decaled the front of the cylinder model, the trick becomes applying the image to the back half without creating a visible seam where the two stamps align along the sides of the model. One way to do this is to write down the values from the **Position** tab on the **Properties Panel**, then line up the map identically for the back half.

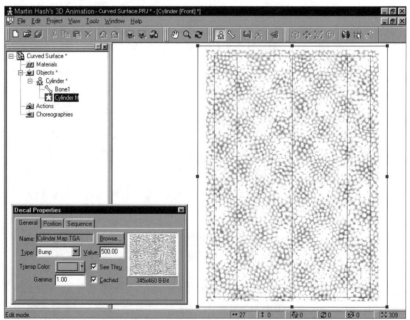

FIGURE *The proper positioning of the bump map before application.*

7.20

However, there's no need to be concerned with keeping track of all those notes. The next few steps describe a method that will make it considerably easier to accomplish the task at hand.

7. Click the **Hide** button to unhide the model.

8. Press the **5** key on the numeric keypad to change to a top view. Use the **Group** tool to select the back half of the model, then click the **Hide** button to hide the front half.

9. Press the **2** key on the numeric keypad to return to a front view. Right-click the **Cylinder Map** item in the **Project Workspace** and select **Position** from the available menu. This will activate the decal in the last position it was in, which also happens to line up perfectly with the first application. This technique actually takes advantage of the infinitely thin nature of a single patch, applying the map from the inside of the cylinder.

10. Right-click within the **Maps** manipulator and select **Apply** from the available menu. Then right-click within the map manipulator once again and select **Stop Positioning**. Click the **Hide** button to unhide the model.

You can rotate the model and render it to see the effect of decaling the model in two halves. Although there is still some smearing or stretching of the image map around the sides of the model, no seam is visible where the two decals meet.

The Bump value of 500 is also a little extreme and will accent the smearing of the map. This smearing effect could actually be of benefit when you're creating models such as dinosaurs or other reptiles. It will result in a very cool look over the nose and center of the head of such a model.

Most people, however, would not see this smearing effect as much of a benefit. A tool in place in the software allows you to decal a model without the undesirable smearing effects. The following exercise will describe how to use this tool.

EXERCISE

DECALING USING FLATTEN

The **Flatten** command allows you actually to squash a model flat before you apply a decal to it. This becomes very useful when the model's surface is varied.

1. Once again, open the *Curved Surface.PRJ* file from the accompanying CD-ROM.

2. Right-click the **Actions** folder in the **Project Workspace** and select **New Action** from the available menu.

3. A **Skeletal Mode Action** window will open that contains the **Cylinder** model. Click the **Muscle Action Mode** button, then press **5** on the numeric keypad to change to a top view.

4. Use the **Group** tool to select just the front half of the model. Click the **Hide** button.

5. Click any of the remaining control points and press the **/** key to Group Connected. Click the **Rotate Manipulator** button to change to a **Rotate Manipulator**.

6. The **Flatten** command works by creating an invisible cylinder around the Blue (Z) axis of the pivot, then splitting the model at the Green (Y) axis. The real trick to using it well is to understand how it will flatten your model. Press the **2** key on the numeric keypad to change back to a front view. Use the **Turn** tool to turn the model to a bird's-eye view.

7. Use the mouse to grab the Blue handle at the end of the Green axis on the pivot. Drag it backwards until it rotates 90 degrees. Watch the **Properties Panel** if necessary until you reach the correct value.

8. Switch to a side view by pressing the **6** key on the numeric keypad. Use the mouse to drag the pivot backwards until it lines up with the open end of the cylinder, as shown in Figure 7.21.

9. Switch back to a front view by pressing the **5** key on the numeric keypad, then right-click inside the **Rotate Manipulator** and select **Flatten** from the available menu.

10. Right-click the **Cylinder** item in the **Objects** section of the **Project Workspace** and select **Import, Decal** from the available menu. Locate the *Flattened Cylinder Map.tga* file on the accompanying CD-ROM. When the map opens, change the type on the **Properties Panel** to *Bump*, enter *500* into the **Value** field, and change the Transparent color to green.

11. Right-click the decal name in the **Project Workspace** and select **Position** from the available menu. Position the map over the

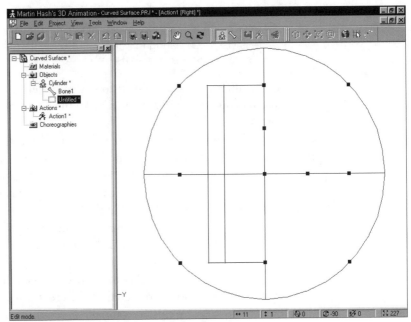

FIGURE *The positioning of the pivot before flattening.*
7.21

flattened model, then right-click within the **Maps Manipulator** and select **Apply** from the available menu. Right-click the decal name in the **Project Workspace** and choose **Stop Positioning** from the available menu.

12. From the **Action** menu, select **Clear** to return the cylinder to an unflattened state. Click the **Hide** button to unhide the back half of the model. Change to a top view and use the **Group** tool to select the back half of the model. Click the **Hide** button to hide the front half of the model.

13. Repeat steps 5 through 9, rotating the pivot in the opposite direction (still toward the open end of the selected points), and translating the pivot toward the open end of the cylinder half.

14. Right-click the decal name in the **Objects** section of the **Project Workspace**. The image map should appear in the **Action** window already in the proper position. Right-click within the **Maps Manipulator** box and select **Apply** from the available menu. Right-click within the **Maps Manipulator** once again and select **Stop Positioning** from the available menu.

15. From the **Action** menu, select **Clear**. Click the **Hide** button to unhide the entire model. Rendering the model now results in a much less visible smearing effect, even though it's still there.

It's very difficult to get a model to flatten perfectly, but there are a couple of techniques you can practice to help make the model as flat as possible before you apply the decal.

One of the major benefits of flattening the object via muscle motion is that you can make changes to the model or spline curvature after flattening, if you feel that the model didn't flatten quite right, or as expected.

Another way to avoid any smearing of the decals is to apply more decals to the surface of the model. For example, in the previous exercise, the cylinder was decaled in two parts. Grouping and hiding the model so that it's decaled in four parts would result in less distortion of the map: The curve of the individual sections is not as pronounced, allowing the model to become more flat. Of course, this method will take a little practice, since it will require the pivot to be directed at different angles to properly flatten the model.

The next step to decaling models is to use multiple maps positioned over one another to create an effect such as a brick wall. The next exercise will walk you through how to do this.

EXERCISE

CREATING A BRICK WALL

Most times, more than one decal will be necessary to get the right look to a model. When several decals are needed, you'll have to position two or more decals atop one another so that they align perfectly. This is so that all of the different map types can be used in conjunction to create the final effect, which may be a scraped-up, dirty wooden table, or the wall of a building in an imaginary downtown.

1. Open the *Brick Wall.PRJ* file from the accompanying CD-ROM. The project will open to a front view of a modeling window that contains a flat plane.

2. Remember that at most times, a single decal will not be enough to make a model look as you want it to. Even this example, a simple brick wall, requires several maps. Right-click the **Wall** item in the **Objects** section of the **Project Workspace** and select **Import, Decal** from the available menus. Locate the *Wall Bump.TGA* file on the CD-ROM.

The decals for this model were made in advance for you, so they'll open to the correct position in the modeler window. The decals were made by first creating the model, then taking a screen shot and painting the maps to fit.

3. On the **General** tab of the **Properties Panel**, select **Bump** from the **Type** drop-down. Change the **Transparent Color** to **Bright Green** and enter *250* into the **Value** field.

4. Right-click the decal in the **Project Workspace** and select **Position** from the available menu. Size the decal to fit the wall. Once the map is in place, click the **Position** tab on the **Properties Panel** and write down the coordinates listed in the four boxes.

5. Right-click within the maps manipulator box and select **Apply** from the available menu. Then right-click within the manipulator box and select **Stop Positioning** from the available menu.

6. Right-click the model name in the **Project Workspace** and select **Import, Decal** from the available menu. Locate the *Wall Image.TGA* file on the CD-ROM.

7. Because you created the bump map from the image map, the coordinates you used to place the bump map will also work for the color map. Had you not created them at the same time, the coordinates from the bump map would not work to position the color map identically. Enter the numbers you wrote down from the bump map into the appropriate fields for the color map. Once you've entered the coordinates, right-click the **Wall Image** item in the **Project Workspace** and select **Position** from the available menu.

8. The color map should appear in the correct position for decaling. Right-click within the **Maps** manipulator and select **Apply** from the available menu, then right-click within the image map manipulator and select **Stop Positioning** from the available menu.

Rendering the model at this point would produce results similar to those shown in Figure 7.22. The image appears darker in the grayscale image for this book than it will when you render. If you find you need to lighten the model a bit, slight adjustments to the Ambiance value should do the trick.

Although the image in Figure 7.22 certainly does look like a brick wall, more details help to sell the model.

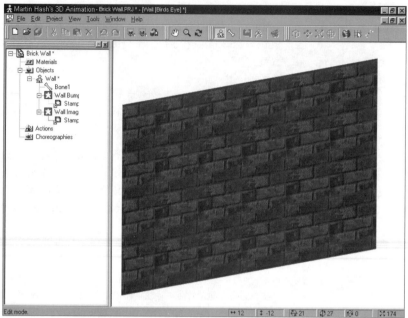

FIGURE **7.22** *The brick wall model with bump and color maps applied.*

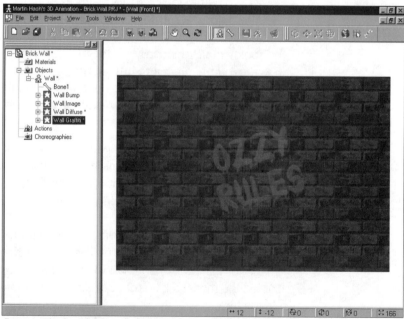

FIGURE **7.23** *The final brick wall model, with two color maps, a bump map, and a diffuse map applied.*

8. Import and apply the *Wall Diffuse.TGA* map to the model. Change the type to **Diffuse**, set the **Transparent Color** to **Green**, and enter *50* into the **Value** field.

9. Finally, import the *Wall Grafitti.TGA* image. Leave the type as *Color,* and enter *75* into the **Value** field.

NOTE

Applying a color map with a value of less than 100 will make the map appear translucent. This is very effective when layering image maps for skin tones, spray paint, or anything else that calls for a variegated surface.

Rendering now produces a better effect, as shown in Figure 7.23. Once again, the image appears dark in the book, so you should make sure to experiment and render this model out to see the effect.

Keep in mind as you use multiple maps on your objects that they appear on the model in the order that they were added to the list. In the previous example, the bump map would be on the bottom, then the brick color map. The diffuse map was added on top of that, and finally the graffiti color map. This is important, because had the graffiti map been applied before the brick color map, it would not show since it would be "covered" by the brick map. In the event that you accidentally put decals onto a model in the incorrect order, you can simply drag and drop the decals in the decal list to reorder them.

Now that you've experienced different techniques for applying maps to models, the next section discusses using anti-aliased versus non-antialiased image maps, and the effects of each on the final render.

ANTIALIASED VERSUS NON-ANTIALIASED IMAGE MAPS

In many images, curved lines or lines that appear at an angle have jagged edges, like those shown in Figure 7.24. This jagginess is referred to as *aliasing* and is obviously an undesirable effect.

A big stumbling block for many users learning Animation:Master is the actual creation of effective image maps. One of the main problems that many people encounter is a "halo" of pixels rendering around their image maps. This halo effect is caused by using tools set to anti-alias.

When creating image maps, you'll be tempted to use the anti-alias option for the tools in your paint program, since they tend to make a more aesthetically pleasing image within the paint program. However, doing so could cause undesirable effects, such as those shown in Figure 7.25.

FIGURE **7.24** *Jagged, or aliased, edges in an image.*

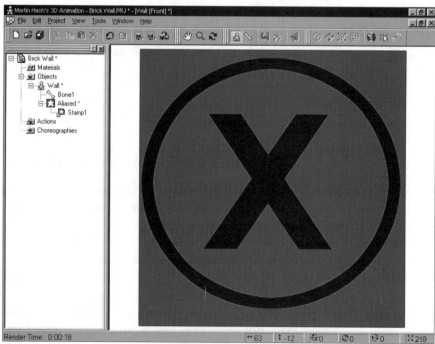

FIGURE **7.25** *An image similar to the one shown in Figure 7.24, created with anti-aliasing tools. Notice that the image renders with an unwanted white halo around its edges.*

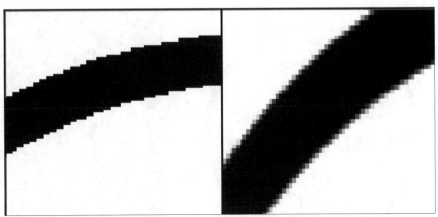

FIGURE   *A close-up of a non anti-aliased line (left) and an anti-aliased line (right).*

7.26

Look closely the anti-aliased image map and non-anti-aliased image map shown in Figure 7.26. Notice how the line on the left side of the image is simply a jagged black-and-white line. Now notice on the right-hand side of the image how the edge of the black line is blended to match the white areas without looking so jagged. When you select white as a transparent color before applying this image map, the left image will remove all of the white pixels, leaving just the black line. However, the right image will remove the white pixels, leaving the pixels close to the black line that are shades of gray from the blending, resulting in the halo.

Therefore, when you create image maps, your best bet is to choose not to anti-alias them as you create them in a paint program. Leave the anti-aliasing to the rendering engine in Animation:Master.

Now that you're familiar with the best way to create image maps, the next section will describe how to create an alpha channel in an image map, and what effect it will have on the map itself.

USING ALPHA CHANNELS IN DECALS

Many times, you'll need to apply a complex image to a model without including the background color upon which it was created. You can do this by utilizing the **Transparent Color** option on the **Properties Panel**, or by creating an alpha channel in the image map.

FIGURE   *The Alpha Channel Cable Company logo.*
7.27

FIGURE   *The alpha channel for the cable company logo*
7.28   *image.*

Alpha channels are an additional 8 bits of data saved into an image that contain transparency information about the image. When you look at an alpha channel, the white areas are where the image will be opaque, and the black areas are transparent. Shades of gray in between cause varying degrees of transparency. Complex images, or images that are going to be used as cookie-cut maps, are a great place to make use of image maps that contain alpha channels.

Figure 7.27 contains a logo image for the imaginary "Alpha Channel Cable Company" that needs to be mapped onto a flat plane as a cookie-cut map that contains an alpha channel for transparency.

To create an alpha channel for this image in Photoshop, select the entire image by pressing **Ctrl+A** on the keyboard. Next, press **Ctrl+C** to Copy the image to the clipboard. Select the **Channels** tab, then click the **New Channel** button. A channel titled "#4" will appear. This is the alpha channel. Press **Ctrl+V** to Paste from the clipboard into the alpha channel.

The image appears in the channel as black on white, which is inverted from what is needed. Select **Image**, **Adjust**, and **Invert** to correct this. The final alpha channel for this map is shown in Figure 7.28, and a rendering of the map is shown in Figure 7.29. Note that you need to save images with alpha channels as 32-bit files, or the alpha channel will be lost.

You will learn a lot as you experiment and take the time to practice different techniques in creating and applying decals. The next section describes a few tips to keep in mind to help you keep on the right track.

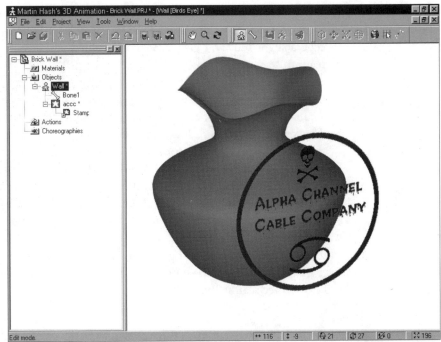

FIGURE   *The cable company logo applied to a flat plane and rendered in front of a simple vase model.*
7.29

TIPS FOR CREATING DECALS

The biggest advantage you can gain in creating decals is experimenting with different combinations of maps, brush types, etc. There is no substitute for first-hand experience when creating image maps, but the following few tips will save you a lot of time in the long run. Some of these are restated from exercises earlier in this chapter.

1. Use *.TGA* format images. Almost every paint program on the market supports the TGA image format, and Animation:Master likes them the best.
2. Do not anti-alias the outside edges of your image maps as you're creating them. Once you become more familiar with what effect this will have on the end product, start experimenting in your spare time. In many situations, anti-aliased maps will make no difference, however, in many more situations, anti-aliasing image maps will cause undesirable effects, such as a pixel "halo" around the image.

3. Blur grayscale images slightly if high detail is not required. Diffuse, transparency, specularity, and reflectivity maps will all benefit from the softer edge a slight blur will give. A Gaussian blur with a small radius is a great place to start.

4. Always set the Transparent Color of a grayscale image map to a color that doesn't exist in the map, such as bright green. This will ensure that no pixels are inadvertently dropped from maps intended to create bumps and the like.

5. Think both before and during the decaling process. Sometimes it can be a real puzzle to do a great mapping job on an object, and being lazy or sloppy won't do justice to the time you spend creating and animating your models.

6. Experiment. Experienced users will be able to guess fairly accurately about the effect any given map or combination of maps will have on the surface of an object, but the only way to tell for certain is to experiment.

The following exercise will give you a nudge in the right direction in your image map thought process. It describes how to create a usable image map of a head from three scanned images.

EXERCISE

CREATING A HEAD IMAGE MAP IN PHOTOSHOP

One pitfall you may run into once you've created your masterpiece human head model is having no idea how to go about making an image map for it. This exercise should help get you rolling in the right direction. Not everyone owns an expensive paint program such as Photoshop, but most paint programs have similar tools, and a little practice to become familiar with your paint program's toolset will pay off over the long haul.

1. Open both the *Martin Hash Front View.TGA* and *Martin Hash Left View.TGA* files from the accompanying CD-ROM into Photoshop.

2. Use the **Lasso** tool or **Path** tools to remove all but the face and ears in each of the three images. What you should end up with is a strange-looking face with no hair or body. The background at this point should be white.

3. Use the **Color Picker** tool to select somewhere on the skin in the *Martin Hash Front View.TGA* image. This will select a skin tone color that should be used to fill the background of the image.

4. Create a new layer on the image and paste the side view of the head into this layer. Adjust the side view image so that it lines up with the front view image. When the two images are aligned, **Copy**, **Paste**, and **Flip**

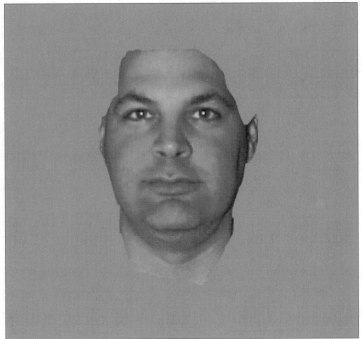

FIGURE **7.30** *The front view of Martin Hash's head on a skin-tone background. It's probably a good idea not to let the person whom you're modeling see themselves in a condition like this, or you may not have many friends left when you're finished.*

Horizontal the layer with the side view of the head on it. This will create the other side of the head. Once you've done this, hide the background and front view layers and merge the two side views onto the same layer.

5. Working on the layer that contains the side views, use the **Magic Wand** tool to select the transparent background of the layer, then select **Invert** from the **Selection Menu**.

6. Pick **Modify, Border** from the **Selection** menu and enter a value of *25*. Pick **OK**. From the **Blur Filter** selections, select **Gaussian Blur**. Set the value at *10* and click **OK**. This will blur the edges of the side views of the head so that they blend more smoothly with the front view.

7. Select the layer of the image that contains the front view and use the **Magic Wand** tool to select the background color. Select **Invert** from the **Selection** menu.

8. Pick **Modify, Border** from the **Selection** menu and enter a value of *25*. Press **Enter**. From the **Blur Filter** selections, select **Gaussian**

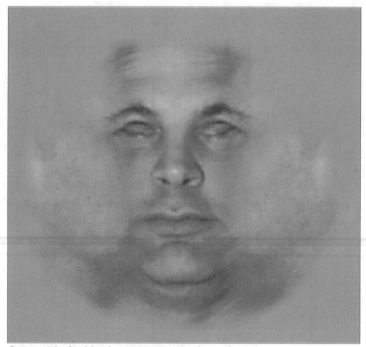

FIGURE   *The final head image map. Remind you of any movies?*
7.31

> **Blur**. Set the value at *10* and click **OK**. This will blur the edges of the front view so that it blends well with the side views.

9. Finally, Flatten the image and do any necessary touch-up work. The **Smear** tool is a good place to start, and some areas of the image may need painting to complete the map.

The image should end up looking something like Figure 7.31. The addition of a bump map for skin texture and some specularity maps for shiny areas of the skin would be beneficial to making a realistic model.

Remember the last few tips that were discussed, as well as the method for creating the image map for the head, and you should be well on your way to creating some killer image maps for your models. If you can afford one, a WACOM drawing tablet is a great addition to a paint program and will make an enormous difference in the precision and end quality of your image maps.

The only question that remains is what to do if you're not very artistic. Some people just aren't natural artists. It can be frustrating when you can see the way the model should look in your head, but you can't magically transfer that image to the computer. The next section discusses an alternative to painting every image map.

TEXTURE MAP ALTERNATIVES

Everybody has their weak areas and their strong areas where using 3D software is concerned. Not everyone is an expert 2D artist who can create jaw-dropping maps with little effort.

If you don't consider yourself a 2D artist and find yourself struggling to create image maps, you may want to consider a program that will allow you to create a map layer by layer, then will render out the final image for use as a decal. One such program is DarkTree Textures from Darkling Simulations.

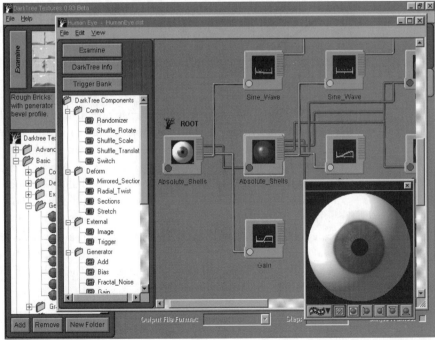

FIGURE   *The interface of the DarkTree textures program. A program such as this is a good idea if*
7.32   *you aren't the artistic type.*

For the non-artistic type, texture programs such as DarkTree make the creation of image maps quick and easy. Figure 7.32 shows a sneak peek of the DarkTree interface.

Textures are created in a similar manner to the materials editor in Animation:Master in that they're created in nodes and the end result is an accumulation of the attributes of each node. Once the texture has been created, color, bump, specularity, and diffuse maps can all be rendered easily, and details will match perfectly between the map types. Since the nature of the editor allows for a huge range of image possibilities, maps for just about any situation are possible.

Such programs are not inexpensive, but the benefits may well offset the cost if the need is there.

SUMMARY

By now, you should have a solid, comprehensive understanding of the different decal types available, how each one works, what the different map types look like with respect to color depths, some common techniques for applying decals, and some tips to keep in mind as you're working along in the software.

A good paint program is a must-have to go hand in hand with a powerful animation system such as Animation:Master. Consider trying out a shareware program such as Paint Shop Pro. Register it if the program fills your needs. A good paint program doesn't have to cost several hundred dollars to be useful. In addition, no matter how much a paint program costs, if you don't sit down and work with it, the program will never seem productive. An alternative method for creating image maps is a texture program such as DarkTree Textures from Darkling Simulations, which will allow flexibility in the creation of textures, then render out the appropriate map types for you.

You've come a long way. At this point, you've created your own models, created and applied materials, and created and applied decals. You still have a ways to go, and some of the most powerful features lie just around the corner. The next chapter starts digging into the meat of the software with Constraints.

8 Constraints

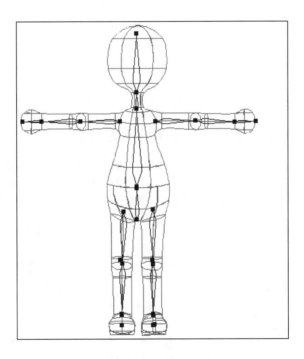

This chapter discusses the types and use of the different constraints available in Animation:Master. Constraints help you mimic natural motion by providing a mechanism for controlling a bone's position or orientation at a given time.

Constraints are time-based, meaning they can be used to aid effectively in the interaction between characters, or between characters and their environments.

This chapter covers the following topics:

- Understanding Constraints
- Types of Constraints
- Using Multiple Constraints
- Animating with Constraints
- Targets

UNDERSTANDING CONSTRAINTS

Most often when a person hears the word *constraint,* the word *restraint* comes to mind. This is not too far from what is actually happening when you apply constraints to your models: The *constraints* restrict or restrain the movement of the bone to which they are applied. Since constraints directly affect the movement of bones, you should understand them before attempting to apply bones to a model as shown in Chapter 9. Understanding what any given bone will do in combination with a constraint will allow you to work faster and more efficiently.

Constraints are very powerful. As such, they can be one of the most difficult concepts to understand in animation.

The first step in using them effectively is to have some idea of what the character or other objects in the scene will do. This allows you to place bones more effectively into the characters and objects in the scene. Scenes such as Thom picking up a coffee cup, in which a character interacts with other models, require proper bone placement in both Thom and the cup for the constraint to work correctly and look decent. Bone and constraints work very closely together for objects to interact within a scene.

The next step is to determine which constraint or combination of constraints is appropriate for each character and object in your scene. A little practice with the constraints and how they work in different situations will aid you in deciding the best or easiest way to achieve the effect you're working toward.

Understanding what each type of constraint is and how it works will help you achieve the results you need quickly. The next section describes each of the seven different types of constraints and walks you through a basic example of how to use each one.

TYPES OF CONSTRAINTS

Animation:Master uses seven different types of constraints to help you create realistic movement for your models. The seven types and how to use them are described in the following sections. Keep in mind that the uses mentioned here are basic and for clear illustration of a point; they are by no means the only use for any given constraint.

AIM AT CONSTRAINTS

The *Aim At* constraint type is one of the most used. When you apply an Aim At constraint to a bone, the bone will literally aim at the target you select. Obviously, Aim At is used quite often to make a camera or light follow an object. Aim At can also be used to make a character's eyes follow an object around a scene, or cause a character's hand to point at an object as it moves.

The following exercise illustrates the use of the Aim At constraint.

EXERCISE

USING THE AIM AT CONSTRAINT

1. Open the *Aim At Constraint.PRJ* file from the accompanying CD-ROM. A project will open that contains a top view of a choreography window containing a simple vase model, a camera, and a light, as shown in Figure 8.1.

2. To make the camera aim at the vase, click the camera in the choreography window to select it (an object manipulator box will appear on the camera). Right-click the camera and select **New Constraint**, then **Aim At** from the available menus.

3. The cursor will change into a picker tool. Use the picker to click on the Vase object. If, for some reason, the picker fails to select the correct object (or any object at all), use the drop-down **Object** list on the **Properties Panel** to select **Shortcut to Vase**.

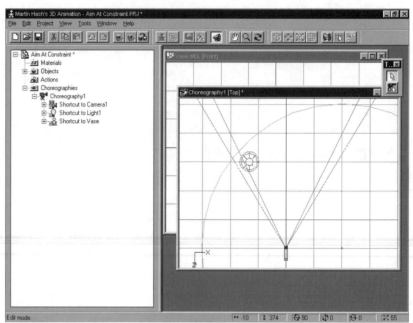

FIGURE 8.1   *The **Aim At Constraint** project on opening.*

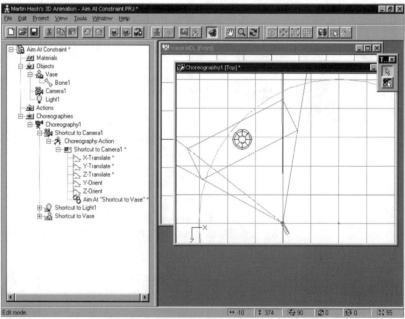

FIGURE 8.2   *The camera with an **Aim At Constraint** applied.*

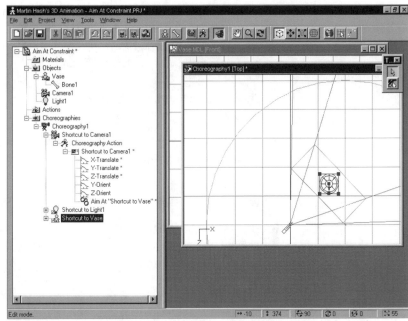

FIGURE   *The camera follows the Vase position anywhere in the **Choreography** window.*

8.3

4. When the Vase is correctly selected, the camera will turn to aim at the Vase model, as shown in Figure 8.2.

5. Click the Vase to select it, then use the mouse to drag the Vase around the **Choreography** window. Notice how the camera will follow, always aiming at the Vase (see Figure 8.3).

Another way to apply constraints is to right-click the object in the **Choreography** section of the **Project Workspace** (in this case, **Shortcut to Camera1** would have been selected) and select **New Constraint** from the available menu. The cursor will still turn into a picker, and you can still manually select the target on the **Properties Panel** if you wish.

NOTE

There's no limit to the number of constraints you can apply to any object, although you need to be careful to avoid circular constraints.

A circular constraint is a tyupe of error that occurs when an object depends on another object's position to determine its own, yet the second object's position is based on the first. This can be illustrated by applying a "Translate To" constraint from the shoulder of a model to the wrist. The shoulder can't be positioned until the wrist is positioned, but the wrist position depends on the shoulder position. If you apply constraints carefully, you won't run into this error too often. However, if you do encounter this error, it can be difficult to fix.

6. Select the light in the scene by clicking on it. An object manipulator will appear around the light.

7. Right-click the Light in the **Choreography** window and select **New Constraint**, then **Aim At** from the available menu.

8. Use the picker to select the Vase, or manually select **Shortcut to Vase** from the **Object** drop-down list on the **Properties Panel**.

9. Once again, move the Vase around the window. Notice that the light doesn't appear to change. This is because the light is a bulb-type light and is omnidirectional (meaning it casts light in all directions). As such, light from this source will illuminate the Vase no matter where in the window it is located. The **Aim At** constraint is applied to the light and can be verified by clicking the light in the scene and noting the direction of the light's bone, shown in Figure 8.4.

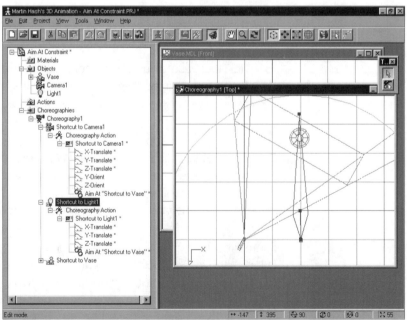

FIGURE
8.4

*The bone of an omnidirectional light indicates the **Aim At** constraints target.*

Keep in mind that constraints affect the bones in a model or object, not necessarily the object itself, as we saw with the bulb-type light. Unexpected results can occur when you forget that the recipient of the constraint's effects is the bone, not the surface points associated with the bone.

You can see from the previous example that the Aim At constraint will likely to be used quite often in your work. The next type of constraint that is discussed is the kinematic constraint.

KINEMATIC CONSTRAINTS

Kinematic constraints are used to help hold a bone in place while other bones higher in the bone hierarchy are moved. As such, they are very effective tools for aiding in interactions between a model and its environment. Kinematic constraints, for example, allow you to constrain a hand to a steering wheel. They affect the hierarchy in such a way that when the steering wheel moves, so does the character's arm.

In the following exercise, kinematic constraints are used to help Thom grab a sphere.

EXERCISE

KINEMATIC CONSTRAINTS

1. Open the *Kinematic Constraint.PRJ* file from the accompanying CD-ROM. A project will open that contains a top view of a choreography window containing the Thom model, as well as a sphere (see Figure 8.5).

Kinematic constraints help with model-to-environment interaction, as is the case in this exercise. For this constraint to look good, bones must be positioned properly in the target object. In this case, notice the three bones in the sphere (listed in the **Project Workspace**). Right and left bones were added to the sides of the sphere near the surface where Thom's hands will be grabbing it.

2. To make Thom grab the sphere, select him by clicking him in the choreography window (an object manipulator will appear), then click the **Skeletal Mode** button on the **Mode** toolbar.

3. The **Choreography** window will change to **Action** mode, and the bones in the selected model will become visible. Click the bone in

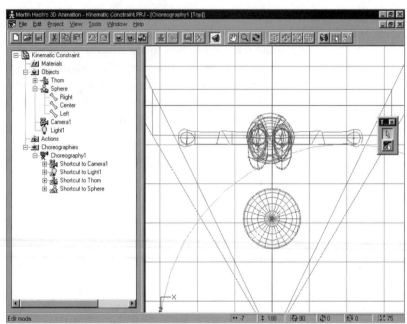

FIGURE
8.5 *The Kinematic Constraint project on opening.*

Thom's right forearm to select it, then right-click the bone and select **New Constraint**, then **Kinematic** from the available menus.

4. The cursor will change to a picker, which you should use to click near the left side of the sphere (your left, not Thom's). Thom's right arm should reach for the sphere, as shown in Figure 8.6.

NOTE

The forearm bones are used to cause Thom to always reach for the sphere with his forearms. This allows a little extra freedom in positioning the hands, as well as providing a better-looking result.

5. Continue by clicking the bone in Thom's left forearm to select it, then right-click the bone and select **New Constraint**, then **Kinematic** from the available menus.

6. The cursor will change to a picker, which you should use to click near the right side of the sphere (your right, not Thom's). The left arm should reach for the sphere, as shown in Figure 8.7.

7. Change back to **Directing Mode** by clicking the **Directing Mode** button on the **Mode** toolbar.

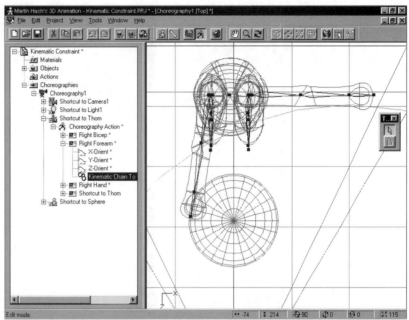

FIGURE
8.6   *Kinematic constraint on Thom's right arm, constraining the forearm bone to the sphere.*

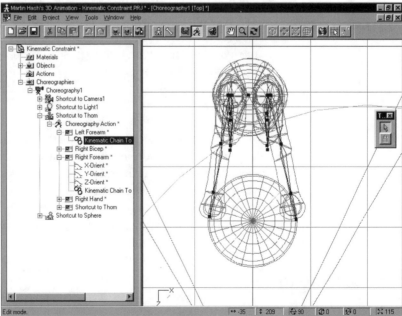

FIGURE
8.7   *Kinematic constraint on Thom's left arm, constraining the forearm bone to the sphere.*

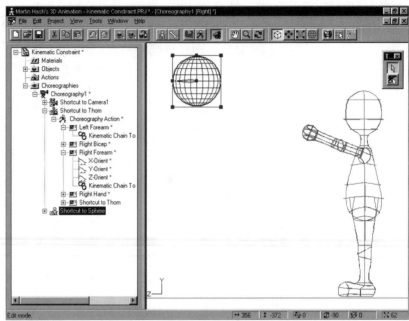

FIGURE
8.8
The model always reaches for the sphere, no matter where in the scene it is placed.

8. Change to a side view by pressing **6** on the numeric keypad. Select the sphere model with the mouse and translate it up and down. Notice how the model's arms follow the sphere no matter where it moves. The arms won't change size if the sphere is moved away from the model; they simply always try to reach for the sphere, as shown in Figure 8.8.

One of the nice things about the kinematic type of constraint is that the hierarchical chain of the model is adjusted automatically, meaning that you only have to make slight adjustments, if any, to make a character appear as though it's interacting with the environment.

Another benefit is that you can move the character (Thom in this case), and the arms will continue to reach for the sphere. Try it out.

PATH CONSTRAINTS

Path constraints are used to place objects on paths to specify where they travel over the course of an animation. Path constraints have a special control, called

Ease, which allows you control over how the object travels the path with regard to speed, acceleration, deceleration, or periods of no motion.

The following exercise describes how to use the path-type constraint, as well as the Ease channel item to make an object travel a path.

EXERCISE

PATH CONSTRAINTS

1. Open the *Path Constraint.PRJ* file from the accompanying CD-ROM. A project will open that contains a top view of a choreography window containing a path, and a model of a bullet, as shown in Figure 8.9.

2. The object of this exercise is to make the bullet travel along the existing path. Do this by selecting the bullet model by clicking on it, then right-clicking the model and selecting **New Constraint, Path** from the available menus.

3. The cursor will change to a picker. Use the picker to click anywhere along the path spline. The bullet will jump to the beginning of the path.

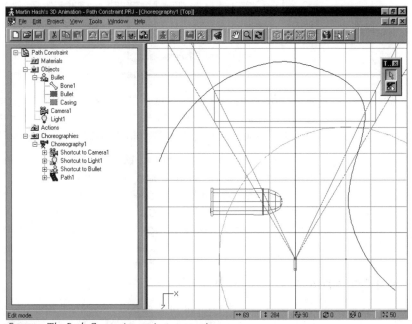

FIGURE   *The Path Constraint project on opening.*

8.9

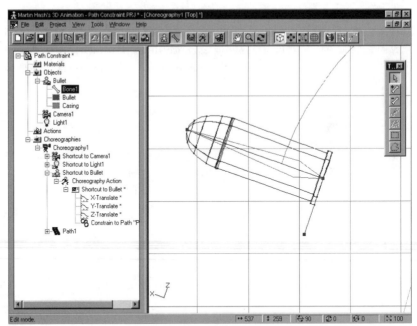

FIGURE   *The Bone1 bone visible in the bullet model.*
8.10

4. Notice the incorrect orientation of the bullet along the path (sideways, rather than lengthwise). This is because the default bone in the model is incorrectly oriented in the model. You can easily correct this problem right in the **Choreography** window. Select the bullet model by clicking on it, then click the **Bones Mode** button on the **Mode** toolbar.

5. In the Model section of the **Project Workspace**, click the **Bone1** item in the **Bullet** section. The bone will become selected inside the wireframe of the model, as shown in Figure 8.10.

6. This bone appears to be oriented correctly, along the length of the model. So what could be causing the problem? The software automatically adds a bone that remains hidden most of the time. This bone defaults to a black color with yellow handles, so depending on the color scheme you're using, it may be difficult to see. To view the position and orientation of the hidden bone, click on the model's name in the **Project Workspace**. Figure 8.11 shows the orientation of the hidden bone.

7. The bone that appears is oriented incorrectly to the body of the bullet model. It needs to be adjusted. Use the mouse to drag the thin end of the bone toward the front of the model, and the wide end of

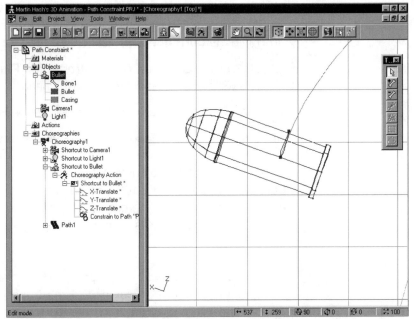

FIGURE   *The default bone in the model that is causing the bullet to sit incorrectly on the*
8.11   *path.*

the bone toward the back of the model. Switch to a side view and position each end of the bone so that it's centered in the model.

8. Click the **Directing Mode** button to switch back to **Directing Mode**, then press the spacebar to refresh the screen. The bullet should now be correctly oriented along the path.

9. Step through a few frames with the plus (**+**) and minus (**–**) keys on the numeric keypad. Notice that the bullet doesn't move. This is because no Ease channel has been set up to tell the bullet where to be at any given time.

NOTE

The Ease channel is expressed as a percent that represents the amount of a path that has been traveled. For example, if the Ease value at frame 15 is 50, the object traveling along the path will be 50% of the way along the path at frame 15. This gives you very precise control over an object's motion when you need it.

10. If the **Frame** toolbar is not visible, make it visible by clicking the border of another toolbar and selecting **Frame** from the list of available Toolbars.

11. Click the path constraint under **Shortcut to Bullet** in the **Project Workspace**. On the **Properties Panel**, locate the **Ease** field. Enter *1* into the **Current Frame** field on the **Frame** toolbar.

12. Click in the **Ease** field on the **Properties Panel** and press **Enter**. This will add a value of 0 to the Ease channel at frame 1.

13. Enter *30* into the **Current Frame** field on the **Frame** toolbar.

14. Enter *100* into the **Ease** field on the **Properties Panel**.

You have just told the bullet that at frame 1, 0% of the path should be traveled, and at frame 30, 100% of the path should be traveled. You can examine the motion this creates by stepping through the frames with the plus (+) and minus (–) keys on the numeric keypad, or the scrub bar on the **Frame** toolbar.

NOTE

The motion of an object along a path is determined by the placement of the hidden bone. For instance, if the bone in the bullet is made shorter (the thin end of the bone moved toward the back), the bullet will express the curves in the path less. Conversely, if the large end of the bone is moved forward, the bullet will express the curves in the path more.

If you would like to view or make changes to the Ease channel, simply expand the constraint branch in the **Project Workspace**, right-click the **Ease** item, and select **Edit** from the available menu. A graph will open with the Ease information in it.

Experiment with making an object slow down gradually or speed up quickly while traveling a path. This is all controlled from the Ease channel and really helps to add believable motion to your animations.

TRANSLATE TO CONSTRAINTS

Applying a *Translate To* constraint to an object makes that object reposition to the location of the target bone. For example, setting a Translate To constraint on the end of a dog's leash, and specifying a character's hand as the target, would cause the end of the dog's leash to always "Translate To" or move to the character's hand, making it look as though the character was holding the leash. The Translate To constraint works by forcing a bone to snap to the location of another bone. Keep in mind that the origin of the bone is considered its position. This type of constraint is again useful in object-to-environment interaction.

EXERCISE

TRANSLATE TO CONSTRAINTS

1. Open the *Translate To Constraint.PRJ* file from the accompanying CD-ROM. A project will open to a top view that contains the Thom model, as well as a sphere (see Figure 8.12).

2. The object of this exercise is to use the Translate To constraint type to make Thom hold the sphere. Click the sphere model to select it, then right-click the model and select **New Constraint, Translate To**.

3. With the picker tool, click on Thom's right hand. The sphere will translate to Thom's hand, as shown in Figure 8.13.

4. As you can see in the screen shot, the center of the sphere seems to have constrained to the target bone. As with the Path constraint,

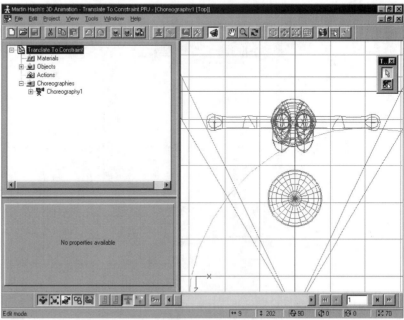

FIGURE *The Translate To Constraint project on opening.*
8.12

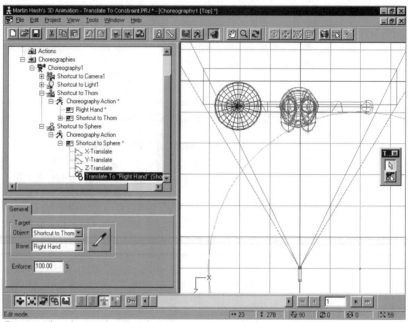

FIGURE   *The sphere with a Translate To constraint applied.*
8.13

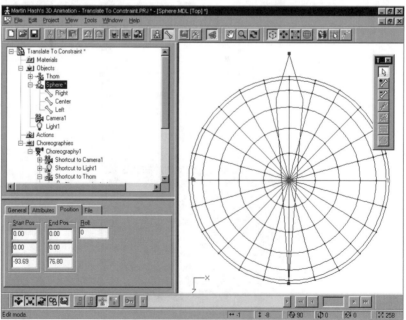

FIGURE   *The new position for the wide end of the default bone.*
8.14

this is because of the default bone location within the sphere. In the **Objects** section of the **Project Workspace**, right-click the **Sphere** item and select **Edit** from the available menu. This will open a modeling window that contains the sphere.

5. Click the **Bones Mode** button on the **Mode** toolbar, then click the **Sphere** item once again to view the location of the default bone. Change to a top view by pressing **5** on the numeric keypad.

6. Notice how the default bone runs from the front edge of the sphere to the center. The base of this bone is what the Translate To constraint is using for positioning. To fix the problem with the sphere's position in Thom's hand, translate the wide end of the bone past the back edge of the sphere, as shown in Figure 8.14. it's necessary to extend the bone beyond the edge of the sphere because it will translate to the base of the target bone, which runs down the center of Thom's arm.

7. Switch back to the **Choreography** window now and observe the changes that took place. The sphere should now be sitting properly in Thom's hand.

Now you've properly constrained the sphere to the model's hand. Anywhere the hand moves, the sphere will move accordingly, always staying attached to the bone to which it's constrained.

Since so much of animation is interaction between objects, you can see that this type of constraint has many uses. Translate To will likely be one of the constraint types that you utilize most.

ORIENT LIKE CONSTRAINTS

The *Orient Like constraint* orients the constrained bone in the same 3D orientation as the target bone. Both the bone and the roll handle of the constrained bone will aim in the same direction as the target bone. Most often, you'll use this type of constraint in conjunction with another constraint, such as Aim At — for example, to make a character's eyes both appear to looking in the same direction at all times.

The next exercise will describe the use of the Orient Like constraint to make two models orient identically in 3D space.

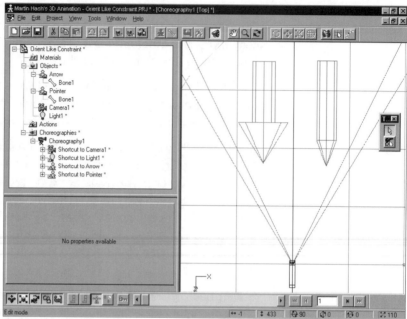

FIGURE   *The Orient Like Constraint project on opening.*
8.15

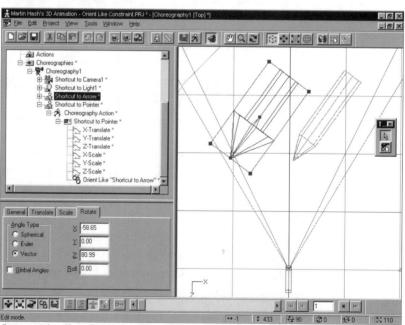

FIGURE   *The effect of an Orient Like constraint.*
8.16

ORIENT LIKE CONSTRAINTS

EXERCISE

1. Open the *Orient Like Constraint.PRJ* file from the accompanying CD-ROM. A project will open to a top view of an arrow-type model, next to which is a pointer model (see Figure 8.15).

2. The object of this exercise is to use the Orient Like constraint type to make two objects orient identically in 3D space. Begin by selecting the pointer model by clicking on it. Right-click the model and select **New Constraint, Orient Like** from the available menus.

3. With the **Picker** tool, click on the arrow model. If for some reason the incorrect object or no object at all gets selected, pick **Shortcut to Arrow** from the **Target** drop-down list on the **Properties Panel**.

4. No obvious changes will occur until you reorient the arrow model. Click on the arrow model to select it, then rotate it by moving either end of the visible bone with the mouse, as shown in Figure 8.16.

No matter which direction the arrow model is pointed, the pointer model will always assume the same X, Y, Z, and roll orientation. As we said in the beginning of this section, this type of constraint is used most often in conjunction with Aim At. For example, a character's left eye could Aim At an object, and the right eye could Orient Like the left. Both eyes would appear to be looking in the same direction, but you would only have to be concerned with one of them.

AIM ROLL AT CONSTRAINTS

The *Aim Roll At constraint* aims the roll handle of the constrained bone at the target bone's pivot. Aim Roll At can be used to create treadmill-type effects, or to help correctly orient a model along a path.

The next exercise will illustrate the use of the Aim Roll At constraint in pointing a gun turret at a target.

AIM ROLL AT CONSTRAINTS

EXERCISE

1. Open the *Aim Roll At Constraint.PRJ* file from the accompanying CD-ROM. A project will open to a top view of a gun turret model (see Figure 8.17).

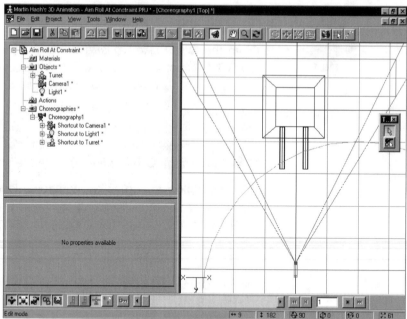

FIGURE
8.17 *The Aim Roll At Constraint project on opening.*

2. The object of this exercise is to use the Aim Roll At constraint type to make a gun turret track a target. Begin by selecting the **Turret** model by clicking it. Right-click the **Turret** and select **New Constraint, Aim Roll At**.

3. Use the **Picker** tool to select the Camera. If for some reason the picker selects no objects, select **Shortcut to Camera1** from the **Target** drop-down list on the **Properties Panel**.

4. Use the mouse to drag the camera around the scene and notice how the gun turret follows it.

Although you might think that an Aim At constraint would have worked in this exercise, it actually would have created more work than necessary. This is because unlike the Aim At constraint, the Aim Roll At constraint does not include tilt. You can test this by changing to a side view in the preceding exercise and translating the camera up and down. The turret will always aim in the general direction of the camera, but won't tilt to aim directly at it.

SPHERICAL LIMITS

Spherical Limits are the most common constraint, because most bones have their freedom of movement restricted in some manner. Your elbows and knees, for example, don't bend backward. Spherical Limits are also one of the most difficult types of constraints to get the hang of. It is possible to animate without them, but you'll be better off if you take the time to learn them now. Spherical Limits make animating easier: Dragging a character's arm won't make the elbow bend backward, so you won't need to adjust it later.

Spherical Limits are usually used on joints. They do exactly what the name says: define part of a sphere within which a particular bone will be allowed to move. Fully unconstrained joints allow full 360 degree motion, making what is referred to as a ball-and-socket joint. Ball-and-socket joints most accurately mimic real-life joints, and they work very well for most other organic objects.

Keep in mind that a subset of the ball-and-socket joint is a hinge joint, which is similar in motion to the joints found on action figures sold in toy stores, and may come in handy at some point in your animations.

The object of the following exercise is to understand how spherical limits affect bone movement. Generally, as is the case here as well, the Spherical Limits constraint is used to restrict movement at joints.

EXERCISE

SPHERICAL CONSTRAINTS

1. Open the *Spherical Constraint.PRJ* file from the accompanying CD-ROM. When the project opens, right-click the **Actions** folder in the **Project Workspace** and select **New Action** from the available menu. A window will open that looks similar to the one shown in Figure 8.18.

2. Begin setting spherical constraints: Select a bone by clicking it. The left calf was chosen for this part of the exercise, because the calf controls (to a point) where the thigh travels.

3. Right-click the left calf bone and select **New Constraint, Spherical Limits** from the available menus. The **Properties Panel** will update and show the current values for the **Longitude, Latitude,** and **Roll** limits on the selected bone.

4. To constrain the motion of Thom's calf, consider your own body's motion for a moment. Your lower leg can move from side to side slightly at the knee joint. To apply this type of motion to the selected

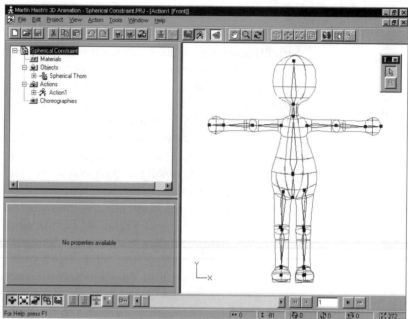

FIGURE *The Spherical Constraint project on opening.*
8.18

bone, enter *–5* into the **Minimum Longitude** field, and *5* into the **Maximum Longitude** field.

5. Your own calf also does not bend forward, but can bend backward (bends at the knee). To apply this range of motion to the calf, enter *–115* into the **Minimum Latitude** field, and *0* into the **Maximum Latitude** field.

NOTE

When you set the constraints on the calf, you should understand the entries you're making as they relate to the movement sphere. The last entry for the forward and back movement of the bone (the bending of the knee joint) is best visualized from a side view. Specifying *0* Maximum Latitude restricts the calf movement to straight down from the thigh; *–115* allows the leg to move backward 115 degrees (0 is straight down, and *–90* is straight back).

6. Once you've made these entries, move the calf bone around with the mouse to test the constraints.

7. To set a constraint along a horizontal axis, such as the elbow joint, click the right forearm bone to select it, then right-click the bone and

select **New Constraint, Spherical Limits** from the available menus.

8. Once again, the **Properties Panel** will update to show the current values applied to this bone.

9. Consider the movement of your elbow. It doesn't bend backward, yet it can move forward as your arm folds. You could represent this movement with a **Minimum Latitude** of *0* and a **Maximum Latitude** of *115*.

10. Consider the elbow joint further. If your arm is bent at a 90-degree angle at the elbow, you can turn your arm so that your hand points down, or back slightly beyond your bicep. You can represent this movement with a **Minimum Longitude** value of *90* and a **Maximum Longitude** value of *270*.

11. After you enter these values, move the forearm bone with the mouse to test the constraints and examine the results.

You should have noticed that although the knee and elbow joints have similar ranges of motion, the values are different. This is because the spherical constraints are set using a sphere of motion that is centered around the wide end of a bone, with the south pole of the sphere always being pointed to by the small end of the selected bone.

Spherical constraints are difficult to grasp unless you really take the time to work with and understand them. Once you do, restricting your model's movement will become much easier. Usually, you'll want to make a one-frame Pose of your character with Spherical Limits applied with which you can clear actions. This will make it possible for you to avoid having to set up the same constraints every time you create a new action for a model.

Now that you've worked with and understand each type of constraint and how each works, the next section describes using several constraints at once to achieve a desired effect.

USING MULTIPLE CONSTRAINTS

Although you can use individual constraints effectively, you can often save work by using different constraint types in conjunction with one another. The next exercises describe two common situations where several constraints can be combined to achieve effective results.

To make eyes follow any given target, as the eyes do in the following exercise, it would certainly be enough to apply two Aim At constraints. However, if you need the eyes to look at different objects as a scene plays out, you would have to change both. This could be hard to follow in a complex choreography. A better technique is to use an Aim At constraint on one of the eyes, and an Orient Like on the other.

EXERCISE

USING AIM AT AND ORIENT LIKE CONSTRAINTS TOGETHER

1. Open the *Eye Constraints.PRJ* file from the accompanying CD-ROM. A project will open to a top view of a **Choreography** window containing two eye models.

2. Begin by clicking the right eye to select it. Right-click the model and select **New Constraint**, then **Aim At** from the available menus.

3. Use the **Picker** tool to click the camera in the scene.

4. Click the other eye model to select it, then right-click the model and select **New Constraint**, then **Orient Like** from the available menus.

5. Use the picker to select the right eye.

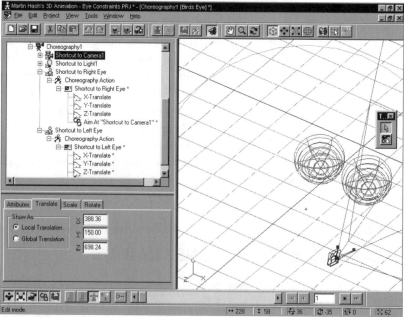

FIGURE   *The right eye aims at the camera, and the left eye orients like the right.*
8.19

Now, anywhere the camera moves, the eyes will follow (see Figure 8.19). If you need to change the target of the eyes, you'll only have to modify the Aim At constraint. The Orient Like constraint will adjust automatically.

Eyes are a common example of how you can use different constraint types at once to save some time. Another good example is the Path constraint. Objects that follow a path tend to need sets of constraints applied to them — for example, a camera following a path, yet aiming at a character in a scene.

This exercise describes how to use a Path constraint with an Aim Roll At constraint to keep an object correctly oriented as it travels a path.

USING PATH AND AIM ROLL AT CONSTRAINTS TOGETHER

1. Open the *Vehicle Constraint.PRJ* file from the accompanying CD-ROM. A project will open to a side view of a choreography window containing a car on a path that forms a loop (see Figure 8.20).

2. Begin by using the plus (+) and minus (–) keys to step through the frames. Notice that the car already has an Ease channel set to make it travel along the path. As you step through the frames, take note of

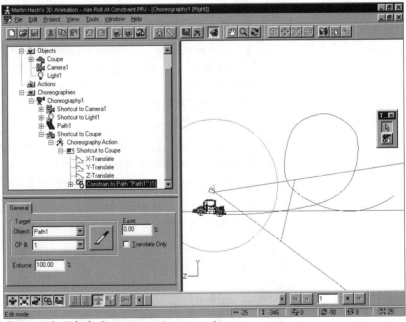

FIGURE
8.20
The Vehicle Constraint project on opening.

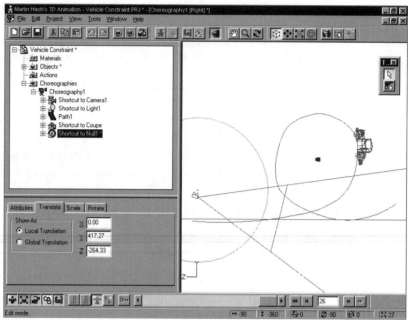

FIGURE *The location of the null object in relation to the looped path.*
8.21

what happens to the car in frame 26. By trying to stay on top of the path, the car flips to the outside of the loop.

3. The problem is fairly easy to fix with something called a *null object*. Null objects are simply bones that won't render. Add one to the choreography by right-clicking the choreography name in the **Project Workspace** and selecting **New**, then **Null Object** from the available menus.

4. The object will appear in both in the choreography window and the **Project Workspace**. Use the mouse to translate the null object to the center of the loop, as shown in Figure 8.21.

5. Right-click the model or the car and select **New Constraint**, then **Aim Roll At** from the available menus.

6. Use the **Picker** to select the null object. The car will flip to correctly orient along the path.

Step through the frames and notice how the vehicle now stays correctly oriented through the entire range of action.

As you can see, many objects will require several constraints to move through a scene in the manner you would like. If you try to concentrate on properly constraining one object at a time (this isn't always possible), you'll have an easier time getting the results you desire without becoming frustrated or confused.

The next section describes how to use different constraints effectively to animate objects.

ANIMATING CONSTRAINTS

One of the hidden powers of the constraint system is the ability to animate with it. This section describes a simple example of animating with constraints, which you'll be able to build on in the future.

The following exercise describes how to use a Kinematic Chain To constraint to aid in animating a character reaching for an object.

EXERCISE

ANIMATING CONSTRAINTS

1. Open the *Animating Constraints1.PRJ* file from the accompanying CD-ROM. A project will open to a front view of a choreography window containing the Thom model and a Vase model.

2. Begin by clicking the Thom model to select him, then click the **Skeletal Action Mode** button on the **Mode** toolbar. Click Thom's right forearm bone, then right-click the bone and select **New Constraint, Kinematic** from the available menus.

3. Use the **Picker** tool to click on the left side of the vase (your left, not Thom's).

4. Click the left forearm bone, then right-click the same bone and select **New Constraint, Kinematic** from the available menus.

5. Use the **Picker** tool to click on the right side of the vase (your right, not Thom's).

6. At this point, both of the model's arms are reaching for the respective sides of the vase. The value that you need to adjust to animate

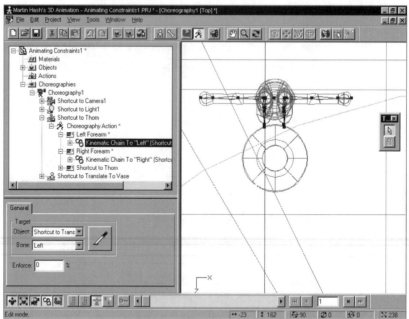

FIGURE
8.22
*The effect that entering 0 into the **Enforce** field has on the constraints.*

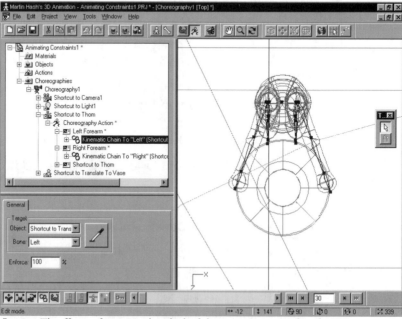

FIGURE
8.23
The effect on frame 30 where both of the constraints are enforced 100%.

with them is located on the **Properties Panel**; it's called **Enforce**. This value tells the software how much of the selected constraint it should use at any given frame.

7. Under **Choreography Action** in the **Project Workspace**, there are two Kinematic Chain To constraints listed (the two that you just applied). Click the first, then enter *0* into the **Enforce** field on the **Properties Panel**. Continue by clicking the second and entering *0* into the **Enforce** field once again. This tells the software that on frame 1 of this animation, it should use 0% of the selected constraints (see Figure 8.22).

8. Enter *30* into the **Current Frame** field on the **Frame Toolbar**.

9. Select the first constraint in the **Project Workspace** and enter *100* into the **Enforce** field on the **Properties Panel**. Enter *100* into the **Enforce** field on the second constraint as well (see Figure 8.23).

10. Enter frame *1* into the **Current Frame** field on the **Frame** toolbar. Use the plus (**+**) and minus (**–**) keys on the numeric keypad to step through the frames and watch as the constraints animate the model reaching for the vase. The movement tends to be a little extreme at the beginning of the movement, since the arms begin straight out. Starting with a more natural pose (arms at the side) would create a smoother motion.

Although it's a rudimentary example, the previous exercise illustrates how simple, time-based manipulations of constraint enforcement can be used to aid you in animation. You can use an unlimited number of constraints in any given scene (provided that they don't cause a circular constraint), and each one has its own time-based enforcement. This gives you an incredibly flexible method for controlling objects.

For even more ease of animating, the next section discusses the use of target bones in a character.

TARGET BONES

Target bones are bones that are applied to a character outside of the wireframe and do nothing but help orient different parts of a model to aid in animating. Some people find it much easier simply to apply a series of bones to a model that can be used to control the model more as a puppeteer controls a puppet, rather than manipulating each bone in the model. This is exactly the purpose of using target bones in your models.

EXERCISE

TARGET BONES

1. Open the *Spherical Thom.MDL* from the accompanying CD-ROM.

2. Right-click the **Actions** folder in the **Project Workspace** and select **New Action**. When the new **Action** window opens, press **6** on the numeric keypad to switch to a side view.

3. Notice the extra bone in front of each knee. Each of these bones could be used in different situations as the target of an Aim At or Orient Like constraint.

Notice that the feet also make use of target bones. Targets come in handy when a character is interacting with its environment, such as climbing stairs. There are countless combinations of constraints that you can use to achieve the desired effect.

SUMMARY

You should now have a firm grasp on the different types of constraints, how they work alone, and how they interact with other constraints. Understanding how constraints work will help you effectively apply bones to the models that you create. Knowing ahead of time what type of actions the model will be performing will help you to construct the most efficient, best-looking model possible.

The next chapter describes how bones work and how to apply them to typical models, such as bipeds.

CHAPTER
9

Bones

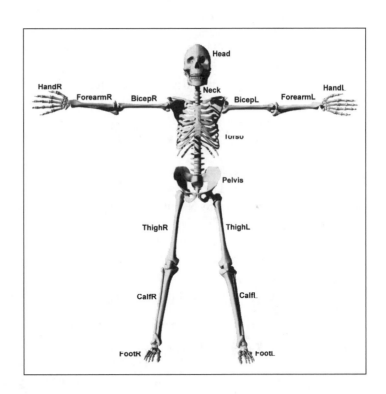

This chapter discusses the application and use of *bones* within your 3D models. Bones are used in every model. Correctly applied, they make animating a character less time-consuming. The essential idea behind bones is that they're added to a model to form an easy-to-manage "skeleton" within it. This skeleton allows you to manipulate the different parts of the model. Even models that you don't add any bones to have two bones by default, which are used for positioning.

As you add bones, you'll notice that they're thicker at one end than the other, and that a handle sticks straight out to the side from the large end. The large end of the bone is the pivot point around which the bone (and the model's associated control points) will rotate. The thin end of the bone is a handle that can be used to manipulate the direction in which the bone points. Finally, the handle sticking out to the side of the large end of the bone is a roll handle (manipulating this causes changes in the roll of the bone and its associated control points).

This chapter describes some techniques used to apply bones to a character, as well as a standard naming convention that can be used to create reusable actions.

This chapter covers the following topics:

- Understanding Joints
- Bone Hierarchies
- A Standard Naming Convention
- Boning Simple Models
- Boning Quadrupeds
- Boolean Operations

UNDERSTANDING JOINTS

It may seem strange that a chapter on bones begins by discussing joints, but if you think about it for a moment, it will make sense. When two bones are added to a model, some type of joint is formed. Depending on the model, it can be anything from a simple hinge joint all the way to a complex joint with spherical limits applied to the latitude, longitude, and roll axes of the bone.

Generally, the bones you add will be creating joints on the arms or legs of a character. Some of the concerns for correct modeling technique were discussed in the modeling chapters. Here, you get to find out why.

The next exercise describes how to add two bones to a simple cylinder to form a joint.

TWO-BONE JOINTS

1. Open the *Two Bone Joint.PRJ* file from the accompanying CD-ROM. The project will open to a modeling window that contains a simple cylinder model with an angled spline in the center. You'll use the angled spline (which was discussed in the modeling chapters) to simulate an elbow joint on this model.

2. Click the **Bones Mode** button. Click the **Add Bone** button on the **Tools** toolbar and add a bone, beginning at the top of the model and reaching down to the center angled spline, as shown in Figure 9.1.

3. Click the **Add Bone** button once again and add a second bone beginning where the first left off and continuing to the bottom of the cylinder, as shown in Figure 9.2.

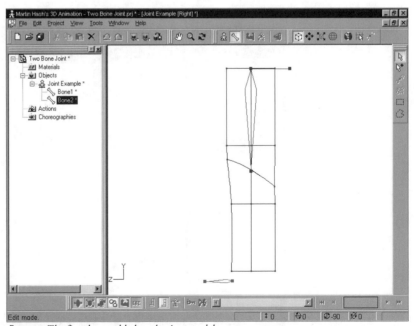

FIGURE *The first bone added to the Arm model.*
9.1

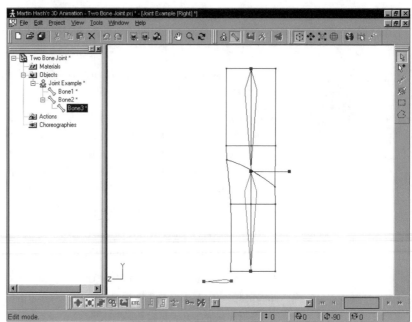

FIGURE *The second bone added to the Arm model.*
9.2

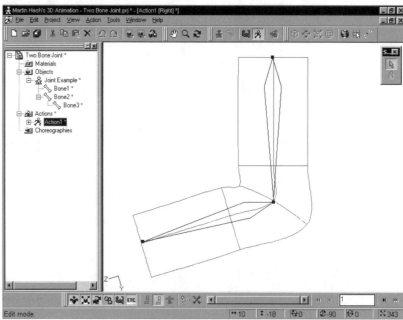

FIGURE *The bent "arm" model. The same technique is used to make effective knee joints.*
9.3

4. Now you need to associate the appropriate control points with the bones. Click the first bone you added to select it, then click the **Group** button.

5. Starting at the top of the model, group all of the control points down to, and including, the angled spline.

6. Click the second bone you added to select it, then click the **Group** button.

7. Group all of the points below the angled spline.

8. Right-click the **Actions** folder in the **Project Workspace** and select **New Action** from the available menu.

9. Switch to a side view and use the mouse to grab the lower, wrist-end bone and drag it. Notice how a fold develops in the joint at the angled spline, similar to Figure 9.3.

NOTE

Take a moment and bend the lower bone upward past 90 degrees. Notice how the fold in the joint begins to become exaggerated. The joint can be enhanced by adjusting the **Magnitude** value of both the spline running through the inside and outside control points of the angled spline. The would minimize the folding effect. Experiment with different values until you develop a joint that suits your modeling style.

For the boning tutorials in this chapter, the previous technique is used. It works well in most cases. However, there will be times when you need more rigid joints that handle a little more tightly than the previous type.

Consider a cylindrical model somewhat like a Slinky toy, where both ends of the model would need to touch the ground, and the model needs to maintain a smooth arch between the ends. Getting the positioning just right on every keyframe would be very tricky, since each joint would likely need to be adjusted on each keyframe. This is where a three-bone joint can be used to do the job. The following exercise describes how to set up such a joint.

EXERCISE

THREE-BONE JOINTS

1. Open the *Three Bone Joint.PRJ* file from the accompanying CD-ROM. A modeling window will open that contains a cylindrical shape similar to the one used in the previous exercise.

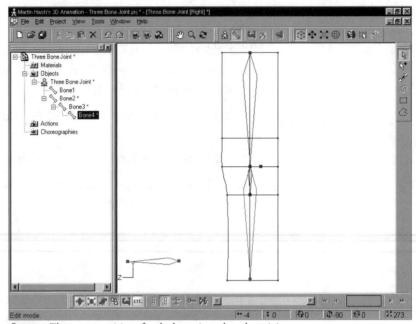

The correct positions for the bones in a three-bone joint.
9.4

2. Click the **Bones Mode** button. Click the **Add Bone** button and add a bone from the top of the model down to the center spline.

3. Click the **Add Bone** button and add a second bone from the center spline to the bottom of the model. With the second bone highlighted, click the **Bone** tab on the **Properties Panel** and make sure that the **Attached to Parent** checkbox is active. If it is not, click in the checkbox.

4. Click the **Add Bone** button once again and add a third bone to the model in the same position as the second, but not extending down to the bottom of the model. Use Figure 9.4 for reference in placing the third bone.

5. Click the **Bone2** item in the **Project Workspace** to select the first bone you added. Use the **Group** tool to select the top two cross-sections of the model.

6. Click the **Bone3** item in the **Project Workspace** to select the second bone you added. Use the **Group** tool to select the bottom two cross-sections of the model.

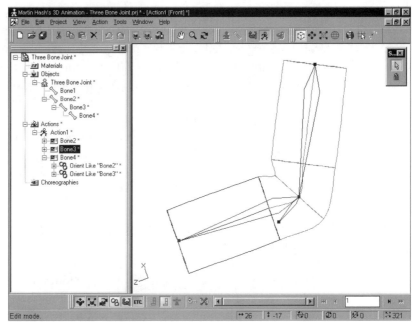

7. Click the **Bone4** item in the **Project Workspace** to select the final bone you added. Use the **Group** tool to select the control points on the center spline of the model.

8. Right-click the **Actions** folder and select **New Action** from the available menu. Right-click **Bone4** (the last bone added) and select **New Constraint, Orient Like** from the available menus.

9. Use the **Picker** tool to select the upper bone in the model.

10. Right-click **Bone4** once again, and select **New Constraint, Orient Like** from the available menus.

11. Use the **Picker** tool to select the lower bone in the model.

12. Use the mouse to manipulate the lower bone and see how the joint reacts. It should look similar to the first joint, except that now the center of the joint always determines its position by blending the two Orient Like constraints that were applied. If necessary, you can "point" the center of the joint by manipulating the center bone. This will help to smooth the curve that develops as the joint is manipulated. Figure 9.5 shows the final three-bone joint.

This joint may seem to be more complex and time-consuming to create, with results that are similar to the joint created in the first exercise. Change the Slinky example used at the beginning of this exercise into a long, flexible tail on a dragon. Certainly, you could use joints with two bones for the tail. However, the three-bone joints give you a higher level of control, since the center splines' positions are based on the location of the bones on either side of the joint.

Now that you've created different types of joints, the next section discusses bone hierarchies and their importance in animating.

BONE HIERARCHIES

Much of the work of applying bones to models can be done in your head before you even sit down to the computer. A little thought before you jump in and begin to add bones haphazardly to a model can save a lot of time in the long run.

Bone hierarchies are huge in the sense that they are what make your characters animatable. You could get away with an improperly set up character, but you would cost yourself an awful lot of time when animating. So, where do you begin? Think about how your character should move. For example, if you move your upper arm, your forearm and hand must also move. This is a hierarchy. The upper arm is the parent, the forearm is the child. Likewise, the forearm is the parent, and the hand is the child. Going one step further, stand up and bend over at the waist. You arms must move when your torso moves. This means that your torso is the parent of your upper arms. The hierarchy continues down through the legs, and up to the head. For the most part, how you move and the hierarchy of your body dictates how bones are added to a character of a similar type (biped).

Although bipeds aren't necessarily the simplest example of a bone hierarchy, keep in mind that bone hierarchies can get extremely complex very quickly. This is where *reusable actions* come into play. Animation:Master allows you to create an action for a character and use it on another character with the same hierarchy and bone names. This flexibility allows you to create a library of actions and a library of characters that you can call on quickly and easily when needed. It also saves huge amounts of time and trouble if you come across two similar characters with complex bone hierarchies. To share actions between characters, you'll need to observe a couple of guidelines. The next section describes these rules.

A STANDARD NAMING CONVENTION FOR BONES

The rules for reusable actions are simple. First, the character you're applying the action to *must* have the same bone hierarchy as the character the action was created on. This means that a quadruped walk cycle cannot be applied to a biped. The only exception to this rule is fingers and toes. An action that is created on a character that does not have fingers or toes in its hierarchy can be applied to a character that does. Of course, no movement will occur on the fingers or toes of the character receiving the action.

The second rule is that both characters *must* have the same naming structure. This is where a standard naming convention comes in. No matter what you call the characters, their bones must be named the same if you want to reuse actions. For example, an action created for a bone with the name "upper arm" will not apply to a bone named "bicep." Figure 9.6 shows a simple standard naming convention that can be used on bipedal characters. Notice that the hands and feet are not articulated (they have no bones in them to make them move) and are simply referred to as handr, handl, footr, and footl.

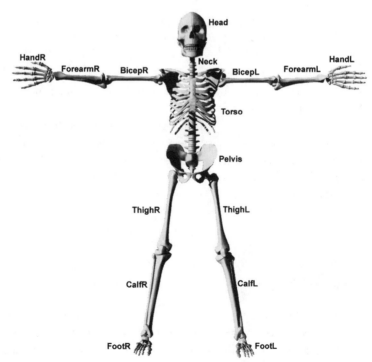

FIGURE *A standard naming convention for the bones in a bipedal character.*
9.6

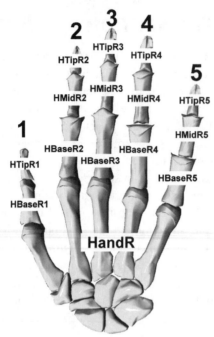

A standard naming convention for a hand
9.7 *or foot. Just change the name accordingly.*

In the event that you decide to create a character whose hands and feet are to be articulated, you can use Figure 9.7 as a guide in naming the individual parts of the hand or foot.

Now that you're familiar with joints, bone hierarchies, and a standard naming convention, it's time to start adding bones to models you've worked with in earlier chapters. The next section begins by describing how to bone a biped.

BONING A BIPED

Killer Bean once again serves as an example in the following exercise. In this exercise, you'll apply bones to the Killer Bean model in a commonly used bipedal hierarchy, then name the bones according to the standard naming convention illustrated in Figure 9.6.

EXERCISE

BONING KILLER BEAN

1. Create a new project and select **Save As** from the **Project** drop-down menu. Type **Bones** for the project name and press **Enter**. Right-click the **Object** item in the **Project Workspace** and select **Import Model**.

2. Open the *Killer Bean no Bones.MDL* file from the accompanying CD-ROM.

3. When the model opens, click the **Bones Mode** button on the **Mode** toolbar.

   When you first access the **Bones Mode** for any given model, you'll notice a default red bone that appears on the screen. This default bone is often used as the *patriarch* (the bone that is the parent to all other bones) in a character.

4. Use the mouse to drag the ends of the patriarch bone until it matches Figure 9.8. After the bone has been positioned properly, click the newly added bone's name in the **Project Workspace** (it

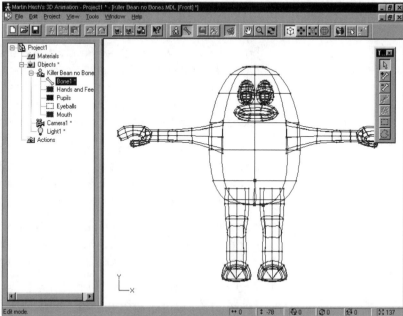

FIGURE *The proper position for the patriarch bone in the Killer Bean model.*

9.8

will be highlighted) and press the **F2** key to rename the bone. Type in *Pelvis* and press **Enter**.

5. The patriarch bone controls all control points by default, so you don't need to specify which control points belong to this bone. However, it is important to check the bone's location within the segment from a side view. If the bone lies outside the wireframe, position it inside the lower body, in the center of the model.

6. Continue by clicking the **Add Bone** button. Clicking above the pelvis bone, with the mouse button down, drag upward toward the chest area of the model (below the mouth). Notice that this bone is a different color than the previous one. As you continue to add bones, the color of each bone will continue to change, as will the color of any control points associated with a given bone. Name this bone *Torso.*

7. With the Torso bone still selected, click the **Group** button and select the two cross-sections on the body just below the mouth. Zoom in if necessary to avoid grouping any of the upper arm's control points. If you accidentally group a control point that should not be associated with the selected bone, click the patriarch (base bone) and select the point to reassign it.

8. With the Torso bone still selected, click the **Add Bone** button once again and create a bone above the torso bone. This mean that the bone you add will become the child of the selected bone (in this case, as in most, the head is the child of the torso). Select all of the points on the body from the top of the head to the cross-section above the one selected for the torso. Include the eyes and mouth. If necessary, use Figure 9.9 for reference. Name this bone *Head.*

9. Begin adding bones to the arms by clicking the Torso bone. This will add the bones to the arms as children of the Torso, which is a child of the Pelvis (patriarch). Click the **Add Bone** button and drag a bone out on Killer Bean's right upper arm.

10. Name this bone *BicepR,* then use the **Group** tool to select all of the points in the upper arm down to and including the elbow spline. Zoom in if necessary to avoid grouping the body control points.

11. Add another bone as a child of the BicepR. Name this bone *ForeArmR.* On the **Properties Panel**, select the **Bone** tab and check the **Attached to Parent** checkbox to create a kinematic chain (this means that when the forearm is pulled, the biceps will follow automatically).

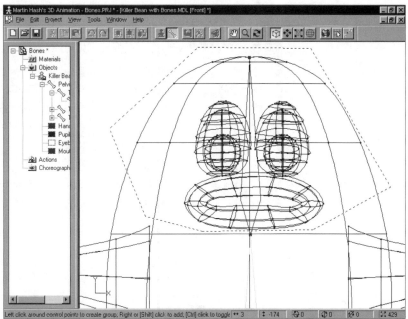

FIGURE   *The correct set of points to group in association with the Head bone.*
9.9

TIP

When adding bones that you know are going to be "Attached to Parent," you can save an extra step. After clicking the **Add Bone** button, click on top of the handle of the previous bone when you drag the new bone out. This will automatically attach the bone you're adding to its parent.

12. With the ForeArmR bone selected, group the last two cross-sections of the arm.

13. Add a bone as the child of the ForeArmR bone, and name it *HandR*. Once again, check the **Attached to Parent** checkbox on the **Bone** tab of the **Properties Panel**. Use the **Group** tool to select all of the control points of the hand.

14. Repeat steps 9–13 for the left arm, changing the names of the bones accordingly. After you add the bones to the left arm, the model should look similar to Figure 9.10.

15. The last parts of the model that need to have bones applied are the legs. Select the Pelvis bone by clicking on it with the mouse, then click the **Add Bone** button and drag a bone out along Killer Bean's right thigh. Name this bone *ThighR*.

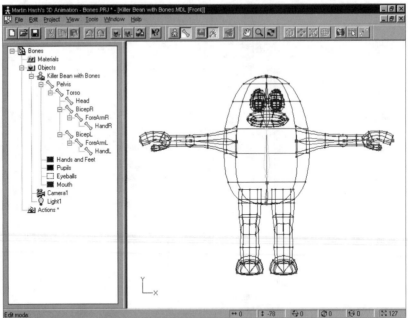

FIGURE   *Killer Bean with bones in his body and arms. Notice that the control points change*
9.10   *color to reflect the bone they're associated with.*

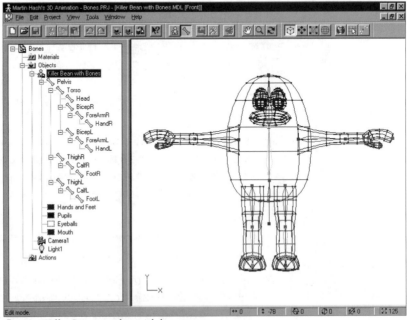

FIGURE   *Killer Bean complete with bones.*
9.11

16. Use the **Group** tool to select all of the control points from the upper leg down to and including the rotated knee spline.

17. Add another bone as a child of the ThighR bone named *CalfR*. Check the **Attached to Parent** checkbox on the **Bone** tab of the **Properties Panel**.

18. Use the **Group** tool to select the two lower cross-sections of the leg. Zoom in if necessary to avoid grouping any of the control points of the foot.

19. Change to a side view, then add a bone as a child of the CalfR bone that reaches from the ankle area to the toe. Name this bone *FootR.*

20. Switch back to a front view and select all of the points that make up Killer Bean's right foot.

21. Repeat steps 15–20 for the left side to finish adding bones to the model. Make the appropriate changes to the bone names.

Figure 9.11 shows the model after all of the bones have been added.

The previous exercise demonstrated the use of bones and their hierarchies. Although Killer Bean serves as a simple example of a very popular and common model type (a body with arms and legs), he is not a typical biped: He has no defined pelvis, torso, neck and head areas. The next section will walk you through adding the final bones to the Thom model to provide a more typical example of bones in a biped.

In a bipedal-type character such as Thom, extra bones are added to the feet to allow them to bend in the middle as Thom walks. There is also a defined neck and head area. As you'll see, this bone hierarchy also expands on the standard naming convention by using more descriptive bone names. Remember that the standard naming convention was just a basic guide. As long as you use the same names for each bone in each character, it makes no difference what you call them.

EXERCISE

FINISHING BONES

1. Create a new project and select **Save As** from the **Project** dropdown. Type **Bones2** for the project name and press **Enter**. Rightclick the **Object** item in the **Project Workspace** and select **Import Model**.

2. Open the *Thom no Bones.MDL* file from the accompanying CD-ROM.

3. When the model opens, click the **Bones Mode** button.

The first thing you notice is that the name of the model is not completely accurate, because there are some bones in the model already. The second thing you should notice is that several bones are missing.

4. Click on the Torso bone with the mouse, then click the **Add Bone** button. Drag a bone from the upper point of the Torso bone (not attached to parent) to the bottom of the head. Name this bone *Neck*. Use the **Group** tool to select the lower cross-section of the head where the Neck bone ends.

5. Add another bone (attached to parent) to the Neck bone that runs from the neck to the top of the head. Name this bone *Head*. Use the **Group** tool to select the points that make up the head of the model.

The upper part of the model is now complete. The next steps will describe the addition of toe bones that allow the foot to bend in the middle.

6. Switch to a side view and use the **Zoom** tool to magnify the area from the ankles down. Notice that there are already bones in each foot, and that the points associated with these bones essentially make up the heels of the feet.

7. Select the bone in the right foot by clicking on it in the **Project Workspace**, then click the **Add Bone** button. Drag the new bone from beyond the second cross-section in from the toe end of the foot (roughly the center of the foot) to the tip of the foot. Use the **Group** tool to select the control points that make up the end of the foot (the last two cross-sections).

NOTE

The best way to select control points in a tight spot such as that in step 7 is to hide the parts of the model that confuse the view. You can do this by selecting the offending bones and clicking the **Wireframe Draw Mode** button on the **Properties Panel**. This means that all of the points associated with the selected bone will not draw in wireframe view; only the bone itself will be visible. If necessary, you can also hide the bone by clicking on it, then clicking in the **Hide Bone** checkbox on the **Properties Panel**.

8. Repeat step 7 on the left foot.

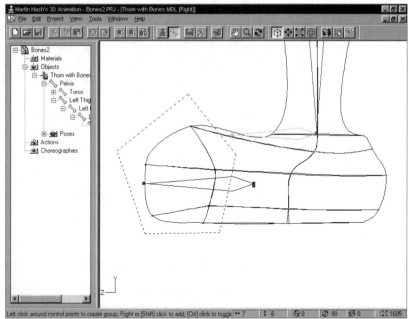

FIGURE *The foot bone and associated points for reference on step 7.*

9.12

Thom's bones are now complete! When it comes time to animate him, bending his feet in the middle will add a little more accuracy to his movements. His head can also now target objects moving through a scene to make it appear as though he is watching the objects move about him without contorting his body.

The next section goes a little further on bones by describing the application of bones into a quadruped. While using basically the same technique, this particular case offers a tail in addition to the a horizontally oriented body and four legs rather than two.

BONING QUADRUPEDS

This section uses the trusty cow model created earlier in this book to demonstrate the addition of bones to a quadruped-type model. Once again, you'll need to give forethought to how the model moves and the hierarchy of the parts, before you sit down and try to apply bones to the model. This situation calls for an extra pair of legs that are hierarchically arranged in a familiar order (upper leg, lower leg, foot) and the addition of enough bones in the tail to allow it to swing back and forth if the cow so desires.

EXERCISE

ADDING THE BASIC BONES

1. Create a new project and select **Save As** from the **Project** drop-down. Type *Bones3* for the project name and press **Enter**. Right-click the **Object** item in the **Project Workspace** and select **Import Model**.

2. Open the *Cow no Bones.MDL* file from the accompanying CD-ROM.

3. When the model opens, click the **Bones Mode** button and change to a side view by pressing the 6 key on the numeric keypad.

4. Click on the default **Bone1** item in the **Project Workspace** to see how the default bone is oriented in relation to the model. Most likely, it will be oriented horizontally along the Z axis running from the back of the model to the front.

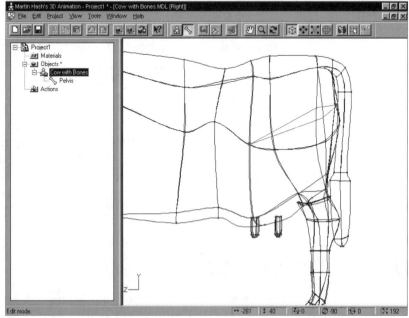

FIGURE *Placement of the cow's Pelvis bone.*
9.13

5. Position the bone so that it lies with one end near the cow's rear end, and the other end forward several cross-sections, as shown in Figure 9.13. Name this bone *Pelvis*.

6. Switch to a top view and verify that the bone is inside the wireframe. If it isn't, drag it with the mouse to adjust it appropriately.

7. Add another bone, not attached to the Pelvis bone, that runs from just in front of the Pelvis bone to just behind where the neck of the cow is located. Name this bone *Torso* and group the appropriate control points on the model. The group of points related to this bone should not include the top of the front legs.

8. Add a bone as a child of the torso that is not attached to its parent. Position this bone to represent the neck of the model. Name this bone *Neck* and group the appropriate control points, shown in Figure 9.14.

9. Add a bone attached to the Neck bone that runs from the neck to the tip of the nose. Name this bone *Head* and use the **Group** tool to group the points forward of the neck's control points. These control points should include the ears on the head of the model.

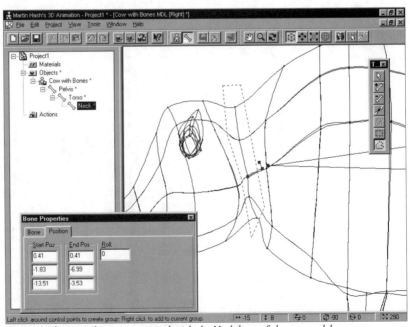

FIGURE *The control points associated with the Neck bone of the cow model.*
9.14

Now that you've added the basic bones to the body, it's time to add bones to the legs of the model. You can name them whatever you want to keep track of them, but try to stick to something descriptive. Most importantly, be consistent in your naming.

EXERCISE

ADDING BONES TO THE LEGS

For the purposes of this exercise, the legs will be referred to as front left, front right, back left, and back right. Each leg is separated into three parts, the upper leg, the lower leg, and the foot. From this description, adding the bones to the legs of the model becomes fairly straightforward.

1. From a side view, click the Torso bone of the model. Click the **Add Bone** button and add a bone running from the top of the front leg to the first cross-section down.

2. From a front view, make any adjustments necessary to align the bone with the front left leg. Name the bone *Front Left Upper Leg.* Use the **Group** tool to group the points that make up the upper leg,

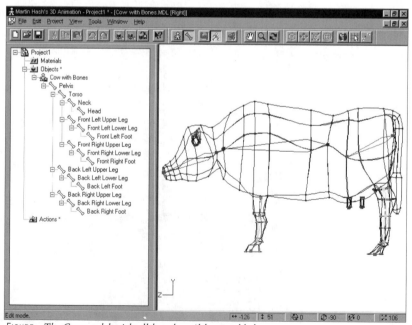

FIGURE *The Cow model with all but the tail bones added.*
9.15

leaving out the points in the center where both legs attach to the body (these points should be associated with the Torso bone).

3. Continue down the leg adding the Front Left Lower Leg and Front Left Foot bones, and grouping the appropriate control points.

4. Continue adding the bones for the front right leg by repeating steps 1–3, changing the names of the bones where needed.

5. Repeat this process twice more for the back legs, using the appropriate name changes as discussed at the beginning of this section. Before adding bones to the back legs, however, select the Pelvis bone.

Figure 9.15 shows the way the model and its bone hierarchy (in the **Project Workspace**) look at this point.

The legs are now complete. The last step in adding bones to this model is the addition of several bones to the tail. These bones will make it possible to make the tail move, if need be.

EXERCISE

ADDING BONES TO THE TAIL

Because no standard naming convention exists for the tail of this model, the name Tail with an appended, incremental number will be used to name the bones added to the tail of the model.

1. From a side view, select the Pelvis bone by clicking on it, then click the **Add Bone** button and add a bone near the base of the tail. Switch to a top view and verify that the position of the bone is correctly aligned with the tail.

2. Name this bone *Tail1*, then use the **Group** tool to select the point shown in Figure 9.16.

3. Add another bone that is attached to the previous one that runs to the next cross-section of the tail. Name this bone *Tail2* and select the end cross-section only.

4. Add a Tail3 bone that is attached to the Tail2 bone and reaches to the next cross-section of the tail. Group the cross-section at the end of the Tail3 bone to associate these points with the bone.

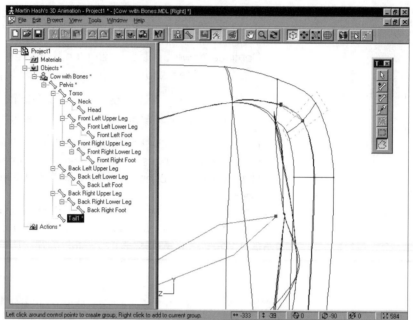

FIGURE
9.16
The control points associated with the first bone added to the tail.

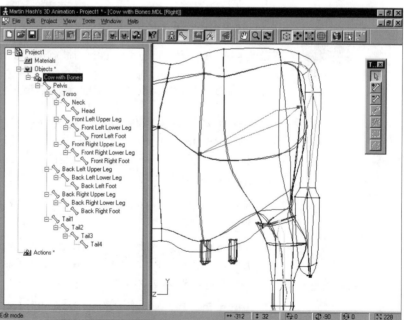

FIGURE
9.17
The tail section of the cow model after all of the bones are added.

5. Add a final bone, Tail4, that reaches from and is attached to the Tail3 bone and runs to the end of the tail of the model. Select the entire end of the tail to associate these points with the newly added bone.

Figure 9.17 shows the bones that were added to the model for the tail.

Adding more resolution (cross-sections) and more bones to the tail of the model would have created a model that could be positioned more precisely, with more detail over the shape of the tail. For this exercise, it was not necessary, but it could come in handy on models such as snakes, electrical cords, wires, or dragons.

There is another use for bones that is not often touched on. A bone can be specified as a *Boolean cutter* and cause the geometry with which it is associated to "cut" away any geometry it intersects. The next section will describe how to use a bone as a Boolean cutter.

BOOLEAN OPERATIONS

Traditionally, *Boolean operations* are reserved for use in modeling, to carve out a difficult shape or help in creating detail. Most of the modelers that allow Boolean operations to be performed on a model are polygonal, so the Boolean functions can be performed by removing or adding polygons where two or more objects intersect.

Unlike polygonal models, the surface of a spline-based model is mathematical, not a physical item that can be manipulated. This means that performing Boolean operations on spline-based models is much more complex. Therefore, Animation:Master implements Boolean operations on a bone level, which also lends to another very cool feature: The Boolean operation can be animated.

The following exercise will describe how to specify a model as a Boolean, and the effect the operation will have.

EXERCISE

SIMPLE BOOLEAN OPERATIONS

1. Open the *Boolean01.PRJ* file from the accompanying CD-ROM. The project file contains a model of a cube with a ball inside, a rod, and ground plane. For now, you'll be working with the cube model, which should be open in a window.

2. As you can see, this model is simply a ball that intersects a cube. To perform a Boolean subtraction, you must specify a bone that controls the control points of the sphere. Click any point on the sphere and press the **/** key to Group Connected. Press the **H** key to hide the unselected points. Only the sphere will remain in the modeler window.

NOTE

The *number one* rule in creating Boolean cutter objects is to make sure that the object is closed on all sides. If a model has a hole in its surface, it will not cut properly. In addition, models that are closed but contain internal patches will likely cause rendering artifacts.

3. Click the **Bones Mode** button. Notice that the default red bone is present. Click the **Add Bone** button and add a bone anywhere on the screen. Name the newly added bone *Cutter*.

4. With the new bone still selected, group all of the points on the sphere with the **Group** tool.

5. Click the **Bone** tab on the **Properties Panel**, and click in the **Boolean Cutter** checkbox. This will cause the geometry associated with the bone to subtract itself from any intersecting objects.

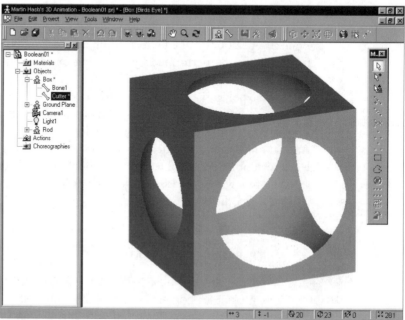

FIGURE   *The resulting render after the sphere is specified as a Boolean cutter.*

9.18

6. Click the **Model Mode** button. Press the **H** key to unhide the model.

7. It appears as though nothing happened. This is because the Boolean cut is performed at render time. Render the image. You should see something similar to Figure 9.18.

NOTE

When you specify a Boolean, only the parts of the same model that it intersects will be subtracted. Therefore, a model can have a hole cut into it that other objects in the scene can pass through.

8. To see the effect the Boolean has on other objects, right-click the **Choreographies** folder and select **New Choreography** from the available menu.

9. Drag the Ground Plane into the choreography and scale it up by dragging the corner of the manipulator box that appears around it.

10. Drag the Cube model into the choreography and place it in the center of the Ground Plane. Check from a side view and make any necessary adjustments to make the model sit on top of the Ground Plane. With the Cube selected, click the **Rotate** tab on the **Properties Panel**. Click the **Euler** radio button and enter **45** into the **Y** field to rotate the model.

11. Drag the Rod model into the choreography. Scale the model up by dragging the corner of the manipulator box that surrounds it. Click the **Rotate** tab on the **Properties Panel**. Enter *90* into the **X** field and *45* into the **Y** field. Position the Rod so that it passes through the center of the model.

12. Position the camera so that it is facing the model and render the image. The rod should be visible passing through the holes cut into the cube.

A project called *Boolean02.PRJ* is on the accompanying CD-ROM and contains a more complex example of a Boolean operation. When you perform a Boolean subtraction, it's a good idea to keep the materials on both the cutter and the surface being cut the same. This is because anywhere the cutter affects the model surface, the material on the cutter will appear. You can get some interesting effects by cutting models that are textured with woodgrain or other interesting patterns.

Experiment with different shapes and materials and see what develops. See what effects you can create by animating a cutter.

SUMMARY

Bone hierarchies are important to the way objects move. Observation and a little thought before you begin to add bones to a model can really make the entire process more efficient for you. Effectively adding bones to a model will become a little easier and less time-consuming with each model you work on. Keep in mind that you need to be consistent in naming and placing the bones in your model, both for reusability and for convenience for you and anyone else you may share data with.

Now that you have experience adding bones to models, the next chapter will describe what's involved in beginning to animate them through a scene. Making models move with both simple and complex path animation is covered. This will help you understand how you can control where your objects are traveling within a scene.

10 Path Animation

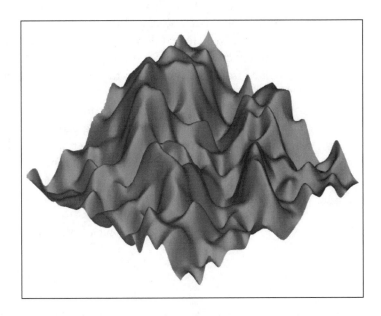

When you boil it down, a path is just a way of telling an object or figure where to go. You travel many paths every day. A trip from the
bedroom to the bathroom involves a path; getting into a car and
driving to work involves a path; even walking your dog involves a path. The
difference between real-life paths and those created on the computer is that
you don't necessarily think of the paths you travel as paths. True, you may consider directions to a particular place while you're driving, but it doesn't stick
out as a path.

Those paths that you create for characters, lights, and even the camera
to follow need some thought. Sometimes, the combination of the correct
path and camera target is used to provide fantastic cinematic effect. Other
times, moving lights may be used to create an eerie effect. On a more complex level, what about making an airplane do some aerobatic stunts? Or
making a vehicle travel along uneven terrain? All of these are accomplished
with effective path animation. The basis for understanding path animation
comes from understanding the movement of objects about the 3D world
you've created.

This chapter discusses what paths are and how they're used. There are several different techniques for creating path animations, from simple translations
to more advanced control of the direction in which a character is going.

This chapter covers the following topics:

- Creating a Simple Path
- Advanced Path Animation
- Controlling Animation along a Path

SIMPLE TRANSLATIONS FOR MOTION

The simplest paths that give you the least control are simple *translation-type
movements*. You create these by placing a model into a scene, changing the
frame number, and moving the model to where it should be at that frame.

There are a couple of drawbacks to this type of movement, however. The
biggest is lack of control for you. If you're unhappy with the movement a character has made, it is difficult to go back and correct the mistake, since there is
no visible path.

The following exercise uses a simple vase model that's already in a choreography to demonstrate simple translations.

EXERCISE

SIMPLE TRANSLATIONS

1. Open the *Simple Translation.PRJ* file from the accompanying CD-ROM. Right-click the **Choreography** name in the **Project Workspace** and select **Edit**. Press **Shift+Z** on the keyboard to zoom out to fit the entire scene in the window.

2. The project should now be open to a top view of a rather sparse choreography. In the top left-hand corner of the main window, there is a Vase object.

3. On the **Frame** toolbar, enter *15* into the **Current Frame** field.

4. Use the mouse to drag the Vase model to the upper right-hand corner of the screen.

5. Enter *30* into the **Current Frame** field.

6. Drag the Vase model to the lower right-hand corner of the main window.

7. Enter *45* into the **Current Frame** field.

8. Drag the vase back to its original position in the upper left-hand corner of the screen.

9. Enter *1* into the **Current Frame** field. Use the **Next Frame** button or the scrub bar to advance through the frames and watch what the vase does.

As you advance through the frames, the vase will move about the screen, ending up at the same position in which you placed it for each keyframe. Technically, you didn't create a path for the model to follow. You simply specified where in the window the vase should be at given frames. Notice that the model doesn't necessarily travel in straight lines as it moves from position to position. This is because the software simply interpolates between the positions you specified.

To reiterate the disadvantages of this, imagine that the vase needed to travel in a perfectly straight line. You would need to add quite a few more keyframes for that to happen. Although this is a simple example with only three keyframes, imagine a complex scene with several objects all moving about. You would have little or no idea where any of the objects would be at any given time, since there is no visible path that you can use to estimate.

Now that you've seen the disadvantages of animation with no paths, the next section will discuss the creation of a simple path, and how to get a character to follow along that path.

CREATING A SIMPLE PATH

This section discusses creating a simple path, and how to apply a model to that path. *Paths* are how you'll tell objects to move through scenes, much as a roller coaster follows a track. When many objects are present, paths can also give you precise control over the timing of movement and the interaction that occurs between objects. Once again, the Vase model will be used, simply for clarity.

EXERCISE

CREATING A SIMPLE PATH

1. Open the *Simple Path.PRJ* file from the accompanying CD-ROM. Right-click the **Choreography1** item in the **Project Workspace** and select **Edit**. Press **Shift+Z** to zoom the objects in the scene to fit.

2. Once again, the Project contains a top view of a sparse choreography. In the top left-hand corner of the main window is the Vase object.

3. Click on the **Add Mode** button. The mode of the main window will switch to **Modeler**, and you'll be allowed to add points to form a path. Adding points to a path is exactly like adding points when modeling, except the **Add Lock** mode is not available.

4. Add four control points to form a curved path, similar to the one shown in Figure 10.1. Notice as you add the points that the software automatically adds the "Path1" object in the choreography section of the **Project Workspace**.

5. To add a model to the path, you must use a path constraint. Click on the Vase model to return to **Directing Mode**, then right-click the model and select **New Constraint, Path**.

6. The pointer will change to a **Picker** tool, which can be used to specify different objects in a scene. Use it to click anywhere along the spline that forms the path created in step 4.

7. The vase should immediately jump to the beginning of the path. Use the **Next Frame** button to advance through several frames and watch as the vase travels along the path.

Modifying this type of path is very simple. All it requires is some manipulation of the existing control points.

8. Click on the path with the pointer, then click the **Modeler Mode** button. Shape the points that form the path into an S shape.

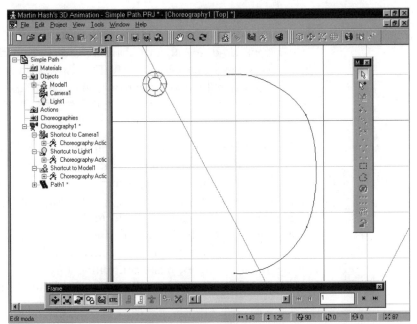

FIGURE
10.1
A simple, four-point, curved path.

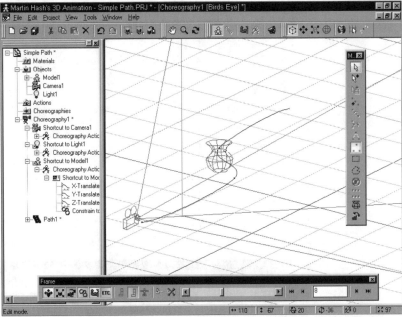

FIGURE
10.2
Bird's-eye view of the Vase model traveling along the newly modified path.

9. Press the spacebar to refresh the screen, and the Vase will jump to the new location at the beginning of the path. Change to a side view and drag any control point upward. Drag a different control point downward. From a Bird's Eye view, examine the Vase as you advance through the frames (see Figure 10.2).

One important thing to keep in mind is the location and orientation of a model's *default bone*. No matter what actions you take when building a model, there is always one bone assigned that is not visible, which controls how an object orients and travels a path. The bone is independent of the first bone that is automatically added to a model in **Bones Mode**.

Notice in Figure 10.3 how the vase seems to be sitting halfway through the path. Technically, this makes no difference, since the path will not render anyway. It can, however, make controlling an object's exact placement difficult. This offset is caused by the position of the hidden bone of the vase model.

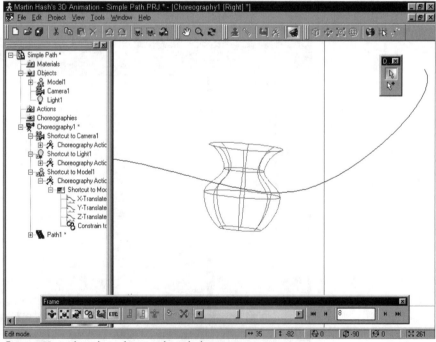

FIGURE *Notice how the path passes through the vase.*
10.3

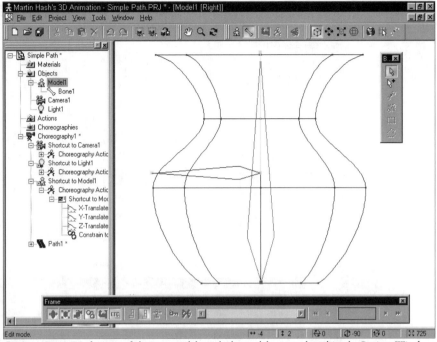

FIGURE   *Bones Mode view of the vase model, with the model name selected in the **Project Window.***
10.4   *A hidden bone becomes visible.*

The way to correct this problem is to look at the vase in **Bones Mode**. While you're in **Bones Mode**, clicking the model name in the **Project Workspace** will display the hidden bone, allowing you to edit its position and orientation. Figure 10.4 shows the position of the hidden bone in the vase model. The horizontal bone is the one that is normally hidden, and as you can see, the path travels through the model at this point. The bone was translated downward to the bottom of the vase, as shown in Figure 10.5. Don't worry if the bones in your models are not exactly like those in the images. The important thing is to recognize and be able to access the hidden bone.

The new position of the default bone now makes the vase sit on top of the path, as shown in Figure 10.6. This allows for much more precise control over the location of an object on a path.

Sometimes, a simple path is all that is required simply to cause an object to move a certain way. But what happens if the model isn't supposed to rotate with the curves in the path? There's an easy way to solve this problem: the **Translate Only** checkbox on the **Properties Panel**.

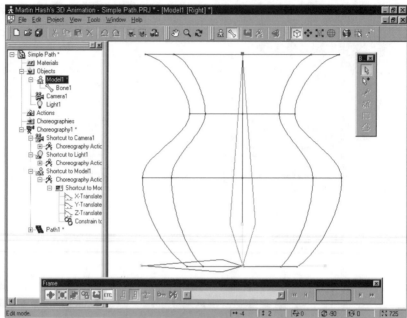

FIGURE **10.5** *The new location of the vase model's hidden bone.*

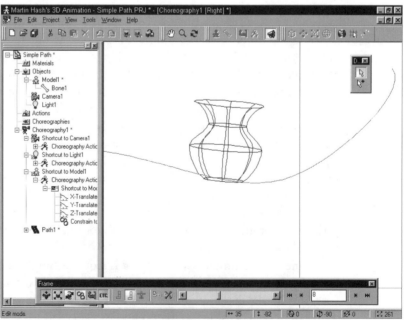

FIGURE **10.6** *The new position of the vase on top of the path.*

EXERCISE

TRANSLATE ONLY

1. Open the *Path Translation Only.PRJ* file from the accompanying CD-ROM.

2. Right-click the **Choreography1** item in the **Project Workspace** and select **Edit**. Press the **6** key on the numeric keypad to change to a side view, and press **Shift+Z** to zoom the objects in the scene to fit within the window.

3. Use the plus (**+**) and minus (**–**) keys on the numeric keypad to step through the frames. Notice what happens between frames 7 and 8. In following the path, the vase flips from the inside of the path to the outside.

4. Since the vase is not supposed to move along the path like a roller coaster (which would use an Aim Roll At constraint to correct the flipping), we need to specify that the vase is simply to follow this path and is not to take any of the rotational values from it. Expand the model item by clicking the plus (**+**) sign to the left of it in the **Project Workspace**. Continue by clicking the plus (**+**) to the left of the **Choreography Action**, then expand the **Action Channel Properties** by clicking the plus (**+**) to the left of the **Shortcut to Model1** item. Finally, Click on the **Constrain to Path** item in the **Project Workspace**.

5. On the **Properties Panel**, click in the checkbox along the right-hand side labeled **Translate Only**.

6. Use the plus (**+**) and minus (**–**) keys on the numeric keypad to step through the frames once again and observe the difference from step 3.

NOTE

While you step through the frames, you'll notice that as the vase travels along the path, it appears to pass through the path at several points. This is because the vase model is not using the rotational values from the path and is concerned only with keeping the end of the hidden bone on the path. If you observe the bottom end of the vase (keeping in mind the new location of the hidden bone from previous discussion), you'll see that it is acting correctly.

Now that you understand how objects travel along a path and how they behave while doing so, the next section will walk you through some advanced path animations. Although all path animation is essentially the same (specifying where an object should go), there are some techniques that will become invaluable as you gain experience telling your stories.

ADVANCED PATH ANIMATION

This section will walk you through two different considerations in creating path animations, traveling along a landscape, and moving between two paths. These techniques take advantage of the flexibility of Animation:Master's path definitions, as well as the capability of creating time-based constraints.

One common occurrence of the need for a path is a vehicle traveling along a landscape. No problem if the vehicle happens to be traveling along a stretch of desert highway where there are few bumps. However, as the terrain becomes less flat, the object gets more difficult to control.

EXERCISE

ADVANCED PATH ANIMATION EXAMPLE 1

1. Open the *Advanced Path1.PRJ* file from the accompanying CD-ROM. Right-click the **Choreography1** item in the **Project Workspace** and select **Edit**. Press **Shift+Z** to zoom the scene to fit within the window.

2. You should have a window open showing a top view of a choreography window with a wireframe grid, and a wireframe torus. When rendered, the grid looks similar to Figure 10.7.

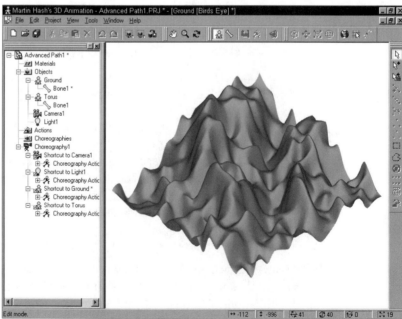

FIGURE *Rendering of the ground plane used in the Advanced Path1 project.*
10.7

Imagine trying to match a path for an object to follow along the surface of this model. Quite a daunting task for even an experienced user.

3. Select the torus model in the lower right-hand corner of the window by clicking on it with the mouse. With the object selected, right-click the torus model, and select **New Constraint, Path** from the available menu.

4. While holding down the **Shift** key, use the **Picker** to click on the 11th spline from the right on the ground plane. Using the **Shift** key with the **Picker** specifies the selection of a spline that is to be designated as a path.

5. Click on the path constraint in the **Project Workspace**. On the **Properties Panel**, locate the **Ease** field. More comprehensive use of Ease will be covered later in this chapter. For now, click in the field and press **Enter** to enter zero into the Ease channel [you'll see a plus (**+**) appear next to the path constraint in the **Project Workspace**].

6. On the **Frame** toolbar, enter *60* into the **Current Frame** field.

7. Enter *100* into the **Ease** field on the **Properties Panel** and press **Enter**.

8. Enter *1* into the **Current Frame** field on the **Frame** toolbar. Use the plus (**+**) and minus (**–**) keys to step through the frames and watch the torus travel along the surface of the ground plane. You may want to use the **Turn** tool to provide a better view.

The file *Advanced Path1.mov,* on the accompanying CD-ROM, is a rendered QuickTime movie of the path animation that was just created. The looks of the animation would be well served by adding shadows to the rendered version, which would help to attach the torus to the ground plane. As is, it serves as an adequate example of this type of path animation.

The next example shows how an object can be made to travel between two paths, using time-based path constraints. Although not as common an occurrence as the previous example, this type of path animation may well come in handy throughout the course of your storytelling.

What if the torus from the previous example was required to jump from one path to another? The next example will demonstrate how this task could be accomplished using two paths, and manipulating the path constraint enforcement as the torus moves between the two paths.

EXERCISE

ADVANCED PATH ANIMATION EXAMPLE 2

1. Open the *Advanced Path2.PRJ* file from the accompanying CD-ROM. Right-click the **Choreography1** item in the **Project Workspace** and select **Edit**. Press the **2** key on the numeric keypad to change to a front view, then press **Shift+Z** to zoom the objects to fit within the window.

2. You should now be looking at a **Choreography** window that shows two curved paths and a wireframe torus. The torus has already been constrained to the path on the left for you.

3. Click the torus model to select it. With the torus selected, right-click the model and select **Path** from the **New Constraint** option that appears. Use the picker to click on the path on the right of the screen.

4. You will notice that the torus jumps partway along the first path. This point is an average of the two path constraints, because you haven't yet adjusted the enforcement. Select the first constraint in the **Project Workspace** by clicking on it. Click in the **Ease** field on the **Properties Panel** and press **Enter** to create a channel for this constraint.

5. Click on the second constraint in the **Project Workspace** to select it. On the **Properties Panel**, enter *0* into the **Enforce** field. This will cause the software to enforce the second constraint 0% (or not at all) at this point in the animation.

6. Enter *15* into the **Current Frame** field on the **Frame** toolbar.

7. Select the first constraint by clicking on it in the **Project Workspace**. On the **Properties Panel**, enter *100* into the **Ease** field and press **Enter**. Enter *100* into the **Enforce** field and press **Enter** to create a channel for the enforcement of the path constraint.

8. Select the second constraint by clicking on it in the **Project Workspace**. Enter *0* into both the **Enforce** and the **Ease** fields, pressing **Enter** after each to enter the data into the paths channel.

9. Enter *16* into the **Current Frame** field on the **Frame** toolbar.

10. Select the first constraint by clicking on it in the **Project Workspace**. Enter *0* into both the **Enforce** and the **Ease** fields, pressing **Enter** after each to enter the data into the paths channel.

11. Select the second constraint by clicking on it in the **Project Workspace**. On the **Properties Panel**, enter *0* into the **Ease** field

and *100* into the **Enforce** field, pressing **Enter** after each entry to enter the data into the appropriate channel.

12. Enter *30* into the **Current Frame** field on the **Frame** toolbar.

13. Select the second constraint if it is not already selected. Enter *100* into the **Ease** field and press **Enter**.

Use the plus (**+**) and minus (**–**) keys on the numeric keypad to step through the frames and watch what happens to the torus. The Ease channel was used to make the torus travel along the paths, and the Enforcement of the path constraints was used to change the influence of each path as needed. As the torus travels along the first path, the second constraint has no influence on it. At frame 16, where the torus changes from the first to the second path, the Enforcement of the first constraint is set to 0 (no influence), and the second constraint is raised to 100. The file *Advanced Path2.mov* is a rendered QuickTime movie of this example.

The path-type constraint allows you the flexibility of making many paths and having control over where the object is at any given time. One way to control object location precisely is to use the *path constraint channels*, which are described in the next section.

CONTROLLING ANIMATION ALONG A PATH

In the previous exercise, you worked with channels to control an object's position and the influence of a constraint over time. Almost everything you do in Animation:Master uses channels that the software builds for you automatically as you work. Different channels have different options, but in the end, they all narrow down to two things: a frame number and a value.

The channel that's used most often is called *Ease*. Ease controls where on a path a character or object is located at any given frame. The movement along a path that is controlled with Ease is completely independent of any other actions that you might apply to a character.

USING EASE

In real life, very few objects, if any, move at a constant rate of speed. Consider the motion of touching the tip of your nose with your fingertip. The motion starts slow, then speeds up as your arm travels the distance. Then you slow down again as you near your nose, and stop when you've attained your goal. This change in speeds is exactly what Ease is for.

The following exercise provides some practice in using the Ease channel.

EXERCISE

USING THE EASE CHANNEL

1. Open the *Ease.PRJ* file from the accompanying CD-ROM. Right-click the **Choreography1** item in the **Project Workspace** and select **Edit** from the available menu. Press **Shift+Z** to zoom the scene to fit within the window. The project is now open to a top view of a window containing a single, four-point path with a vase constrained to it.

2. Click the plus (**+**) sign to the left of the **Choreography1** item in the **Project Workspace**. Expand the tree further by clicking the plus (**+**) to the left of the **Shortcut to Vase** item. Continue expanding the vase's tree by clicking the plus signs that appear to the left of the items in the list. Once you've expanded the tree all the way, you can begin working with Ease by clicking the path constraint item in the **Project Workspace**.

3. Since the Ease channel simply specifies a value (percent of the path that has been traveled) at a given frame, you simply need to determine where along a path your model should be at any given time. You must begin the Ease channel by clicking in the **Ease** field on the **Properties Panel** and pressing **Enter**. Click the plus (**+**) that appears next to the constraint in the **Project Workspace**. A channel tree will expand (with only one branch in this case), with a description of the channels available to you (Ease).

4. Traveling a path linearly is simple. The object is 0% of the way along the path at frame 1, and 100% along the path at the end frame of the animation. For nonlinear motion, you can use varying values. Advance to frame 10 and enter *5* into the **Ease** field on the **Properties Panel**.

5. Advance to frame 25 and enter *80* into the **Ease** field.

6. Advance to frame 40 and enter *100* into the **Ease** field.

7. Return to frame 1 and step through the frames with either the scrub bar or the plus (**+**) and minus (**−**) keys. You will see that the object starts traveling the path by going backward a bit, then slowly forward, speeding up along the middle of the path and slowing down as it reaches the end of the path.

8. To see the channel that was generated, right-click the **Ease** item in the path constraint tree and select **Edit**.

9. A graph will open with frames across the bottom and a scale up and down the left side. You'll notice control points on the grid where you specified them (frames 1,10, 25, and 40) with a spline running through each point.

NOTE

Splines within a channel window can be manipulated and edited manually for precise data entry when necessary. The curvature of a channel's splines can affect an object's motion, as it does here to the vase if you look closely.

10. While stepping through the first few frames, you'll notice that the vase wavers along the path before it heads in a continuous direction. Looking at the Ease channel spline, you should see that the curvature of the spline between the control points at frames 1 and 10 causes the vase to travel backward slightly before advancing. Figure 10.8 shows a full-screen view of the channels window for reference.

There are two different ways to correct the wavering of the vase, both of which require making adjustments to the spline in the channels window.

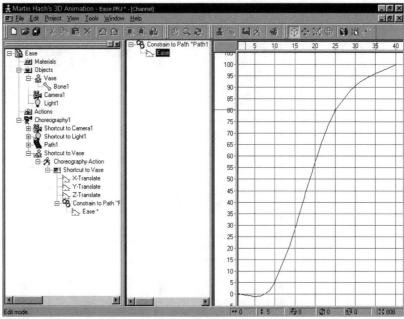

FIGURE   *Full-screen view of the Ease channel created in this exercise.*
10.8

11. The first method for correcting this problem is to select the offending control point by clicking on it, then make the appropriate changes on the **Properties Panel**. For this spline, select the **Linear Interpolation** radio button and make adjustments to the handles on the control point until the path runs smoothly in a straight line between the control points.

12. The second method of correcting this problem would be to select the Ease channel in the **Project Workspace** by clicking on it, then select the appropriate interpolation type on the **Properties Panel**. This method affects the entire channel, so it's effective for making changes to large channels that would otherwise be too tedious.

NOTE

This description of how to control the movement of an object on a path using an Ease channel is rather limited, because it takes some practice and experience to understand how the graph affects the motion of a model along the path.

Keep in mind that you can adjust control points up a little to get the curve out of the negative area of the graph if need be. Another way is to adjust the Magnitude on the control point at frame 10 to again move the spline out of the negative area.

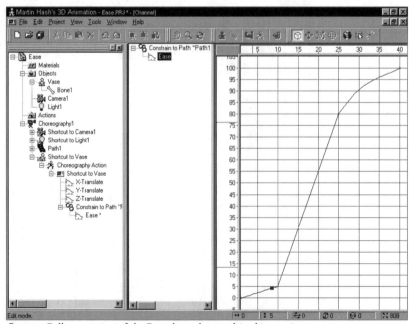

FIGURE   *Full-screen view of the Ease channel created in this exercise.*

10.9

A spline adjusted similarly to the one shown in Figure 10.9 will correct the problem with the vase in this exercise.

From the preceding examples, you can see how channels add a powerful tool for making characters and objects move about a choreography. Getting the motion to look just right will take a little practice. The more time you spend experimenting with the channels, the easier they will become to use, and the more efficient and effective you'll become with them.

SUMMARY

Path animation is a crucial ingredient in effective character animation. As you've seen, there are several different methods that you can use in creating paths for your characters and the other objects in a scene to travel. Be creative, and don't be afraid to experiment.

Now that you've learned how to make an object travel along a path, the next chapter describes how to make some individual actions for your characters. There are two main types of motion used in character animation: skeletal and muscle. Both are described in the next chapter.

11

Creating Actions

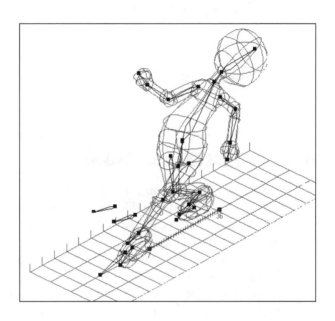

The world is energetic and powerful. Everywhere you look, there's activity, movement, action. Actions bring to life your models. With motion libraries, lip-synch, and skeletal and muscle motion, creating actions for your models has never been easier. You can create any action you can imagine.

This chapter discusses what skeletal and muscle motion are, as well as how poses, dopesheets, and the different types of motion all work together. It also discusses keyframing techniques for both skeletal and muscle motion, squash and stretch with both skeletal and muscle motion, poses, lip-synch, motion libraries, and rotoscoping actions.

This chapter covers the following topics:

- Creating Skeletal Actions
- Creating Muscle Actions
- Creating Poses
- Lip-Synch
- Motion Libraries

CREATING SKELETAL ACTIONS

Skeletal actions make up a huge amount of the animation you will likely be doing for your characters. Skeletal-type motions include walking, running, sitting, and so on. Almost any motion that requires the movement of a limb is done with skeletal motion.

Creating skeletal motions essentially boils down to moving to a particular frame and positioning a character's bones where you want them to be at that frame. The software will then interpolate linearly between these keyframes. Much of the nuance of motion won't be obvious when you first start animating, because subtleties aren't accounted for in the interpolation between keyframes. Rather, you would start with a basic walk cycle, then go back and tweak the action to suit your character's needs. The following exercise describes how to create a simple walk cycle for the Thom model.

EXERCISE

CREATING A SIMPLE WALK CYCLE

1. Open the *Walk Cycle.PRJ* file from the accompanying CD-ROM.

2. This project currently contains the Thom model. Right-click the **Actions** folder in the **Project Workspace**, and select **New Action**. A window will open in **Skeletal** mode that contains the model.

3. Right-click the **Action1** item that appears beneath the **Action** folder and select **Save As** from the pop-up menu that appears. Type **Walk** as the filename and press **Enter**.

4. A good technique to use when creating actions is to open two **Action** windows, with two different views of the model. To do this, click the title bar of the **Action** window you just opened to activate it, then select **New Window** from the **Window** menu. A second **Action** window will appear.

5. Select **Tile Vertically** from the **Window** menu to set the two windows side by side. Click on the left-hand window and press **Shift+Z** to zoom the model to fit the window.

6. Click the right-hand window and press **6** on the numeric keypad to switch to a side view. Press **Shift+Z** to zoom the model to fit within this view.

7. If it isn't already visible, open the **Frame** toolbar. The screen should look similar to Figure 11.1.

8. Using Figure 11.2 for reference, position the Thom model to begin the walk cycle. Make sure the **Current Frame** field on the **Frame**

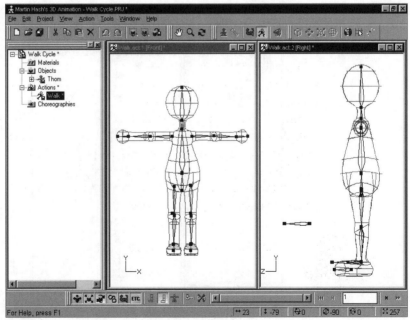

FIGURE *The screen layout used to create a walk cycle.*
11.1

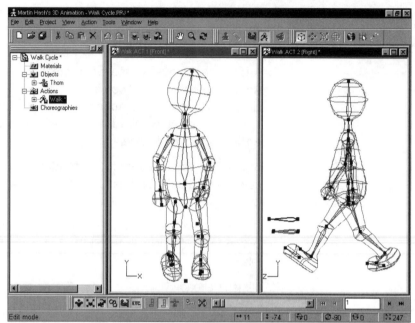

FIGURE
11.2
The screen layout used to create a walk cycle.

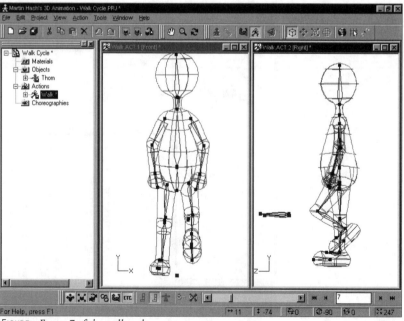

FIGURE
11.3
Frame 7 of the walk cycle.

toolbar is set to 1. Use the mouse to select bones and drag them into position. The right foot should be forward, as is the left arm.

9. Advance to frame 7 with the plus (**+**) key on the numeric keypad and position the model similarly to Figure 11.3.

10. Advance to frame 15 with the plus (**+**) key on the numeric keypad and position the model similarly to Figure 11.4.

11. Advance to frame 24 with the plus (**+**) key on the numeric key pad and position the model similarly to Figure 11.5.

12. Type *1* into the **Current Frame** field to return to the first frame of the action.

13. Select **Copy Keyframe** from the **Edit** menu. Type *30* into the **Current Frame** field and select **Paste Keyframe** from the **Edit** menu.

Because the walk cycle is a loop, steps 12 and 13 copy the first frame of the action to the last. This ensures that the model is in the same position at the end of the cycle as it was at the beginning, which keeps the motion smooth. Since the action is 30 frames long, you'll need to render 29 frames or use the Overlap feature on multiple occurrences of the action to avoid a stutter or delay when frame

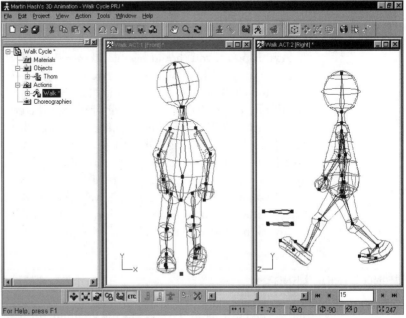

FIGURE *Frame 15 of the walk cycle.*

11.4

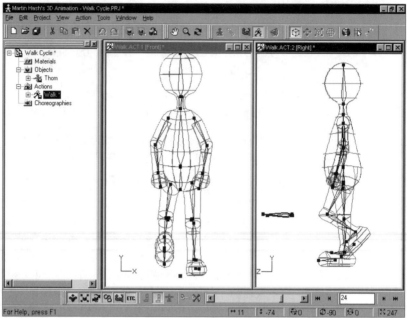

> 30 from the first action, then frame 30 from the second action are
> played in succession.

At this point, you should be able to step through the frames with the plus
(+) and minus (–) keys on the numeric keypad, or use the scrub bar to view
your action. It should look something like a walk. Notice how A:M automatically fills in, or "'tweens," the positions between the keys that you set at frames
1, 7, 15, and 24. To experiment, go back and see where you think the motion
could use a little tweaking. One place to start working with is the feet, which
could be made to bend as the foot comes down. Another place to experiment
would be to accent the bounce in the walk.

Now that you've created a simple walk action, you need a way to keep the
character's feet from slipping as he travels a path. The next section describes
how to do this with a tool called **Stride Length**.

USING STRIDE LENGTH

One of the most daunting tasks facing an animator is to prevent foot slippage,
which causes the character to appear to skate as it travels along a path. This

problem can be compounded by the fact that after everything is in place and ready to go, a slight change in the length of the path the character is traveling could throw everything off.

Animation:Master has a special tool called **Stride Length** for just this problem. **Stride Length** allows you to define the length of a character's step, then saves that information with the action cycle. When you place the character on a path, the software now knows how far the character will go in one cycle of the action, regardless of the path length. This makes it very easy to control or minimize skating. The following exercise walks you through setting up **Stride Length** on an action for the Thom character.

EXERCISE

STRIDE LENGTH

1. Open the *Stride Length.PRJ* file from the accompanying CD-ROM. If a **Choreography** window doesn't open, right-click the **Choreography1** item in the **Project Workspace** and select **Edit** from the available menu. Press the **1** key on the numeric keypad to change to a camera view.

2. From the camera view, you should see the Thom model on a path. Step through the frames and notice how his feet slide as he moves along the path.

3. Right-click the **Sneak** item in the **Actions** section of the **Project Workspace** and select **Edit** from the available menu. Maximize the **Action** window, and press **Shift+Z** for a clearer view of the model. As you can see, this window contains Thom with the sneak action applied. The screen should look similar to Figure 11.6.

4. In the **Actions** section of the **Project Workspace**, right-click the **Sneak** item and select **Properties** to display the **Properties Panel**. To begin adding **Stride Length** to this action, you first must tell the software that you want to use it. Do this by clicking in the **Has Stride Length** checkbox on the **Properties Panel**. A ruler will appear along the bottom of the character, with numbers at each end that represent the length of the character's stride in frames. If no stride has been set, as is the case here, the ruler may appear as a single point with a number below it.

5. Use the plus (**+**) key on the numeric keypad to start stepping through the frames slowly until the front foot of the character touches the ground (frame 7). This is where Thom's stride begins.

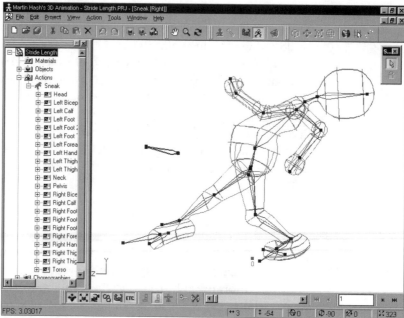

FIGURE   *A **Skeletal Mode** window that contains the Thom figure with the Sneak action*
11.6   *applied. **Skeletal Mode** is where Stride Length is applied to an action.*

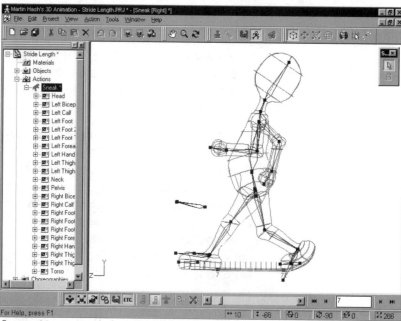

FIGURE   *Measure out the beginning of the stride where the character's foot first touches the*
11.7   *ground.*

6. Use the mouse to drag the front end of the ruler beneath the character's leg. Try to find some reference point with which you can align the ruler to make setting the stride easier. In this case, the ruler was aligned just about in the lower corner of the heel. Figure 11.7 shows the character and ruler positions for reference. Enter 7 into the **Start** field on the **Properties Panel**.

7. Continue to step through the frames until just before the character lifts the same foot off the ground, roughly around frame 36. Use the mouse to drag the back end of the ruler to beneath the same reference point used for the front of the ruler. It isn't always possible to line them up in a straight line, so estimate if necessary.

8. Enter the current frame number (36) into the **End** field on the **Properties Panel**. This tells the software that Thom's step begins on frame 7 and ends on frame 36. The **Length** field automatically calculates and displays the length of the step in centimeters. Figure 11.8 shows the approximate position of the character and the ruler on frame 36.

9. Use the **Turn** tool to rotate the view to a bird's eye view of the model. Notice the reference ground plane beneath the character's

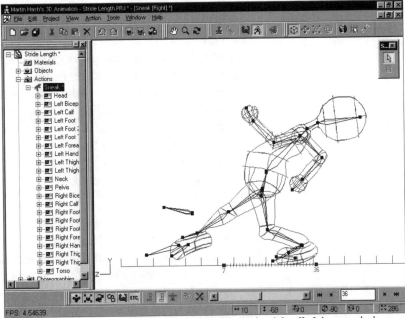

FIGURE
11.8
Measure out the entire step until just before the foot lifts off of the ground, then use the mouse to drag the back of the ruler into position.

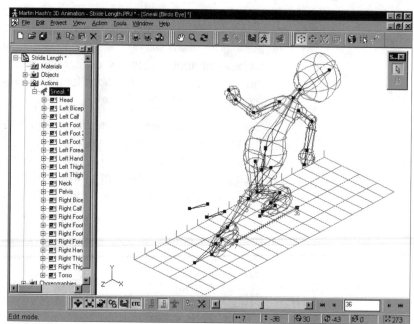

FIGURE *The reference plane beneath the character helps you judge ground speed.*
11.9

feet (Figure 11.9). As you step through the frames, this reference plane moves at the speed the character will travel when placed on a path.

The reference plane can be used from a bird's-eye or side view effectively to make any small adjustments necessary to minimize any remaining foot slippage. Pick a spot or a reference post nearest to a reference point on the character's foot, and watch both as you step through the frames. If the character's foot gets out of line with the reference point on the plane, make small adjustments to the ruler to fix them. Most often, it doesn't have to be exact to work. Getting close will likely stop any noticeable slipping that might occur.

10. Change back to the **Choreography** window. Click the **Shortcut to Sneak [1-72]** item in the **Choreography** section of the **Project Workspace**. This is the shortcut to the action that is applied to the character. In the **How to Execute** section of the **Properties Panel**, click on the **Use Stride Length** checkbox.

11. Step through the frames and notice that the character's feet no longer slide.

Two QuickTime movies are included on the CD-ROM, one called *Stride Length OFF.MOV* and another called *Stride Length ON.MOV*. These two movies illustrate the difference before and after the addition of **Stride Length** to a character.

The first time you stepped through the frames in this project, the software had no instructions to use in helping the character take enough steps to travel the path without his feet slipping. Therefore, Thom simply took one step every 36 frames or so, with no regard for the length of the path.

However, the second time through, Thom was instructed to take one step every 64.52 centimeters he traveled, resulting in many more steps. The path in this case was about 400 centimeters long, resulting in a need for roughly six steps.

There are two major benefits of using **Stride Length**. The first is that you only have to create and work with one walk cycle. You don't have to try to add and loop one walk action enough times to keep the feet from slipping. This means that no matter how long a choreography is, a simple change to the **End** value for the **Shortcut to Sneak Properties** will automatically adjust the length of the action.

The second advantage comes when the length of the path is changed (go ahead, try it!). Thom automatically adjusts the number of steps he takes to match the length of the path.

Now that you have a little background on how to make objects move with Skeletal actions, the next section describes how to squash and stretch an object using only Skeletal Mode.

SKELETAL SQUASH AND STRETCH

Squash and stretch is a very commonly used animation technique. It can help to add personality to an inanimate object, or to emphasize motions such as the bouncing of a ball. Squash and stretch can be performed easily as a skeletal action and can really add some life to your characters. The following exercise describes the creation of a skeletal action that uses squash and stretch.

EXERCISE

SKELETAL SQUASH AND STRETCH

1. Open the *Cereal Box.PRJ* file from the accompanying CD-ROM. The project will open with a front view of both a **Choreography** window and an **Action** window. This project uses an imaginary box of Dust Bunnies cereal from the MH3D company to illustrate squash and stretch technique.

2. Maximize the **Action** window. You can easily accomplish squash and stretch via skeletal motion if you work with the patriarch bone. This is because any translation or scaling changes you make to the patriarch will affect the other bones in the hierarchy.

3. Switch to a side view by pressing the **6** key on the numeric keypad. In the cereal box model, the horizontal bone at the bottom of the box is the patriarch. Click the patriarch bone to select it.

4. Enter *5* into the **Current Frame** field. On the **Translate** tab of the **Properties Panel**, enter *500* into the **Y** field. This will cause the entire model to move upward along the Y axis.

5. Enter *10* into the **Current Frame** field. Enter *0* into the **Y Translate** field. The box should now be resting back in its original position.

6. Step through the frames and notice the action on the box. The movement is very linear and mechanical. You can alter this by adjusting the **Y Translate Channel** item. Right-click the **Y Translate** item beneath the **Bounce** item in the **Project Workspace** and select

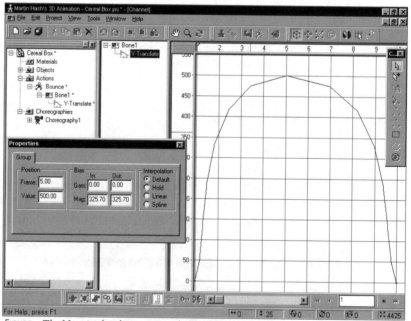

FIGURE *The Magnitude adjustment to the motion graph to flatten the curve somewhat. The*
11.10 *Magnitude for the center point was adjusted to 325.70.*

Edit. A channel window will open showing the motion you just created for the box.

7. Click on the point at the top of the motion curve (frame 5). Adjust the Magnitude of this point to flatten out the curve somewhat, similar to what is shown in Figure 11.10.

Step through the frames of the action once again and notice the changes that took place in the motion. The box now jumps up into the air very quickly, then hangs there for a moment before coming back down. Now that the jump is in place, the next few steps will describe how to make the box squash when it hits the ground.

8. From a side view, select the patriarch bone by clicking on it. Enter 1 into the **Current Frame** field. On the **Scale** tab of the **Properties Panel**, enter *70* into the **Y** field, and *130%* into both the **X** and **Z** fields. This will keep the volume of the box roughly the same, while changing the dimensions somewhat.

9. Enter *2* into the **Current Frame** field. Set the **X**, **Y**, and **Z Scale** fields to *100*. This will make the box appear to snap back to original shape as it leaves the ground.

10. Since the box appears to leap into the air a little quickly, right-click the **Y Translate** item in the **Project Workspace**. Click the **Add** button and click on the spline between the first and second control points. A new control point will be inserted into the graph. With the new control point selected, enter *2* into the **Frame** field on the **Properties Panel**, and *0* into the **Value** field. Enter *0* into both the **Mag In** and **Mag Out** fields to make the curve peak.

11. Click the **Add** button once again, and click on the spline in the graph near frame 8. This will add a new control point to the opposite side of the graph. With the new control point selected, enter *9* into the **Frame** field on the **Properties Panel**, and *0* into the **Value** field. Enter *0* into both the **Mag In** and **Mag Out** fields to make the curve peak. Figure 11.11 shows the shape of the curve at this point.

12. Enter *10* into the **Current Frame** field. From a side view, click on the patriarch bone. On the **Properties Panel**, enter **70** into the **Y Scale** field, and *130* into both the **X** and **Z** fields.

13. Enter *9* into the **Current Frame** field and set the **X**, **Y**, and **Z Scale** to *100*.

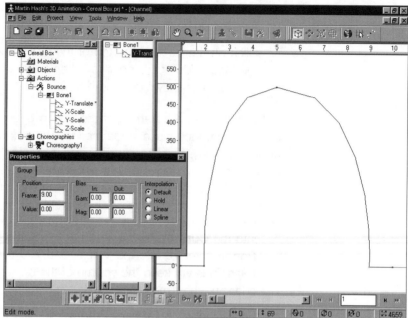

FIGURE *The horseshoe shape of the motion graph for the squashing of the cereal box as it*
11.11 *hits the ground.*

This would be a good time to do a test render and see what effect these changes have had on the box. The channel settings have made the box appear squashed as it sits on the ground, then leap into the air, hang there for a moment, and fall back to the ground where it squashes once again. *Squash.mov* on the accompanying CD-ROM is a wireframe render of the action after step 13. The next few steps describe how to make the model stretch as it leaps into the air.

14. From a side view, select the patriarch bone by clicking on it. Enter *3* into the **Current Frame** field. At this point, the model has left the ground and is on the way up. On the **Scale** tab of the **Properties Panel**, enter *105* into the **Y Scale** field and *95* into both the **X** and **Z** fields.

15. Enter *5* into the **Current Frame** field. This is the apex of the jump. Enter *100* into the **X**, **Y**, and **Z Scale** fields on the **Properties Panel**.

16. Enter *8* into the **Current Frame** field. This part of the action is the downside of the leap. Enter *105* into the **Y Scale** field and *95* into both the **X** and **Z** fields.

If you take the time to render after step 16, you'll now see the motion of the box, with a squash when the box hits the ground, and a stretch as it leaps into the air. The QuickTime movie *Stretch.mov* on the accompanying CD-ROM is a wireframe render of the action to this point. The main part of the squash and stretch action is done, but the action can be made more interesting by adding a second leap. The next few steps will describe how to do this.

17. From a side view, select the patriarch. Enter *1* into the **Current Frame** field and select **Copy Keyframe** from the **Edit** menu. Enter *11* into the **Current Frame** field and select **Paste Keyframe** from the **Edit** menu.

18. Continue creating the second leap for the box by copying frame 2 to frame 12, 3 to 13, 5 to 15, 8 to 18, 9 to 19, and 10 to 20. The box will now leap twice over a period of 20 frames.

19. To make the cereal box bounce from side to side as it jumps, enter *10* into the **Current Frame** field, then set the **X Translate** value on the **Properties Panel** to *150.* Set the **X Translate** to *0* on frame 20.

20. Step through the frames and notice that the box appears to drag on the ground as it leaps into the air. You can correct this by editing the **X Translate Channel** item in the **Project Workspace**. Adjust the **Magnitude** of the center point (frame 10) to smooth the curve.

21. Add four points to the graph at frames 2, 9, 12, and 19. Set the value for the points at frames 2 and 19 to *0,* and *150* for the points at frames 9 and 12. Set the **Mag In** and **Mag Out** values to *0* for all four points. You should now have a graph that is flat on top and curved down the sides.

22. To complete the action, add two more control points to the graph, at frames 5 and 15. Set the value for both points to *50.* Smooth the sides of the curve by entering *100* into the **Mag In** and **Mag Out** values for both points. The graph should look similar to the one shown in Figure 11.12.

23. Render the animation to see the results.

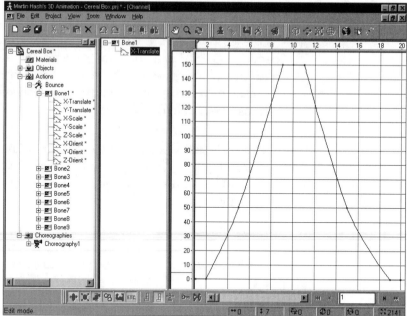

FIGURE   *The final look of the X-Translate Channel.*
11.12

Skeletal actions make it easy to add life to inanimate objects, or to make a character walk and interact with its environment. Another type of motion that is commonly used is called *Muscle motion*. Muscle motion lets you change the location of a model's control points over time. Combined with Skeletal actions, Muscle motions can really bring your characters to life. The next section describes how to create Muscle actions.

CREATING MUSCLE ACTIONS

Muscle actions are the true beauty of quality character animation. A nice walk cycle draws an interested stare, but showing emotion really makes the character seem alive and believable.

The movements of the individual control points that make up a model are called *Muscle motion*. Muscle motion is very powerful and, because of the spline-based nature of the software, rather easy to create. Making them look good, however, takes time, patience, and practice.

The next exercise will describe how to add a simple muscle motion to make a Mask model smile.

EXERCISE

CREATING A SIMPLE MUSCLE MOTION

1. Open the *Smile.PRJ* file from the accompanying CD-ROM.

2. This project currently contains the Mask model. Right-click the **Actions** folder in the **Project Workspace** and select New Action. A window will open in **Skeletal** mode that contains the model.

3. Click the **Action1** item that appears beneath the **Action** folder and press the **F2** key to rename the item. Type *Smile* and press **Enter**.

4. Click the **Muscle Mode** button to change from a **Skeletal Mode**. All of the control points that make up the model will become visible.

5. Use the **Group** tool to select the points at the corners of the mouth.

6. Advance to frame 10 on the **Frame** toolbar and drag the corners of the mouth upward, as shown in Figure 11.13.

   Use the plus (**+**) or minus (**–**) keys on the numeric keypad or the scrub bar to advance through the frames and check out your handiwork — a simple smile created entirely with muscle motion. As with skeletal motions, keyframes for muscle motion are created at any frame where a control point is moved.

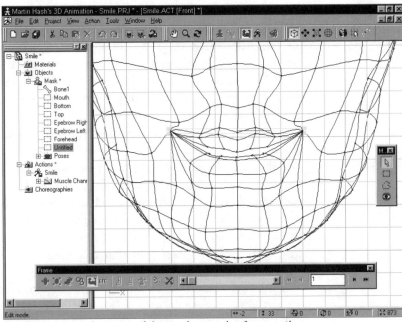

FIGURE *Dragging the corners of the mouth upward to form a smile.*
11.13

If you come across a situation where a keyframe is needed and no points have been moved, click the **Key** button on the **Frame** toolbar. In the smile example, points were only moved on frame 10, so the software interpolates between the default location of the control points and the keyframe that was created.

Although the previous exercise was very easy, it did demonstrate simple muscle motion. Obviously, most muscle actions are going to be more complex than a simple smile. For complex muscle actions, it is best to work with named groups on a model. The next section discusses naming groups and using them in muscle actions.

NAMING GROUPS

Naming groups on the surface of a model makes it fast and easy to select control points to work with. Examine the list of named groups associated with the *Smile.PRJ* model (they're listed in the **Model** section of the **Project Workspace**).

The entire mouth, upper lip, lower lip, left eyebrow, right eyebrow, and forehead were already named. You could add several more with groups for the cheeks, eyes, and possibly nostrils.

With named groups in place, you can simply go to the frame you want to work on, click the named group in the **Project Workspace**, and make any necessary changes. Take a moment and select a few of the named groups in the **Project Workspace** to see how the control points in a group become selected. If necessary, you can select multiple groups by holding down the **Shift** key while you click the group names.

As your experience grows, the real benefit of working with named groups will start to show. The little movement of facial muscles while a character studies an object, the raising of eyebrows in curiosity, or the furrowing of a brow in frustration all add to the personality of a character. A useful technique to aid in facial expressions or motions is to purchase a small mirror (preferably one that does not cause a distorted reflection and can stand on its own), and keep it near your computer. When your character is angry, make an angry face in the mirror and study it. When your character speaks, look in the mirror and say the lines, watching your entire face (not just the mouth).

If you prefer not to sit at your desk staring into a mirror, consider a book such as *Cartooning the Head and Figure* by Jack Hamm. This book includes 150 facial expressions, as well as a detailed description of the facial muscles and how they affect your face.

The next section describes how you can use Poses to save individual facial expressions and use them in an action at a later time.

POSES

A big part of facial animation is the expression of emotions. Many times, it is necessary to exaggerate these expressions on digital characters so that a viewer can read them faster. One of the tools in place in Animation:Master that can help you quickly create and utilize expressions is *Poses*. The next section walks you through the creation of some expressions, as well as how to use them in an action.

CREATING POSES

Poses are essentially one-frame "actions" that can be used to define skeletal motion, muscle motion, constraints, or any combination of the three. Poses can be used as a powerful animation tool, since you can create and save them individually, then drag and drop them into a larger action to create keyframes.

When used properly, Poses can become a big weapon in your character animation arsenal. These one-frame actions can be called up and utilized very quickly. Under certain conditions, they can even be used from character to character.

One use for Poses could be the creation of single-frame facial expressions, which, when needed, could simply be dropped into place in an action. The next exercise describes how to create Poses and drop them into an action.

EXERCISE

CREATING EMOTION POSES

1. Continue working with the *Smile.PRJ* file from the previous exercise on Creating a Simple Muscle Motion. If an existing action has been applied to the model, remove it by clicking on the action name in the **Project Workspace** and pressing the **Delete** key.

2. Right-click the **Mask** item in the **Objects** section of the **Project Workspace**. Select **New**, then **Pose** from the available menus. A **Poses** folder will appear within the **Models** folder. Poses are

always stored with a model to make them easy to use and locate when animating.

3. Click the **Pose1** item in the **Project Workspace**, then press the **F2** key to edit the item name. Type *Angry* and press **Enter**.

4. Because this pose will be constructed of just muscle motion, click the **Muscle Mode** button on the **Mode** toolbar.

5. Adjust the control points of the model to create an angry look. Try lowering the brow, squinting the eyes, lowering the corners of the mouth slightly, and lifting the outside corners of the eyes up slightly. Figure 11.14 shows the control points in a decent-looking "angry" position.

6. To create another new Pose, right-click the **Poses** folder and select **New Pose** from the available menu.

7. Click the **Pose1** item in the **Project Workspace** and press the **F2** key. Type *Happy* and press **Enter**.

8. Each Pose is independent of the others, and when a new Pose is created, there is no reference to the previous one. Notice that the

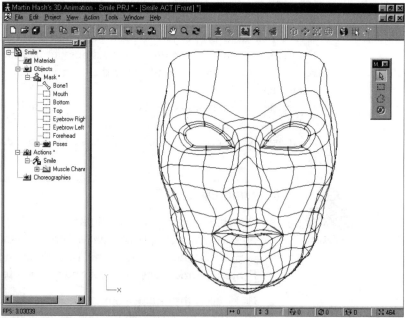

FIGURE *The face adjusted to look angry.*
11.14

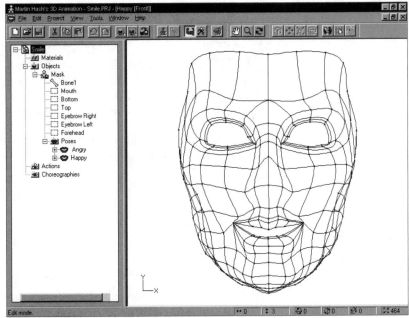

FIGURE   *The face in a happy pose.*

11.15

New Pose window opens in **Skeletal Mode**. Click the **Muscle Mode** button on the **Mode** toolbar.

9. Raise the corners of the mouth into a smile, separate the lips a bit, lift the brow up, widen the eyes, and lower the outside corners of the eyes. Figure 11.15 shows the Happy Pose.

NOTE

If you want to make any adjustments to an existing Pose, right-click the Pose name in the **Project Workspace** and select **Edit** from the available menu. A **Pose** window will open to allow you to make modifications. To save the changes to the Pose, save the model.

10. Now that you've created both the Angry and Happy Poses, you can easily drop them into an action to make the face go from happy to angry. Right-click the **Actions** folder, and select **New Action** from the pop-up menu.

11. To use a Pose in an action, all you need to do is drag the Pose from the **Project Workspace** and drop it on the model in the **Action** window. With the **Current Frame** field set to *1,* drag the Happy Pose onto the model and drop it. The model will change to reflect the Pose.

12. Enter *15* into the **Current Frame** field and drag the Angry Pose onto the model. Once again, the model will change to reflect the Pose.

Use the plus (**+**) and minus (**–**) keys on the numeric keypad to step through the frames and watch as the expression on the face of the model changes. You can see from this example how easily you can create Poses and use them to animate with.

Now that you've become familiar with how both Muscle motion and Poses are created and utilized, the next section will describe how to combine the two to do lip-synch.

LIP-SYNCH

The unique capabilities of Muscle Poses offers a fantastic opportunity for fast, efficient *lip-synching*. For obvious reasons, lip-synching is immensely

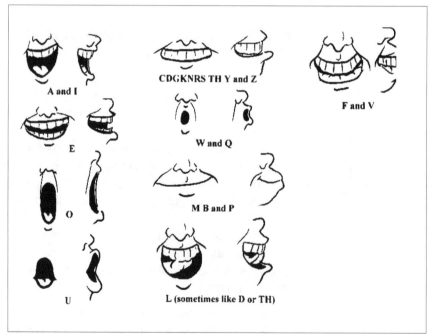

FIGURE *Mouth shapes for reference in creating Poses.*
11.16

important to character animation. You don't want hours of your hard work wrecked by a mouth that appears to be chattering or, worse yet, doesn't even come close to matching the soundtrack, reminiscent of a bad audio dub on an old karate flick.

To use Poses for lip-synching, you'll need to create mouth shape Poses for each of the phonemes required, and then drop the appropriate Pose into the action as needed. Figure 11.16 shows a chart that you can use for reference in creating your own mouth shapes for characters.

The following exercise describes how to create a simple lip-synch word using only Muscle Poses.

EXERCISE

SIMPLE LIP-SYNCH

1. Open the *Hello.PRJ* file from the accompanying CD-ROM.

2. Click the plus (**+**) to the left of the **Action** folder in the **Project Workspace**. Right-click the **Say Hello** item and select **Edit** from the available menu. An **Action** window will open to a front view containing a simple head model. Several mouth shapes have already been created for this model.

3. Enter *6* into the **Current Frame** field and drag the "Heh" Pose onto the model.

4. Enter *11* into the **Current Frame** field and drag the "El" Pose onto the character.

5. Enter *13* into the **Current Frame** field and drag the "Oh" Pose onto the character.

6. Enter *21* into the **Current Frame** field and drop the "Ooo" Pose onto the model.

7. Finally, enter *1* into the **Current Frame** field and select **Copy Keyframe** from the **Edit** menu. Enter *30* into the **Current Frame** field and select **Paste Keyframe** from the **Edit** menu.

8. Render the action and see how it looks.

The final action passes as a fair representation of the word Hello (if you're good at reading lips), but it's not as close as it could be. This is because the motion was simply timed out by looks, without the use of a dopesheet to keep track of the action. *Dopesheets* are a list of what position a mouth or other object is in on any given frame. They've traditionally been done with pencil and paper.

Animation:Master uses an electronic form of dopesheet. These electronic dopesheets are a way for you to sound out words, then place the proper Pose and related framer number into a document.

This is what the contents of a dopesheet file for Animation:Master look like:

```
[DOPESHEETFILE]
[MATERIALS]
[ENDMATERIALS]
[OBJECTS]
[ENDOBJECTS]
[ACTIONS]
[DOPESHEET]
[DOPEFRAME]
Name=default
Frame=1
[ENDDOPEFRAME]
[DOPEFRAME]
Name=default
Frame=9
[ENDDOPEFRAME]
[DOPEFRAME]
Name=U
Frame=10
[ENDDOPEFRAME]
[DOPEFRAME]
Name=A I
Frame=12
[ENDDOPEFRAME]
[DOPEFRAME]
Name=rest
Frame=14
[ENDDOPEFRAME]
[ENDDOPESHEET]
[ENDACTIONS]
[CHOREOGRAPHIES]
[ENDCHOREOGRAPHIES]
[ENDDOPESHEETFILE]
```

Each *dopeframe* section in the dopesheet file specifies the name of the Pose to use, as well as the frame number to which it will be applied. This example is an excerpt from a much larger file, and as you can probably guess, dopesheets can get quite large. The Poses referred to in the dopesheet file must exist for the model that you intend to use them on.

Once you've created a dopesheet, you can load it by right-clicking the **Actions** folder in the **Project Workspace**, then selecting **Import, Dopesheet** from the available menu. Now you can use the dopesheet like an action file by dragging and dropping it onto the appropriate model.

Creating a dopesheet manually can become quite a chore. Since computers are here to make life easier, a program called *LipSYNC* is part of the Animation:Master suite. LipSYNC makes the process of creating dopesheets less tedious. The next section discusses the LipSYNC program and tells a little bit about how it works.

LipSYNC

A more powerful and much more accurate alternative to the dopesheet method is *LipSYNC,* a program that comes with the Animation:Master suite. LipSYNC allows you to load a sound file and mark the frames where sounds occur. You can then specify the Pose name to associate with that sound, and LipSYNC will export a perfect dopesheet for you. The following exercise shows you how to do lip-synch with LipSYNC.

EXERCISE

LipSYNC

1. Start the LipSYNC program. Click the **New** button and open the *Animation is Hard.WAV* file from the accompanying CD-ROM.

2. Select **Import Pose Bank** from the **File** menu and locate the *LipSYNC.lip* file on the accompanying CD-ROM. Pose Banks are somewhat of a librarian for mouth-shape images. When you import a Pose Bank, a series of mouth shapes will open along the right-hand side of the screen. If you wish, you can render your characters' mouth shapes and use them in the Pose Bank to see exactly what the synch will look like on your character. Refer to the LipSYNC online help for tips on this.

3. Use the markers in the center portion of the interface where the waveform is displayed to scrub through the audio. When you've isolated a phoneme sound, click the appropriate mouth shape along the right-hand side of the screen and drag to the area just left of the waveform.

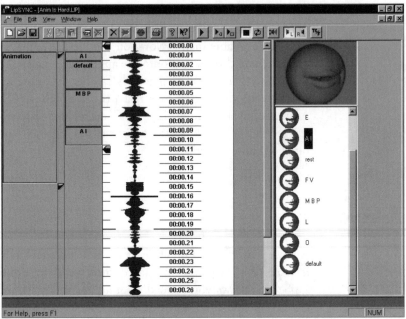

FIGURE *The LipSYNC interface, with a work in progress.*
11.17

4. A box will appear with the name of the mouth shape you've chosen. This box can be expanded or contracted as necessary to align the mouth shape up with the audio.

5. The process of scrubbing through the audio continues until the entire waveform has been mapped. At this point, select **File, Dopesheet Export** to save a dopesheet file. Once saved, a dopesheet can be easily imported into Animation:Master.

LipSYNC really does make the task of creating accurate lip-synch almost fun. One of the real benefits to using LipSYNC is the small box that draws the mouth shapes as you specify them (as they occur in the sound file). Being able to see the mouth move as the audio is played back makes it easy to correct any problems that may arise as the dopesheet is being created. This is much easier than having to run multiple rendering tests to get the lips and the sound to line up perfectly.

Remember that although a program like LipSYNC is both incredibly powerful and fast, you are still the animator, and you still need to play a part to ensure the quality of the end product. LipSYNC uses Poses that you've created.

This means that if you choose not to make any facial motions other than the mouth, the final result will look rather odd. A good technique for avoiding this pitfall is to make one pass on the action to get the dialog matched well with the audio. Then, you can go back and take the time to create a separate set of actions for the eyebrows, forehead, and rest of the face. Once the second action is complete, you can drop it on the first in the choreography to combine the two. This technique, called *Action Overloading*, comes in pretty handy for lip-synch and facial animation.

All of these different motion files can add up quickly and become quite confusing. Animation:Master includes a way for you to create libraries of motions so that you can keep track of them and easily recall them. The next section describes the idea of *motion libraries*.

MOTION LIBRARIES

Many of the actions performed by much of the population every day are repeated, and easily done by almost any other member of the population. For example, you walk. Although your walk may be a little different from anyone else's, you still have two legs, two arms, a head, torso, pelvis, and so on. Because actions in real life are repetitive, actions for your 3D characters also must be repetitive — and reusable. Imagine how quickly you could get rolling if you could just load a basic walk cycle onto a character, then make any necessary adjustments to match the size and personality of the character. This is exactly the idea behind *motion libraries*.

The requirement for reusing Skeletal motion is that the two characters that will share the actions must have the same number of bones, in the same hierarchy, with the same names. The only exception is fingers and toes, which can be omitted without causing any problems other than a stiff-looking hand or foot.

After different motions have been created and saved, you can store them in Libraries. To create a new library, right-click in the **Library** window and select **Add/Remove Libraries**. When the **Libraries** dialog appears, click the **New Library** button. Enter the name you want to call the library and press **Enter** to save it. The new library will appear on a tab in the **Library** window. Now, any actions that are not embedded in a project file can simply be dragged into the library window and dropped for storage. You can easily recall them and insert them into the project. You may choose to organize your actions into Walks, Runs, or Misc.

Libraries can also include models, materials, and Poses. Consider a time when a client or associate comes to you and asks for a character to walk into the street and get hit by a car. This animation is need for a demonstration within the next day or two. Load the car from your Vehicles library, the character from your Biped library, and a walk cycle from your Action library. Place the models on paths, set up the camera and lights, and have the rendering going in no time.

SUMMARY

Skeletal and Muscle animation really are all there is to making a character move. The real trick is in how you use the actions. If you're willing to sit down and study the art of animation, you'll be well rewarded with the capabilities these types of motion offer, especially when combined with the powerful constraint systems available in the software.

Of course, the truth of the matter is that not everyone is an artist, or has the time to dedicate to this skilled practice. In that case, consider using rotoscopes in creating actions that are as accurate as the video you've captured into your computer.

The character has been constructed, textured, and boned, and has had actions created for it. The next big step is the environment in which the character(s) will be placed. Sometimes, very detailed sets are needed. At other times, simple environments that just get the point across are enough. Whichever type you need, the following chapter will help you develop methods that will produce effective, appealing environments.

12 Environments

This chapter discusses different methods you can use to create and populate environments for your models to interact with. There are several different techniques used, from simple ground planes on up to very high quality detailed scenes. You'll have to decide which will work best for you on any given project.

This chapter covers the following techniques:

- What Constitutes an Environment?
- Creating Simple Environments
- More Complex Environments
- Mixing CG Characters with Real Life

WHAT CONSTITUTES AN ENVIRONMENT?

In a computer-generated world, an *environment* can consist of just about anything from a simple background color or ground plane up to a very detailed complex city scene, complete with dirt and graffiti on the sides of buildings. As the artist, you must first decide what type of environment you'll use, then you must go about creating it. Much like a bad set for a stage show, poorly created environments can easily detract from your characters. That's not to say that simple sets won't add to a good piece such as "Fluffy."

Take the time to make your environment work for you. Every little detail can make a difference, because even though the environment may be functional to a CG character, humans are very quick to notice when something is wrong or out of place. Therefore, if you're trying to achieve a photorealistic look, observe real-life objects, then work toward that on the computer.

This chapter describes several different techniques you can use to create backgrounds and environments, from the ever popular simple ground plane to different techniques for providing fuller (360-degree) backdrops. The amount of detail you choose to populate your world with is up to you. Many times you only need to decide what will be seen, or what objects will play a part in the final cut (such as the camera passing behind a tree to add a little depth to the scene).

The next section discusses creating simple environments with techniques such as ground planes, background colors, and backdrops.

CREATING SIMPLE ENVIRONMENTS

Many times, for test rendering, and even in the finished product in some cases, you can use simple ground planes, background colors, and fog. The following section will describe how to set up and use each of these techniques.

SIMPLE GROUND PLANES

Using *simple ground planes* to start out is a good idea. As you progress, you'll likely move toward more complex environments.

The benefits of simple ground planes are that they're easy and fast to create, always a reliable standby if you happen to be in a crunch for time, and render quickly. They're also extremely easy to texture.

EXERCISE

SIMPLE GROUND PLANES

1. Start Animation:Master and click the **New** button. Select **Model** from the menu that appears.

2. Press the **5** key on the numeric keypad to switch to a top view.

3. Select **Options** from the **Tools** menu and click the **Modeling** tab.

4. Check the **Display Grid** checkbox, if it isn't already checked. Enter *25* into the **Grid Spacing** field. Click **OK**.

5. Click on the right-hand side of the **Status Bar**, on the View data. Enter *100* into the **Zoom** field of the dialog that appears, then click **OK**.

6. Add a single vertical spline that starts on the upper left of the window and runs downward 16 grid spaces (it may be necessary to expand the **Modeler** window).

7. Press the **/** key to **Group Connected**, then right-click within the yellow manipulator box and select **Snap to Grid**. The control points at the ends of the spline should snap to the nearest grid intersection.

8. Click the **Snap Manipulators to Grid** button, then click the **Extrude** button. Drag the extrusion horizontally 16 units.

9. Notice how the sides of the plane default to smooth drawing modes. Press the **/** key to **Group Connected**, then click the **Peak** button.

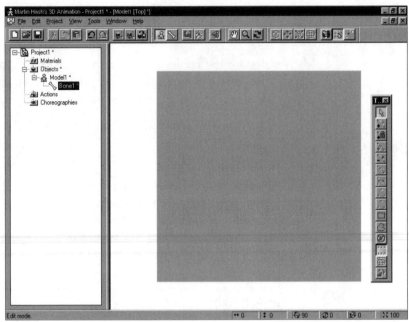

FIGURE *Rendered single patch plane.*
12.1

10. You should now have a perfect one-patch square on your screen, that when rendered looks similar to the one shown in Figure 12.1.

11. Select **Save As** from the **Project** drop-down menu, and enter *Ground Plane* as the name of the project.

Now that you've created the ground plane, all that's left is to drop it into a choreography to "try it on for size."

12. Right-click the **Choreographies** icon in the **Project Workspace** and select **New Choreography** from the available menu. A choreography window will open to a top view.

13. Drag the plane model from the **Models** area of the **Project Workspace** into the **Choreography** window and drop it. In relation to the rest of the scene, the plane is rather small. You can scale it up to fit your needs as necessary.

Scaling the ground plane up and rendering from the camera view would result in a scene similar to the one shown in Figure 12.2.

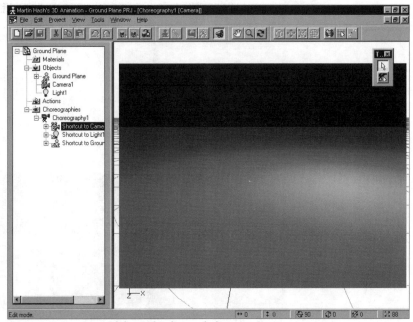

FIGURE *Camera view of the rendered ground plane.*
12.2

Although this model certainly qualifies as a simple ground plane, you can still make it a little less plain, and a little more interesting, beginning with adding some texture.

14. Click on the **Ground Plane** item in the **Objects** section of the **Project Workspace**. On the **Properties Panel**, select the **Attributes** tab.

15. Change the color to a brownish shade. RGB values of *103*, *62*, and *24* should suffice. Enter *20* into the **Roughness Height** field, and *150* in the **Roughness Scale** field.

Rendering now would result in a more interesting view of the ground plane, as it has a much more "ground-like" look.

Taking the entire scene into consideration, it's clear that the lighting needs a little adjustment.

16. Click the **Light1** item in the **Objects** section of the **Project Workspace**. The properties for the light will appear on the **Properties Panel**.

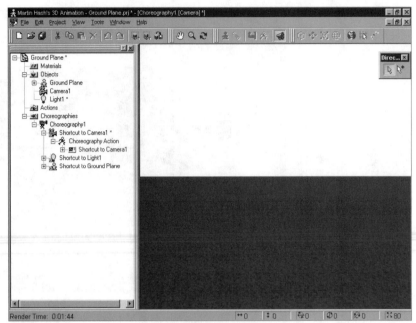

FIGURE **12.3** *The ground plane model with some texture added, as well as an adjustment to the lighting in the scene.*

17. Click the **Sun** button to change the light type, then change the color of the light to white. Position the light from the top view to the left of the camera, from a side view above the camera, and pointing down toward the ground plane.

Rendering the scene now offers results similar to those shown in Figure 12.3. The scene is coming together now. It's more interesting to look at than the original. But it still feels as though something is missing.

Looking at Figure 12.3, you might notice that one of the strange-looking things about this scene is that the ground plane goes on into an empty background.

18. Click on the **Shortcut to Camera1** in the **Choreographies** section of the **Project Workspace**.

19. On the **Properties Panel**, set the **Background Color** to *129* **Red**, *154* **Green**, and *243* **Blue**.

Upon rendering, the scene would now include the ground plane and a light blue background color. However, it's easy to see where the

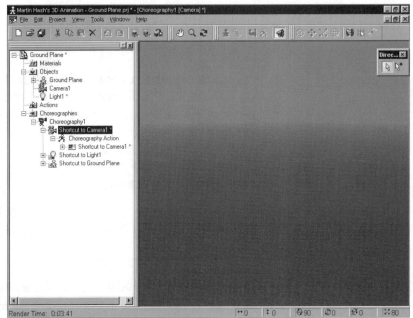

FIGURE
12.4
A rendered view of the ground plane with textures, background color, lighting, and fog added. For this image, the fog distance was set to 3500.

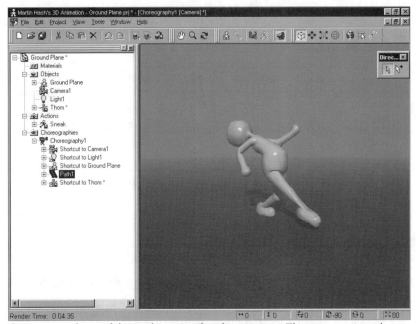

FIGURE
12.5
A rendering of the simple scene with a character in it. This scene contains only a ground plane, one light, one character, and one camera.

ground plane comes to an abrupt end and where the background color takes over. This hard "horizon" can be broken up somewhat with an atmospheric effect called *fog*.

20. With the **Shortcut to Camera1** still selected, enter values into the **Fog** field on the **Properties Panel** and notice the effect. As you look from the camera view, the increasing value of **Fog** specifies how far from the camera the objects you see should start to become washed out. Your view of the reference grid will change as you enter values. Experiment with the values until you find one that offers results similar to those shown in Figure 12.4.

You can see that the final result of this technique is much more interesting than just using the plane itself. Now when you add a character, weak surroundings won't make the character look bad.

The previous exercise described how to create a simple scene that can be created quickly and easily. As your models become more complex, so will the scenes in which you place them. The next section describes some techniques used to create more complex scenes.

COMPLEX ENVIRONMENTS

This section builds on the technique you used to create the simple ground plane in the previous exercise. One of the first steps in producing a more complex environment is to create a more interesting ground. This section describes creating a complex ground plane from a grid.

EXERCISE

MORE COMPLEX GROUND PLANE

1. Start Animation:Master and click the **New** button. Select **Model** from the list of available menu items.

2. Switch to a top view by pressing **5** on the numeric keypad.

3. Select **Options** from the **Tools** menu, and click the **Modeling** tab.

4. Enter *25* into the **Grid Spacing** field and verify that the **Display Grid** item is checked.

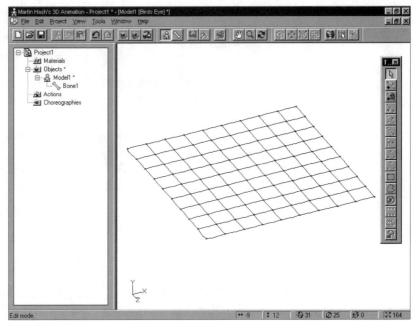

5. Click the **Add Lock** button on the **Tool** panel and add a vertical spline to the left of the screen that contains 10 control points. Try to add the points as close to grid intersections as possible. When you're finished, press the **Escape** key or right-click to stop adding points, then click the last control point that was added to select it.

6. Press the **/** key to **Group Connected**, then right-click the group and select **Snap to Grid**.

7. Click the **Snap Manipulator to Grid** button, then click the **Extrude** button. Drag the extrusion one grid unit to the right. Continue to click the **Extrude** button and drag the extrusion to the right until you have a 10 unit by 10 unit grid, similar to the one shown in Figure 12.6 (the model was rotated in this figure to avoid confusion with the grid lines in the interface).

A rendering of the grid at this point would look like the simple plane model used in the previous section: Even though the grid model has more resolution, all of the control points still lie flat along the X plane.

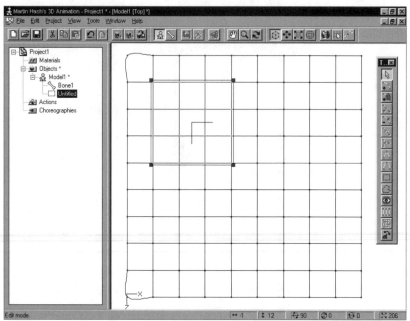

FIGURE   *Start forming a terrain by grouping these points.*
12.7

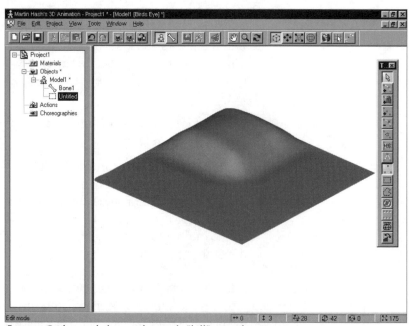

FIGURE   *Grid ground plane with a single "hill" created on it.*
12.8

Once you've created a grid model, you can form terrain by simply pushing and pulling points or groups of points along the Y axis.

8. Working from a top view, use the **Group** tool to select the points shown in Figure 12.7 (the grid was turned off for clarity).

9. With the group still selected, switch to a front view by pressing the **2** key on the numeric keypad. If necessary, press **Shift+Z** to fit the entire grid in the view.

10. Press and hold the **2** key along the top of the keyboard while you use the mouse to drag the selected group upward. This will restrict the group's movement to the Y axis only. Move the group up roughly two grid units.

11. Switch back to a top view by pressing **5** on the numeric keypad. Use the **Group** tool to group the four control points that make up the center of the currently selected group (the previously selected group will deselect when you click to the bound group).

12. Once again, switch back to the front view by pressing **2** on the numeric keypad. Holding down the **2** key along the top of the keyboard, drag the selected group upward to form a smooth, curved "hill" on the surface of the grid.

13. Adjust any other points necessary to keep the bump you just created smooth. Rendering the model at this point would give a result similar to Figure 12.8.

Repeat the process of selecting groups of points and translating them along the Y axis to form hills and valleys in the grid model until you create a surface that suits your needs. Once the model is done, save it and experiment with placing it into a scene.

The grid used to create the ground model in the previous exercise was fairly small (10×10), but clearly illustrates a good technique for creating complex, organic-looking terrain.

Larger ground planes can be made from grids of any size, although you'll probably want to keep the size of most grids below 5000×5000 cm (the default size of the visible ground reference grid in choreography), since large, complex models can become unwieldy.

As you can probably imagine, creating large, complex grid models could become tedious and time consuming very quickly. To save time and effort, a utility called *Grid Maker* is available on the World Wide Web that will create a grid to your specifications, then save the file wherever you specify. The next exercise describes how to create terrain using the Grid Maker program.

EXERCISE

USING GRID MAKER TO CREATE GROUND PLANES

For this exercise, you'll need to be able to connect to the World Wide Web. Most online services provide some type of Web browser, and more experienced Internet users with Netscape or Internet Explorer should have no problems at all.

1. Begin by pointing your browser to Todd's Wholesale Monkey Farm: reality.sgi.com/employees/shafer_mfg/Hash_stuff/hash_grid_maker.html.

2. A page will open that allows you to make five entries to specify the type of grid you'd like to create, and a button that actually creates the grid. This program creates the grids in a vertical plane rather than a horizontal one, so the finished product will have to be rotated in the modeler before it can be used.

Take a moment to look over each entry field that is available for Grid Maker.

The first field is for the X size of the grid. This specifies how many units across the grid will be. For example, entering *10* here would create a grid that was 10 units across. The second field is for the Y size of the grid. This entry works exactly like the X entry, only along the Y axis. The third field, **Step Size**, specifies the distance (in grid units) between each control point. The **Step Size** will determine the size of the squares that make up the grid.

The **Variability of Z** field is what actually makes the bumps in the surface of the model. This number specifies how perturbed the surface of the model should be. Entries between 0 and 150 are reasonable. Using values beyond 150 creates grids that look confusing.

The **Variability of X/Y** field alters the locations of the grid points to give a somewhat more organic look to the grids you create. Varying this number creates a grid with fewer right angles in it.

Figures 12.9 through 12.11 shows several example grid models that are included on the accompanying CD-ROM.

Once you've created a grid that you can work with, the model can be opened by clicking the **New** button, selecting **Model** from the available menu, then right-clicking the model name in the **Project Workspace** and selecting **Import**, then **V4 Segment** from the available menus. The most effective way to utilize the Grid Maker program is to generate a grid

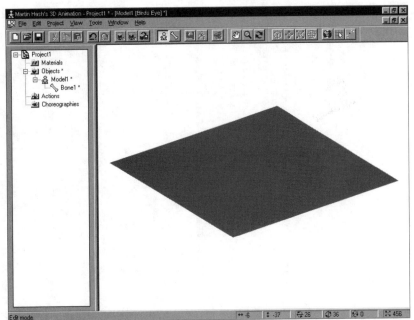

FIGURE
12.9
Grid Maker–generated ground plane created with the default settings.

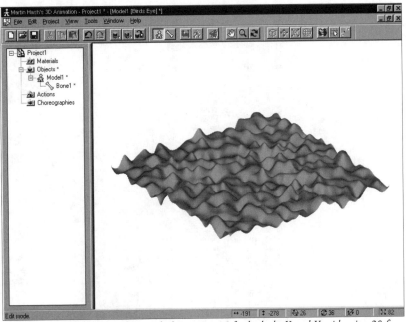

FIGURE
12.10
Grid Maker created ground plane using 25 for both the X and Y grid units, 20 for the grid scale, and 50 for the Z Variability.

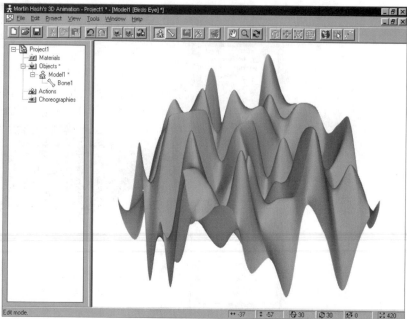

FIGURE
12.11
Grid Maker created ground plane using 10 for both the X and Y grid units, 10 for the grid scale, and 100 for the Z Variability.

FIGURE
12.12
An image of the sky opened as a camera rotoscope.

that comes close to what you need, then make any necessary adjustments in the modeler, saving the final product. Don't expect Grid Maker to create a perfect terrain for you.

NOTE

If you think you may be able to use the same landscape in different places by making only minor modifications, remember that you can make Poses and save them with the model. This will allow you to select the appropriate Pose for your scene without destroying the original model.

In the previous exercises, you've learned how to create both simple and complex ground planes, as well as how to use the background color and fog to help give your scenes a feeling of depth. Another way to create an interesting background is to paint one in a program such as Photoshop, or take a photograph and scan it into the computer. Either way, these images can be used to create an interesting backdrop, and don't require as much time as building all of the models.

One way to utilize an image as a backdrop is to open the image as a *camera rotoscope*. This is done by right-clicking the **Shortcut to Camera** item in the **Choreographies** section of the **Project Workspace** and selecting **Import Rotoscope**.

This will open the selected image in the camera view, as shown in Figure 12.12.

There are several drawbacks to using camera rotoscopes as backdrops. The most important is that if and when the camera moves, the rotoscoped image stays in the camera view. This means that no matter what is going on in a scene, regardless of camera movement, the image used for the backdrop will always be the same. Some of this difficulty can be averted by using animated rotoscopes, but setting the scene up to match the action in an animated rotoscope can be tedious.

Other drawbacks of using camera rotoscopes are that they're not affected by fog effects, and they will not reflect or refract through any objects in a scene. This can be significant, depending on what a scene calls for.

To avoid these problems, there are basically three methods you can use to create a full environment in 3D software. These methods utilize cylinders, hemispheres, and spheres to create the illusion of an environment. The following sections will discuss how to create and use each effectively.

CYLINDRICAL BACKDROPS

The simplest of the three types of backgrounds makes use of a *cylinder* model that has an image mapped onto it. You then create the scene within the cylinder. With this technique, the camera will "see" the cylinder in the background of the scene, and as the camera turns, the background will stay still. The cylinder can also be rotated slowly to give the effect of clouds drifting in the sky.

EXERCISE

CREATING CYLINDRICAL BACKDROPS

1. Click the **New** button and select **Model** from the available list of items.

2. From **Tools**, select the **Options** menu, then click the **Modeling** tab. Set the **Lathe Precision** to 8. Enter 25 into the **Grid Spacing** field, and verify that the **Display Grid** checkbox is enabled. Click **OK**.

3. Adjust the **Zoom** value to 100 with either the **Zoom** tool or by clicking on the **View Settings** on the **Status Bar** and entering the value manually.

4. To the right of the Y axis marker, create a horizontal spline with two control points on it that is roughly 10 units long. Click the **Lathe** button.

5. Switch to a top view by pressing the **5** key on the numeric keypad and use the **Group** tool to select the points in the middle of the circle that was just created. Press the **Delete** key.

6. Change back to a front view by pressing the **2** key on the numeric keypad. Click on any point in the spline and press the **/** key to **Group Connected**.

7. Click the **Snap Manipulator to Grid** button. Click the **Extrude** button, then while holding down the **2** key on the top of the keyboard, drag the extrusion upward 10 units.

   Figure 12.13 shows the procedure you'll follow for decaling the cylinder.

8. Change to a top view by pressing the **5** key on the numeric keypad, and use the **Group** tool to select just the front two of the eight cylinder faces. Click the **Hide** button to hide the rest of the model.

9. Change back to a front view by pressing the **2** key on the numeric keypad, then press **Shift+Z** to zoom the visible model to fill the screen.

10. Click on the control point in the upper left-hand corner of the screen. On the **Properties Panel**, click the **Selected CP** tab, and on a piece of paper make a note that says "Upper Left." Beneath

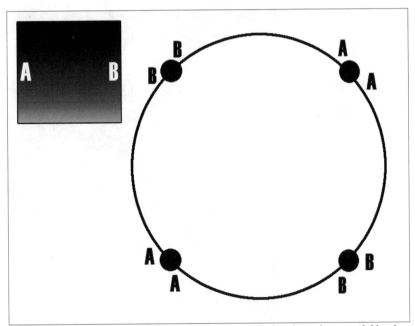

FIGURE *The sky map will be applied normally, then reversed so that it becomes tilable where*
12.13 *it meets the previous application of the map.*

this, write down the X and Y coordinates. In this example, the X value was –176.44, and the Y value was 250, but your values may be different.

11. Click on the lower right-hand control point, and make a note that says "Lower Right." Once again, write down the X and Y coordinates. For this example, the X value was 176.44, and the Y value was 0. These four numbers are very important, as they provide the key to precisely aligning the applications of the decal.

12. Right-click the **Model1** item in the **Objects** section of the **Project Workspace** and select **Import**, then **Decal** from the available menus. Locate the *NightSky.TGA* file on the accompanying CD-ROM.

13. After a few moments, the map information will appear on the **Properties Panel**. Set the transparent color to bright green to avoid any holes in the map.

14. Right-click the **NightSky** item in the **Objects** section of the **Project Workspace** and select **Position**. When the map appears in the **Modeler** window with a manipulator around it, click the **Position** tab on the **Properties Panel**.

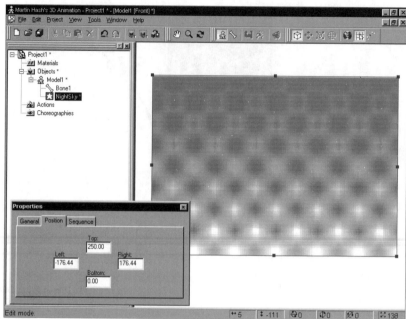

15. For the **Top** field, enter the highest Y value you wrote down (in this example, 250). For the **Left** field, enter the lowest X value (–176.44). In the **Bottom** field, enter the lowest Y value (0). Finally, for the **Right** field, type in the highest X value (176.44). The decal should now be lined up perfectly with the edges of the model, as shown in Figure 12.14.

16. Right-click within the image map manipulator and select **Apply** from the pop-up menu. Click the **Stamp1** item that appears in the **Project Workspace**, press **F2** to **Edit** the name, and type in *Front*. This will make it easy to distinguish where each decal stamp is located on the surface of the model.

17. Right-click within the image map manipulator and select **Stop Positioning** from the available menu.

18. Press the **Hide** button to unhide the model. Switch to a top view and use the **Group** tool to select the opposite, or back, face of the cylinder. Click the **Hide** button to hide the rest of the model, and change back to the front view.

From the front view, the correct Zoom value is already set, since the software will remember what the last settings used in that view were.

The coordinates for decaling the back face are identical to those of the front face, except that the map on the back needs to be reversed along the X axis when it's applied (refer to Figure 12.13).

19. Right-click the **NightSky** item in the **Objects** section of the **Project Workspace** and select **Position**. After a few moments, the map will appear in the **Modeler** window with a manipulator around it. The decal will appear in exactly the same position you set in the previous steps. The **Position** tab on the **Properties Panel** should already be selected. Swap the values in the **Left** and **Right** fields to reverse the map. The **Left** field should now be 176.44, and the Right should be −176.44. Right-click within the map boundary and select **Apply**.

20. Right-click within the image map manipulator and select **Stop Positioning** from the available menu. Click the **Stamp1** item in the **Objects** section of the **Project Workspace**, press **F2** to edit the name, and type in *Back*.

21. Click the **Hide** button to unhide the rest of the model. Switch to a top view and select the faces on the right side of the model. Press the **6** key on the numeric keypad to change to a side view, and press **Shift+Z** to zoom the visible model to fit the window.

22. The positioning values for the left and right faces will be the same as the front and back, so the only thing that requires some attention is the orientation of the decal. According to the reference diagram in Figure 12.13, the right face image is applied reversed. Right-click the image map name in the **Project Workspace** and select **Position** from the available menu. When the map appears, notice that the settings are still correct (with the image reversed) from the application to the back face. Right-click within the image boundary and select **Apply**.

23. Right-click within the image maps manipulator and select **Stop Positioning** from the available menu. Click the **Stamp1** item in the **Objects** section of the **Project Workspace** and press **F2** to edit the name. Enter *Right* and press **Enter**.

24. Click the **Hide** button to unhide the model, and from the top view, group the faces that make the left side of the cylinder. Click the **Hide** button to hide the rest of the model, and press **6** on the numeric keypad to switch to a right-hand view.

25. Click the **NightSky** item in the **Project Workspace**. The left side of the cylinder is to be decaled with the map in a normal orientation, so

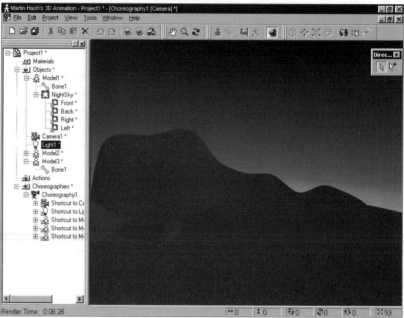

FIGURE *A cylinder backdrop used in a simple scene.*
12.15

swap the Left and Right values on the **Properties Panel**. Right-click the **NightSky** item and select **Position** from the available menu.

26. When the map appears in the **Modeler** window, right-click within the boundary of the map and select **Apply**. Right-click anywhere on the image map and select **Stop Positioning**. Name this stamp *Left*.

27. Unhide the rest of the model, and test render it from a few different angles to see what effect the application of the map has had.

You can now drop the cylinder into a choreography and build a scene inside it. Remember to scale the cylinder up close to the size of the default grid in the **Choreography** window — otherwise you'll severely limit the size of the scene you can construct, and any depth in the scene will be difficult to accent with effects such as fog.

The example shown in Figure 12.15 was lit with a single sun-type light that was bluish in color. The Ambiance value of the cylinder model was raised to 80 to make it look "bright," and the hills were added to break up the horizon line.

Populating this environment with buildings, characters, and other props would create a believable look, with only two problems.

The first is where the maps meet. Keep any clouds or unusual patterns to a minimum along the map edges. This is because even though the images line up perfectly, the edges where the maps meet can begin to look like an ink-blot test, which is very distracting.

The second problem can be a little more serious. If the camera points upward either on purpose or accidentally, the entire effect created by the cylinder is blown. Cylinders as backdrops should be kept to scenes that will not contain a lot of camera movement, or will have very controlled camera movement, such as following a car down a street.

If more erratic camera movement is needed, or there is the potential for a camera shot that will be pointing upward, a different technique can be used. The next section will discuss the creation of this type of environment, a dome.

DOME BACKDROPS

Cylindrical backdrops do have their place. But more complex, erratic camera motion, such as following a jet or spaceship across the sky, requires a more complete backdrop such as a *dome*. Once a dome has been added to a scene, it serves as a full "sky." The next exercise describes how to create and integrate a dome into a scene.

EXERCISE

ENVIRONMENT MAPS

1. Open the *Dome.PRJ* file from the accompanying CD-ROM. The project contains a prebuilt dome model.

2. One way to use a dome for an environment is to apply the image that you're going to use for the surface of the dome as an *environment map*. This will get the map onto the surface of the model with a minimum of distortion and work. The correct way to apply such a map is in the front view, and the model should be facing front, as the dome is in this project.

3. Right-click the ***Materials*** icon in the **Project Workspace** and select **New Material** from the available menu. When the new material appears in the **Project Workspace**, click the plus (**+**) to the left of the **Material1** item to expand the material tree.

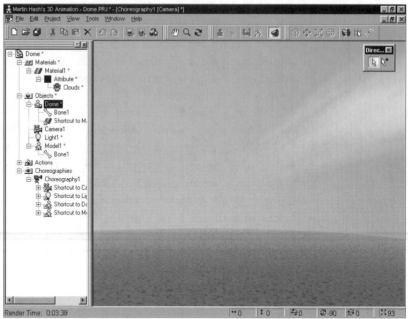

FIGURE *The end result of applying a texture to the dome model as an Environment Map.*
12.16

4. Right-click the **Attribute** item beneath the new material and select **Import Environment Map** from the available menu. Locate the *Clouds.TGA* file on the accompanying CD-ROM.

5. When the map opens, set the transparent color on the **Properties Panel** to a color that does not appear in the image, such as bright green. This will prevent any "holes" from appearing in the map when it is rendered.

6. Now drag the **Material1** item down to the **Dome** item in the **Project Workspace** and drop the material on the model name.

7. You can now place the dome into a choreography. Note that you'll need to rotate the model –90 degrees to properly orient it as a sky. You'll also need to scale up the model to create a large area to work in.

Figure 12.16 shows the result of applying a map to the dome in this manner.

As you can see from the final result, this technique is very effective in creating 180 degree backdrops. The other benefit of this technique is its speed. All seven steps of the exercise take no longer than a minute or two to complete.

Another technique that can be used to apply an image to a dome model is to flatten the model, then apply the image as a decal. The next exercise describes how to do this.

EXERCISE

DECALING A DOME

1. Once again, open the *Dome.PRJ* file from the accompanying CD-ROM.

2. To decal the dome without destroying the map with distortion, the dome model must first be flattened. You do this in Action. Right-click the ***Actions*** icon in the **Project Workspace** and select **New Action** from the available menu.

3. Click the **Muscle** button to change to **Muscle Action Mode**, then click any point on the dome and press the **/** key to **Group Connected**.

4. Switch to a side view and zoom out if necessary until the entire model is visible. Click the **Rotate Manipulator** button.

5. Rotate the pivot so that the green axis is oriented such that it points out the open end of the hemisphere. Watch the **Properties Panel** until the value reaches 90 degrees.

6. Drag the pivot backward until it lines up with the open edge of the hemisphere, as shown in Figure 12.17.

7. Change to a front view. Right-click within the manipulator and select **Flatten** from the available menu. The model should look similar to the one shown in Figure 12.18.

8. Once a model has been flattened, if any control points seem out of place or skewed, you can drag them into position with the mouse.

9. Right-click the model name in the **Project Workspace** and select **Import**, Decal from the available menus. Locate the *Clouds.TGA* file on the accompanying CD-ROM. Right-click the **Clouds** item in the **Project Workspace** and select **Position** from the available menu.

10. In the front view, use the mouse to position the map so that it covers all of the flattened model, as shown in Figure 12.19. Once the map is in position, right-click within the boundary of the image and select **Apply** to decal the dome.

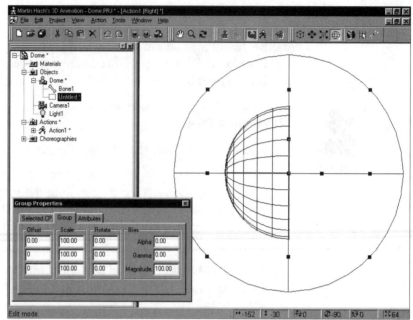

FIGURE
12.17
Correct positioning of the pivot to properly flatten a hemisphere.

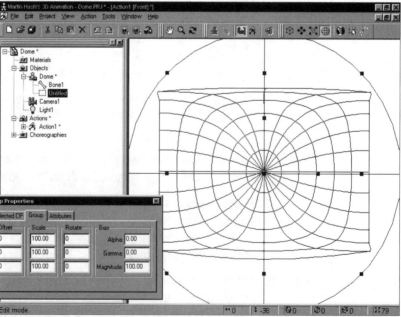

FIGURE
12.18
A front view of the dome model after it has been flattened.

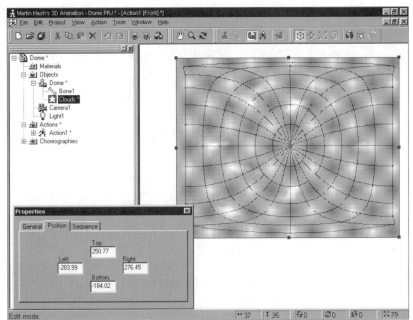

FIGURE
12.19 *Before applying the decal to the flattened model, the image must be positioned properly to cover the entire model.*

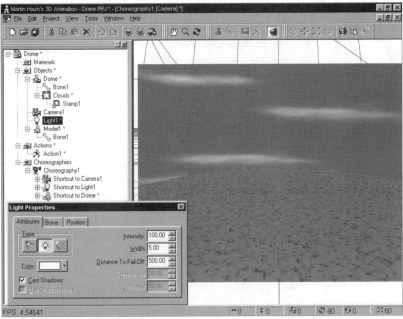

FIGURE
12.20 *The dome shape in the Choreography window, rendered from the camera view.*

11. Right-click inside of the image manipulator and select **Stop Positioning** from the available menu.

12 Select **Clear** from the **Action** menu to return the model to its original, unflattened state.

13. Change to the **Choreography** window, and position your scene within the dome. The dome model will look better with an increased Ambiance value, much like the cylindrical backdrop.

At times, the Flatten function may cause patches to flatten behind other patches, making them "miss" being decaled. You can't always be sure when this will happen, but it helps if you don't try to flatten objects with patches that go around the back of the model. Remember that you can manipulate a flattened model before decaling without destroying the original model. It's best to work with the Flatten function to get the flattest possible end result (for best decaling), and test render the model before using it in an animation.

You may also notice some stretching of the map around the edges of the model. Once you get the hang of what Flatten is doing to the model, you'll be able to adjust your image maps accordingly and avoid this problem.

There is one more technique that is often used in creating environments. Although cylindrical and dome backdrops are suitable for most situations, there is one particular use that neither of them can cover: space.

The next exercise describes a technique you can use to make backdrops for any animations that may need a full, 360-degree background.

SPHERICAL BACKDROPS

Spherical backdrops are the only solution when full 360-degree visibility is required. Most often, this technique is used to create starfields. The following exercise describes creating and using a spherical environment.

EXERCISE

SPHERICAL ENVIRONMENTS

1. Open the *Sphere.PRJ* file from the accompanying CD-ROM. The project will open with a sphere already modeled and ready for mapping in an **Action** window.

2. The most reasonable method for decaling the sphere involves doing half at a time (much like the dome shape), so click the **Muscle** button

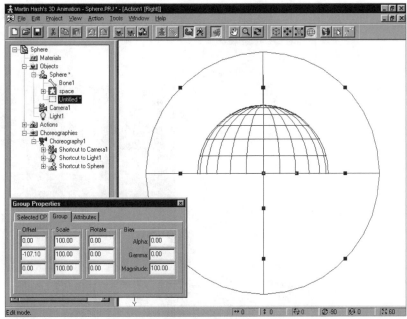

FIGURE   *Proper pivot placement for flattening a hemisphere.*

12.21

to change to **Muscle Action Mode**, and use the **Group** tool to select the top half of the sphere, including the middle horizontal spline. Click the **Hide** button to hide the lower half of the model.

3. Switch to a side view and zoom out if necessary to see the entire model. Use the **Group** tool to select all of the control points in the **Muscle** window. Click the **Rotate Manipulator** button.

4. Rotate the pivot so that the green axis points straight down. Drag the pivot by the center handle and position it even with the lowest cross-section on the sphere, as shown in Figure 12.21.

5. Right-click anywhere within the manipulator and select **Flatten** from the available menu.

6. Right-click the model name in the **Project Workspace** and select **Import**, then **Decal** from the available menus. Locate the *Space.TGA* file on the accompanying CD-ROM. On the **Properties Panel**, select a color that does not appear in the image map for the Transparent Color (such as bright green). Change to a top view by pressing the **5** key on the numeric keypad.

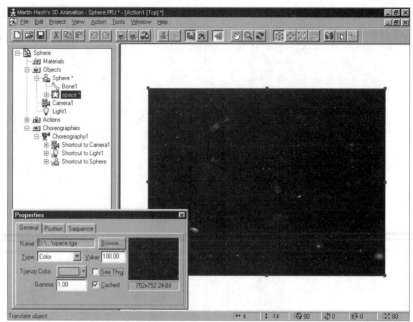

FIGURE *Proper positioning of the* Space.TGA *image map is necessary so that it covers the*
12.22 *entire flattened mesh before applying.*

7. Right-click the **Space** item in the **Project Workspace**, and use the mouse to position the map so that it covers all of the flattened model, as shown in Figure 12.22. When the map is positioned properly, right-click within the boundary of the image and select **Apply** to decal the top hemisphere.

8. Right-click within the image boundary and select **Stop Positioning** from the available menu.

9. Select **Clear** from the **Action** drop-down menu to return the sphere to its original shape. From a front view, use the **Group** tool to select the bottom half of the sphere, including the center horizontal spline, then click the **Hide** button to hide the top half of the model.

10. From a side view, use the **Group** tool to select the visible control points. Zoom out to see the entire hemisphere if necessary. Click the **Rotate Manipulator** button.

11. The orientation of the pivot is already correct, so don't rotate it. Use the mouse to translate the pivot even with the top cross-section of the hemisphere, as shown in Figure 12.23.

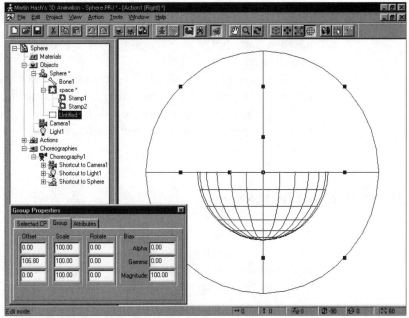

FIGURE *Correct positioning of the pivot for flattening the lower hemisphere.*
12.23

12. Right-click within the manipulator and select **Flatten** from the available menu.

13. Change to a top view, zooming out if necessary to fit the entire flattened model in the view. Right-click the **Space.TGA** decal name in the **Project Workspace** and select **Position** from the available menu.

14. Make any adjustments that are necessary to position the map so that it covers all of the flattened model. Right-click within the boundary of the image and select **Apply** to decal the bottom hemisphere. Right-click anywhere on the image map and select **Stop Positioning** from the available menu.

15. Select **Clear** from the **Action** menu to return the hemisphere to its original state, then click the **Hide** button to unhide the rest of the model. Click on the **Choreography** window.

To reiterate a point made earlier in this chapter, one of the benefits of mapping a flattened model in Action is that if it flattens oddly, you can make adjustments to the control points before you apply the map. Spheres can be tricky to get flattened just right, so it may be easier for you to map them in quarters rather than halves.

A trick you can use to add "depth" to your space scenes, once you get the hang of flattening and decaling spheres, is to nest one sphere inside of another, and apply space maps as cookie cutters or with alpha channels to both spheres.

You have now practiced three commonly used techniques for creating environments (other than compositing). The next section discusses a technique for integrating computer animation with live action. This technique can also be used to put together computer-generated characters and scenes that were created separately.

FRONT PROJECTION MAPPING

Front projection mapping is a simple, yet powerful technique used to combine live-action images with computer-generated characters. This technique is used to add shadows or reflections to a scene that make your character appear to be part of it. You can create some excellent effects using this technique.

EXERCISE

USING FRONT PROJECTION MAPS

1. Click the **New** button and select **Choreography** from the available menu.

2. Right-click the **Shortcut to Camera1** in the **Project Workspace**, and select **Import Rotoscope** from the pop up menu. Locate the *Projection.TGA* file on the accompanying CD-ROM. When the file opens, set the Transparent Color on the **Properties Panel** to a bright green (since this color does not appear in the image).

3. Click in the **Front Projection Map** checkbox on the **Properties Panel** for the rotoscope to specify that this map is a projection map.

4. Right-click the *Objects* icon in the **Project Workspace** and select **New**, then **Model** from the available menus. Select **Options** from the **Tools** menu, then click the **Modeling** tab. Set the grid spacing to *15*, and make sure that the **Display Grid** item is checked.

5. Change to a top view in the **Modeler** window, and to the right of the Z axis marker, create a single horizontal spline that is roughly three grid units long. Click the **Lathe** button to create a disk shape.

FIGURE 12.24 *Alignment of the plane model projection target with the rotoscoped image.*

6. Group the control points that make up the inner circle of the disk, and enter *1* into both the X and Z scale fields on the **Properties Panel**.

7. Drag the model into the **Choreography** window from a top view. Align the disk as well as possible with the circular bricks in the middle of the rotoscope. The alignment doesn't have to be perfect, but it needs to be close. Figure 12.24 shows a good position for the model for the purposes of this exercise. Placing the model can be hard, since you're really matching the camera angle, as well as the angle and distance of the object.

8. With the disk model selected, click the **General** tab on the **Properties Panel**. Click in the **Front Projection Target** checkbox to specify that this model is to be a projection map target.

Rendering the image at this point would produce something similar to Figure 12.25. The dark area in the center of the image is the disk model; it appears dark because no adjustments have been made to the scene yet.

Correcting the problem of dark models can turn out to be one of the difficult tasks in using projection maps effectively: matching the lighting in a scene. If you look closely at the rotoscoped image, you'll see very

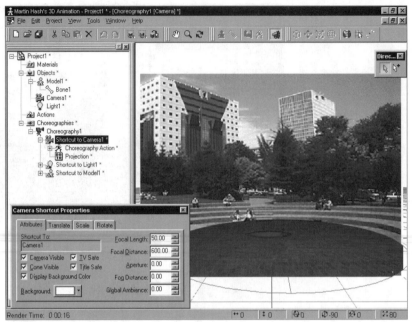

FIGURE   *Rendering of the projection mapped scene with no adjustments made to the lighting.*
12.25

few shadows: It's an outdoor scene on a clear day. With this information, you can effectively estimate the lighting in the scene.

9. Click the **Light1** item in the **Objects** section of the **Project Workspace**. On the **Properties Panel**, change the default light type to a sun (since the scene is outdoors), and make the light color white.

10. Change to a side view, and click on the **Shortcut to Light1** item in the **Choreographies** section of the **Project Workspace**. Move the light directly above the scene and point it downward at the disk model. This light positioning is how you match the lighting in the photograph as closely as possible.

11. To finish making adjustments, switch to a Camera view and test-render the scene. If the disk model appears too dark or too light, adjust the Ambiance setting of the model on the **Properties Panel**. Some more adjustments to the light in the scene may also be necessary.

Rendering the scene after step 10 produces results like those shown in Figure 12.26. The disk model is still in the scene and will receive any

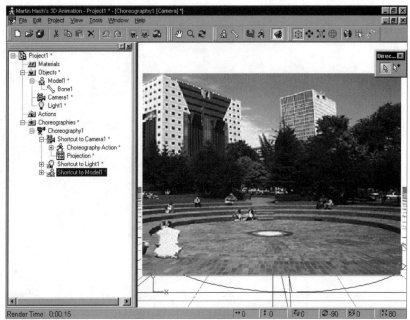

FIGURE
12.26
Rendering of the projection map with adjustments made to the lighting and ambiance of the model.

shadows cast by a model passing through, but it is "invisible," since the background image is matched seamlessly.

12. Right-click the **Objects** icon in the **Project Workspace** and select **Import Model**. Locate the *Thom.MDL* file on the accompanying CD-ROM.

13. Drag the model into the **Choreography** and Scale him appropriately to fit the scene. From a side view, make sure that the model appears to be standing on the disk model.

14. Position Thom in a cute pose and render him. Thom will cast shadows on the disk model that is projection mapped with the background image, making him appear to be standing in the scene. For surfaces such as wooden or linoleum floors, windows, or countertops, adding a little reflectivity to the projection mapped surface will really help you pull off the effect.

Figure 12.27 shows the wireframe view of the final scene, and Figure 12.28 shows a rendered view.

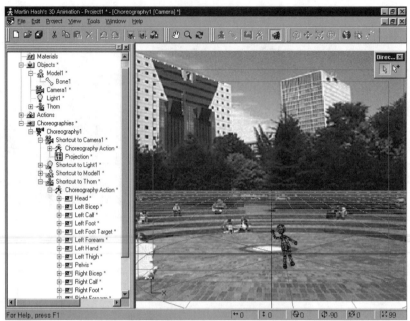

FIGURE *A wireframe view of the final scene.*
12.27

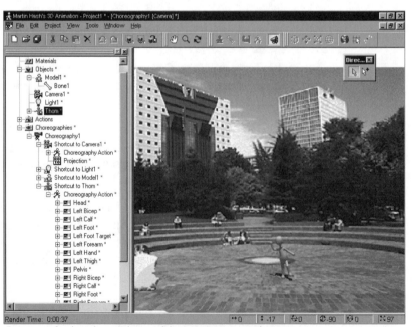

FIGURE *A final quality rendering of the projection mapped scene.*
12.28

Projection maps are an incredibly powerful tool for mixing live action and computer-generated characters, but it can take some practice to get the technique right. Setting up the camera to match the angle used in the backdrop and matching the lighting are the most time-consuming. The rest is fairly straightforward.

SUMMARY

You now have some experience with the main types of environments used in creating a full scene in which your action can take place. The modeling skills you've acquired through experience and the exercises contained in this book should be useful to you in creating props for your scenes. A few trees in the background or some buildings can go a long way toward adding a full look to a scene, rather than leaving it sparse and barren.

Now that you know how to create environments and how they work in relation to a scene, the next chapter will discuss your role as a director, some of the tools you have at your disposal, and some tips to keep a piece interesting.

13 You as Director

Director is most likely the most important role you'll play in telling your story. Good directing can make or break a story very quickly, and sometimes even the best-looking models won't help. Everybody has seen a good actor in a poorly directed film. You may also have seen someone you never heard of in a low-budget film that turned out to be really good — because of the directing.

This chapter discusses some lighting and camera techniques that should get you rolling in the right direction as you continue to develop your animation skills. Some people are great artists, others are great directors, and many fall somewhere in between. Directing well is hard, so expect it to take some time and practice. Experimenting with different camera angles, lighting, and so on, is always helpful as well.

This chapter covers the following techniques:

- Direction and the Mood of the Story
- The Camera
- Lighting Technique
- Background Color and Fog
- Motion Blur

DIRECTION AND THE MOOD OF THE STORY

As you arrange your characters, lights, and cameras in a scene, remember that you need to keep with the mood. If you're trying to compose an eerie scene, use low-intensity lights positioned somewhat low to create long, drawn-out shadows. Conversely, if you're trying to create a bright, happy mood, use bright lights, as well as brighter colors on your models.

Probably some of the best experience you can gain is to observe techniques from other directors. This can be as easy as a trip to the local video store to rent movies. For example, directors such as James Cameron (*The Terminator*, *T2*) make extensive use of moving cameras. Spielberg uses suspense and very believable situations to tell his stories. Something that can be especially useful is a LaserDisc player (or DVD) with frame-by-frame capabilities. This gives you a chance to really slow down the action and see what the camera, lights, and actors are doing at any given point.

The camera is the eye with which you tell your story. The next section should get you headed in the right direction by describing some different camera techniques.

THE CAMERA

What the camera is doing at any given moment can be very important to your viewers. Move it too fast, and you may make them miss some of the action; move it too slowly, and you'll downplay any urgency that you're trying to convey. You should use the camera in such a way that it adds to whatever is happening in a given scene, rather than detracting from it with confusing movements or unnecessary motion.

The following exercise describes a couple of different ways to use a camera to follow an object through a scene. Use these techniques as a starting point in developing your next masterpiece.

EXERCISE

TRACKING OBJECTS WITH THE CAMERA

1. Open the *The Camera.PRJ* file from the accompanying CD-ROM.

2. Click the plus (**+**) sign to the left of the **Choreography1** item in the **Project Workspace**.

3. Right-click the **Choreography1** item and select **Edit**. This will open a **Choreography** window that contains a camera, a car, a light, and two paths.

4. Press the **1** key on the numeric keypad to change to a camera view, and use the plus (**+**) and minus (**–**) keys to step through the frames and see what happens. Around frame 26, the car passes out of the camera's field of view.

5. You can make this scene a little more interesting if you first change to a top view by pressing the **5** key on the numeric keypad. Next, select the camera by clicking on it. Then right-click the camera and select **New Constraint**, then **Aim At** from the available menus.

NOTE

You can also add a constraint to the camera by right-clicking the **Shortcut to Camera1** item in the **Project Workspace**, then selecting **New Constraint, Aim At** from the available menus.

6. When the cursor changes to a picker, click the Coupe model. You'll notice that the camera angle drops a bit, and the coupe is now centered in the viewing window, as shown in Figure 13.1.

7. Once again, use the plus (**+**) and minus (**–**) keys to step through the frames. Notice that the camera now follows the car, making this

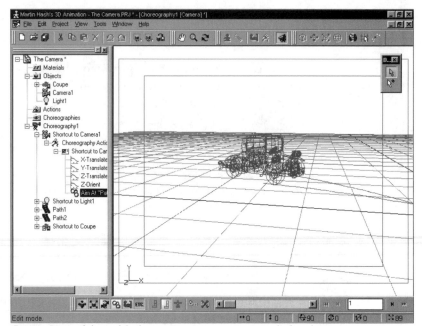

FIGURE   *View of the model after an Aim At constraint is applied to the camera.*

13.1

sequence more interesting to look at than watching the car simply drive out of the camera's view.

If you're interested in seeing the final rendering with the Aim At constraint, feel free to render the animation and watch the action. A wireframe render of the scene after step 7 is included on the CD-ROM.

Although this technique is clearly effective when compared to the original, you can do still more to make the scene a little more exciting.

8. Change to a top view, then click the camera to select it. Right-click the camera, then select **New Constraint**, then **Path** from the available menus.

9. When the cursor changes into a **Picker** tool, click the second path in the choreography (not the one that the coupe is on).

10. You'll notice when the camera is applied to the path that it no longer points at the coupe model (the effect of the Aim At seems to have been lost). This is because constraints are ordered, and a Path type constraint that occurs after an Aim At constraint will override the Aim

At. To correct this, simply drag the "Path" constraint above the Aim At constraint in the **Project Workspace** and drop it. The constraints will reorder automatically, and pressing the spacebar to refresh the window should show that the camera is now correctly aimed at the car.

11. You'll need to set the Ease value for the camera, to tell it how to travel along the path. Click the Path constraint in the **Project Workspace**, and on the **Properties Panel**, enter *0* into the **Ease** field. Enter *60* into the **Current Frame** field on the **Frame** toolbar, and enter *100* into the **Ease** field on the **Properties Panel**. The camera will now travel the path smoothly over the course of the animation.

12. Change to a camera view by pressing the **1** key on the numeric keypad, and step through the frames with the plus (**+**) and minus (**–**) keys. Notice how the camera drags across the ground reference plane. To correct this, select the path that the camera is on, and from a side view, drag the path upward and away from the car. While you're moving it, the camera will remain aimed at the coupe.

13. Once again, use the plus (**+**) and minus (**–**) keys to step through the frames and watch the action.

As you can see, a simple example of a camera on a path aiming at an object on a path can hold some interest. You could change the shape or length of the path to make it more interesting; adding a little more scenery wouldn't hurt, either. Now that you're familiar with working with a single camera, the next exercise will discuss working with multiple cameras.

MULTIPLE CAMERAS

Now that you have some practice with a camera, this section will show a short example of working with *multiple cameras*. Make sure you practice with this technique before you try to plug it into a scene, since it can take away from action when misused.

Consider all of those quick cuts that occur in a movie when the action is shown from many different angles. To set up such a scene in real life, the film crew films the same action with many cameras at once, then the best footage is used during the editing process. Like a real-life movie set, Animation:Master allows you to add many cameras, which you can use to add a nice effect to your finished pieces.

EXERCISE

MULTIPLE CAMERAS

1. This exercise continues where the previous one left off. You should still have the project open, with the camera aimed at the coupe and traveling along "Path2" in the choreography.

2. Add another camera to the scene by right-clicking the **Choreography1** item in the **Project Workspace** and selecting **New**, then **Camera** from the available menus. The second camera will appear in the scene, as well as in the **Project Workspace**.

3. The only real trick to using multiple cameras is knowing which camera should be used to render a given sequence. For example, in this case, Camera1 will be used to "film" the coupe for the first 30 frames. Then, Camera2 will be used to complete the sequence from a stationary position.

4. Right-click the **Camera2** item in the **Project Workspace**, then select **New Constraint, Aim At** from the available menus. When the cursor changes to a picker, select the Coupe model.

5. Right-click within the **Choreography** window, then select **View, Camera1** from the available menus. Use the **Render to File** button to render frames 1 to 30 to a .*TGA* sequence, named *Coupe000.TGA*. The software will continue the numbering automatically.

6. Right-click within the **Choreography** window, then select **View, Camera2** from the available menus. Render frames 30 to 60 to .*TGA* files, using the same name as in the previous step, and placing them in the same folder as the previous render.

    A program such as Adobe Premiere would now be very effective for making the .*TGA* files into an AVI or QuickTime. The example cut demonstrated in this exercise was specifically intended to show the use of multiple cameras. As such, it's not of a beautiful cinematic quality. However, it does get the point across.

Now that you've gotten rolling with cameras, it's time to take a look at lighting. The next exercise will walk you through a basic three-light technique on which you can build to create intricately lit scenes.

LIGHTING

Lighting is vitally important to your animations. Proper lighting can make a scene work beautifully; bad lighting can kill it by unintentionally washing out objects.

The following figures demonstrate how different lighting conditions can be used to create different moods on the same subject. Figure 13.2 shows a cute little bunny lit with basic *three-point lighting.*

Figure 13.3 shows the same cute bunny, lit only by one *sun-type light* set at a distance. Like real sunlight, sun-type lights do not have any dropoff.

Finally, Figure 13.4 shows the bunny lit with one *klieg-type light* placed beneath and in front of the model. This gives a somewhat eerie feeling, as if Mr. Fuzzy is about to head off to that great rabbit hutch in the sky.

In addition to setting the mood, lighting also help to "attach" objects to the ground (or whatever they may be resting on) by casting shadows. Examine Figures 13.5 and 13.6 for a moment.

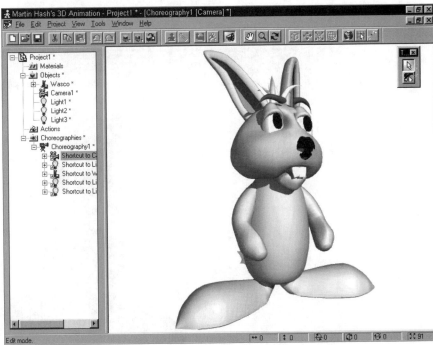

FIGURE *A cute bunny lit with basic three-point lighting.*
13.2

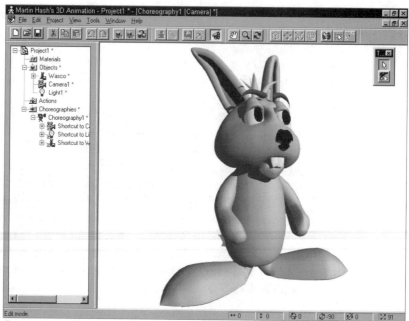

FIGURE
13.3
A cute bunny lit with just one sun-type light.

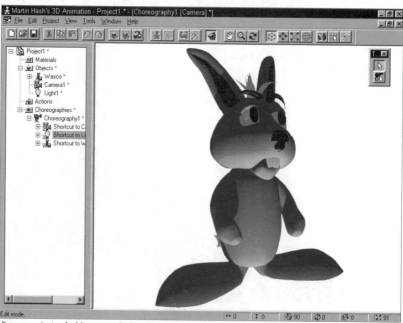

FIGURE
13.4
A single klieg-type light placed beneath and in front of a character can be used to set an eerie mood.

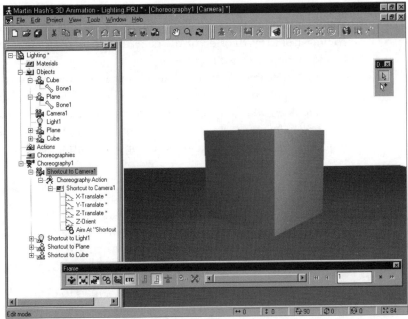

FIGURE *A simple cube rendered on a plane with no shadows.*
13.5

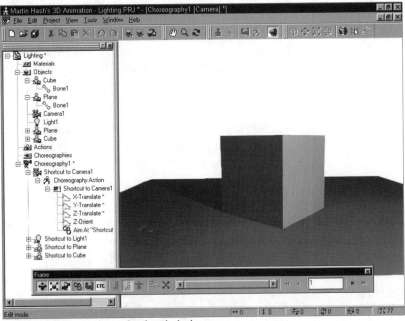

FIGURE *The same cube rendered with shadows.*
13.6

Both images are identical, except the first is rendered without shadows, and the second with. Figure 13.5 still clearly illustrates the direction the light is coming from (by the side of the cube that is more brightly lit), but the cube looks flat, and also as if it's floating.

With that said, keep in mind that at least one shadow-casting light in a scene is important. However, don't overdo it. Multiple shadows can be confusing to look at, take away from the realism of a scene, and increase render times.

The following exercise describes how to create a simple, three-light technique on which you can build more complex lighting schemes.

EXERCISE

BASIC LIGHTING TECHNIQUE

1. Open the *Lighting.PRJ* file from the CD-ROM accompanying the book. Right-click the **Choreography1** item in the **Project Workspace** and select **Edit** from the available menu.

2. Press the **1** key on the numeric keypad to change to a camera view. You should see a cube resting on a plane similarly to the one shown in the previously discussed images.

3. The three-light technique is based on a *key light* (named because it's the main, or key, light), a *fill light* that's intended to lighten dark areas of a scene or model slightly, and a *back light,* which serves to define the edges of the model being lit. Press the **5** key on the numeric keypad to change to a top view. Click the **Shortcut to Light1** item in the **Project Workspace**. The default bulb-type light should become selected to the lower right of the screen (it may be necessary to zoom out a bit to see it). This light will be the key light.

4. To change the attributes of this light, click the name *Light1* in the **Object** tree of the **Project Workspace**. Press the **F2** key to edit the name of this light, type *Key*, then press **Enter**. With the light still selected, the **Properties Panel** will show the settings available for this light.

5. Click the **Klieg** button (far left) to change the light type. Enter *60* into the Intensity field, and leave all of the remaining settings at the default values, except for the color, which should be changed to white. Notice that klieg lights offer the ability to use shadow maps, which are a less costly method in terms of rendering for shadows.

6. Notice that the light is actually pointing away from the object that is to be lit. Right-click the **Shortcut to Light1** item and select **New**

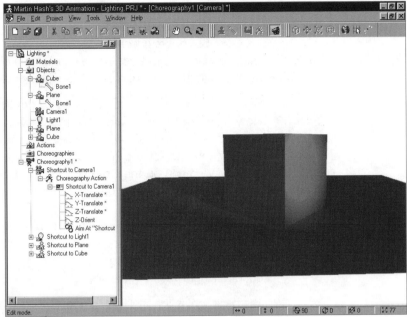

FIGURE *Rendering of the cube on a plane with the key light in place.*
13.7

Constraint, Aim At. When the cursor changes to a picker, click the cube object. If you inadvertently hit the ground plane, select the cube from the drop-down menu on the **Properties Panel** for the constraint. Rendering the model at this point produces results similar to those shown in Figure 13.7.

7. Since the key light is coming from the right of the object, a fill light needs to be added to the left of the camera. Right-click the **Choreography1** item in the **Project Workspace** and select **New**, then **Light** from the available menus. It's best to do this from the top view, since lights can be difficult to position from the camera view.

8. Use the mouse to select and drag the newly added light to the left of the camera, in line with the key light. Check the light position from a side view as well, since objects are generally added at 0 Y (aligned with the ground reference grid).

9. Click the **Light2** item in the Objects section of the **Project Workspace**. Press the **F2** key, type *Fill*, then press **Enter**.

10. On the **Properties Panel**, change the light color to white. Once again, change the light type to **Klieg**. Since this light is the fill light, uncheck the **Cast Shadows** checkbox. Generally, the fill light will have very low intensity, since it is used strictly to brighten the darkest area of a model slightly. With this in mind, enter *10* into the Intensity field.

11. Right-click this lights shortcut in the **Project Workspace** and select **New Constraint**, then **Aim At** from the available menus. When the cursor changes to a picker, click the cube object in the scene. If you inadvertently select the ground plane, select the cube from the drop-down menu on the **Constraint Properties Panel**. Rendering the model after this light has been added should produce results similar to Figure 13.8.

    The difference between the two renderings (with and without the fill light) is very subtle, but noticeable. The fill light illuminates the side of the cube just enough to make it look evenly lit without washing out or taking away from the key light.

12. The back light is the final light to add. Switch to a top view by pressing the **5** key on the numeric keypad. Right-click the **Choreography1**

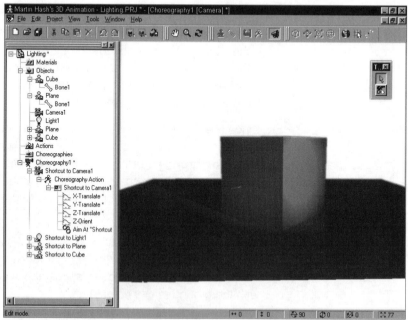

FIGURE **13.8** *Rendering of the cube object with both the key and fill lights in place. Notice that the left side of the cube is now slightly lighter.*

item in the **Project Workspace**, and select **New**, then **Light** from the available menus.

13. From the top view, drag and drop this light behind the cube, in line with the camera. Perfect positioning is not crucial, and the light can be moved later if necessary. Check the light position from a side view to verify that it is not on or below the ground plane.

14. Click the **Light3** item in the **Objects** section of the **Project Workspace**. Press the **F2** key to change the name, type *Back* and press **Enter**.

15. With the **Light3** item still selected, change the light type to klieg on the **Properties Panel**, and enter *20* into the **Intensity** field. Uncheck the **Cast Shadows** checkbox and change the light color to white.

16. Right-click the shortcut to the back light in the **Choreographies** section of the **Project Workspace** and select **New Constraint**, then **Aim At** from the available menus. When the cursor changes to a picker, click the cube object, or select it on the constraints **Properties Panel**.

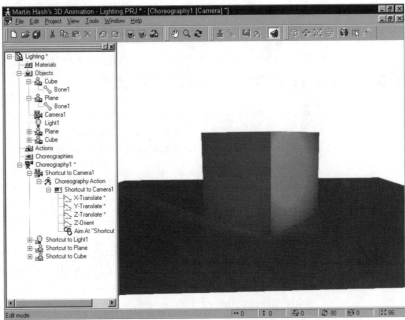

FIGURE *Rendering of the cube model with key, fill, and back lights in place.*
13.9

The final rendering should look similar to Figure 13.9, which offers no noticeable change from Figure 13.8. This is because the light that was added between the two renderings is a back light, blocked mostly by the cube. The use of a back light in defining the edges of a model will become more apparent as you build on this technique to light more complex objects.

Keep in mind as you light your scenes that you have your choice of colors and light types to work with. As you're deciding on colors, light types, and the values associated with lights, be aware that they're time-based. This is very important, because if you decide to change the color of a light while your current frame is set to 20, the software will automatically interpolate the light color from frame 1 to the light color set at frame 20. When used correctly, time-based lights can add great effects, such as blinking lights. However, if you're not paying attention, they can lead to some strange-looking renders.

Now that you're familiar with basic camera and lighting techniques, the next section briefly discusses how *fog* and *background color* are used. These tools offer yet a little more flexibility in setting the mood for your scene.

FOG AND BACKGROUND COLOR

Every camera you add to a scene gives you the option of a different *background color*. This can be useful for filling in small holes in a scene, or for giving a "continuing" feeling to the scene (such as a ground plane that extends to a blue horizon).

Background color is most useful when it's mixed with another effect called *fog*. Fog works by progressively washing out the scene until it reaches the background color. It can be used to create very nice environmental effects.

The default value for fog is zero, meaning that no fog is visible. The value used to describe fog is measured in a distance from the camera at which falloff begins. For example, the cube from the previous exercise rendered with a Fog value of 100 would result in a completely white rendering, since the fog starts too close (100 units) to the camera. A value of 1000 would result in a more suitable image, similar to the one shown in Figure 13.10.

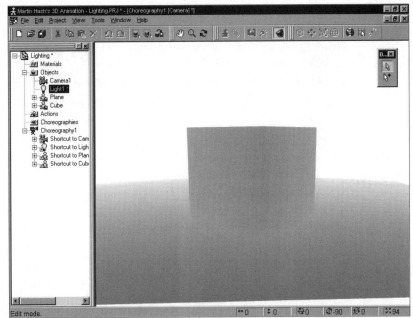

FIGURE *Rendering of the cube object with fog set to a distance of 1000 units.*
13.10

One of the real benefits of the fog effect is that if you're creative, the results can be fantastic. Fog can be used to simulate very accurately the dropoff of light underwater. Also, like everything else in the software, fog is time-based — you can make it roll in and out, or shimmy in place.

The final section in this chapter discusses one more consideration in setting the mood for a choreography: *motion blur*. Although it's a direct function of the renderer, motion blur deserves mention here since it can be used to add some nice effects to an animation.

MOTION BLUR

Everyone has seen *motion blur* in action. From the old Road-Runner cartoons, to digital effects like those seen in *The Mask*, motion blur is a reliable standby in exaggerating or expressing motion.

The settings for motion blur are actually set on the render panel. There are generic presets, but you can enter your own values if you like.

Be careful when you consider using motion blur: Anything moving in a scene will be blurred. Obviously, you can work around this by rendering the blurred object separately from the rest of the scene, then compositing the two together later.

At any rate, keep motion blur in mind as one more weapon in your "director's arsenal." It is covered more in depth in the next chapter.

SUMMARY

It can be hard to get the hang of directing. Not everyone has an eye for what makes an effective, engaging scene. As with most processes in animation, a healthy amount of practice never hurt anyone. Starting with basic, one-camera, three-light setups will help, and it will create a solid foundation on which you can build your own techniques. Remember to study other people's work, and practice some of the techniques you see elsewhere.

With effects like fog and motion blur, it's best to remember that too much of a good thing usually isn't good. Don't be excessive in using these techniques, or it will look as if you're trying to mask your shortcomings as an animator. Instead, use them to accent your work and really grab the attention of the audience.

The next chapter describes the renderer that Animation:Master uses, and some of the common terms related to rendering. Although the real "guts" of the renderer are not described in agonizing detail, it's very helpful to understand a little better just what is going on when you click the Render button.

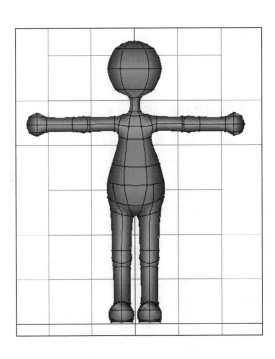

This chapter discusses the type of renderer Animation:Master uses, and defines many of the common terms used in describing rendering. It also helps you to understand the types of output you're creating when you render, and the differences between them. Having a better idea of the kind of output available to you will make it easier for you to decide what will work best in any given situation.

This chapter covers the following technical information:

- The Hybrid Renderer
- Understanding Final Output
- Alpha Buffer Output
- Using Motion Blur

THE HYBRID RENDERER

Animation:Master uses a renderer called a *hybrid*. The term hybrid comes from the fact that the renderer uses true raytracing when necessary to create realistic shadows, reflections, and transparent objects, and a combination of fast *shaders* the remainder of the time.

One of the shaders is referred to as an *a-buffer*, or *accumulation buffer*, so named because it adds, or accumulates, in memory the results of the rendering operations being performed on a given scene. The second type of shader is referred to as a *z-buffer shader*. The z-buffer is simply a comparison of the Z values of two objects, with the lesser value (the object or pixel closer to the camera) being displayed.

The combination of these rendering methods allows for very high image quality without long render times. The trade-off, obviously, is the need for enough physical memory (RAM) to hold the image being rendered.

FLAT SHADING

Flat shading is the simplest form of rendering available in Animation:Master. When an object is flat-shaded, it actually receives no shading at all, resulting in a very flat-looking image. When you select flat shading in the rendering

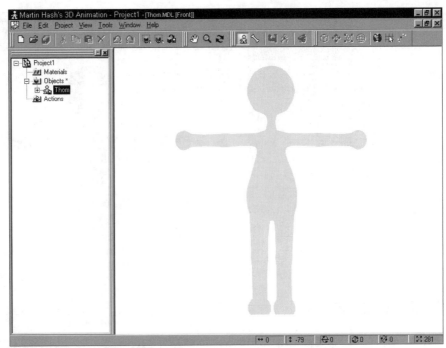

FIGURE   *Flat shaded image of Thom.*
14.1

preferences, the software will simply look at an object, find a patch, and color it accordingly. No shadow or other surface information is rendered, which means that the image will be rendered very quickly, but at a quality that is not suitable for final output. Flat shading is used most often for rough previews of scenes, because it doesn't provide any detail. However, it can be used to create accurate templates for creating decals.

Z-BUFFER

The next type of renderer is called a *z-buffer*. It is very common, and very fast, as long as the computer has enough physical memory to render the image. In z-buffer rendering, each patch is assigned a Z value. Then, pixel by pixel, the patch with the smallest value is displayed.

The biggest disadvantage of z-buffer rendering is the large amounts of memory required to store the information needed to correctly render a scene.

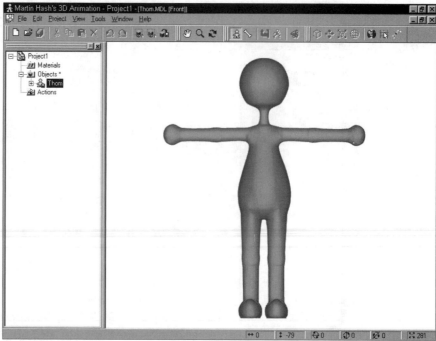

FIGURE *z-Buffer rendering of Thom.*
14.2

The z-buffer works in conjunction with the raytracer in creating transparent, refractive, reflective, and shadowed surfaces.

A-BUFFER

The renderer that provides the fidelity in an image is called an *a-buffer*. The "a" stands for accumulation, which describes the way the renderer works.

Each screen pixel is divided into 32 subpixels. Information from each pixel's rendering results is stored in a buffer as the renderer calculates Z values, whether or not it is necessary to cast any rays, etc. When the entire 32-subpixel grid has been filled by the accumulation of rendering results, the pixel is done, and the renderer continues to the next one. Because each pixel is subdivided, the a-buffer provides very high-quality output that goes well beyond the viewing resolution.

This explanation barely scratches the surface of the complex calculations the renderer is performing. However, it's enough to help you understand the differences between a and z buffers, and how they work.

GOURAUD SHADING

Gouraud shading is the type of rendering available when using a graphics accelerator mode such as Direct 3D, Quick Draw 3D, or OpenGL. This type of renderer subdivides each patch on the model according to the specifications set in the **Render Settings** dialog, locates the surface normals, calculates the color of each, then interpolates between them to form a shaded area.

Gouraud shading provides fast feedback and smooth surfaces.

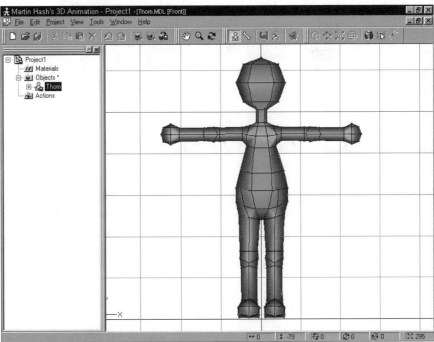

FIGURE
14.3
A Direct 3D rendering of the Thom model with the patch subdivision set to 1 polygon per patch. Notice the angles of the surface, and the lack of a smooth curve.

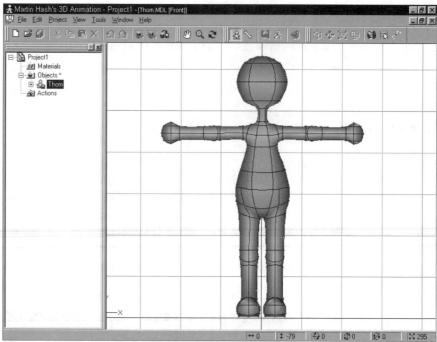

FIGURE   *A Direct 3D rendering of Thom model with the patch subdivision set to Variable polygons*
14.4   *per patch. Notice the smooth curves.*

UNDERSTANDING FINAL OUTPUT

After all the hard work is finished and you're ready to render, you're left with a
decision to make about what kind of output to use. A *full-motion video* (*AVI*
on PC, *QuickTime Movie* on the PowerMac) will usually be the choice if the
only planned use for the animation is desktop playback. If you expect to put
your animation on videotape, or need higher quality output, you'll want to
save your work as a series of *.TGA (TARGA)* files.

AVI

AVI stands for *Audio Video Interleave* and is the standard for video on the
Windows platform. AVI files offer fair compression and playback quality, but

often require a great deal of storage space. These files use something called a *CODEC (COmpression/DECompression)* to help reduce the amount of redundant or unchanging information from frame to frame in the video file. There are many different CODECs, some of the most common being *Microsoft Video 1, Cinepak,* and *Indeo.* Animation:Master allows you to choose a compressor from those available on your system when you create your movie files.

QuickTime MOV

MOV is the Apple *QuickTime* movie format, the standard for video on the PowerMac platform. QuickTime movies offer compression ratios as high as 50:1, as well as high-quality playback. Like AVI files, QuickTime movies tend to have high storage requirements.

QuickTime movies also use CODECs to compress the data in a movie file. Animation:Master will allow you to choose one of the several CODECs available on the PowerMac platform.

QuickTime movies can also be played on a Windows-based machine, with *QuickTime for Windows.* The QuickTime movie has become very popular on the PC because of the high quality it offers.

TGA (TARGA) File Format

TARGA files are the best choice for output when you plan to go to videotape. When files are rendered to a TARGA sequence, they're saved with the filename, then a frame number appended to the end (*file0001.tga, file0002.tga,* etc.). Once a sequence has been rendered, you can run it to tape using one of many available methods. Keep in mind that the trade-off for this quality is the cost of transfer, which can add up quickly. Sequences of TARGA files can also be compressed into a movie file with a program such as Adobe Premiere.

TARGA files have several advantages over the available movie formats. They can render to large resolutions much more easily, because large movie files tend to get unwieldy very quickly and require huge amounts of system resources.

TARGA files are less likely to be lost in the event of a system crash or power outage because once a frame has been rendered, it is saved to the hard drive, and the next one is worked on. Movie formats, on the other hand, must be stored somewhere and kept open for access until all frames are completed and can be compressed. Consider the disappointment in rendering a 100-frame movie if you crash on frame 99. You would have to start rendering again from the beginning.

ALPHA BUFFER

Alpha buffers are 8 bits of additional information that are stored in output files when the alpha buffer rendering option is selected. *Alpha channels* are essentially a grayscale version of your render that describe the transparent values in the image. Totally opaque areas of a frame will be white in the alpha channel; transparent objects are black. Varying levels of transparency appear as shades of gray.

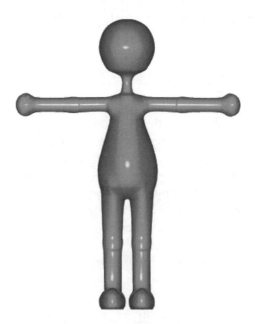

FIGURE *Rendered output of the Thom model with an alpha buffer. Notice that you can't see any*
14.5 *visible signs that the alpha buffer exists in this image.*

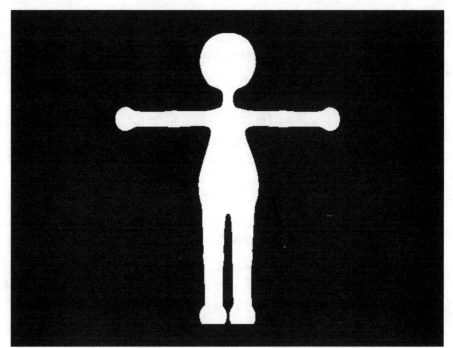

FIGURE *This image shows what the alpha buffer from the rendering shown in Figure 14.5 looks like.*
14.6

Alpha channels are used most often during rendering to a sequential frame output where the plan is to composite the output with other images. The alpha channel makes it possible to combine two images cleanly without the need for color keys or special tools to remove the background color.

Now that you have a little background on the rendering processes and terminology, the next section will discuss motion blur and walk you through an exercise demonstrating its effect.

MOTION BLUR

Motion blur is a rendering technique that gives the effect of speed, or accents slow-motion scenes by blurring the object or objects that are moving. Everyone has seen this effect before — in any Road-Runner cartoon.

As the Road-Runner is running, his feet appear only as a blurred circle, giving the illusion that they're moving very fast. Another example would be the propeller of an airplane. The propeller spins so fast that all that remains visible is a blurred "circle."

Keep in mind when you're planning to use motion blur that anything in the scene that is moving will blur. In addition, don't overdo it. Blurring everything you do will make your animation look confusing, as well as tiring to look at. Use motion blur sparingly, to accent motion.

The following exercise will describe using motion blur on a simple model of a tornado.

EXERCISE

USING MOTION BLUR

1. Begin by opening the *Motion Blur.PRJ* file from the accompanying CD-ROM. The project will open to a **Choreography** window containing a funnel shape on a path, with a plain white backdrop.

2. The point of this exercise is not necessarily to see how the funnel and associated materials and paths were created, but to see the effect of motion blur on a model. You may want to take a moment to examine the objects and materials, as well as the path constraint and associated Ease channel, to see how the model was made to move.

3. Click the **Render To File** button. Change the output to save either an AVI or QuickTime movie that is 320 × 240. The **Frame Range** should be 1–60 (this should be set correctly already).

4. On the **Quality** tab, click the **Final** radio button. On the **Final Quality Options** tab, click in both the **Filter Textures** and the **Shadows** checkboxes. Click in the **Motion Blur** checkbox to activate the motion blur options, and select the **360 Degree** radio button. These settings control the amount of blur that you'll see as the model moves along its path.

5. Click the **Start** button and allow the animation to render. Because the **Filter Textures** and **Shadows** options are selected, and because the tornado has some transparency, render time will be a little longer. If you're working on a slower machine, you may want to try turning off **Filter Textures** or **Shadows** to speed up the render times.

NOTE

Notice that on the first frame of the animation, no motion blur is present. This is because the model is not yet moving. If you require blur on the first frame of your animation, render out a TARGA file sequence, then drop the first frame and composite the remaining frames into the final output.

As the animation plays back, adjust the speed and notice the difference in the effect. Remember not to expect motion blur to cover poorly animated characters. Instead, use it to enhance their motions.

SUMMARY

Although it certainly isn't crucial to know how the renderer works its magic, it is important to understand your output options, and what you're asking of your computer. Many of the terms described in this chapter are tossed about carelessly at times. Knowing a little bit of background of the terminology you're using is important in understanding both the software, and the output that you're left with in the end.

The next chapter will cover compositing with MultiPlane, a robust, layer-based compositing tool included in the Animation:Master suite.

CHAPTER 15

Compositing

The process of merging multiple images into a single image is called compositing. The Animation:Master software suite includes a program called *MultiPlane*, which was specifically designed for 3D compositing. MultiPlane is named after the multiplane camera crane that Walt Disney used in adding perspective and depth into the compositing of many layers.

This chapter introduces the interface and basic working ideas of the MultiPlane compositor.

Topics described in this chapter include:

- The Art of Digital Compositing
- The MultiPlane Interface
- Simple Layer Animations
- Working with Multiple Layers
- Using Color Key and Lens Flare Effects

THE ART OF DIGITAL COMPOSITING

The art of *digital compositing* is fairly new to the desktop PC. It was long reserved for high-end finishing work for movies and television. The possibilities of such a program on the desktop are practically endless. Animation:Master allows you to create anything you can imagine, and MultiPlane allows you to put it together with backgrounds, live action, and effects such as lens flares.

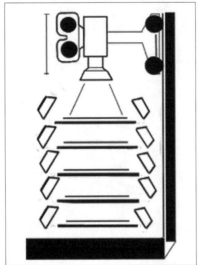

FIGURE   *The multiplane camera crane that gave*
15.1   *many Disney cartoons their look of depth.*

As mentioned in the introduction, the MultiPlane program is the desktop replacement for the ever-popular multiplane camera crane, a drawing of which is shown in Figure 15.1.

This digital version of a multiplane camera adds much more flexibility and power in the form of ease of use and a practically unlimited number of layering possibilities.

SCENE COMPOSITION

Any artist would agree that *scene composition* is significant to the end result. As you look at an image, your mind must decipher many visual cues to understand that image. Without such cues, the incredible array of information coming from the image would be impossible to comprehend.

When you consider the importance of the individual components of scene composition, providing a feeling of *depth* should be near the top of the list. This is because depth always makes it easier to decipher an image quickly. Is a character walking behind trees, or in front of them? Is an airplane flying into clouds? This kind of information is important in defining the location of different objects throughout a scene.

Another important component would be the *background image.* This could be just the image of a sky, or both the sky and the ground plane. Picture a painting or animation for a moment. Neither of them consists of objects simply floating over a sea of blackness; other objects are visible, such as the sky, ground, or other scenery. The background scenery helps again to develop the depth of the scene, in addition to providing an environment where the action takes place. With these few details in mind, it's easy to see how every scene can be broken down and composed of many individual layers.

Blending the separate layers into a single image adds richness to the story. The better the individual layers integrate into a scene, the better the resulting image. The design of MultiPlane keeps the idea of 3D animation in mind, as opposed to the single-picture compositing provided in most paint programs.

Keep in mind that compositions can be as simple as a single image, or as complex as layers of thousands of sequential images. Compositing the thousands of frames that make up an animation is a repetitive task that is best left to a computer, which can work unattended.

Each of the images or sequences of images in a given composition is called a *layer.* An example of how MultiPlane handles layers is shown in Figure 15.2. The sky image is on one layer, and the P51 Airplane image is on another layer. Each of these individual layers can be translated, scaled, or rotated, or can have effects applied to it; each of these attributes can change from frame to frame to

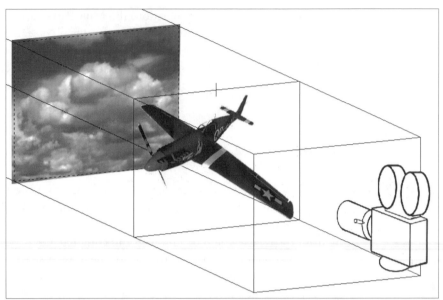

FIGURE *The cloud image and the P51 image are on separate layers.*
15.2

FIGURE *The final image produced by compositing the layers shown in Figure 15.2.*
15.3

achieve the desired effect. When the layers are combined (composited), the end result is a single image, such as the one shown in Figure 15.3.

Now that the introductions are complete, and you know a little about compositing, it's time to become familiar with the MultiPlane interface. The next section describes each part of the MultiPlane interface briefly, as well as discussing which parts of the program are used to perform certain functions.

THE MULTIPLANE INTERFACE

The *MultiPlane interface,* shown in Figure 15.4, is composed of several main sections. Each section performs an important function in the compositing process. The main sections of the interface are the menu bar, **Composition** window, **Object List**, **Attribute Panel**, and **Tool Panel**. The integration of these tools and a high-quality compositing engine are what make it easy to achieve high-quality results quickly.

The next section briefly describes those tools available from the menu bar.

FIGURE   *The MultiPlane interface, with a single layer loaded into the Object List.*
15.4

THE MENU BAR

The *menu bar* is located across the top of the interface. It includes drop-down menus for **File**, **Edit**, **Window**, and **Help** functions.

The **File** drop-down menu is shown in Figure 15.5. The **File** drop-down menu contains options used to create New compositions, Open existing compositions, Save compositions, or Save compositions As a new name. Files that are saved from MultiPlane have a *.CMP* extension on them.

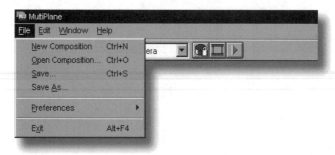

FIGURE   *The **File** drop-down menu from MultiPlane.*
15.5

Global **Preferences** such as Memory and Undo levels, as well as Channel Window preferences, are also accessed from the **File** drop-down menu. The **Exit** item will close the current composition and exit the MultiPlane program.

The **Edit** drop-down menu is shown in Figure 15.6. From the **Edit** menu, **Undo** and **Redo** allow you to undo and redo your previous actions.

In MultiPlane, you can make individual layers travel along a path, just as you can with an object within the Animation:Master program. Selecting a

FIGURE   *The **Edit** drop-down menu from MultiPlane.*
15.6

point along a path, then selecting **Complement Path** from the **Edit** menu will invert the points selected on the path. Likewise, selecting a point on a path and selecting **Group Path** from the **Edit** menu will cause the entire path to become selected.

If a layer or several layers are selected in the **Object List**, picking **Complement All** will cause all of the selected layers to become deselected, and all of the deselected layers to become selected.

Ungroup All and **Group All** also affect the selected layers. **Ungroup All** will deselect all selected layers, and **Group All** will select all layers. These are useful when certain layers need to be moved in unison.

FIGURE   *The **Window** drop-down menu from MultiPlane.*
15.7

The **Window** drop-down menu is shown in Figure 15.7. The **Window** menu contains many of the same items as the one in the main Animation:Master interface, and these options affect the windows in the same way.

- Selecting **New Window** will open another occurrence of the selected window. This allows you to open several windows and work while viewing several angles at once.
- **Close** will close the selected window.
- The **Show Panels** section of the **Window** drop-down is used to control which panels are visible.
- **Close All, Tile, Tile Vertically, Cascade, Twin View,** and **Quad View** are all preset window arrangements that you can select to help you organize several windows on the screen.

- The **Arrange Icons** option is useful if you have several minimized windows along the bottom of the screen.
- Finally, selecting **View** from the **Window** drop-down menu will allow you to enter X and Y offset values, Roll, Tilt, and Swivel view angles, and Zoom values. All of these values match the operation of the View controls within the Animation:Master interface.

Now that you're familiar with the contents of the drop-down menus available, the next section describes the **Composition Window**.

THE COMPOSITION WINDOW

The **Composition Window,** shown in Figure 15.8, is the main part of the interface. This is where layers are positioned, moved over time, displayed, and preview rendered.

FIGURE *The Composition Window, where layers are arranged and the composition is preview*
15.8 *rendered.*

The controls used to affect the individual layers are located on both the **Tool** and **Attribute Panels**. They give you precise control over the image positioning and scaling. The next section discusses the tools available on the **Tool Panel**.

THE TOOL PANEL

The **Tool Panel**, shown in Figure 15.9, contains many of the tools that are used to make adjustments to an individual layer within a composition.

FIGURE **15.9** *The **Tool Panel**, which is used for making changes to the individual layers in a composition.*

The **Edit** mode button is selected by default on the **Tool Panel**. **Edit** mode allows you to select layers, change layer settings, add effects, etc.

Other buttons are provided for **Channels** (allowing precise time-based control over a layers attributes), **Translate**, **Scale**, **Rotate**, and **Translate** the selected layer's **Pivot**. The pivot position is important, since is the point around which a layer will rotate or scale.

The next section describes the **Attribute Panel**, which provides numerical entry fields for the selected layer's settings (such as Scale and Translation).

THE ATTRIBUTE PANEL

The **Attribute Panel**, shown in Figure 15.10, provides numerical fields that display the values associated with the effect a tool is having on a layer. For example, if you select a layer, then select the **Scale** tool, watching the values on the

FIGURE
15.10
*The **Attribute Panel** allows direct input of numerical data. It can also be used for feedback on a given layer.*

Attribute Panel will tell you when to stop scaling. Likewise, if you're planning to scale a layer down to exactly 50%, you can simply enter *50* directly into both the X and Y Scale fields on the **Attribute Panel**.

The panel is divided into five main sections:

- The **Translate** section allows you to see or enter X, Y, and Z values for a selected layer.
- The **Pivot** section allows you to specify the X and Y position of the selected layer's pivot.
- The **Scale** section allows you to see or enter X and Y scale values for a selected layer.
- The **Roll** field allows you to turn a layer about the Y axis, rotating it in 3D.
- Finally, the **Transparency** field allows you to specify how transparent the selected layer should look. This is a useful tool for cloud or fog effects.

Now you're familiar with all of the sections of the interface except the **Object List**, which is described in the next section.

THE OBJECT LIST

The **Object List** is where layers are added and deleted, effects are applied, and Layer Settings are changed. Figure 15.11 shows the **Object List**.

FIGURE *The **Object List**, where layers are added and deleted, effects are applied, and Layer*
15.11 *Settings are modified.*

The **Object List** is a useful and important part of the compositing process, because it gives you a quick look at how a selected layer is set. The right-hand side of the **Object List** contains a condensed form of valuable information, such as the image sequence and play mode settings, scaling quality, and subpixel compositing.

Now that you've been briefly familiarized with the MultiPlane interface, the next section describes how to begin working in MultiPlane by creating a simple, single-layer animation.

LAYER ANIMATION

On the simplest level, you can use MultiPlane to create many of the rotating, zooming, and scaling effects you've seen when television shows head to or return from a break. You can create these effects easily with simple manipulation of a few settings for an individual layer. The next exercise will describe how to do a simple translate and zoom move on a single layer.

EXERCISE

LAYER ANIMATION

1. Start MultiPlane and click the **New** button to begin a new composition.

2. On the **Object List**, click the **Add** button and locate the *Single Layer Animation.TGA* file on the accompanying CD-ROM.

3. Click the layer you just added in the **Object List** to activate it, and enter 5 into both the **X** and **Y Scale** fields on the **Attributes Panel**.

4. Click the **Translate** button on the toolbar and drag the layer to the upper left-hand corner of the **TV/Title Safe** region on the screen.

5. Enter 30 into the **Current Frame** field.

6. Enter 0 into the **X** and **Y Translate** fields to return the layer to its original position. You'll notice that a white spline path appears as you make these changes. Each control point along the spline has a number under it representing the frame at which changes were made for that point.

7. Enter 45 into the **Current Frame** field, and enter 100 into both the **X** and **Y Scale** fields.

8. The animation for this layer now causes the layer to start out small in the upper left-hand corner, travel to the center of the screen, then "zoom" in until it fills the window. A little more motion wouldn't hurt, so enter 37 into the **Current Frame** field and enter 180 into the **Y Pivot** field. This will move the layer off-center from the pivot.

9. Enter 30 into the **Current Frame** field, and enter 0 into the **Y Pivot** field so that the layer will not begin to offset until frame 30.

10. Finally, enter 45 into the **Current Frame** field and enter 0 into the **Y Pivot** field to return the layer to its original location.

   Render the animation and see how it looks. You should get something similar to the *Single Layer.MOV* file on the accompanying CD-ROM.

Now that you're familiar with how to manipulate a single layer in MultiPlane, the next step is working with several layers at once. The next section describes how to create a simple composition out of three individual layers.

WORKING WITH MULTIPLE LAYERS

The true power of working with MultiPlane comes when you need to add several layers to a composition. This might include a *background*, an *effects layer*, a *fog layer*, a *layer with a 3D character* on it, and perhaps a *titling layer*. As mentioned earlier, every layer can be manipulated individually — so now the flexibility and power of the program comes to light.

Although it doesn't include any fancy translations or scaling, the next exercise describes how to create and work with a composition containing multiple layers.

MULTILAYER COMPOSITIONS

1. Click the **New** button to begin a new composition.

2. Click the **Add** button on the **Object List** and locate the *Foreground.TGA* file on the accompanying CD-ROM.

3. Click the **Add** button on the **Object List** and locate the *Background.TGA* file on the CD-ROM.

4. Click the **Add** button on the **Object List** once more, and locate the *Titling.TGA* file on the CD-ROM.

5. Right-click the **Filmstrip** button on the menu bar and change the output resolution to D1 (720×486). This will match the output size to the size of the individual layers that you added in the previous three steps. The screen should look similar to Figure 15.12.

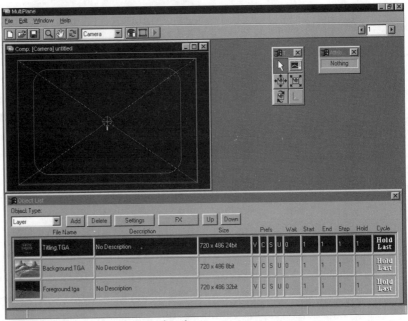

FIGURE *A composition containing three layers.*
15.12

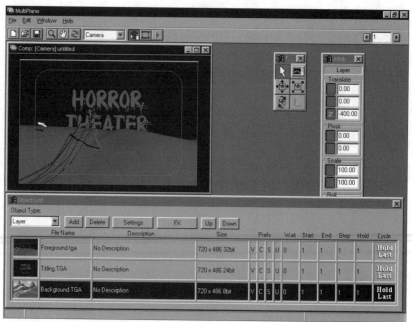

FIGURE
15.13
A rendering of the composition after the layers are reordered. Although the layers are in the correct positions, the background image is blocked out by the black background of the middle layer.

6. If you rendered the composition at this point, the titling would be the only visible layer, since you added it last. To move this layer between the background and foreground, click the *Titling.TGA* layer, and click the **Down** button on the **Object List** once.

7. Now the titling is in the correct position, but the foreground and background are incorrect. Click the *Foreground.TGA* layer to select it, then click the **Up** button on the **Object List** once. This will move the foreground in front of the titling.

8. Finally, click the *Background.TGA* file on the **Object List**, and click the **Down** button twice to move this layer to the back of the image.

9. When rendered, the image looks like Figure 15.13. The background image is blocked out by the black background of the titling layer.

10. This can be corrected by applying a color key to the titling image. To do this, click the *Titling.TGA* layer in the **Object List**, then click the **FX** button.

11. Click the **Add** button, then select the **Keying** tab.

FIGURE *The composition with the background color of the titling layer keyed out. The*
15.14 *background layer is now visible.*

12. Click the **Key Color** item and select **OK**.

13. On the **FX** List, click the **Key Color** item, then click the **Settings** button. For the Transparent color, set the **RGB** sliders to *0,0,0*. This will remove all black from the selected image.

14. Close the **FX List** and render the scene. The output should look similar to Figure 15.14.

15. To aid in adding a little depth to the scene, click the *Background.TGA* layer and click the **FX** button.

16. Click the **Add** button and select the **Blur** item.

17. Select the **Blur** item in the **FX List** and click the **Settings** button. Set the **Blur Radius** to *1*.

18. The final step is to make the text scroll across the screen. Select the *Titling.TGA* layer in the **Composition Window** by clicking on it. It may be necessary to use the **Turn** tool to rotate the view.

19. On the **Attribute** panel, enter *–200* into the **Y Translate** field.

20. Enter *120* into the **Current Frame** field.

21. Enter *500* into the **Y Translate** field on the **Attributes Panel**. This will cause the text to scroll from below the foreground hill upward off the screen.

The *Multiple Layer.MOV* file on the CD-ROM is the resulting render from the composition that you just created. Take a little time and experiment with different movements of the titling layer. See what kind of results you can produce.

You've gotten a small taste of the effects in MultiPlane with the simple color key you used in the previous exercise. The next section looks at *color keys* and *lens flares* a little more closely, since these are two of the more commonly used effects.

EXAMPLE EFFECTS

Effects are a must in the production environment. Consider where movies and special effects would be today if there were no way to combine live actors with miniature sets, or to place well-known stars into perilous situations with no risk. Some of these situations are handled by professional stunt people. Others are filmed in front of a green or blue screen, then left to the digital finishing company to fill in the blanks.

One of the effects used commonly is a *color key*. Color key was used in a simple form in the previous exercise. The following exercise looks a little more closely at the color key effect.

EXERCISE

COLOR KEY

1. Start MultiPlane, and click the **New** button to begin a new composition.

2. Click the **Add** button on the **Object List** and locate the *Color Key.TGA* file on the accompanying CD-ROM.

3. The *Color Key.TGA* image is a white-to-black gradient to help illustrate the color key effect. With the *Color Key.TGA* layer selected, click the **FX** button on the **Object List**, then click the **Add** button.

4. Select the **Keying** tab and click the **Color Key** item. Click **OK**.

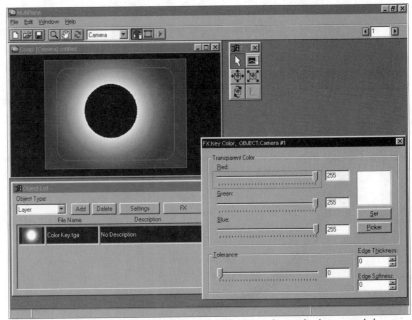

FIGURE **15.15** *A gradient image with a color key applied. Notice the rough edges around the center where the white pixels were removed.*

5. In the **FX List**, select the **Blur** item, then click the **Settings** button. Set the **Transparent Color** to white by moving each of the **RGB** sliders to *255*.

6. Render the image. It should look similar to Figure 15.15. Notice how rough the center appears where the white pixels were keyed out of the image.

7. Enter *2* into both the **Edge Thickness** and **Edge Softness** fields to lessen the effect of the sharp edges.

8. Use the **Tolerance** slider to adjust the tolerance of the color key. This key out pixels that are varying shades of white, depending on the value.

9. Continue to experiment with the **Tolerance** slider, as well as the **Edge** fields, to see what kind of results you can produce.

The **Color Key** filter is very useful when you're combining puter-generated layers. It also works well when you're combin was shot in front of a green screen with computer-generated im

Another often-used effect is the *lens flare*. If you choose to use them in your work, do so sparingly; this effect has been overused and worn out by many of today's science fiction television shows. A sound idea is to stick with using them in situations where a visible light is needed, such as the sun or the headlights of a car.

The following exercise describes how to use lens flares in Animation:Master with the aid of MultiPlane.

EXERCISE

LENS FLARES

1. Start Animation:Master and open the *Flare.PRJ* file from the accompanying CD-ROM. This project contains only a light, a camera, and a path.

2. The Lens Flare effect in MultiPlane uses the light information in a rendered TARGA file to determine where a flare is traveling through a scene. Therefore, to make a lens flare effect, all you need is a light that's visible in the rendered image. Right-click the **Shortcut to Light1** item in the **Project Workspace** and select **New Constraint, Path** from the available menu.

3. When the cursor changes into a **Picker** tool, select the existing path by clicking on it in the **Choreography** window. If you inadvertently miss the path object with the **Picker** tool, use the drop-down list on the **Properties Panel** to select the path.

4. The color and light type are not important, but the light width is. Click the **Shortcut to Light1** item in the **Project Workspace** and enter *100* into the **Width** field on the **Properties Panel**.

5. The lens flare effect uses the names of the lights that you specified in the rendered scene. To keep track of lights you intend to use to create a flare, it's a good idea to name them accordingly. Click the **Shortcut to Light1** item in the **Project Workspace** to select it, then press the **F2** key to edit the name. Type *Flare* and press **Enter**.

6. Click on the **Path Constraint** item in the **Project Workspace**. On the **Properties Panel**, enter *0* into the **Ease** field. Enter *30* into the **Current Frame** field and enter *100* into the **Ease** channel. This will cause the light to travel from the beginning of the path to the end in 30 frames.

7. Click the **Render to File** button and render a 30-frame sequence of *.TGA* files to a folder on your hard drive. Name the output file *Frame000.TGA*.

8. Start MultiPlane and click the **New** button to begin a new composition.

9. Click the **Add** button on the **Object List**, and locate the *Frame001.TGA* file that was just rendered. When the image opens, click the **Settings** button and enter *30* into the **End** field.

10. Right-click the **Filmstrip** button and set the output resolution size to 320×240.

11. Click the **FX** button, then click the **Add** button and select the **Render** tab. Click the **Lens Flare** item and select **OK**.

12. Highlight the **Lens Flare** item in the **FX List** and click the **Settings** button. A dialog box similar to the one shown in Figure 15.16 will open.

13. Notice that the name of the light appears in the **Light Name** list along the right side of the lens flare settings. Click the **Flare** item in

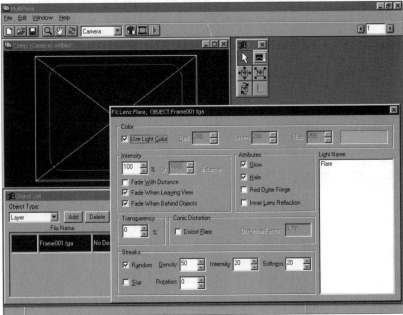

FIGURE *The dialog box with the settings for a lens flare.*
15.16

this list to select the only light in the scene, then uncheck the **Use Light Color** checkbox.

14. Set the **Red** field to *255,* and both the **Green** and **Blue** fields to *200.* This will give the flare a reddish tint.

15. Uncheck the **Fade When Leaving View** and **Fade When Behind Objects** checkboxes, and place a check in the **Fade With Distance** checkbox. This will cause the flare to fade out as it travels away from the camera, giving the appearance of depth.

16. Click the **Filmstrip** button and render a 30-frame movie of the lens flare at 320×240. For reference, the *Flare.MOV* file on the CD-ROM should be similar to your results.

NOTE It's very important to remember that Animation:Master stores the light information for lens flares in the rendered image files. If you were to open one of these images in a paint program and save it back, all of the lighting information would be lost.

Experiment with the Flare Rotation and Streak settings to see what kind of effect they have on the final flare. Also take some time to experiment with the **Inner Lens Reflection** checkbox and see what effect that produces in the final renderings.

Remember that, as with many of the other techniques you've learned, if you plan out how you'd like to use the **Lens Flare** tool, you can come up with an interesting effect without too much effort.

SUMMARY

This chapter illustrates how an animation program and a compositing program work together to produce a dynamic end result. Anything you create in Animation:Master can be placed in front of different backgrounds, either CG or live action.

When you consider using the MultiPlane effects in a finished piece, remember to plan it out, and to use them sparingly. Too many effects make it look as if you're trying to cover something up.

ABOUT THE CD-ROM

The CD included with this book contains many of the models shown in the tutorials so that they may be opened within Animation:Master and examined. These models are provided in Animation:Master v5 format as a learning tool for your private, non commerical use and may not be distributed or converted to other formats.

Wherever possible, all supporting image maps, materials, and patch color information is included with the model files so that you can fully understand the construction of these characters, and how each of these parts combine to achive the final goal. Also included are several example animations created with Animation:Master that show the capabilities of the software. These are for private use as well and may not be distributed or converted to any other format.

INSTALLATION

WINDOWS '95/NT

Place the AM Handbook in your CD-Rom drive. If autoplay is enabled on the machine you are using, the installer will automatically run. If not, follow the instuctions below:

Double Click the setup folder
Double Click the Intel Folder
Double Click MH3Dinst.EXE
Follow the instructions in the installer

NOTE: If a release/registered version of MH3D/AM has already bee installed on the system, do not install the demo version.

NOTE: On systems with icon sizes set below 32 pionts, reoccuring crashes in Windows Explorer or Module KERNL32.DLL can be fixed by deleting the HASHICON.DLL file from the Windows\System folder. It may be necessary to delete this file from a DOS prompt.

POWERMAC

Place the AM Handbook CD in your CD-ROM drive
Double Click the Setup folder
Double Click the PowerMac folder
Double Click MH3D5 Demo Installer
Follow the instructions in the installer

NOTE: The CD is a 32-bit hybrid (cross platform) CD. Therefore, if your machine is unable to read the CD, verify that ISO-9660, High Serra, and Foreign File Access extensions are present and active.

Please note that Conix OpenGL for the PowerMac is included in the installer. When memory is alloted to MH3D on the Mac, be aware that OpenGL runs in *system memory*, not program memory. This means that if your system has 40MB RAM, you do not want to specify 36MB to MH3D, because there will be no room for OpenGL to perform within system memory.

Index

A

A-buffer, 414, 416–417
Accumulation buffer, 414, 416–417
Action, 18, 22
  menu, 23
  Options tab, 29
  Overloading, 359
  unconstrained, 23
Actions, 12
  lip-synch, 354–359
  motion libraries, 359–360
  muscle, 348–351
  poses, 351–354
  reusable, 296, 297
  skeletal, 334–348
Adobe Photoshop, 122, 232, 235, 241, 375
  alpha channels, 252
  head image map, 254–256
Adobe Premiere, 419
Aim At constraints, 261–265, 399–401
Aim Roll At constraints, 277–278
Airbrush, use of, 235
Airplane, 176–183
Alpha buffer, 420–421
Alpha channels, 420–421
  using, 251–253
Ambiance, 198, 380
  maps, 236–237

Animation, using constraints, 285–287
  See also Actions; Path animation
Anti-aliasing, 227, 249–251, 253
Appearance tab, 27
Arms, 164–165
  extrusions for, 67–70
Attribute panel, MultiPlane, 433–434
AVI (Audio Video Interleave), 418–419

B

Babylon 5, 183
Backbone curvature, 157
Backdrops
  cylindrical, 375–381
  dome, 381–386
  spherical, 386–390
Background image, 427
Back light, 406, 410
Base attributes, 194–198
Biped, 59–76
  bones, 298–305
Bones, 35, 265, 314
  biped, 298–305
  Boolean operations, 311–313
  default or hidden, 272, 299–300, 320–322
  hierarchies, 296
  understanding joints, 290–296
  quadrupeds, 305–311

standard naming convention, 297–298
target, 287–288
See also Constraints
Boolean cutter, 311–313
Brick wall, 246–249
Brightness. *See* Ambiance
Buildings, 170–176
Bump maps, 230–232

C
Camera
   rotoscope, 375
   techniques, 399–402
Cameron, James, 398
Cartooning the Head and Figure, 350
Channel
   Options tab, 30
   window, 329
Character
   combining with images, 390–395
   development, 4–5
   simple, 42–58
   See also Modeling
Checker combiner, 204–207
Chest area, 157–158
Choreography, 12, 18, 331, 359, 380
   Options tab, 29–30
Chrome, 215–218
Cinepak, 419
Circular constraint, 263–264
CODEC (COmpression/DECompression), 419
Color, 196
   background, 410–411
   key exercise, 440–441
   lighting, 410
   maps, 227–228, 249
   See also Patch coloring
Combiners, 203–211
Commands tab, 24

Complement All, 20
Complement spline, 20
Compositing
   digital, 426–429
   effects, 440–444
   layer animation, 435–436
   MultiPlane interface, 429–435
   multiple layers, 436–440
Composition window, MultiPlane, 432–433
Constraints, 260–261
   animating, 285–287
   using multiple, 281–285
   target bones, 287–288
   time-based, 324, 325
   types of, 261–281
Control points, 20, 38, 116, 304, 350
Cookie-cut maps, 238–239, 252
Cow
   body, 77–80
   bones, 306–308
   finishing, 85–86
   head, 79–80
   legs, 80–83
      bones in, 308–309
   tail, 83–85
      bones in, 309–311
Creases, 89, 113, 114–121, 134
   mouth corner, 137–140
Curved surface, 120–121
   decaling of, 240–243
Customizing tools menu, 23–27
Cylindrical backdrops, 375–381

D
Darkling Simulations, 257
DarkTree Textures, 257–258
Decals, 31, 258, 415
   alpha channels, 251–253
   dome exercise, 383–386

reordering, 249
techniques for, 240–251
texture map alternatives, 257–258
tips for creating, 253–257
types of, 226–240
Depth, 390, 427
Diffuse maps, 233–235
Digital compositing, 426–429
Direct 3D, 417, 418
Directing
  camera use, 399–402
  fog and background color, 410–411
  lighting, 403–410
  Mode, 32
  mood of story, 398
  motion blur, 411–412
Disney, Walt, 426
Displacement maps, 239
Dockable toolbars, 32–33
Dome backdrops, 381–386
Doors and windows, 173–176
Dopesheets, 356–357, 358
Drop-down menus, 17–18
  Action, 23
  edit, 19–20
  file, 18–19
  Project, 20–21
  Tools, 23–31
  View, 21–22
  Window, 31
DXF files, exporting, 93

E

Ease channel, 269, 271, 272
  using, 327–331
Edge Threshold, 207–208
Edit menu, 19–20
Effects, 440–444
Emotions, expression of, 351–354

Environments, 360, 362
  complex, 368–395
  map, 381–382
  simple, 363–368
Exercises
  Aim At and Orient Like constraints, 282–283
  Aim At constraints, 261–264
  Aim Roll At constraints, 277–278
  airplane
    fuselage, 177–182
    rotoscopes, 176–177
  animating constraints, 285–287
  arm extrusion, 67–70
  arms, 164–165
  boning Killer Bean, 299–303
  bones, finishing, 303–305
  bones, target, 288
  Boolean operations, simple, 311–313
  brick wall, 246–249
  building, simple, 170–172
  cameras, multiple, 402
  color key, 440–441
  cow
    body, 77–78
      shaping, 80
    bones, 306–308
    head, 79–80
    legs, 80–83
      bones in, 308–309
    tail, 83–85
      bones in, 309–311
  cylindrical backdrops, 376–380
  decaling
    a dome, 383–386
    curved surfaces, 241–243
    using Flatten, 243–246
  doors and windows, 173–176
  Ease channel, 328–331
  emotion poses, 351–354

environment maps, 381–382
eyes, 53–56
  cornea, 154–155
  creation, 150–151
  pupil, 152–153
  surface around, 140–146
face, closing patches of, 133–135
facial features, 53–56
  basic, 127–129
  resolution, 129–132
  shaping, 135–136
feet, 44–48
front projection maps, 390–394
Grid Maker to create ground planes, 372–375
ground plane
  complex, 368–371
  simple, 363–368
hands, 49–52, 75
head image map in Photoshop, 254–256
head shape, basic, 125–126
hole, adding with hooks, 90–92
interface, 33–37
joints, three-bone, 293–295
joints, two-bone, 291–293
Kinematic constraints, 265–268
layer animation, 435–436
legs, 166–167
legs and feet, 59–62
lens flares, 442–444
lighting technique, basic, 406–410
LipSYNC, 357–358
lip-synch, simple, 355
martini glass, 213–214
material library, 223
materials, combining, 221–222
materials, complex, 218–220
metal material, 215–218
motion blur, 422–423
mouth, 56–58
  corner creases, 137–140
multilayer compositions, 437–440

muscle motion, simple, 349–350
neck and head, 74–75
nose, creating a, 146–149
Orient Like constraints, 277
patch coloring, 199–203
path, simple, 318–320
Path and Aim Roll At constraints, 283–284
path animation
  advanced example 1, 324–325
  advanced example 2, 326–327
Path constraints, 269–272
pelvis, 162–164
  and torso, 63–67
Property Panel, 13–14
rotoscopes, setting up, 123–124
shoulders, 70–74
skeletal squash and stretch, 343–347
spaceship, 184–189
specularity, 196–197
Spherical constraints, 279–281
spherical environments, 386–389
Status Bar, 16–17
stride length, 339–343
torso, 155–162
tracking objects with camera, 399–401
translate only, 323
Translate To constraints, 273–275
translations, simple, 317
20-minute man, 59–76
Tyrannosaurus rex
  arms, 100–105
  back legs, 105–108
  body, 97–100
  head, 108–111
  tail, 95–96
walk cycle, simple, 334–337
Window Workspace, 15
Extrusion, 28, 112, 191
  arms, 67–70
Eyes, human, 4–5
  constraints, 282–283

modeling, 150–155
surface around, 140–146

F

Facial expressions, 350, 351
Facial features, 52–58
  muscles, 350
  resolution and, 127–150
Feet, 44–48, 298
  slippage, 338–339, 342, 343
File
  menu, 18–19
  toolbar, 32
Fill light, 406
Flat shading, 414–415
Flatten, 243–246, 383, 386, 389
Fog, 368, 375, 410–411
Fractal maps, 240
Frame toolbar, 32
Front projection mapping, 390–395
Full-motion video output, 418

G

Gaussian blur, 232, 254, 255–256
Gizmo, 4, 5
Glass, 212–214, 218
Global tab, 27–28
Gouraud shading, 417
Gradient combiner, 207–208
Gremlins, 4
Grid, 371–372
Grid Maker, 371–375
Ground plane
  complex exercise, 368–371
  exercise, 363–368
  from *Grid Maker,* 372–375
Group Connected, 20

H

"Halos", 249, 250, 251, 253
Hamm, Jack, 350

Hands, 48–52, 75, 298
Hash, Inc., 122, 183
Hash, Martin, 122, 254–256
Head
  image map, 254–256
  modeling, 121–126
Hierarchies, bone, 296, 314
Holes, 90–92, 174, 410
Hooks, 88–94
  Tyrannosaurus rex creation, 94–114
Horizon, hard, 368, 410
Human body, modeling, 155–168
Human face, modeling
  features and resolution, 127–150
  head, 121–126
Hybrid renderer, 414–418

I

Image maps, 173, 189
  antialiased vs. non-antialiased, 249–251
  See also Decals; *specific types*
Images, combining with characters, 390–395
Indeo, 419
Interface, 10–11, 39
  drop-down menus, 17–31
  exercise, 33–37
  Project Workspace, 11–12
  Properties Panel, 13–14
  Status Bar, 16–17
  Window Workspace, 14–15
Interface, MultiPlane, 429
  Attribute Panel, 433–434
  Composition Window, 432–433
  Menu bar, 430–432
  Object List, 435
  Tool Panel, 433

J

Joints, 69, 279, 281, 290–296
Jurassic Park, 94

K

Keyboard Shortcuts tab, 24, 26, 27
Key light, 406
Killer Bean, 42–43
  boning, 299–303
  patch coloring, 198–203
Kinematic constraints, 265–268
Klieg-type light, 403–404

L

LaserDisc player, 398
Lathe Precision, 28
Lathe tool modeling, 42–43, 112, 113, 191
  cow's udder and ears, 85–86
  facial features, 52–56
  feet, 44–48
  hands, 48–52
  mouth, 56–58
Layer animation, 435–436
  multiple, 436–440
Layers, 427–429
Legs and feet, 59–62, 166–167
Lens flare, 442–444
Libraries, 33
  actions, 296–298
  eye color maps, 150
  material, 222–224
  motion, 359–360
Lighting, 392, 395, 403–410
  lens flare, 442–444
  underwater, 411
LipSYNC, 357–359
Lip-synch, 354–359

M

Manipulator toolbar, 33
Mannerisms, 5
Map edges, 381
Mapping
  front projection, 390–395

See also Decals
Mask, The, 411
Materials editor, 12, 18
  combiners, 203–211
  complex techniques, 218–222
  glass and metal, 212–218
  libraries, 222–224
Mechanical modeling
  airplane, 176–183
  buildings, 170–176
  spaceship, 183–192
Memory, physical, 414, 415
Menu bar, MultiPlane, 430–432
Metal, 212, 214–218
Microsoft Video 1, 419
Model, 18
Modeling
  hooks, 88–114
  human body, 155–168
  human eyes, 150–155
  human face, 121–155
  lathe tool, 42–58
  Mode, 32
  Options tab, 28–29
  unibody construction, 58–76
  unibody quadruped, 76–86
Mode toolbar, 32–33
Motion
  blur, 411–412, 421–423
  libraries, 359–360
  See also Actions; Ease channel; Path animation
Mouth, 56–58, 137–140
  shapes for Poses, 354, 358
  smile, 349–350
Movie formats, 419–420
MultiPlane, 423, 426–427
  effects, 440–444
  interface, 429–435
  layer animation, 435–436
  multiple layers, 436–440

Multiple cameras, 401–402
Muscle
  Mode, 23, 32
  motion, 348–351
    facial, 350

N
Naming
  convention, bones, 297–298
  groups, 199, 350
Navigation toolbar, 33
Neck and head, 74–75
Noise combiner, 208–210
Nose, 146–149

O
Object list, MultiPlane, 435
Objects, 12
180-degree backdrops, 381–382
OpenGL, 417
Options, tool menu, 27–31
Orient Like constraints, 275–277
Output, final, 418–420

P
Patch-based modeler, 37
Patch coloring, 198–203
Patches, 38–39
  three-point on curved surface, 120–121
  three rules of creating, 39
Path animation
  advanced, 324–327
  controlling, 327–331
  simple, 318–323
  translation-type movements, 316–317
Path constraints, 268–272, 283–284, 400–401
Patriarch, 299–300
PC computer, 122, 418, 419, 426
Pelvis and torso, 63–67, 162–164
Physical memory, 414, 415

Polygonal-based modelers, 37
  Boolean operations, 311
  displacement maps, 239
Poses, 23, 351–354
  lip-synch, 354–359
PowerMac, 418, 419
Projection maps, 390–395
Project
  menu, 20–21
  Workspace, 11–12
Properties Panel, 13–14

Q
Quadruped, 77–86
  bones, 305–311
Quick Draw 3D, 417
QuickTime MOV, 418, 419

R
RAM, 414, 415
Raytracing, 414, 416
Realization, 7
Recent files, 19, 21
Reflectivity, 197
  maps, 235–236
Refraction, 198
Rendering
  alpha buffer, 420–421
  final output, 418–420
  hybrid renderer, 414–418
  motion blur, 421–423
  Options tab, 30–31
Resolution, 311
  high attached to low, 92, 113
Road-Runner cartoons, 411, 421, 422
Rotate Manipulator, 27–28
Rotoscopes, 122–125, 167, 360
  airplane, 176–177
  camera, 375
Roughness Height and Scale, 198

S

Saving data, 12, 18, 21
Scene composition, 395, 427–429
Screen resolution, 10
Shaders, 414–418
Shadows, 403, 405–406
Shoulders, 70–74
Skeletal
  actions, 334–348
  Mode, 32
  squash and stretch, 343–347
"Sky", 381
Smearing effect, 243, 246
Snap Group to Grid, 20
Space scenes, 386–390
Spaceship, 183–192
Specular highlights, 153
Specularity, 196–197
  maps, 232–233
Speed, changes in, 327–331
Spherical
  backdrops, 386–390
  combiner, 210–211
  Limits constraints, 279–281
Spielberg, Steven, 398
Splines, 37–39, 56
  continuous, doubling back, 118–119
  extruded, 28
  noncontinuous, 115–117
Squash and stretch, skeletal, 343–347
SR-71 Blackbird, 176, 180, 182–183
Standard toolbar, 32
Starfields, 386
Star Trek, 183
Status Bar, 16–17, 21
Story
  boarding, 6
  definition of, 2–3
  telling, 2, 3–6

Stride length, 338–343
Sun-type light, 403–404
Surface
  ambiguities, 39, 114–121
  creating a, 38–39
  detail, spaceship, 189–192
  integrity, 89

T

T2, 398
TARGA (.TGA) file format, 122, 226, 253,
    418, 419–420, 423
Target bones, 287–288
Telepresence, 183
Terminator, The, 398
Terminology, 38–39, 350
  bone hierarchies, 296–298
Texture map alternatives, 257–258
Texturing
  base attributes, 194–198
  material libraries, 222–224
  material techniques, 212–222
  patch coloring, 198–203
  three-dimensional textures, 203–211
Thom model, 93–94
  base attributes, 194–198
  kinematic constraints, 265–268
  stride length, 339–343
  walk cycle, 334–338
Three-dimensional textures, 203–211
Three-point lighting, 403
Three-point patches, 120–121
360-degree background, 386–390
Tilt, 228
Time-based manipulation, 287, 324–225
Toolbars
  dockable, 32
  tab, 23–24
  types of, 32–33

Tool panel, MultiPlane, 433
Tools menu
  customize, 23–27
  Options, 27–31
Tools tab, 24
Tools toolbar, 32
Torso, 63–67, 155–162
Tracking objects, 399–401
Translate To constraints, 272–275
Translations
  motion, 316–317
  path, 323
Transparency, 198
  maps, 173, 228–230
"Tweens", 338
20-minute man, 59–76
Tyrannosaurus rex creation, 94–114

U
Underwater lighting, 411
Unibody construction, 58–59
  arm extrusion, 67–70
  legs and feet, 59–62
  pelvis, 63–67
  quadruped, 76–86
  shoulders, head, and hands, 70–75

V
Videotape output, 418, 419
View
  menu, 21–22
  Settings, 16, 17
Voices, use of, 5

W
WACOM drawing tablet, 256
Walk cycle exercise, 334–338
Weird Science, 160
Window
  menu, 31
  Workspace, 14–15
Windows and doors, 173–176
Wood, 218–220
Workbook, 22
World Wide Web, 371, 372

Z
Z-buffer, 414, 415–416

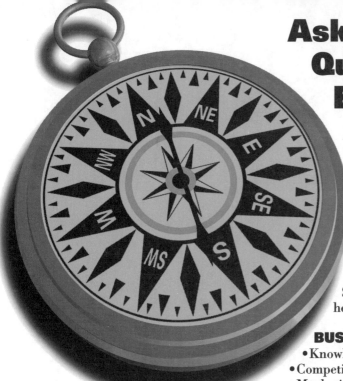

Ask a Tough Question. Expect Solid Direction.

Help on the Horizon. Arnold Information Technology points corporations and organizations to information that get results. Access our experienced professionals who can help senior managers identify options and chart a course.

Since 1991, we've proven we can help in a range of capacities:

BUSINESS DEVELOPMENT
- Knowledge Management
- Competitive Intelligence
- Marketing & Sales
- Acquisitions & Mergers
- Patent Evaluations
- Technology Startups

INFORMATION TECHNOLOGY SERVICES
- Intranets, and Extranets
- Web-based Technologies
- Database Management
- Digital Work Flow Planning
- Information Engineering

ACTION FROM IDEAS. We helped build the service known as the Top 5% of the Internet, found at www.lycos.com. Our latest competitive intelligence tool can be explored at abcompass.com. It builds a personal daily news feed that only you receive.

A TEAM WITH STRATEGIC VISION. Our seasoned consultants can build, research, prototype, budget, plan, assess, and tackle some of the toughest jobs in information technology. Our managers have taken a leadership role in U.S. corporations and elsewhere in the world.

GET WHERE YOU WANT TO GO. TODAY. We move corporations and organizations into the future. Our work spans a variety of industries, including publishing, telecommunications, government agencies, investment banks, and startups. We welcome confidential, informal discussions of your challenges and opportunities.

CONTACT:

Stephen E. Arnold, President
Arnold Information Technology
P.O. Box 320
Harrods Creek, Kentucky 40027
Voice: 502 228-1966
E-Mail: ait@arnoldit.com
Facsimile: 502 228-0548